STUDENT'S SOLUTIONS MANUAL

NUMERICAL ANALYSIS
SECOND EDITION

Timothy Sauer
George Mason University

PEARSON

Boston Columbus Indianapolis New York San Francisco Upper Saddle River
Amsterdam Cape Town Dubai London Madrid Milan Munich Paris Montreal Toronto
Delhi Mexico City Sao Paulo Sydney Hong Kong Seoul Singapore Taipei Tokyo

The author and publisher of this book have used their best efforts in preparing this book. These efforts include the development, research, and testing of the theories and programs to determine their effectiveness. The author and publisher make no warranty of any kind, expressed or implied, with regard to these programs or the documentation contained in this book. The author and publisher shall not be liable in any event for incidental or consequential damages in connection with, or arising out of, the furnishing, performance, or use of these programs.

Reproduced by Pearson from electronic files supplied by the author.

ISBN-13: 978-0-321-78392-9
ISBN-10: 0-321-78392-1

1 2 3 4 5 6 OPM 16 15 14 13 12

www.pearsonhighered.com

Table of Contents

Chapter 5   Numerical Differentiation and Integration

Chapter 6   Ordinary Differential Equations

Chapter 7   Boundary Value Problems

Chapter 8   Partial Differential Equations

Chapter 9   Random Numbers and Applications

Chapter 10 Trigonometric Interpolation and the FFT

Chapter 11 Compression

Chapter 12 Eigenvalues and Singular Values

Chapter 13 Optimization

CHAPTER 0
Fundamentals

EXERCISES 0.1 Evaluating a Polynomial

1 (a) $P(x) = 1 + x(1 + x(5 + x(1 + x(6))))$.

$P(\frac{1}{3}) = 6(\frac{1}{3})^4 + (\frac{1}{3})^3 + 5(\frac{1}{3})^2 + \frac{1}{3} + 1 = 1 + \frac{1}{3}(1 + \frac{1}{3}(5 + \frac{1}{3}(1 + \frac{1}{3}(6)))) = 2.$

1 (b) $P(x) = 1 + x(-5 + x(5 + x(4 + x(-3))))$

$P(\frac{1}{3}) = -3(\frac{1}{3})^4 + 4(\frac{1}{3})^3 + 5(\frac{1}{3})^2 - 5(\frac{1}{3}) + 1 = 1 + \frac{1}{3}(-5 + \frac{1}{3}(5 + \frac{1}{3}(4 + \frac{1}{3}(-3)))) = 0$

1 (c) $P(x) = 1 + x(0 + x(-1 + x(1 + x(2))))$

$P(\frac{1}{3}) = 2(\frac{1}{3})^4 + (\frac{1}{3})^3 - (\frac{1}{3})^2 + 1 = 1 + \frac{1}{3}(0 + \frac{1}{3}(-1 + \frac{1}{3}(1 + \frac{1}{3}(2)))) = 77/81.$

3 $P(\frac{1}{2}) = 1 + (\frac{1}{2})^2(2 + (\frac{1}{2})^2(-4 + (\frac{1}{2})^2(1))) = 81/64.$

5 (a) $P(\frac{1}{2}) = 4 + \frac{1}{2}(4 + (\frac{1}{2} - 1)(1 + (\frac{1}{2} - 2)(3 + (\frac{1}{2} - 3)(2)))) = 5$

5 (b) $P(-\frac{1}{2}) = 4 - \frac{1}{2}(4 + (-\frac{1}{2} - 1)(1 + (-\frac{1}{2} - 2)(3 + (-\frac{1}{2} - 3)(2)))) = 41/4$

7 $P(x) = c_1 + (x - r_1)(c_2 + (x - r_2)(c_3 + (x - r_3)(c_4 + \ldots + (x - r_n)c_{n+1})))$ is the degree n polynomial with base points. The operations needed are n multiplications and $2n$ additions.

COMPUTER PROBLEMS 0.1

1 The MATLAB command nest(50,ones(51,1),1.00001) gives 51.01275208274999, differing from $(x^{51} - 1)/(x - 1)$ with $x = 1.00001$ by 4.76×10^{-12}.

EXERCISES 0.2 Binary Numbers

1 (a) $(64)_{10} = (2^6)_{10} = (1000000)_2$

1 (b) $(17)_{10} = (16 + 1)_{10} = (10001)_2$

1 (c)

$$79 \div 2 = 39 \text{ R } 1$$
$$39 \div 2 = 19 \text{ R } 1$$
$$19 \div 2 = 9 \text{ R } 1$$
$$9 \div 2 = 4 \text{ R } 1$$
$$4 \div 2 = 2 \text{ R } 0$$
$$2 \div 2 = 1 \text{ R } 0$$
$$1 \div 2 = 0 \text{ R } 1, \text{ so } (79)_{10} = (1001111)_2$$

1 (d)

$$227 \div 2 \;=\; 113 \,\text{R}\,1$$
$$113 \div 2 \;=\; 56 \,\text{R}\,1$$
$$56 \div 2 \;=\; 28 \,\text{R}\,0$$
$$28 \div 2 \;=\; 14 \,\text{R}\,0$$
$$14 \div 2 \;=\; 7 \,\text{R}\,0$$
$$7 \div 2 \;=\; 3 \,\text{R}\,1$$
$$3 \div 2 \;=\; 1 \,\text{R}\,1$$
$$1 \div 2 \;=\; 0 \,\text{R}\,1$$

Therefore $(227)_{10} = (11100011)_2$.

3 (a) $10.5 = 10 + 0.5$. Integer part: $(10)_{10} = (8+2)_{10} = (1010)_2$. Fractional part: $(0.5)_{10} = (0.1)_2$, so $(10.5)_{10} = (1010.1)_2$.

3 (b)

$$\frac{1}{3} \times 2 \;=\; \frac{2}{3} + 0$$
$$\frac{2}{3} \times 2 \;=\; \frac{1}{3} + 1$$
$$\frac{1}{3} \times 2 \;=\; \frac{2}{3} + 0$$
$$\vdots$$

Therefore $(\frac{1}{3})_{10} = (0.\overline{01})_2$.

3 (c)

$$\frac{5}{7} \times 2 \;=\; \frac{3}{7} + 1$$
$$\frac{3}{7} \times 2 \;=\; \frac{6}{7} + 0$$
$$\frac{6}{7} \times 2 \;=\; \frac{5}{7} + 1$$
$$\frac{5}{7} \times 2 \;=\; \frac{3}{7} + 1$$
$$\frac{3}{7} \times 2 \;=\; \frac{6}{7} + 0$$
$$\vdots$$

Therefore $(\frac{5}{7})_{10} = (0.\overline{101})_2$.

3 (d) $(12.8)_{10} = (12)_{10} + (0.8)_{10}; (12)_{10} = (1100)_2.$

$$0.8 \times 2 \;=\; 0.6 + 1$$
$$0.6 \times 2 \;=\; 0.2 + 1$$
$$0.2 \times 2 \;=\; 0.4 + 0$$
$$0.4 \times 2 \;=\; 0.8 + 0$$
$$0.8 \times 2 \;=\; 0.6 + 1$$
$$\vdots$$

Therefore $(12.8)_{10} = (1100.\overline{1100})_2.$

3 (e) $(55.4)_{10} = (55)_{10} + (0.4)_{10}; (55)_{10} = (32 + 16 + 4 + 2 + 1)_{10} = (110111)_2.$

$$0.4 \times 2 \;=\; 0.8 + 0$$
$$0.8 \times 2 \;=\; 0.6 + 1$$
$$0.6 \times 2 \;=\; 0.2 + 1$$
$$0.2 \times 2 \;=\; 0.4 + 0$$
$$0.4 \times 2 \;=\; 0.8 + 0$$
$$\vdots$$

Therefore $(55.4)_{10} = (110111.\overline{0110})_2.$

3 (f)

$$0.1 \times 2 \;=\; 0.2 + 0$$
$$0.2 \times 2 \;=\; 0.4 + 0$$
$$0.4 \times 2 \;=\; 0.8 + 0$$
$$0.8 \times 2 \;=\; 0.6 + 1$$
$$0.6 \times 2 \;=\; 0.2 + 1$$
$$0.2 \times 2 \;=\; 0.4 + 0$$
$$\vdots$$

Therefore $(0.1)_{10} = (0.0\overline{0011})_2.$

5 $(\pi)_{10} = (3)_{10} + (\pi - 3)_{10}$

$$
\begin{aligned}
0.14159265 \times 2 &= 0.28318531 + 0 \\
0.28318531 \times 2 &= 0.56637061 + 0 \\
0.56637061 \times 2 &= 0.13274123 + 1 \\
0.13274123 \times 2 &= 0.26548246 + 0 \\
0.26548246 \times 2 &= 0.53096491 + 0 \\
0.53096491 \times 2 &= 0.06192983 + 1 \\
0.06192983 \times 2 &= 0.12385966 + 0 \\
0.12385966 \times 2 &= 0.24771932 + 0 \\
0.24771932 \times 2 &= 0.49543864 + 0 \\
0.49543864 \times 2 &= 0.99087728 + 0 \\
0.99087728 \times 2 &= 0.98175455 + 1 \\
0.98175455 \times 2 &= 0.96350910 + 1 \\
0.96350910 \times 2 &= 0.92701821 + 1
\end{aligned}
$$

$$\vdots$$

Therefore $(\pi)_{10} = (11.0010010000111\ldots)_2$.

7 (a) $(1010101)_2 = (2^0 + 2^2 + 2^4 + 2^6)_{10} = (1 + 4 + 16 + 64)_{10} = (85)_{10}$

7 (b) $(1011.101)_2 = (2^3 + 2^1 + 2^0 + 2^{-1} + 2^{-3})_{10} = (11 + \frac{1}{2} + \frac{1}{8})_{10} = (93/8)_{10}$.

7 (c) $(10111.\overline{01})_2 = (2^4 + 2^2 + 2^1 + 2^0)_{10} + (0.\overline{01})_2$. Set $x = (0.\overline{01})_2$. Then $2^2 x - x = (01)_2 = 1$ implies $x = \frac{1}{3}$. Therefore $(10111.\overline{01})_2 = (23 + \frac{1}{3})_{10} = (70/3)_{10}$.

7 (d) $(110.\overline{10})_2 = (2^2 + 2^1)_{10} + (0.\overline{10})_2$. Set $x = (0.\overline{10})_2$. Then $2^2 x - x = (10)_2$ implies $x = \frac{2}{3}$. Therefore $(110.\overline{10})_2 = (6 + \frac{2}{3})_{10} = (20/3)_{10}$.

7 (e) $(10.\overline{110})_2 = (2)_{10} + (0.\overline{110})_2$. Set $x = (0.\overline{110})_2$. Then $2^3 x - x = (110)_2 = 6$ implies $x = 6/7$. Therefore $(10.\overline{110})_2 = (2 + \frac{6}{7})_{10} = (20/7)_{10}$.

7 (f) $(110.1\overline{101})_2 = (6)_{10} + (\frac{1}{2})_{10} + (0.0\overline{101})_2 = (\frac{13}{2} + \frac{x}{2})_{10}$, where $x = (0.\overline{101})_2$. Since $2^3 x - x = (101)_2 = 5$, $x = 5/7$. Therefore $(110.1\overline{101})_2 = (\frac{13}{2} + \frac{5\frac{1}{7}}{2})_{10} = (48/7)_{10}$.

7 (g) $(10.010\overline{1101})_2 = (2)_{10} + (\frac{1}{4})_{10} + \frac{1}{8}(0.\overline{1101})_2$. Set $x = (0.\overline{1101})_2$. Then $2^4 x - x = (1101)_2 = 13$, implying that $x = \frac{13}{15}$. Therefore $(10.010\overline{1101})_2 = (\frac{9}{4} + \frac{1}{8}\frac{13}{15})_{10} = (283/120)_{10}$.

7 (h) $(111.\overline{1})_2 = (7)_{10} + (0.\overline{1})_2 = (7)_{10} + x$, where $x = (0.\overline{1})_2$. Since $2^1 x - x = (1)_2$, $x = 1$, and $(111.\overline{1})_2 = (7 + 1)_{10} = (8)_{10}$.

EXERCISES 0.3   Floating Point Representation of Real Numbers

1 (a) $(\frac{1}{4})_{10} = (0.01)_2$; $\text{fl}(\frac{1}{4}) = +1.0 \times 2^{-2}$.

1 (b) $(\frac{1}{3})_{10} = (0.\overline{01})_2 =$

$+1.\boxed{0101010101010101010101010101010101010101010101010101}\, 0101\ldots \times 2^{-2}.$

The Rounding to Nearest Rule says to round down when the 53rd bit is 0.

$\text{fl}(\frac{1}{3}) = +1.\boxed{0101010101010101010101010101010101010101010101010101} \times 2^{-2}.$

1 (c) $(\frac{2}{3})_{10} = (0.\overline{10})_2 =$

$+1.\boxed{0101010101010101010101010101010101010101010101010101}\, 0101\ldots \times 2^{-1}.$

$\text{fl}(\frac{2}{3}) = +1.\boxed{0101010101010101010101010101010101010101010101010101} \times 2^{-1}.$

1 (d) $(0.9)_{10} = (0.1\overline{1100})_2 =$

$+1.\boxed{1100110011001100110011001100110011001100110011001100}\, 1100\ldots \times 2^{-1}.$

The Rounding to Nearest Rule says to round up since the 53rd bit is nonzero, and further bits are nonzero.

$\text{fl}(0.9) = +1.\boxed{1100110011001100110011001100110011001100110011001101} \times 2^{-1}.$

3 Note that $\text{fl}(5) = 1.01 \times 2^2$. Adding 1 as bit $3, 4, \ldots, 52$ of the mantissa will not incur rounding error. These correspond to 2^{-k} for $k = 1, 2, \ldots, 50$.

5 (a) $1 + (2^{-51} + 2^{-53}) =$

$+1.\boxed{0000000000000000000000000000000000000000000000000010}\, 1 \times 2^0.$

$\text{fl}(1 + (2^{-51} + 2^{-53})) =$

$+1.\boxed{0000000000000000000000000000000000000000000000000010} \times 2^0$, using the Rounding to Nearest Rule. Therefore $\text{fl}((1 + (2^{-51} + 2^{-53})) - 1) =$

$.\boxed{0000000000000000000000000000000000000000000000000010}$

$= 1.\boxed{0000000000000000000000000000000000000000000000000000} \times 2^{-51} = 2^{-51}.$

5 (b) $1 + (2^{-51} + 2^{-52} + 2^{-53}) =$

$+1.\boxed{0000000000000000000000000000000000000000000000000011}\, 1 \times 2^0.$

$\text{fl}(1 + (2^{-51} + 2^{-52} + 2^{-53})) =$

$+1.\boxed{0000000000000000000000000000000000000000000000000100} \times 2^0$, using the Rounding to Nearest Rule. Therefore $\text{fl}((1 + (2^{-51} + 2^{-52} + 2^{-53})) - 1) =$

$.\boxed{0000000000000000000000000000000000000000000000000100}$

$= 1.\boxed{0000000000000000000000000000000000000000000000000000} \times 2^{-50} = 2^{-50}.$

7 (a) $(8)_{10} = (1000.)_2 = 1.0 \times 2^3$. The biased exponent is $3 + 1023 = 1026$, which is $2^{10} + 2$. The sign is 0 (positive), so the sign/exponent is represented by the binary string 0100 0000 0010. The mantissa is 52 zeros, so the machine representation is the 64 bits

$\boxed{\text{0100 0000 0010 0000 0000 0000 0000 0000 0000 0000 0000 0000 0000 0000 0000 0000}}$

or 4020000000000000 in hex format.

7 (b) $(21)_{10} = (10101.)_2 = 1.0101 \times 2^4$. The biased exponent is $4 + 1023 = 1027 = 2^{10} + 3$, represented by 100 0000 0011. The machine representation is

0100 0000 0011 0101 0000 0000 0000 0000 0000 0000 0000 0000 0000 0000 0000 0000

or `4035000000000000` in hex format.

7 (c) $(1/8)_{10} = 1.0 \times 2^{-3}$. The biased exponent is $-3 + 1023 = 1020 = 2^{10} - 4$, represented by 011 1111 1100. The machine representation is

0011 1111 1100 0000 0000 0000 0000 0000 0000 0000 0000 0000 0000 0000 0000 0000

or `3fc0000000000000` in hex format.

7 (d) $(1/3)_{10} = 1.\overline{01} \times 2^{-2}$, and after rounding down, $\mathrm{fl}(1/3) = 1.0101\ldots0101 \times 2^{-2}$. The biased exponent is $-2 + 1023 = 1021 = 2^{10} - 3$, represented by 011 1111 1101. The machine representation is

0011 1111 1101 0101 0101 0101 0101 0101 0101 0101 0101 0101 0101 0101 0101 0101

or `3fd5555555555555` in hex format.

7 (e) $(2/3)_{10} = 1.\overline{01} \times 2^{-1}$, and after rounding down, $\mathrm{fl}(1/3) = 1.0101\ldots0101 \times 2^{-1}$. The biased exponent is $-1 + 1023 = 1022 = 2^{10} - 2$, represented by 011 1111 1110. The machine representation is

0011 1111 1110 0101 0101 0101 0101 0101 0101 0101 0101 0101 0101 0101 0101 0101

or `3fe5555555555555` in hex format.

7 (f) $(0.1)_{10} = 1.\overline{1001} \times 2^{-4}$, and after rounding up, $\mathrm{fl}(0.1) = 1.1001\ldots1001\ 1010 \times 2^{-4}$. The biased exponent is $-4 + 1023 = 1019 = 2^{10} - 5$, represented by 011 1111 1011. The machine representation is

0011 1111 1011 1001 1001 1001 1001 1001 1001 1001 1001 1001 1001 1001 1001 1010

or `3fb999999999999a` in hex format.

7 (g) $(-0.1)_{10} = -1.\overline{1001} \times 2^{-4}$, and after rounding, $\mathrm{fl}(-0.1) = -1.1001\ldots1001\ 1010 \times 2^{-4}$. The biased exponent is $-4 + 1023 = 1019 = 2^{10} - 5$, represented by 011 1111 1011. The machine representation is

1011 1111 1011 1001 1001 1001 1001 1001 1001 1001 1001 1001 1001 1001 1001 1010

or `bfb999999999999a` in hex format.

7 (h) $(-0.2)_{10} = -1.\overline{1001} \times 2^{-3}$, and after rounding, $\mathrm{fl}(-0.2) = -1.1001\ldots1001\ 1010 \times 2^{-3}$. The biased exponent is $-3 + 1023 = 1020 = 2^{10} - 4$, represented by 011 1111 1100. The machine representation is

1011 1111 1100 1001 1001 1001 1001 1001 1001 1001 1001 1001 1001 1001 1001 1010

or `bfc999999999999a` in hex format.

9 (a) $(7/3)_{10} = 1.00\overline{10} \times 2^1$, and after rounding, $\mathrm{fl}(7/3) = 1.0010\ldots1010\ 1011 \times 2^1$. $(4/3)_{10} = 1.\overline{01} \times 2^0$, and after rounding, $\mathrm{fl}(4/3) = 1.01\ldots0101\ 0101 \times 2^0$. Subtracting gives

$$1.\boxed{0010101010101010101010101010101010101010101010101011}0 \times 2^1$$

$$-\ 0.\boxed{1010101010101010101010101010101010101010101010101010}1 \times 2^1$$

$$=\ 0.\boxed{1000000000000000000000000000000000000000000000000000}1 \times 2^1$$

that is normalized to

$$=\ 1.\boxed{0000000000000000000000000000000000000000000000000001} \times 2^0,$$

which is $1 + \epsilon_{mach}$. After subtracting 1, the result is that the double precision floating point version of $(7/3 - 4/3) - 1$ is ϵ_{mach}.

9 (b) $(4/3)_{10} = 1.\overline{01} \times 2^0$, and after rounding, $fl(4/3) = 1.01 \dots 0101\ 0101 \times 2^0$. $(1/3)_{10} = 1.\overline{01} \times 2^{-2}$, and after rounding, $fl(1/3) = 1.01 \dots 0101\ 0101 \times 2^{-2}$. Subtracting gives

$$1.\boxed{0101010101010101010101010101010101010101010101010101}\ 00 \times 2^0$$
$$-\ 0.\boxed{0101010101010101010101010101010101010101010101010101}\ 01 \times 2^0$$

$$=\ 0.\boxed{1111111111111111111111111111111111111111111111111111}\ 11 \times 2^0$$

that normalizes to

$$=\ 1.\boxed{1111111111111111111111111111111111111111111111111111}\ 1 \times 2^{-1}$$

and rounds to

$$=\ 10.\boxed{0000000000000000000000000000000000000000000000000000} \times 2^{-1}$$

which is 1.0×2^0. After subtracting 1, the result is machine zero, not ϵ_{mach}.

11 The associative law of addition fails for floating point addition with the Rounding to Nearest Rule, for example, because $1 + (\epsilon_{mach}/2 + \epsilon_{mach}/2) = 1 + \epsilon_{mach} > 1$, while $(1 + \epsilon_{mach}/2) + \epsilon_{mach}/2 = 1$, because $1 + \epsilon_{mach}/2 = 1$.

13 (a) 2, represented by $010 \dots 0$ (b) 2^{-511}, represented by $0010 \dots 0$ (c) 0, represented by $10 \dots 0$. When bit 4 through 12 is the nonzero bit, the floating point number is positive but less than 2^{-511}. When bit 13 through 64 is the nonzero bit, the number is positive and subnormal, so less than 2^{-511}.

15(a) $(8.3)_{10} = 1.0000\overline{1001} \times 2^3$, and rounded, $fl(8.3) = 1.0000\ 1001\ 1001 \dots 1001\ 1010 \times 2^3$. $(7.3)_{10} = 1.110\overline{1001} \times 2^2$, and rounded, $fl(7.3) = 1.1101\ 0011\ 0011 \dots 0011\ 0011 \times 2^2$. Subtracting gives

$$1.\boxed{0000100110011001100110011001100110011001100110011010}\ 0 \times 2^3$$
$$-\ 0.\boxed{1110100110011001100110011001100110011001100110011001}\ 1 \times 2^3$$

$$=\ 0.\boxed{0010000000000000000000000000000000000000000000000000}\ 1 \times 2^3$$

that is normalized to

$$=\ 1.\boxed{0000000000000000000000000000000000000000000000000100} \times 2^0,$$

which is $1 + 2^{-50}$. After subtracting 1, the result is that the double precision floating point version of $(8.3 - 7.3) - 1$ is 2^{-50}.

15(b) $(8.4)_{10} = 1.0000\overline{0110} \times 2^3$, and rounded, $\mathrm{fl}(8.4) = 1.0000\ 1100\ 1100\ldots1100\ 1101 \times 2^3$.
$(7.4)_{10} = 1.11\overline{0110} \times 2^2$, and rounded, $\mathrm{fl}(7.4) = 1.1101\ 1001\ 1001\ldots1001\ 1010 \times 2^2$.
Subtracting gives

$$
\begin{array}{r}
1.\boxed{0000110011001100110011001100110011001100110011001101} \times 2^3 \\[2pt]
-\quad 0.\boxed{1110110011001100110011001100110011001100110011001101} \times 2^3 \\[2pt]
\hline
=\quad 0.\boxed{0010000000000000000000000000000000000000000000000000} \times 2^3
\end{array}
$$

which is 1. After subtracting 1, the result is that the double precision floating point version of
$(8.4 - 7.4) - 1$ is 0.

15(c) $(8.8)_{10} = 1.000\overline{1100} \times 2^3$, and rounded, $\mathrm{fl}(8.8) = 1.0001\ 1001\ 1001\ldots1001\ 1010 \times 2^3$.
$(7.8)_{10} = 1.11\overline{1100} \times 2^2$, and rounded, $\mathrm{fl}(7.8) = 1.1111\ 0011\ 0011\ldots0011\ 0011 \times 2^2$.
Subtracting gives

$$
\begin{array}{r}
1.\boxed{0001100110011001100110011001100110011001100110011010}\,0 \times 2^3 \\[2pt]
-\quad 0.\boxed{1111100110011001100110011001100110011001100110011001}\,1 \times 2^3 \\[2pt]
\hline
=\quad 0.\boxed{0010000000000000000000000000000000000000000000000000}\,1 \times 2^3
\end{array}
$$

that is normalized to

$$
=\quad 1.\boxed{0000000000000000000000000000000000000000000000000100} \times 2^0,
$$

which is $1 + 2^{-50}$. After subtracting 1, the result is that the double precision floating point
version of $(8.8 - 7.8) - 1$ is 2^{-50}.

EXERCISES 0.4   Loss of Significance

1 (a) For x near $2\pi n$ for integer n, $\sec x \approx 1$, and the numerator exhibits subtraction of nearly
equal numbers. An algebraically equivalent expression avoids the difficulty:

$$
\begin{aligned}
\frac{1 - 1/\cos x}{\tan^2 x} &= \frac{\cos x - 1}{\cos x \tan^2 x} \\[6pt]
&= \frac{\cos x - 1}{\sec x \sin^2 x} \cdot \frac{\cos x + 1}{\cos x + 1} \\[6pt]
&= \frac{\cos^2 - 1}{\sec x \sin^2 x (\cos x + 1)} \\[6pt]
&= -\frac{1}{1 + \sec x}
\end{aligned}
$$

1 (b) For x near 0, the numerator subtracts nearly equal numbers. Simplifying to

$$\frac{1-(1-x)^3}{x} = \frac{1-(1-3x+3x^2-x^3)}{x} = 3-3x+x^2$$

eliminates the loss of significance.

1 (c) For x near 0, there is subtraction of nearly equal numbers. Using common denominators eliminates the problem:

$$\frac{1}{1+x} - \frac{1}{1-x} = \frac{1-x-(1+x)}{(1+x)(1-x)} = \frac{2x}{x^2-1}$$

3 Since b is positive, the roots should be calculated as in (0.13):

$$x_1 = -\frac{b+\sqrt{b^2+4\times10^{-12}}}{2}$$

$$x_2 = \frac{2\times10^{-12}}{b+\sqrt{b^2+4\times10^{-12}}}$$

COMPUTER PROBLEMS 0.4

1 (a) Compare the original expression to the revised version $-1/(1+\sec x)$ from Exercise 1(a).

x	original	revised
0.10000000000000	−0.49874791371143	−0.49874791371143
0.01000000000000	−0.49998749979096	−0.49998749979166
0.00100000000000	−0.49999987501429	−0.49999987499998
0.00010000000000	−0.49999999362793	−0.49999999875000
0.00001000000000	−0.50000004133685	−0.49999999998750
0.00000100000000	−0.50004445029084	−0.49999999999987
0.00000010000000	−0.51070259132757	−0.50000000000000
0.00000001000000	0	−0.50000000000000
0.00000000100000	0	−0.50000000000000
0.00000000010000	0	−0.50000000000000
0.00000000001000	0	−0.50000000000000
0.00000000000100	0	−0.50000000000000
0.00000000000010	0	−0.50000000000000
0.00000000000001	0	−0.50000000000000

1 (b) Compare the original expression to the revised version $3 - 3x + x^2$ from Exercise 1(b).

x	original	revised
0.10000000000000	2.71000000000000	2.71000000000000
0.01000000000000	2.97010000000001	2.97010000000000
0.00100000000000	2.99700100000000	2.99700100000000
0.00010000000000	2.99970000999905	2.99970001000000
0.00001000000000	2.99997000008379	2.99997000010000
0.00000100000000	2.99999700015263	2.99999700000100
0.00000010000000	2.99999969866072	2.99999970000001
0.00000001000000	2.99999998176759	2.99999997000000
0.00000000100000	2.99999991515421	2.99999999700000
0.00000000010000	3.00000024822111	2.99999999970000
0.00000000001000	3.00000024822111	2.99999999997000
0.00000000000100	2.99993363483964	2.99999999999700
0.00000000000010	3.00093283556180	2.99999999999970
0.00000000000001	2.99760216648792	2.99999999999997

3 Since a is large and negative, the expression represents subtraction of nearly equal numbers. Multiply numerator and denominator by the conjugate:

$$a + \sqrt{a^2 + b^2} = \frac{(a + \sqrt{a^2 + b^2})(a - \sqrt{a^2 + b^2})}{a - \sqrt{a^2 + b^2}} = \frac{-b^2}{a - \sqrt{a^2 + b^2}} \approx 6.1272 \times 10^{-13}.$$

5 Set $x = 3344556600$ and $y = 1.2222222$. The difference between the lengths of the hypotenuse and the longer leg is

$$\sqrt{x^2 + y^2} - x = (\sqrt{x^2 + y^2} - x)\frac{\sqrt{x^2 + y^2} + x}{\sqrt{x^2 + y^2} + x} = \frac{y^2}{\sqrt{x^2 + y^2} + x}$$

where we have rewritten the expression to eliminate the subtraction of nearly equal numbers. Although calculating the leftmost expression in double precision yields no correct significant digits, the rightmost expression gives the correct answer 2.23322×10^{-10}.

EXERCISES 0.5 Review of Calculus

1 (a) Since $f(0)f(1) = (1)(-2) < 0$, there exists c between 0 and 1 such that $f(c) = 0$ by the Intermediate Value Theorem.

1 (b) Since $f(0)f(1) = (1)(-9) < 0$, $f(c) = 0$ for some c between 0 and 1 as in (a).

1 (c) Since $f(0)f(1/2) = (1)(-1/2) < 0$, $f(c) = 0$ for some c between 0 and 1/2 by the Intermediate Value Theorem, thus $0 \le c \le 1$.

3 (a) According to the Mean Value Theorem for Integrals, there exists c between 0 and 1 satisfying $f(c) = \dfrac{\int_0^1 x \cdot x\, dx}{\int_0^1 x\, dx} = \dfrac{1/3}{1/2} = \dfrac{2}{3}$. Since $f(x) = x$, choose $c = 2/3$.

3 (b) According to the Mean Value Theorem for Integrals, there exists c between 0 and 1 satisfying

$$f(c) = \frac{\int_0^1 x^3\, dx}{\int_0^1 x\, dx} = \frac{1/4}{1/2} = \frac{1}{2}.$$

Since $f(x) = x^2$, this implies $c^2 = 1/2$, or $c = 1/\sqrt{2}$.

3 (c) According to the Mean Value Theorem for Integrals, there exists c between 0 and 1 satisfying $f(c) = \dfrac{\int_0^1 xe^x\, dx}{\int_0^1 e^x\, dx} = \dfrac{1}{e-1}$. Since $f(x) = x$, choose $c = \dfrac{1}{e-1}$.

5 (a) The derivatives evaluated at $x = 0$ are $f(0) = 1, f'(0) = 0, f''(0) = 2, f'''(0) = 0, f^{(iv)}(0) = 12$, and $f^{(v)}(0) = 0$. Then the degree 5 Taylor polynomial is $P(x) = 1 + x^2 + \frac{1}{2}x^4$.

5 (b) The derivatives evaluated at $x = 0$ are $f(0) = 1, f'(0) = 0, f''(0) = -4, f'''(0) = 0, f^{(iv)}(0) = 16$, and $f^{(v)}(0) = 0$. The degree 5 Taylor polynomial is $P(x) = 1 - 2x^2 + \frac{2}{3}x^4$.

5 (c) The derivatives at $x = 0$ are $f(0) = 0, f'(0) = 1, f''(0) = -1, f'''(0) = 2, f^{(iv)}(0) = -6$, and $f^{(v)}(0) = 24$. The degree 5 Taylor polynomial is $P(x) = x - \frac{1}{2}x^2 + \frac{1}{3}x^3 - \frac{1}{4}x^4 + \frac{1}{5}x^5$.

5 (d) The derivatives at $x = 0$ are $f(0) = 0, f'(0) = 0, f''(0) = 2, f'''(0) = 0, f^{(iv)}(0) = -8$, and $f^{(v)}(0) = 0$. The degree 5 Taylor polynomial is $P(x) = x^2 - \frac{1}{3}x^4$.

7 (a) The derivatives at $x = 1$ are $f(1) = 0, f'(1) = 1, f''(1) = -1, f'''(1) = 2$, and $f^{(iv)}(1) = -6$. The degree 4 Taylor polynomial is $P(x) = x - 1 - \frac{1}{2}(x-1)^2 + \frac{1}{3}(x-1)^3 - \frac{1}{4}(x-1)^4$.

7 (b) $f(0.9)$ can be approximated by $P(0.9) = -0.105358\overline{3}$. Likewise, $f(1.1) \approx P(1.1) = 0.095308\overline{3}$.

7 (c) The remainder term is $(x-1)^5/(5c^5)$, where c lies between x and 1. At $x = 0.9$, the error is $(0.1)^5/(5c^5) \le (0.1)^5/(5(0.9)^5) \approx 0.000003387$, where the upper bound results from evaluating c at the worst case $c = 0.9$. At $x = 1.1$, the error is $(0.1)^5/(5c^5) \le (0.1)^5/(5(1.0)^5) \approx 0.000002$. On the basis of the remainder, we predict smaller error at $x = 1.1$.

7 (d) The error at $x = 0.9$ is $|f(0.9) - P(0.9)| = 0.00000218$, and the error at $x = 1.1$ is $|f(1.1) - P(1.1)| = 0.00000185$.

9 The degree one Taylor polynomial is $P(x) = 1 + \frac{1}{2}x$, with Taylor remainder $E = x^2/(8(1+c)^{3/2})$ for c between x and 0. Setting $x = 0.02$, $E \le (0.02)^2/(8(1)^{3/2}) = 0.00005$. The actual values are $\sqrt{1.02} \approx 1.0099505$ and $1 + \frac{1}{2}(0.02) = 1.01$, which is a difference of 0.0000495, slightly less than the upper bound E.

CHAPTER 1
Solving Equations

EXERCISES 1.1   The Bisection Method

1 (a) Check that $f(x) = x^3 - 9$ satisfies $f(2) = -1$ and $f(3) = 27 - 9 = 18$. By the Intermediate Value Theorem, $f(2)f(3) < 0$ implies the existence of a root between $x = 2$ and $x = 3$.

1 (b) Define $f(x) = 3x^3 + x^2 - x - 5$. Check that $f(1) = -2$ and $f(2) = 21$, so there is a root in $[1, 2]$.

1 (c) Define $f(x) = \cos^2 x - x + 6$. Check that $f(6) > 0$ and $f(7) < 0$. There is a root in $[6, 7]$.

3 (a) Start with $f(x) = x^3 + 9$ on $[2, 3]$, where $f(2) < 0$ and $f(3) > 0$. The first step is to evaluate $f\left(\frac{5}{2}\right) = \frac{53}{8} > 0$, which implies the new interval is $[2, \frac{5}{2}]$. The second step is to evaluate $f\left(\frac{9}{4}\right) = \frac{729}{64} - 9 > 0$, giving the interval $[2, \frac{9}{4}]$. The best estimate is the midpoint $x_c = \frac{17}{8}$.

3 (b) Start with $f(x) = 3x^3 + x^2 - x - 5$ on $[1, 2]$, where $f(1) > 0$ and $f(2) < 0$. Since $f\left(\frac{3}{2}\right) > 0$, the second interval is $[1, \frac{3}{2}]$. Since $f\left(\frac{5}{4}\right) > 0$, the third interval is $[1, \frac{5}{4}]$. The best estimate is the endpoint $x_c = \frac{9}{8}$.

3 (c) Start with $f(x) = \cos^2 x + 6 - x$ on $[6, 7]$, where $f(6) > 0$ and $f(7) < 0$. Since $f(6.5) > 0$, the second interval is $[6.5, 7]$. Since $f(6.75) > 0$, the third interval is $[6.75, 7]$. The best estimate is the midpoint $x_c = 6.875$.

5 (a) Setting $f(x) = x^4 - x^3 - 10$, check that $f(2) = -2$ and $f(3) = 44$, so there is a root in $[2, 3]$.

5 (b) According to (1.1), the error after n steps is less than $(3-2)/2^{n+1}$. Ensuring that the error is less than 10^{-10} requires $\left(\frac{1}{2}\right)^{n+1} < 10^{-10}$, or $2^{n+1} > 10^{10}$, which yields $n > 10/\log_{10}(2) - 1 \approx 32.2$. Therefore 33 steps are required.

COMPUTER PROBLEMS 1.1

1 (a) There is a root in $[2, 3]$ (see Exercise 1.1.1). In MATLAB , use the textbook's Program 1.1, `bisect.m`. Six correct decimal places corresponds to error tolerances 5×10^{-7}, according to Def. 1.3. The calling sequence

```
>> f=@(x) x^3-9;
>> xc=bisect(f,2,3,5e-7)
```

returns the approximate root 2.080083.

1 (b)   Similar to (a), on interval $[1, 2]$. The command

```
>> xc=bisect(@(x) 3*x^3+x^2-x-5,1,2,5e-7)
```

returns the approximate root 1.169726.

1 (c)   Similar to (a), on interval $[6, 7]$. The command

```
>> xc=bisect(@(x) cos(x)^2+6-x,6,7,5e-7)
```

returns the approximate root 6.776092.

3 (a)   Plots for parts (a) - (c) are:

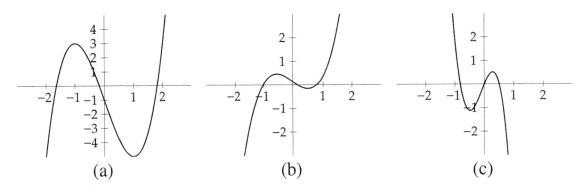

(a)   (b)   (c)

In part (a), it is clear from the graph that there is a root in each of the three intervals $[-2, -1]$, $[-1, 0]$, and $[1, 2]$. The command

```
>> bisect(@(x) 2*x^3-6*x-1,-2,-1,5e-7)
```

yields the first approximate root -1.641783. Repeating for the next two intervals gives the approximate roots -0.168254 and 1.810038.

3 (b)   There are roots in $[-2, -1]$, $[-0.5, 0.5]$, and $[0.5, 1.5]$. Using `bisect` as in part (a) yields the approximate roots -1.023482, 0.163823, and 0.788942.

3 (c)   There are roots in $[-1.7, -0.7]$, $[-0.7, 0.3]$, and $[0.3, 1.3]$. Using `bisect` as in part (a) yields the approximate roots -0.818094, 0, and 0.506308.

5 (a)   There is a root in the interval $[1, 2]$. Eight decimal place accuracy implies an error tolerance of 5×10^{-9}. The command

```
>> bisect(@(x) x^3-2,1,2,5e-9)
```

yields the approximate cube root 1.25992105 in 27 steps.

5 (b)   There is a root in the interval $[1, 2]$. Using `bisect` as in (a) gives the approximate cube root 1.44224957 in 27 steps.

5 (c)   There is a root in the interval $[1, 2]$. Using `bisect` as in (a) gives the approximate cube root 1.70997595 in 27 steps.

7   Trial and error, or a plot of $f(x) = \det(A) - 1000$, shows that $f(-18)f(-17) < 0$ and $f(9)f(10) < 0$. Applying `bisect` to $f(x)$ yields the roots -17.188498 and 9.708299. The backward errors of the roots are $|f(-17.188498)| = 0.0018$ and $|f(9.708299)| = 0.00014$.

9 The desired height is the root of the function $f(H) = \pi H^2(1 - \frac{1}{3}H) - 1$. Using

```
>> bisect(@(H) pi*H^2*(1-H/3)-1,0,1,0.001)
```

gives the solution 636 mm.

EXERCISES 1.2   Fixed-Point Iteration

1 (a) $\dfrac{3}{x} = x \Rightarrow x^2 = 3 \Rightarrow x = \pm\sqrt{3}$

1 (b) $x^2 - 2x + 2 = x \Rightarrow x^2 - 3x + 2 = 0 \Rightarrow x = 1, 2$

1 (c) $x^2 - 4x + 2 = x \Rightarrow x^2 - 5x + 2 = 0 \Rightarrow x = \dfrac{5 \pm \sqrt{17}}{2}$

3 (a) Check by substitution. For example, $\dfrac{1^3 + 1 - 6}{6(1) - 10} = 1$.

3 (b) Check by substitution.

5 (a) No, $g(\sqrt{3}) \neq \sqrt{3}$.

5 (b) Yes, $g(\sqrt{3}) = \dfrac{2\sqrt{3}}{3} + \dfrac{1}{\sqrt{3}} = \sqrt{3}$.

5 (c) No, $g(\sqrt{3}) \neq \sqrt{3}$.

5 (d) Yes, $g(\sqrt{3}) = 1 + \dfrac{2}{\sqrt{3} + 1} = \sqrt{3}$.

7 (a) $g'(x) = \frac{2}{3}(2x - 1)^{-\frac{2}{3}}$, and $|g'(1)| = \frac{2}{3} < 1$. Theorem 1.6 implies that FPI is locally convergent to $r = 1$.

7 (b) $g'(x) = \frac{3}{2}x^2$, and $|g'(1)| = \frac{3}{2} > 1$; FPI diverges from $r = 1$.

7 (c) $g'(x) = \cos x + 1$, and $|g'(0)| = 2 > 1$; FPI diverges from $r = 0$.

9 (a) Solve $\frac{1}{2}x^2 + \frac{1}{2}x = x$ to find the fixed points $r = 0, 1$. The derivative $g'(x) = x + \frac{1}{2}$. By Theorem 1.6, $|g'(0)| = \frac{1}{2} < 1$ implies that FPI converges to $r = 0$, and $|g'(1)| = \frac{3}{2} > 1$ implies that FPI diverges from $r = 1$.

9 (b) Solve $x^2 - \frac{1}{4}x + \frac{3}{8} = x$ to find the fixed points $r = \frac{1}{2}, \frac{3}{4}$. The derivative $g'(x) = 2x - \frac{1}{4}$. $|g'(\frac{1}{2})| = \frac{3}{4} < 1$ implies that FPI is locally convergent to $r = \frac{1}{2}$. $|g'(\frac{3}{4})| = \frac{5}{4} > 1$ implies that FPI diverges from $r = \frac{3}{4}$.

11 (a) There is a variety of answers, obtained by rearranging the equation $x^3 - x + e^x = 0$ to isolate x. For example, $x = x^3 + e^x$, $x = \sqrt[3]{x - e^x}$, $x = \ln(x - x^3)$.

11 (b) As in (a), rearrange $3x^{-2} + 9x^3 = x^2$ to isolate x. For example, $x = \dfrac{3}{x^3} + 9x^2$, $x = \dfrac{1}{9} - \dfrac{1}{3x^4}$, $x = \dfrac{x^5 - 9x^6}{3}$.

13 (a) Solving the fixed point equation $x = g(x) = 0.39 - x^2$ yields the fixed points $r = 0.3$ and -1.3.

13 (b) $g'(x) = -2x$ so $|g'(0.3)| = 0.6$ and $|g'(-1.3)| = 2.6$. By Theorem 1.6, Fixed Point Iteration is locally convergent to $r = 0.3$.

13 (c) Convergence by FPI is at the rate $e_{i+1} \approx 0.6 e_i$, which is slower than the Bisection Method.

15 Check that $\sqrt{5}$ is a fixed point for each iteration. Then calculate convergence rates for the three iterations. (A) $g'(x) = \dfrac{4}{5} - \dfrac{1}{x^2}, g'(\sqrt{5}) = \dfrac{4}{5} - \dfrac{1}{\sqrt{5}^2} = \dfrac{3}{5}$.

(B) $g'(x) = \dfrac{1}{2} + \dfrac{5}{2}\left(-\dfrac{1}{x^2}\right), g'(\sqrt{5}) = \dfrac{1}{2} - \dfrac{1}{2} = 0$.

(C) $g'(x) = -\dfrac{4}{(x+1)^2}, g'(\sqrt{5}) = -\dfrac{4}{(\sqrt{5}+1)^2} \approx -0.382$.

From fastest to slowest: (B), (C), (A).

17 Solving $x^2 = \dfrac{1-x}{2}$ for x results in the two separate equations $g_1(x) = \sqrt{\dfrac{1-x}{2}}$ and $g_2(x) = -\sqrt{\dfrac{1-x}{2}}$. First notice that $g_1(x)$ returns only positive numbers, and $g_2(x)$ only negative. Therefore -1 cannot be a fixed point of $g_1(x)$, and $\frac{1}{2}$ cannot be a fixed point of $g_2(x)$. Check that $g_1(\frac{1}{2}) = \frac{1}{2}$ and $g_1'(x) = -\dfrac{1}{2\sqrt{2-2x}}$. $|g_1'(\frac{1}{2})| = \frac{1}{2} < 1$ confirms that FPI with $g_1(x)$ is locally convergent to $r = \frac{1}{2}$. Likewise, $g_2(-1) = -1$, $g_2'(x) = \dfrac{1}{2\sqrt{2-2x}}$ and $|g_2'(-1)| = \frac{1}{4}$ implies that FPI with $g_2(x)$ is locally convergent to $r = -1$.

19 Define $g(x) = (x + A/x^2)/2$. Since $|g'(\sqrt[3]{A})| = \frac{1}{2} < 1$, FPI is locally convergent to the cube root $\sqrt[3]{A}$.

21 (a) Substitute roots and check.

21 (b) $g'(x) = -5 + 15x - \frac{15}{2}x^2$. FPI diverges from all three roots, because $|g'(1 - \sqrt{3/5})| = |g'(1 + \sqrt{3/5})| = 2$ and $|g'(1)| = 2.5$.

23 The slopes of g at r_1 and r_3 imply that the graph of $y = g(x)$ must pass through the line $y = x$ at $x = r_2$ from below the line to above the line. Therefore $g'(r_2)$ must belong to the interval $(1, \infty)$.

25 Let x belong to $[a, b]$. By the Mean Value Theorem, $|g(x_0) - r| \leq B|x_0 - r| < |x_0 - r|$. Since r belongs to $[a, b]$, $x_1 = g(x_0)$ does also, and by extension, so does x_2, x_3, etc. Similarly, $|x_1 - r| \leq B|x_0 - r|$ extends to $|x_i - r| \leq B^i |x_0 - r|$, which converges to zero as $i \to \infty$.

27 (a) Solving $x - x^3 = x$ yields $x^3 = 0$, or $x = 0$.

27 (b) Assume $0 < x_0 < 1$. Then $x_0^3 < x_0$, and so $0 < x_1 = x_0 - x_0^3 < x_0 < 1$. The same argument implies by induction that $x_0 > x_1 > x_2 > ... > 0$.

27 (c)   The limit $L = \lim\limits_{i \to \infty} x_i$ exists because the x_i form a bounded monotonic sequence. Since $g(x)$ is continuous, $g(L) = g(\lim\limits_{i \to \infty} x_i) = \lim\limits_{i \to \infty} g(x_i) = \lim\limits_{i \to \infty} x_{i+1} = L$, so L is a fixed point, and by (a), $L = 0$.

29 (a)   Set $g(x) = \dfrac{x^3 + (c+1)x - 2}{c}$. Then $g'(x) = \dfrac{3x^2 + (c+1)}{c}$, and $|g'(1)| = |\dfrac{4+c}{c}| < 1$ for $c < -2$. By Theorem 1.6, FPI is locally convergent to $r = 1$ if $c < -2$.

29 (b) $g'(1) = 0$ if $c = -4$.

31   By factoring or the quadratic formula, the roots of the equation are $-\frac{5}{4}$ and $\frac{1}{4}$. Set $g(x) = \frac{5}{16} - x^2$. Using the cobweb diagram of $g(x)$, it is clear that initial guesses in $(-\frac{5}{4}, \frac{5}{4})$ converge to $r_2 = \frac{1}{4}$, and initial guesses in $(-\infty, -\frac{5}{4}) \cup (\frac{5}{4}, \infty)$ diverge to $-\infty$ under FPI. Initial guesses $-\frac{5}{4}$ and $\frac{5}{4}$ limit on $-\frac{5}{4}$.

33 (a)   Choose $a = 0$ and $|b| < 1$, c arbitrary. Since $a = 0$, $r = 0$ is a fixed point, and $g'(x) = b + 2cx$ implies $|g'(0)| = |b| < 1$, so FPI is locally convergent to 0 by Theorem 1.6.

33 (b)   Choose $a = 0$ and $|b| > 1$ to make initial guesses move away from the fixed point 0.

COMPUTER PROBLEMS 1.2

1 (a)   Define $g(x) = (2x + 2)^{\frac{1}{3}}$, for example. Using the `fpi` code, the command

```
>> x=fpi(@(x) (2*x+2)^(1/3),1/2,20)
```

yields the solution 1.76929235 to 8 correct decimal places.

1 (b)   Define $g(x) = \ln(7 - x)$. Using `fpi` as in part (a) returns the solution 1.67282170 to 8 correct decimal places.

1 (c)   Define $g(x) = \ln(4 - \sin x)$. Using `fpi` as in part (a) returns the solution 1.12998050 to 8 correct decimal places.

3 (a)   Iterate $g(x) = (x + 3/x)/2$ with starting guess 1. After 4 steps of FPI, the results is 1.73205081 to 8 correct places.

3 (b)   Iterate $g(x) = (x + 5/x)/2$ with starting guess 1. After 5 steps of FPI, the results is 2.23606798 to 8 correct places.

5   Iterating $g(x) = \cos^2 x$ with initial guess $x_0 = 1$ results in 0.641714 to six correct places after 350 steps. Checking $|g'(0.641714)| \approx 0.96$ verifies that FPI is locally convergent by Theorem 1.6.

7 (a)   Almost all numbers between 0 and 1.

7 (b)   Almost all numbers between 1 and 2.

7 (c)   Any number greater than 3 or less than -1 will work.

EXERCISES 1.3   Limits of Accuracy

1 (a)   The forward error is $|r - x_c| = |0.75 - 0.74| = 0.01$. The backward error is $|f(x_c)| = |4(0.74) - 3| = 0.04$.

1 (b) $FE = |r - x_c| = 0.01$ as in (a). $BE = |f(0.74)| = (0.04)^2 = 0.0016$.

1 (c) $FE = |r - x_c| = 0.01$ as in (a). $BE = |f(0.74)| = (0.04)^3 = 0.000064$.

1 (d) $FE = |r - x_c| = 0.01$ as in (a). $BE = |f(0.74)| = (0.04)^{\frac{1}{3}} = 0.342$.

3 (a)   Check derivatives: $f(0) = f'(0) = 0$, $f''(0) = \cos 0 = 1$. The multiplicity of the root $r = 0$ is 2.

3 (b)   The forward error is $|r - x_c| = |0 - 0.0001| = 0.0001$. The backward error is $|f(x_c)| = |1 - \cos 0.0001| \approx 5 \times 10^{-9}$.

5   The root of $f(x) = ax - b$ is $r = b/a$. If x_c is an approximate root, the forward error is $FE = |b/a - x_c|$ while the backward error is $BE = |f(x_c)| = |ax_c - b| = |a||\frac{b}{a} - x_c| = |a|FE$. Therefore the backward error is a factor of $|a|$ larger than the forward error.

7 (a) $W'(x) = (x - 2) \cdots (x - 20) + (x - 1)(x - 3) \cdots (x - 20) + \ldots + (x - 1) \cdots (x - 19)$, so $W'(16) = (16 - 1)(16 - 2) \cdots (16 - 15)(16 - 17)(16 - 18)(16 - 19)(16 - 20) = 15!4!$

7 (b)   For a general integer j between 1 and 20,
$W'(j) = (j - 1)(j - 2) \cdots (1)(-1)(-2) \cdots (j - 20) = (-1)^j(j - 1)!(20 - j)!$

COMPUTER PROBLEMS 1.3

1 (a)   Check the derivatives of $f(x) = \sin x - x$ to see that $f(0) = f'(0) = f''(0) = 0$ and $f'''(0) = -\cos 0 = -1$, giving multiplicity 3.

1 (b)   `fzero` returns $x_c = -2.0735 \times 10^{-8}$. The forward error is 2.0735×10^{-8} and MATLAB reports the backward error to be $|f(x_c)| = 0$. This means the true backward error is likely less than machine epsilon.

3 (a)   The MATLAB command

```
>> xc=fzero(@(x) 2*x*cos(x)-2*x+sin(x^3),[-0.1,0.2])
```

returns $x_c = 0.00016881$. The forward error is $|x_c - r| = 0.00016881$ and the backward error is reported by MATLAB as $|f(x_c)| = 0$.

3 (b)   The bisection method with starting interval $[-0.1, 0.2]$ stops after 13 steps, giving $x_c = -0.00006103$. Neither method can determine the root $r = 0$ to more than about 3 correct decimal places.

5 To use (1.21), set $f(x) = (x-1)(x-2)(x-3)(x-4)$, $\epsilon = -10^{-6}$ and $g(x) = x^6$. Then near the root $r = 4$, $\Delta r \approx -\epsilon g(r)/f'(r) = 4^6/6 \approx 0.00068267$. According to (1.22), the error magnification factor is $|g(r)|/|rf'(r)| = 4^6/24 \approx 170.7$. `fzero` returns the approximate root 4.00068251, close to the guess 4.00068267 given by (1.21).

EXERCISES 1.4   Newton's Method

1 (a) $x_1 = x_0 - (x_0^3 + x_0 - 2)/(3x_0^2 + 1) = 0 - (-2)/(1) = 2$; $x_2 = 2 - (2^3 + 2 - 2)/(3(2^2) + 1) = 18/13$.

1 (b) $x_1 = x_0 - (x_0^4 - x_0^2 + x_0 - 1)/(4x_0^3 - 2x_0 + 1) = 1$; $x_2 = 1$.

1 (c) $x_1 = x_0 - (x_0^2 - x_0 - 1)/(2x_0 - 1) = -1$; $x_2 = -\frac{2}{3}$.

3 (a) According to Theorem 1.11, $f'(-1) = 8$ implies that convergence to $r = -1$ is quadratic, with $e_{i+1} \approx |f''(-1)/(2f'(-1))|e_i^2 = |-40/(2)(8)|e_i^2 = 2.5e_i^2$; $f'(0) = -1$ implies convergence to $r = 0$ is quadratic, $e_{i+1} \approx 2e_i^2$; $f'(1) = f''(1) = 0$ and $f'''(1) = 12$ implies that convergence to $r = 1$ is linear, $e_{i+1} \approx \frac{2}{3}e_i$.

3 (b) $f'(-\frac{1}{2}) = -27/4$ implies that convergence to $r = -\frac{1}{2}$ is quadratic, with error relationship $e_{i+1} \approx |27/2(-\frac{27}{4})|e_i^2 = 2e_i^2$; $f'(1) = f''(1) = 0$ and $f'''(1) = 18$ implies that convergence to $r = 1$ is linear, $e_{i+1} \approx \frac{2}{3}e_i$.

5 Convergence to $r = 0$ is quadratic since $f'(0) = -1 \neq 0$, so Newton's Method converges faster than the Bisection Method. Convergence to $r = \frac{1}{2}$ is linear since $f'(\frac{1}{2}) = f''(\frac{1}{2}) = 0$ and $f'''(\frac{1}{2}) = 24$, with $e_{i+1} \approx \frac{2}{3}e_i$. Since $S = \frac{2}{3} > \frac{1}{2}$, Newton's Method will converge to $r = \frac{1}{2}$ slower than the Bisection Method.

7 Computing derivatives, $f'(2) = f''(2) = 0$ and $f'''(2) = 6$ implies that $r = 2$ is a triple root. Therefore Newton's Method does not converge quadratically, but converges linearly and $e_{i+1}/e_i \to \frac{2}{3}$ according to Theorem 1.12.

9 Since $f'(x) = 2x$, Newton's Method is

$$x_{i+1} = x_i - \frac{x_i^2 - A}{2x_i} = \frac{x_i}{2} + \frac{A}{2x_i} = \frac{x_i + A/x_i}{2}.$$

11 The nth root of A is the real root of $f(x) = x^n - A = 0$. Newton's Method applied to the equation is

$$x_{i+1} = x_i - \frac{x_i^n - A}{nx_i^{n-1}} = \frac{n-1}{n}x_i + \frac{A}{nx_i^{n-1}} = \frac{(n-1)x_i + A/x_i^{n-1}}{n}.$$

Since $f'(A^{\frac{1}{n}}) = nA^{\frac{n-1}{n}}$, Theorem 1.11 implies that Newton's Method converges quadratically as long as $A \neq 0$.

13 (a)   Newton's Method converges quadratically to $r = 2$ since $f'(2) = 8 \neq 0$, and $e_5 \approx$ $f''(2)/(2f'(2))e_4^2 = \frac{3}{4}(10^{-6})^2 = 0.75 \times 10^{-12}$.

13 (b)   Since $f'(0) = -4$ and $f''(0) = 0$, Theorem 1.11 implies that $\lim_{i \to \infty} e_{i+1}/e_i^2 = 0$, and no useful estimate of e_5 follows. Essentially, convergence is faster than quadratic. Reverting to the definition of Newton's Method, $x_{i+1} = x_i - \dfrac{x_i^3 - 4x_i}{3x_i^2 - 4} = \dfrac{2x_i^3}{3x_i^2 - 4}$, and because $r = 0$,

$e_{i+1} = \left| \dfrac{2e_i^3}{3e_i^2 - 4} \right|$. Substituting $e_4 = 10^{-6}$ yields $e_5 = \left| \dfrac{2 \times 10^{-18}}{3 \times 10^{-12} - 4} \right| \approx 0.5 \times 10^{-18}$.

COMPUTER PROBLEMS 1.4

1 (a)   Newton's Method is $x_{i+1} = x_i - (x_i^3 - 2x_i - 2)/(3x_i^2 - 2)$. Setting $x_0 = 1$ yields $x_7 = 1.76929235$ to eight decimal places.

1 (b)   Applying Newton's Method with $x_0 = 1$ yields $x_5 = 1.67282170$ to eight places.

1 (c)   Applying Newton's Method with $x_0 = 1$ yields $x_3 = 1.12998050$ to eight places.

3 (a)   Newton's Method converges linearly to $x_c = -0.6666648$. Subtracting x_c from x_i shows error ratios $|x_{i+1} - x_c|/|x_i - x_c| \approx \frac{2}{3}$, implying a multiplicity 3 root. Applying Modified Newton's Method with $m = 3$ and $x_0 = 0.5$ converges to $x_c = -\frac{2}{3}$.

3 (b)   Newton's Method converges linearly to $x_c = 0.166666669$. The error ratios $|x_{i+1} - x_c|/|x_i - x_c| \approx \frac{1}{2}$, implying a multiplicity 2 root. Applying Modified Newton's Method with $m = 2$ and $x_0 = 1$ converges quadratically to $0.166666667 \approx \frac{1}{6}$. In fact, one checks by direct substitution that the root is $r = \frac{1}{6}$.

5   The volume of the silo is $400 = 10\pi r^2 + \frac{2}{3}\pi r^3$. Solving for r by Newton's Method yields 3.2362 meters.

7   Newton's Method converges quadratically to -1.197624 and 1.530134, and converges linearly to the root 0. The error ratio is $|x_{i+1} - 0|/|x_i - 0| \approx \frac{3}{4}$, implying that $r = 0$ is a multiplicity 4 root. This can be confirmed by evaluating the first four derivatives.

9   Newton's Method converges quadratically to 0.8571428571 with quadratic error ratio $M = \lim_{i \to \infty} e_{i+1}/e_i^2 \approx 2.4$, and converges linearly to the root 2 with error ratio $S = \lim_{i \to \infty} e_{i+1}/e_i \approx \dfrac{2}{3}$.

11   Solving the ideal gas law for an initial approximation gives $V_0 = nRT/P = 1.75$. Applying Newton's Method to the non-ideal gas Van der Waal's equation with initial guess $V_0 = 1.75$ converges to $V = 1.701$.

13 (a)   The equation is equivalent to $1 - 3/(4x) = 0$, and has the root $r = \frac{3}{4}$.

13 (b)   Newton's Method applied to $f(x) = (1 - 3/(4x))^{\frac{1}{3}}$ does not converge.

13 (c) $f(x)$ is not differentiable at 0.

EXERCISES 1.5   Root-Finding without Derivatives

1 (a) Applying the Secant Method with $x_0 = 1$ and $x_1 = 2$ yields $x_2 = x_1 - \dfrac{(x_1 - x_0)f(x_1)}{f(x_1) - f(x_0)} = \dfrac{8}{5}$
and $x_3 \approx 1.742268$.

1 (b) Using the Secant Method formula with $x_0 = 1$ and $x_1 = 2$ as in (a) returns $x_2 \approx 1.578707$
and $x_3 \approx 1.660160$.

1 (c) The Secant Method yields $x_2 \approx 1.092907$ and $x_3 \approx 1.119357$.

3 (a) Applying IQI with $x_0 = 1$, $x_1 = 2$ and $x_2 = 0$ yields $x_3 = -\frac{1}{5}$ and $x_4 \approx -0.11996018$
from formula (1.37).

3 (b) Applying the IQI formula gives $x_3 \approx 1.75771279$ and $x_4 \approx 1.66253117$.

3 (c) Applying IQI as in (a) and (b) yields $x_3 \approx 1.13948155$ and $x_4 \approx 1.12927246$.

5 Setting $A = f(a)$, $B = f(b)$, $C = f(c)$, and $y = 0$ in (1.35) gives

$$
\begin{aligned}
P(0) &= \frac{af(b)f(c)}{(f(a) - f(b))(f(a) - f(c))} + \frac{bf(a)f(c)}{(f(b) - f(a))(f(b) - f(c))} \\
&\quad + \frac{cf(a)f(b)}{(f(c) - f(a))(f(c) - f(b))} \\
&= \frac{a\frac{f(b)-f(c)}{f(a)} + b\frac{f(c)-f(a)}{f(b)} + c\frac{f(a)-f(b)}{f(c)}}{(1 - \frac{f(b)}{f(a)})(\frac{f(a)}{f(c)} - 1)(1 - \frac{f(c)}{f(b)})} \\
&= \frac{as(1 - qs) + bqs(r - q) + c(q - 1)}{(q - 1)(r - 1)(s - 1)} \\
&= c + \frac{as(1 - r) + br(r - q) - c(r^2 - qr - rs + s)}{(q - 1)(r - 1)(s - 1)} \\
&= c - \frac{(c - b)r(r - q) + (c - a)s(1 - r)}{(q - 1)(r - 1)(s - 1)}.
\end{aligned}
$$

7 (a) (A) is the Bisection Method, which cuts uncertainty in half on each step.
(B) Check that $f'(2^{1/4}) = (4)2^{3/4} \neq 0$. Therefore the Secant Method converges superlinearly.
(C) $2^{1/4}$ is a fixed point because $g(2^{1/4}) = \dfrac{2^{1/4}}{2} + \dfrac{1}{2^{3/4}} = \dfrac{2^{1/4} + 2^{1/4}}{2} = 2^{1/4}$.
Note that $g'(x) = \dfrac{1}{2} - \dfrac{3}{x^4} \Rightarrow g'(2^{1/4}) = \dfrac{1}{2} - \dfrac{3}{(2^{1/4})^4} = \dfrac{1}{2} - \dfrac{3}{2} = -1$.

(D) $2^{1/4}$ is a fixed point because $g(2^{1/4}) = \dfrac{2^{1/4}}{3} + \dfrac{1}{(3)2^{3/4}} = \dfrac{2 + 1}{(3)2^{3/4}} = 2^{1/4}$.
Note that $g'(x) = \dfrac{1}{3} - \dfrac{3}{3x^4} \Rightarrow g'(2^{1/4}) = \dfrac{1}{3} - \dfrac{1}{(2^{1/4})^4} = \dfrac{1}{3} - \dfrac{1}{2} = -1/6$.

Fastest to slowest: (B), (D), (A); (C) does not converge to $2^{1/4}$.

7 (b) Newton's Method will converge faster than the four above choices.

COMPUTER PROBLEMS 1.5

1 (a)   Applying the Secant Method formula shows convergence to the root 1.76929235

1 (b)   1.67282170

1 (c)   1.12998050.

3 (a)   Applying formula (1.37) for Inverse Quadratic Interpolation shows convergence to 1.76929235.

3 (b)   Similar to part (a). Converges to 1.67282170

3 (c)   Similar to part (a). Converges to 1.129998050.

5   The MATLAB command

```
>> fzero(@(x) 1/x,[-2,1])
```

converges to zero, although there is no root there.

CHAPTER 2
Systems of Equations

EXERCISES 2.1   Gaussian Elimination

1 (a)   Subtracting $\frac{5}{2}$ times the first equation from the second equation yields $\frac{3}{2}y = 3$, or $y = 2$. Substituting $y = 2$ into the first equation gives $2x - 3(2) = 2$, or $x = 4$.

1 (b)   Subtracting 2 times the first equation from the second equation yields $-y = 3$, or $y = -3$. Substituting into the first equation gives $x - 6 = -1$, or $x = 5$.

1 (c)   Subtracting -3 times the first equation from the second yields $7y = 21$, or $y = 3$. Substituting into the first equation gives $-x + 3 = 2$, or $x = 1$.

3 (a) $5z = 5$ implies $z = 1$; $3y - 4(1) = -1$ implies $y = 1$; $3x - 4(1) + 5(1) = 2$ implies $x = \frac{1}{3}$.

3 (b) $-3z = 3$ implies $z = -1$; $4y - 3(-1) = 1$ implies $y = -\frac{1}{2}$; $x - 2(-\frac{1}{2}) + (-1) = 2$ implies $x = 2$.

5   If n increases to $3n$, the approximate operation count changed from $2n^3/3$ to $2(3n)^3/3 = 54n^3/3$, which will take 27 times as long.

7   It is given that $(4000)^2$ operations require 0.002 seconds, corresponding to $500(4000)^2$ operations per second. Using the operation count $2n^3/3$, it will take about $(2(9000)^3/3)/(500(4000)^2) \approx 61$ seconds, to solve a general 9000×9000 system.

COMPUTER PROBLEMS 2.1

1 (a)   Putting together the code fragments from the bottom of pages 79 and 81 gives the program

```
for j=1:n-1
  for i=j+1:n
    if abs(a(j,j))<eps; error('zero pivot encountered'); end
    mult = a(i,j)/a(j,j);
    for k = j+1:n
      a(i,k) = a(i,k) - mult*a(j,k);
    end
    b(i) = b(i) - mult*b(j);
  end
end
for i = n:-1:1
  for j = i+1:n
```

```
    b(i) = b(i) - a(i,j)*x(j);
  end
  x(i) = b(i)/a(i,i);
end
```

Define the coefficient matrix a=[2 -2 -1;4 1 -2;-2 1 -1], b=[-2;1;-3] and apply the preceding MATLAB program. The result is $x = [1, 1, 2]$.

1 (b) Proceed as in (a); the result of the MATLAB program is $x = [1, 1, 1]$.

1 (c) Proceed as in (a); the result is $x = [-1, 3, 2]$.

EXERCISES 2.2   The LU Factorization

1 (a) Subtracting 3 times the top row from the second row yields the upper triangular matrix $U = \begin{bmatrix} 1 & 2 \\ 0 & -2 \end{bmatrix}$. The matrix of multipliers is $L = \begin{bmatrix} 1 & 0 \\ 3 & 1 \end{bmatrix}$. Check by multiplication:

$$LU = \begin{bmatrix} 1 & 0 \\ 3 & 1 \end{bmatrix}\begin{bmatrix} 1 & 2 \\ 0 & -2 \end{bmatrix} = \begin{bmatrix} 1 & 2 \\ 3 & 4 \end{bmatrix}.$$

1 (b) Subtracting 2 times the top row from the second row yields

$$U = \begin{bmatrix} 1 & 3 \\ 0 & -4 \end{bmatrix} \text{ and } L = \begin{bmatrix} 1 & 0 \\ 2 & 1 \end{bmatrix}.$$

Check by multiplication:

$$LU = \begin{bmatrix} 1 & 0 \\ 2 & 1 \end{bmatrix}\begin{bmatrix} 1 & 3 \\ 0 & -4 \end{bmatrix} = \begin{bmatrix} 1 & 3 \\ 2 & 2 \end{bmatrix}.$$

1 (c) Subtracting $-\frac{5}{3}$ times the top row from the second row yields

$$U = \begin{bmatrix} 3 & -4 \\ 0 & -\frac{14}{3} \end{bmatrix} \text{ and } L = \begin{bmatrix} 1 & 0 \\ -\frac{5}{3} & 1 \end{bmatrix}.$$

Check by multiplication:

$$LU = \begin{bmatrix} 1 & 0 \\ -\frac{5}{3} & 1 \end{bmatrix}\begin{bmatrix} 3 & -4 \\ 0 & -\frac{14}{3} \end{bmatrix} = \begin{bmatrix} 3 & -4 \\ -5 & 2 \end{bmatrix}.$$

3 (a) Subtracting 2 times the top row from the second row gives the factorization

$$LU = \begin{bmatrix} 1 & 0 \\ 2 & 1 \end{bmatrix}\begin{bmatrix} 3 & 7 \\ 0 & 13 \end{bmatrix}.$$

Solving $Lc = b$, or

$$\begin{bmatrix} 1 & 0 \\ 2 & 1 \end{bmatrix} \begin{bmatrix} c_1 \\ c_2 \end{bmatrix} = \begin{bmatrix} 1 \\ -11 \end{bmatrix},$$

yields $c_1 = 1$ and $2(1) + c_2 = -11$, or $c_2 = -13$. Solving $Ux = c$, or

$$\begin{bmatrix} 3 & 7 \\ 0 & -13 \end{bmatrix} \begin{bmatrix} x_1 \\ x_2 \end{bmatrix} = \begin{bmatrix} 1 \\ -13 \end{bmatrix},$$

gives $x_2 = 1$ and $3x_1 + 7 = 1$, or $x_1 = -2$. Thus $x = [-2, 1]$.

3 (b) Subtracting 2 times the top row from the second row gives the factorization

$$LU = \begin{bmatrix} 1 & 0 \\ 2 & 1 \end{bmatrix} \begin{bmatrix} 2 & 3 \\ 0 & 1 \end{bmatrix}.$$

Solving $Lc = b$, or

$$\begin{bmatrix} 1 & 0 \\ 2 & 1 \end{bmatrix} \begin{bmatrix} c_1 \\ c_2 \end{bmatrix} = \begin{bmatrix} 1 \\ 3 \end{bmatrix},$$

yields $c_1 = 1$ and $2(1) + c_2 = 3$, or $c_2 = 1$. Solving $Ux = c$, or

$$\begin{bmatrix} 2 & 3 \\ 0 & 1 \end{bmatrix} \begin{bmatrix} x_1 \\ x_2 \end{bmatrix} = \begin{bmatrix} 1 \\ 1 \end{bmatrix},$$

gives $x_2 = 1$ and $2x_1 + 3(1) = 1$, or $x_1 = -1$. Thus $x = [-1, 1]$.

5 Since A is already factored as LU, only the back substitution is needed. Solving $Lc = b$, or

$$\begin{bmatrix} 1 & 0 & 0 & 0 \\ 0 & 1 & 0 & 0 \\ 1 & 3 & 1 & 0 \\ 4 & 1 & 2 & 1 \end{bmatrix} \begin{bmatrix} c_1 \\ c_2 \\ c_3 \\ c_4 \end{bmatrix} = \begin{bmatrix} 1 \\ 1 \\ 2 \\ 0 \end{bmatrix},$$

yields $c_1 = 1, c_2 = 1, c_3 = -2$, and $c_4 = -1$. Solving $Ux = c$, or

$$\begin{bmatrix} 2 & 1 & 0 & 0 \\ 0 & 1 & 2 & 0 \\ 0 & 0 & -1 & 1 \\ 0 & 0 & 0 & 1 \end{bmatrix} \begin{bmatrix} x_1 \\ x_2 \\ x_3 \\ x_4 \end{bmatrix} = \begin{bmatrix} 1 \\ 1 \\ -2 \\ -1 \end{bmatrix},$$

yields $x_4 = -1, x_3 = 1, x_2 = -1$, and $x_1 = 1$. Thus $x = [1, -1, 1, -1]$.

7 To solve 1000 upper-triangular 500×500 systems requires 1000 back substitutions, or approximately $1000(500)^2$ operations. To solve one full 5000×5000 system requires approximately

$2(5000)^3/3 + 2(5000)^2 \approx 2(5000)^3/3$ operations. The number of seconds to solve the latter is the ratio

$$\frac{2(5000)^3/3}{1000(500)^2} = \frac{1000}{3} \approx 333 \text{ seconds},$$

or 5 minutes, 33 seconds (or 5 minutes, 34 seconds if the $2(5000)^2$ term is not neglected).

9   The first problem $Ax = b_0$ requires approximately $2n^3/3$ multiplications, while the 100 subsequent problems require $2n^2$ each. Setting the two equal gives the equation $\dfrac{2n^3}{3} = 200n^2$, or $n = 300$.

COMPUTER PROBLEMS 2.2

1 The elimination part of the code must be supplemented by filling in the entries of L and U. The diagonal entries of L are ones, and the remaining entries are the multipliers from `mult`. It is also necessary to change the k loop to go from j to n, in order to place a zero in the eliminated location of U. MATLAB code follows:

```
l=diag(ones(n,1));
for j = 1:n-1
  for i = j+1:n
    if abs(a(j,j))<eps; error('zero pivot encountered'); end
    mult = a(i,j)/a(j,j);l(i,j)=mult;
    for k = j:n
      a(i,k) = a(i,k) - mult*a(j,k);
    end
  end
end
l
u=a
```

EXERCISES 2.3   Sources of Error

1 (a)   The matrix infinity norm is the maximum of the absolute row sums, in this case the maximum of 3 and 7. So $||A||_\infty = 7$.

1 (b)   The maximum of the absolute row sums is $|1| + |-7| + |0| = 8$.

3 (a)   The solution of the system

$$\begin{bmatrix} 1 & 1 \\ 1.0001 & 1 \end{bmatrix} \begin{bmatrix} x_1 \\ x_2 \end{bmatrix} = \begin{bmatrix} 2 \\ 2.0001 \end{bmatrix},$$

is $[1, 1]$. The forward error is $||[1, 1] - [-1, 3]||_\infty = 2$. The backward error is the infinity norm of

$$b - Ax_c = \begin{bmatrix} 2 \\ 2.0001 \end{bmatrix} - \begin{bmatrix} 1 & 1 \\ 1.0001 & 1 \end{bmatrix} \begin{bmatrix} -1 \\ 3 \end{bmatrix} = \begin{bmatrix} 0 \\ 0.0002 \end{bmatrix},$$

which is 0.0002. The error magnification factor is the ratio of the relative forward and backward errors, or $(2/1)/(0.0002/2.0001) = 20001$.

3 (b) The forward error is $||[1, 1] - [0, 2]|| = 1$. The backward error is the infinity norm of

$$b - Ax_c = \begin{bmatrix} 2 \\ 2.0001 \end{bmatrix} - \begin{bmatrix} 2 \\ 2 \end{bmatrix} = \begin{bmatrix} 0 \\ 0.0001 \end{bmatrix},$$

which is 0.0001. The error magnification factor is the ratio of the relative forward and backward errors, or $(1/1)/(0.0001/2.0001) = 20001$.

3 (c) The calculation is similar to (a) and (b). The forward error is $||[1, 1] - [2, 2]|| = 1$, the backward error is $||[-2, -2.0001]|| = 2.0001$, and the error magnification factor is $(1/1)/(2.0001/2.0001) = 1$.

3 (d) Forward error is $||[1, 1] - [-2, 4]|| = 3$, the backward error is $||[0, 0.0003]|| = 0.0003$, and the error magnification factor is $(3/1)/(0.0003/2.0001) = 20001$.

3 (e) Forward error is $||[1, 1] - [-2, 4.0001]|| = 3.0001$, the backward error is $||[0.0001, 0.0002]|| = 0.0002$, and the error magnification factor is $(3.0001/1)/(0.0002/2.0001) = 30002.5$.

5 (a) The solution of the system

$$\begin{bmatrix} 1 & -2 \\ 3 & -4 \end{bmatrix} \begin{bmatrix} x_1 \\ x_2 \end{bmatrix} = \begin{bmatrix} 3 \\ 7 \end{bmatrix},$$

is $[1, -1]$. The forward error is $||[1, -1] - [-2, -4]||_\infty = 3$, and the relative forward error is $3/||[1, -1]|| = 3$. The backward error is the infinity norm of

$$b - Ax_c = \begin{bmatrix} 3 \\ 7 \end{bmatrix} - \begin{bmatrix} 1 & -2 \\ 3 & -4 \end{bmatrix} \begin{bmatrix} -2 \\ -4 \end{bmatrix} = \begin{bmatrix} -3 \\ -3 \end{bmatrix},$$

and the relative backward error is is $||[-3, -3||/||[3, 7]|| = 3/7$. The error magnification factor is the ratio of the relative forward and backward errors, or $3/\frac{3}{7} = 7$.

5 (b) The forward error is $||[1, -1] - [-2, -3]||_\infty = 3$, and the relative forward error is $3/1 = 3$. The backward error is the infinity norm of

$$b - Ax_c = \begin{bmatrix} 3 \\ 7 \end{bmatrix} - \begin{bmatrix} 1 & -2 \\ 3 & -4 \end{bmatrix} \begin{bmatrix} -2 \\ -3 \end{bmatrix} = \begin{bmatrix} 0 \\ 1 \end{bmatrix},$$

and the relative backward error is is $||[0, 1||/7 = 1/7$. The error magnification factor is the ratio $3/\frac{1}{7} = 21$.

5 (c) The forward error is $||[1, -1] - [0, -2]||_\infty = 1$, and the relative forward error is $1/1 = 1$. The backward error is the infinity norm of $[-1, -1]$, and the relative backward error is is $1/7$. The error magnification factor is the ratio of the relative forward and backward errors, or $1/\frac{1}{7} = 7$.

5 (d) The forward error is $||[1, -1] - [-1, -1]||_\infty = 2$, and the relative forward error is $2/1 = 2$. The backward error is $||[3, 7] - [1, 1]||_\infty = 6$, and the relative backward error is is $6/7$. The error magnification factor is $2/\frac{6}{7} = 7/3$.

5 (e) The inverse matrix is

$$A^{-1} = \begin{bmatrix} -2 & 1 \\ -\frac{3}{2} & \frac{1}{2} \end{bmatrix}.$$

The condition number of A is $||A|| \cdot ||A^{-1}|| = 7 \cdot 3 = 21$.

7 The maximum row of the 5×5 Hilbert matrix is the top row $[1, \frac{1}{2}, \frac{1}{3}, \frac{1}{4}, \frac{1}{5}]$, and $||H||_\infty = 1 + \frac{1}{2} + \frac{1}{3} + \frac{1}{4} + \frac{1}{5} = \frac{137}{60}$.

9 (a) The three properties that define a vector norm must be checked.
(i) $||x||_\infty \geq 0$ is guaranteed by the definition $||x||_\infty = \max|x_i|$, and if $||x||_\infty = 0$, then all components x_i must be zero.
(ii) For a scalar α,

$$\begin{aligned} ||\alpha x||_\infty &= \max\{|\alpha x_1|, \ldots, |\alpha x_n|\} \\ &= \max\{|\alpha||x_1|, \ldots, |\alpha||x_n|\} \\ &= |\alpha| \max\{|x_1|, \ldots, |x_n|\} \\ &= |\alpha| \cdot ||x||_\infty. \end{aligned}$$

(iii)

$$\begin{aligned} ||x + y||_\infty &= \max\{|x_1 + y_1|, \ldots, |x_n + y_n|\} \\ &\leq \max\{|x_1| + |y_1|, \ldots, |x_n| + |y_n|\} \\ &\leq \max\{|x_1|, \ldots, |x_n|\} + \max\{|y_1|, \ldots, |y_n|\} \\ &= ||x||_\infty + ||y||_\infty \end{aligned}$$

9 (b) The three properties:
(i) $||x||_1 \geq 0$ is guaranteed by the definition $||x||_1 = |x_1| + \ldots + |x_n|$, and if $||x||_1 = 0$, all components x_i must be zero.
(ii) For a scalar α,

$$\begin{aligned} ||\alpha x||_1 &= |\alpha x_1| + \ldots + |\alpha x_n| \\ &= |\alpha|(|x_1| + \ldots + |x_n|) \\ &= |\alpha| \cdot ||x||_1 \end{aligned}$$

(iii) The triangle inequality is

$$\begin{aligned} ||x + y||_1 &= |x_1 + y_1| + \ldots + |x_n + y_n| \\ &\leq |x_1| + |y_1| + \ldots + |x_n| + |y_n| \\ &= ||x||_1 + ||y||_1 \end{aligned}$$

11   For a matrix A, the operator norm of the vector infinity norm is $\max \dfrac{||Ax||_\infty}{||x||_\infty}$. where the maximum is taken over all vectors x. By property (ii) of vector norms, this is equal to the maximum $||Ax||_\infty$, where the maximum is taken over all unit vectors x in the infinity norm, or $\max ||Ax||_\infty = \max\{a_{11}x_1 + \ldots + a_{1n}x_n, \ldots, a_{n1}x_1 + \ldots + a_{nn}x_n\}$ where $|x_1|, \ldots, |x_n| \leq 1$. In fact, the maximum is reached when all x_i are $+1$ or -1, where the sign of x_i is chosen to match the sign of a_{i1}. Here i denotes the largest row in the sense of the infinity vector norm. Therefore $||A||_\infty = $ maximum absolute row sum of $A = \max\limits_{||x||=1} ||Ax|| = \max\limits_{x} \dfrac{||Ax||_\infty}{||x||_\infty}$.

13 (a)   The unit vector that maximizes $||Ax||_\infty$ is $x = [1, 1]$, so that $Ax = \begin{bmatrix} 1 & 2 \\ 3 & 4 \end{bmatrix} \begin{bmatrix} 1 \\ 1 \end{bmatrix} = \begin{bmatrix} 3 \\ 7 \end{bmatrix}$. Note that $||x||_\infty = 1$, $||Ax||_\infty = 7$, and $||A||_\infty = 7$. Any scalar multiple of x will work as well.

13 (b)   The unit vector that maximizes $||Ax||_\infty$ is $x = [1, -1, 1]$. The signs are chosen to maximize row 3 of Ax. Since

$$Ax = \begin{bmatrix} 1 & 5 & 1 \\ -1 & 2 & -3 \\ 1 & -7 & 0 \end{bmatrix} \begin{bmatrix} 1 \\ -1 \\ 1 \end{bmatrix} = \begin{bmatrix} -3 \\ -6 \\ 8 \end{bmatrix},$$

we have $||x||_\infty = 1$, $||Ax||_\infty = 8$, and $||A||_\infty = 8$. Any scalar multiple of x will also work.

15   Applying Gaussian elimination yields the matrices

$$\begin{bmatrix} 10 & 20 & 1 \\ 1 & 1.99 & 6 \\ 0 & 50 & 1 \end{bmatrix} \longrightarrow \begin{bmatrix} 10 & 20 & 1 \\ 0 & -0.01 & 5.9 \\ 0 & 50 & 1 \end{bmatrix} \longrightarrow \begin{bmatrix} 10 & 20 & 1 \\ 0 & -0.01 & 5.9 \\ 0 & 0 & 29501 \end{bmatrix}$$

where the last multiplier is $l_{32} = -5000$. The LU-factorization is

$$LU = \begin{bmatrix} 1 & 0 & 0 \\ 0.1 & 1 & 0 \\ 0 & -5000 & 1 \end{bmatrix} \begin{bmatrix} 10 & 20 & 1 \\ 0 & -0.01 & 5.9 \\ 0 & 0 & 29501 \end{bmatrix},$$

and the largest magnitude multiplier is -5000.

COMPUTER PROBLEMS 2.3

1 (a) Since the answers depend on rounding errors, they will vary slightly with the exact sequence of operations used. For example, using the naive Gaussian elimination code of Computer Problem 2.1.1 gives the forward error $\|x - x_c\|_\infty \approx 6.6 \times 10^{-10}$ and error magnification factor $\approx 4.6 \times 10^6$, while the MATLAB backslash command, a more sophisticated algorithm, returns forward error $\approx 5.4 \times 10^{-10}$ and error magnification factor $\approx 3.7 \times 10^6$. The condition number of A is approximately 7×10^7.

1 (b) The MATLAB code of Computer Problem 2.1.1 gives forward error $\|x - x_c\|_\infty \approx 1.5 \times 10^{-3}$ and error magnification factor $\approx 6.2 \times 10^{12}$, while the MATLAB backslash command returns forward error $\approx 1.1 \times 10^{-3}$ and error magnification factor $\approx 9.1 \times 10^{12}$. The condition number of A is approximately 1.3×10^{14}.

3 Using naive Gaussian elimination as in Computer Problem 2.1.1, the results are:

n	FE	EMF	cond (A)
100	5.3×10^{-11}	1.2×10^3	1.0×10^4
200	5.8×10^{-10}	6.3×10^3	4.0×10^4
300	3.0×10^{-9}	8.7×10^3	9.0×10^4
400	4.5×10^{-9}	7.0×10^3	1.6×10^5
500	9.6×10^{-9}	4.8×10^4	2.5×10^5

The MATLAB backslash command is slightly more efficient, yielding the results:

n	FE	EMF	cond (A)
100	5.7×10^{-12}	6.3×10^3	1.0×10^4
200	3.4×10^{-11}	1.9×10^4	4.0×10^4
300	6.2×10^{-11}	3.2×10^4	9.0×10^4
400	1.8×10^{-10}	9.6×10^4	1.6×10^5
500	2.6×10^{-10}	1.1×10^5	2.5×10^5

5 The exact n depends slightly on the code, as in Computer Problem 1. Using the naive Gaussian elimination code of Computer Problem 2.1.1, the solution for $n = 11$ rounds to the correct solution $x = [1.0, \ldots, 1.0]$ within one correct decimal place, while the solution for $n = 12$ does not. If the MATLAB backslash command is used, the $n = 12$ solution rounds correctly to one decimal place and $n = 13$ does not.

EXERCISES 2.4   The PA=LU Factorization

1 (a)

$$\begin{bmatrix} 1 & 3 \\ 2 & 3 \end{bmatrix} \longrightarrow \begin{array}{c} P = \begin{bmatrix} 0 & 1 \\ 1 & 0 \end{bmatrix} \\ \text{exchange rows 1 and 2} \end{array} \longrightarrow \begin{bmatrix} 2 & 3 \\ 1 & 3 \end{bmatrix} \xrightarrow[\text{from row 2}]{\text{sub } \frac{1}{2} \text{ x row 1}} \begin{bmatrix} 2 & 3 \\ \frac{1}{2} & \frac{3}{2} \end{bmatrix}$$

$$\begin{bmatrix} 0 & 1 \\ 1 & 0 \end{bmatrix} \begin{bmatrix} 1 & 3 \\ 2 & 3 \end{bmatrix} = PA = LU = \begin{bmatrix} 1 & 0 \\ \frac{1}{2} & 1 \end{bmatrix} \begin{bmatrix} 2 & 3 \\ 0 & \frac{3}{2} \end{bmatrix}$$

1 (b)

$$\begin{bmatrix} 2 & 4 \\ 1 & 3 \end{bmatrix} \xrightarrow[\text{from row 2}]{\text{subtract } \frac{1}{2} \text{ x row 1}} \begin{bmatrix} 2 & 4 \\ \frac{1}{2} & 1 \end{bmatrix}$$

$$\begin{bmatrix} 1 & 0 \\ 0 & 1 \end{bmatrix} \begin{bmatrix} 2 & 4 \\ 1 & 3 \end{bmatrix} = PA = LU = \begin{bmatrix} 1 & 0 \\ \frac{1}{2} & 1 \end{bmatrix} \begin{bmatrix} 2 & 4 \\ 0 & 1 \end{bmatrix}$$

1 (c)

$$\begin{bmatrix} 1 & 5 \\ 5 & 12 \end{bmatrix} \longrightarrow \begin{array}{c} P = \begin{bmatrix} 0 & 1 \\ 1 & 0 \end{bmatrix} \\ \text{exchange rows 1 and 2} \end{array} \longrightarrow \begin{bmatrix} 5 & 12 \\ 1 & 5 \end{bmatrix} \xrightarrow[\text{from row 2}]{\text{sub } \frac{1}{5} \text{ x row 1}} \begin{bmatrix} 5 & 12 \\ \frac{1}{5} & \frac{13}{5} \end{bmatrix}$$

$$\begin{bmatrix} 0 & 1 \\ 1 & 0 \end{bmatrix} \begin{bmatrix} 1 & 5 \\ 5 & 12 \end{bmatrix} = PA = LU = \begin{bmatrix} 1 & 0 \\ \frac{1}{5} & 1 \end{bmatrix} \begin{bmatrix} 5 & 12 \\ 0 & \frac{13}{5} \end{bmatrix}$$

1 (d)

$$\begin{bmatrix} 0 & 1 \\ 1 & 0 \end{bmatrix} \longrightarrow \begin{array}{c} P = \begin{bmatrix} 0 & 1 \\ 1 & 0 \end{bmatrix} \\ \text{exchange rows 1 and 2} \end{array} \longrightarrow \begin{bmatrix} 1 & 0 \\ 0 & 1 \end{bmatrix}$$

$$\begin{bmatrix} 0 & 1 \\ 1 & 0 \end{bmatrix} \begin{bmatrix} 0 & 1 \\ 1 & 0 \end{bmatrix} = PA = LU = \begin{bmatrix} 1 & 0 \\ 0 & 1 \end{bmatrix} \begin{bmatrix} 1 & 0 \\ 0 & 1 \end{bmatrix}$$

3 (a)

$$\begin{bmatrix} 3 & 7 \\ 6 & 1 \end{bmatrix} \longrightarrow \begin{array}{c} P = \begin{bmatrix} 0 & 1 \\ 1 & 0 \end{bmatrix} \\ \text{exchange rows 1 and 2} \end{array} \longrightarrow \begin{bmatrix} 6 & 1 \\ 3 & 7 \end{bmatrix} \xrightarrow[\text{from row 2}]{\text{sub } \frac{1}{2} \text{ x row 1}} \begin{bmatrix} 6 & 1 \\ \frac{1}{2} & \frac{13}{2} \end{bmatrix}$$

$$\begin{bmatrix} 0 & 1 \\ 1 & 0 \end{bmatrix} \begin{bmatrix} 3 & 7 \\ 6 & 1 \end{bmatrix} = PA = LU = \begin{bmatrix} 1 & 0 \\ \frac{1}{2} & 1 \end{bmatrix} \begin{bmatrix} 6 & 1 \\ 0 & \frac{13}{2} \end{bmatrix}$$

$Lc = Pb$:

$$\begin{bmatrix} 1 & 0 \\ \frac{1}{2} & 1 \end{bmatrix} \begin{bmatrix} c_1 \\ c_2 \end{bmatrix} = \begin{bmatrix} 0 & 1 \\ 1 & 0 \end{bmatrix} \begin{bmatrix} 1 \\ -11 \end{bmatrix} = \begin{bmatrix} -11 \\ 1 \end{bmatrix}$$

Solving from the top,

$$c_1 = -11$$

$$\frac{1}{2}(-11) + c_2 = 1 \Rightarrow c_2 = \frac{13}{2}$$

$Ux = c$:

$$\begin{bmatrix} 6 & 1 \\ 0 & \frac{13}{2} \end{bmatrix} \begin{bmatrix} x_1 \\ x_2 \end{bmatrix} = \begin{bmatrix} -11 \\ \frac{13}{2} \end{bmatrix}$$

From the bottom,

$$\frac{13}{2}x_2 = \frac{13}{2} \Rightarrow x_2 = 1$$

$$6x_1 + 1(1) = -11 \Rightarrow x_1 = -2$$

The solution is $x = [-2, 1]$.

3 (b)

$$P = \begin{bmatrix} 0 & 1 & 0 \\ 1 & 0 & 0 \\ 0 & 0 & 1 \end{bmatrix}$$

$$\begin{bmatrix} 3 & 1 & 2 \\ 6 & 3 & 4 \\ 3 & 1 & 5 \end{bmatrix} \longrightarrow \text{ exchange rows 1 and 2 } \longrightarrow \begin{bmatrix} 6 & 3 & 4 \\ 3 & 1 & 2 \\ 3 & 1 & 5 \end{bmatrix}$$

$$\begin{array}{c} \text{subtract } \frac{1}{2} \text{ x row 1} \\ \longrightarrow \quad \text{from row 2} \quad \longrightarrow \end{array} \begin{bmatrix} 6 & 3 & 4 \\ \boxed{\tfrac{1}{2}} & -\frac{1}{2} & 0 \\ 3 & 1 & 5 \end{bmatrix}$$

$$\begin{array}{c} \text{subtract } \frac{1}{2} \text{ x row 1} \\ \longrightarrow \quad \text{from row 3} \quad \longrightarrow \end{array} \begin{bmatrix} 6 & 3 & 4 \\ \boxed{\tfrac{1}{2}} & -\frac{1}{2} & 0 \\ \boxed{\tfrac{1}{2}} & -\frac{1}{2} & 3 \end{bmatrix} \qquad \begin{array}{c} \text{subtract 1 x row 2} \\ \longrightarrow \quad \text{from row 3} \quad \longrightarrow \end{array} \begin{bmatrix} 6 & 3 & 4 \\ \boxed{\tfrac{1}{2}} & -\frac{1}{2} & 0 \\ \boxed{\tfrac{1}{2}} & \boxed{1} & 3 \end{bmatrix}$$

$$\begin{bmatrix} 0 & 1 & 0 \\ 1 & 0 & 0 \\ 0 & 0 & 1 \end{bmatrix} \begin{bmatrix} 3 & 1 & 2 \\ 6 & 3 & 4 \\ 3 & 1 & 5 \end{bmatrix} = PA = LU = \begin{bmatrix} 1 & 0 & 0 \\ \frac{1}{2} & 1 & 0 \\ \frac{1}{2} & 1 & 1 \end{bmatrix} \begin{bmatrix} 6 & 3 & 4 \\ 0 & -\frac{1}{2} & 0 \\ 0 & 0 & 3 \end{bmatrix}$$

Solve $Lc = Pb$:

$$\begin{bmatrix} 1 & 0 & 0 \\ \frac{1}{2} & 1 & 0 \\ \frac{1}{2} & 1 & 1 \end{bmatrix} \begin{bmatrix} c_1 \\ c_2 \\ c_3 \end{bmatrix} = \begin{bmatrix} 0 & 1 & 0 \\ 1 & 0 & 0 \\ 0 & 0 & 1 \end{bmatrix} \begin{bmatrix} 0 \\ 1 \\ 3 \end{bmatrix} = \begin{bmatrix} 1 \\ 0 \\ 3 \end{bmatrix}$$

Starting at the top,

$$c_1 = 1$$

$$\frac{1}{2}(1) + c_2 = 0 \Rightarrow c_2 = -\frac{1}{2}$$

$$\frac{1}{2}(1) + 1(-\frac{1}{2}) + c_3 = 3 \Rightarrow c_3 = 3$$

Solve $Ux = c$:

$$\begin{bmatrix} 6 & 3 & 4 \\ 0 & -\frac{1}{2} & 0 \\ 0 & 0 & 3 \end{bmatrix} \begin{bmatrix} x_1 \\ x_2 \\ x_3 \end{bmatrix} = \begin{bmatrix} 1 \\ -\frac{1}{2} \\ 3 \end{bmatrix}$$

Starting at the bottom,

$$3x_3 = 3 \quad \Rightarrow \quad x_3 = 1$$

$$-\frac{1}{2}x_2 = -\frac{1}{2} \quad \Rightarrow \quad x_2 = 1$$

$$6x_1 + 3(1) + 4(1) = 1 \quad \Rightarrow \quad x_1 = -1$$

Therefore the solution is $x = [-1, 1, 1]$.

5 According to Theorem 2.8, simply exchange rows 2 and 5 of the identity matrix.

$$P = \begin{bmatrix} 1 & 0 & 0 & 0 & 0 \\ 0 & 0 & 0 & 0 & 1 \\ 0 & 0 & 1 & 0 & 0 \\ 0 & 0 & 0 & 1 & 0 \\ 0 & 1 & 0 & 0 & 0 \end{bmatrix}$$

7 The matrix has been changed by moving row 1 to row 4, row 4 to row 3, and row 3 to row 1. According to Theorem 2.8, this can be done by multiplying on the left with a permutation

matrix constructed by applying the same changes to the identity matrix. Therefore the leftmost
matrix is

$$\begin{bmatrix} 0 & 0 & 1 & 0 \\ 0 & 1 & 0 & 0 \\ 0 & 0 & 0 & 1 \\ 1 & 0 & 0 & 0 \end{bmatrix}.$$

9 (a)

$$\begin{bmatrix} 1 & 0 & 0 & 1 \\ -1 & 1 & 0 & 1 \\ -1 & -1 & 1 & 1 \\ -1 & -1 & -1 & 1 \end{bmatrix} \longrightarrow \begin{bmatrix} 1 & 0 & 0 & 1 \\ -1 & 1 & 0 & 2 \\ -1 & -1 & 1 & 2 \\ -1 & -1 & -1 & 2 \end{bmatrix}$$

$$\longrightarrow \begin{bmatrix} 1 & 0 & 0 & 1 \\ -1 & 1 & 0 & 2 \\ -1 & -1 & 1 & 4 \\ -1 & -1 & -1 & 4 \end{bmatrix} \longrightarrow \begin{bmatrix} 1 & 0 & 0 & 1 \\ -1 & 1 & 0 & 2 \\ -1 & -1 & 1 & 4 \\ -1 & -1 & -1 & 8 \end{bmatrix}$$

The PA=LU factorization is

$$\begin{bmatrix} 1 & 0 & 0 & 0 \\ 0 & 1 & 0 & 0 \\ 0 & 0 & 1 & 0 \\ 0 & 0 & 0 & 1 \end{bmatrix} \begin{bmatrix} 1 & 0 & 0 & 1 \\ -1 & 1 & 0 & 1 \\ -1 & -1 & 1 & 1 \\ -1 & -1 & -1 & 1 \end{bmatrix} = \begin{bmatrix} 1 & 0 & 0 & 0 \\ -1 & 1 & 0 & 0 \\ -1 & -1 & 1 & 0 \\ -1 & -1 & -1 & 1 \end{bmatrix} \begin{bmatrix} 1 & 0 & 0 & 1 \\ 0 & 1 & 0 & 2 \\ 0 & 0 & 1 & 4 \\ 0 & 0 & 0 & 8 \end{bmatrix}$$

9 (b) Following the pattern in (a), $P = I$, since partial pivoting results in no row exchanges. The
entries of L are 1 on the main diagonal, and -1 in all lower triangular locations. The matrix
U is the identity matrix except for column n, which is $[2^0, 2^1, 2^2, \ldots, 2^{n-1}]^T$.

EXERCISES 2.5   Iterative Methods

1 (a) The Jacobi equations are

$$u_{k+1} = \frac{5 + v_k}{3}$$
$$v_{k+1} = \frac{4 + u_k}{2}$$

Starting with $[u_0, v_0] = [0, 0]$, the first two steps are

$$\begin{bmatrix} u_1 \\ v_1 \end{bmatrix} = \begin{bmatrix} \frac{5}{3} \\ 2 \end{bmatrix}, \begin{bmatrix} u_2 \\ v_2 \end{bmatrix} = \begin{bmatrix} \frac{7}{3} \\ \frac{17}{6} \end{bmatrix}.$$

The Gauss-Seidel equations are

$$u_{k+1} = \frac{5 + v_k}{3}$$
$$v_{k+1} = \frac{4 + u_{k+1}}{2}$$

Starting with $[u_0, v_0] = [0, 0]$, the first two steps are

$$\begin{bmatrix} u_1 \\ v_1 \end{bmatrix} = \begin{bmatrix} 5/3 \\ 17/6 \end{bmatrix}, \begin{bmatrix} u_2 \\ v_2 \end{bmatrix} = \begin{bmatrix} \frac{47}{18} \\ \frac{119}{36} \end{bmatrix}.$$

1 (b)   The Jacobi equations are

$$u_{k+1} = \frac{v_k}{2}$$
$$v_{k+1} = \frac{u_k + w_k + 2}{2}$$
$$w_{k+1} = \frac{v_k}{2}$$

Starting with $[u_0, v_0, w_0] = [0, 0, 0]$, the first two steps are

$$\begin{bmatrix} u_1 \\ v_1 \\ w_1 \end{bmatrix} = \begin{bmatrix} 0 \\ 1 \\ 0 \end{bmatrix}, \begin{bmatrix} u_2 \\ v_2 \\ w_2 \end{bmatrix} = \begin{bmatrix} \frac{1}{2} \\ 1 \\ \frac{1}{2} \end{bmatrix}.$$

The Gauss-Seidel equations are

$$u_{k+1} = \frac{v_k}{2}$$
$$v_{k+1} = \frac{u_{k+1} + w_k + 2}{2}$$
$$w_{k+1} = \frac{v_{k+1}}{2}$$

Starting with $[u_0, v_0, w_0] = [0, 0, 0]$, the first two steps are

$$\begin{bmatrix} u_1 \\ v_1 \\ w_1 \end{bmatrix} = \begin{bmatrix} 0 \\ 1 \\ \frac{1}{2} \end{bmatrix}, \begin{bmatrix} u_2 \\ v_2 \\ w_2 \end{bmatrix} = \begin{bmatrix} 1/2 \\ 3/2 \\ 3/4 \end{bmatrix}.$$

1 (c)　The Jacobi equations are

$$u_{k+1} = \frac{6 - v_k - w_k}{3}$$

$$v_{k+1} = \frac{3 - u_k - w_k}{3}$$

$$w_{k+1} = \frac{5 - u_k - v_k}{3}$$

Starting with $[u_0, v_0, w_0] = [0, 0, 0]$, the first two steps are

$$\begin{bmatrix} u_1 \\ v_1 \\ w_1 \end{bmatrix} = \begin{bmatrix} 2 \\ 1 \\ \frac{5}{3} \end{bmatrix}, \begin{bmatrix} u_2 \\ v_2 \\ w_2 \end{bmatrix} = \begin{bmatrix} 10/9 \\ -2/9 \\ 2/3 \end{bmatrix}.$$

The Gauss-Seidel equations are

$$u_{k+1} = \frac{6 - v_k - w_k}{3}$$

$$v_{k+1} = \frac{3 - u_{k+1} - w_k}{3}$$

$$w_{k+1} = \frac{5 - u_{k+1} - v_{k+1}}{3}$$

Starting with $[u_0, v_0, w_0] = [0, 0, 0]$, the first two steps are

$$\begin{bmatrix} u_1 \\ v_1 \\ w_1 \end{bmatrix} = \begin{bmatrix} 2 \\ \frac{1}{3} \\ \frac{8}{9} \end{bmatrix}, \begin{bmatrix} u_2 \\ v_2 \\ w_2 \end{bmatrix} = \begin{bmatrix} \frac{43}{27} \\ \frac{14}{81} \\ \frac{262}{243} \end{bmatrix}.$$

3 (a)　The SOR equations are

$$u_{k+1} = (1 - \omega)u_k + \omega \frac{5 + v_k}{3}$$

$$v_{k+1} = (1 - \omega)v_k + \omega \frac{4 + u_{k+1}}{2}$$

where $\omega = 1.5$. Starting with $[u_0, v_0] = [0, 0]$, the first two steps are

$$u_1 = -\frac{1}{2}u_0 + \frac{3(5 + v_0)}{6} = \frac{5}{2}$$

$$v_1 = -\frac{1}{2}v_0 + \frac{3(4 + u_1)}{4} = \frac{39}{8}$$

and

$$u_2 = -\frac{1}{2}u_1 + \frac{3(5 + v_1)}{6} = \frac{59}{16}$$

$$v_2 = -\frac{1}{2}v_1 + \frac{3(4 + u_2)}{4} = \frac{213}{64}$$

3 (b) The SOR equations are

$$u_{k+1} = (1 - \omega)u_k + \omega\frac{v_k}{2}$$

$$v_{k+1} = (1 - \omega)v_k + \omega\frac{u_{k+1} + w_k + 2}{2}$$

$$w_{k+1} = (1 - \omega)w_k + \omega\frac{v_{k+1}}{2}$$

where $\omega = 1.5$. Starting with $[u_0, v_0, w_0] = [0, 0, 0]$, the first two steps are $[u_1, v_1, w_1] = [0, \frac{3}{2}, \frac{9}{8}]$ and $[u_2, v_2, w_2] = [\frac{9}{8}, \frac{39}{16}, \frac{81}{64}]$.

3 (c) The SOR equations are

$$u_{k+1} = (1 - \omega)u_k + \omega\frac{6 - v_k - w_k}{3}$$

$$v_{k+1} = (1 - \omega)v_k + \omega\frac{3 - u_{k+1} - w_k}{3}$$

$$w_{k+1} = (1 - \omega)w_k + \omega\frac{5 - u_{k+1} - v_{k+1}}{3}$$

where $\omega = 1.5$. Starting with $[u_0, v_0, w_0] = [0, 0, 0]$, the first two steps are $[u_1, v_1, w_1] = [3, 0, 1]$ and $[u_2, v_2, w_2] = [1, \frac{1}{2}, \frac{5}{4}]$

5 (a) By dividing an eigenvector v associated to λ by its largest magnitude entry, we can find an eigenvector whose largest magnitude entry v_m is exactly 1. The mth row of the eigenvalue equation $Av = \lambda v$ is therefore

$$A_{m1}v_1 + \ldots + A_{m,m-1}v_{m-1} + A_{mm} + A_{m,m+1}v_{m+1} + \ldots + A_{mn}v_n = \lambda.$$

Since $|v_i| \leq 1$ for all $1 \leq i \leq n$, it follows that

$$|A_{mm} - \lambda| = |A_{m1}v_1 + \ldots + A_{m,m-1}v_{m-1} + A_{m,m+1}v_{m+1} + \ldots + A_{mn}v_n|$$

$$\leq \sum_{j \neq m}|A_{mj}|.$$

5 (b) If $\lambda = 0$ is an eigenvalue of A, then by the Gerschgorin Circle Theorem there exists an m such that $|A_{mm}| \leq \sum_{j \neq m}|A_{mj}|$, which contradicts strict diagonal dominance.

COMPUTER PROBLEMS 2.5

1 The MATLAB program `jacobi.m` can be used to solve the system after defining A and b with an altered version of `sparsesetup.m`. The initial vector is set to $[0, \ldots, 0]$. By checking the infinity norm error of the solution x, say by the command `norm(x-1,inf)`, the Jacobi method can be iterated until the error is less than 0.5×10^{-6}. For $n = 100$, 36 Jacobi steps are required. For $n = 100000$, 36 steps are required. In both cases, the backward error is approximately 4.6×10^{-7}.

3 The Gauss-Seidel method can be coded in MATLAB as follows:

```
% Gauss-Seidel
% Inputs: sparse matrix a, r.h.s b,
%         d = diagonal of a, r = rest of a,
%         numsteps = number of Jacobi iterations
% Output: solution x
function x = gaussseidel(a,b,k)
n=length(b);            % find n
d=diag(diag(a)); u=triu(a,1);l=tril(a,-1);
x=zeros(n,1);           % Initialize vector x
for j=1:k               % loop for GS iteration
  b1=b-u*x;
  for i=1:n
    x(i)=(b1(i)-l(i,:)*x)/d(i,i);
  end
end
```

5 Using the code from Computer Problem 3, 21 steps of Gauss-Seidel iteration, starting from $x = [0, \ldots, 0]$, are needed to converge to the correct solution within 6 decimal places. Using the code from Computer Problem 4, 16 steps of SOR with $\omega = 1.2$, starting from $x = [0, \ldots, 0]$, are needed to converge to the correct solution within 6 decimal places.

7 The results will depend on the computer. Using the sparse matrix capability of MATLAB and the Gauss-Seidel code from Computer Problem 3, typical results for one second of computation are given in the table.

n	steps	forward error
400	50	1.1×10^{-8}
800	15	1.7×10^{-3}
1200	7	2.5×10^{-2}

EXERCISES 2.6   Methods for Symmetric Positive-Definite Matrices

1 (a) For $x = [x_1, x_2] \neq 0$,

$$x^T A x = \begin{bmatrix} x_1 & x_2 \end{bmatrix} \begin{bmatrix} 1 & 0 \\ 0 & 3 \end{bmatrix} \begin{bmatrix} x_1 \\ x_2 \end{bmatrix} = x_1^2 + 3x_2^2 > 0.$$

1 (b) For $x = [x_1, x_2] \neq 0$,

$$x^T A x = \begin{bmatrix} x_1 & x_2 \end{bmatrix} \begin{bmatrix} 1 & 3 \\ 3 & 10 \end{bmatrix} \begin{bmatrix} x_1 \\ x_2 \end{bmatrix} = x_1^2 + 6x_1 x_2 + 10x_2^2 = (x_1 + 3x_2)^2 + x_2^2 > 0.$$

1 (c) For $x = [x_1, x_2, x_3] \neq 0$,

$$x^T A x = \begin{bmatrix} x_1 & x_2 & x_3 \end{bmatrix} \begin{bmatrix} 1 & 0 & 0 \\ 0 & 2 & 0 \\ 0 & 0 & 3 \end{bmatrix} \begin{bmatrix} x_1 \\ x_2 \\ x_3 \end{bmatrix} = x_1^2 + 2x_2^2 + 3x_3^2 > 0.$$

3 (a) Clearly $R^T R = \begin{bmatrix} \sqrt{1} & 0 \\ 0 & \sqrt{3} \end{bmatrix} \begin{bmatrix} \sqrt{1} & 0 \\ 0 & \sqrt{3} \end{bmatrix}$ is a Cholesky factorization; alternatively, R can be chosen to be the negative of this matrix.

3 (b) The top row of R is $R_{11} = \sqrt{a_{11}} = 1$, followed by $R_{12} = u = \dfrac{[3]}{\sqrt{a_{11}}} = 3$. Subtracting the outer product uu^T from the lower principal submatrix $[10]$ leaves $10 - 3 = 1$. Repeating the factorization step for the remaining 1×1 matrix yields $R_{22} = \sqrt{1} = 1$. Therefore $R = \begin{bmatrix} 1 & 3 \\ 0 & 1 \end{bmatrix}$ satisfies $R^T R = \begin{bmatrix} 1 & 0 \\ 3 & 1 \end{bmatrix} \begin{bmatrix} 1 & 3 \\ 0 & 1 \end{bmatrix} = \begin{bmatrix} 1 & 3 \\ 3 & 10 \end{bmatrix}.$

3 (c) Clearly $R^T R = \begin{bmatrix} \sqrt{1} & 0 & 0 \\ 0 & \sqrt{2} & 0 \\ 0 & 0 & \sqrt{3} \end{bmatrix} \begin{bmatrix} \sqrt{1} & 0 & 0 \\ 0 & \sqrt{2} & 0 \\ 0 & 0 & \sqrt{3} \end{bmatrix}$ is a Cholesky factorization; alternatively, R can be chosen to be the negative of this matrix.

5 (a) The top row of R is $R_{11} = \sqrt{a_{11}} = 1$, followed by $R_{12} = u = \dfrac{[2]}{\sqrt{a_{11}}} = 2$. Subtracting the outer product uu^T from the lower principal submatrix $[8]$ leaves $8 - 4 = 4$. Repeating the factorization step for the remaining 1×1 matrix yields $R_{22} = \sqrt{4} = 2$. Therefore $R = \begin{bmatrix} 1 & 2 \\ 0 & 2 \end{bmatrix}$ satisfies $R^T R = \begin{bmatrix} 1 & 0 \\ 2 & 2 \end{bmatrix} \begin{bmatrix} 1 & 2 \\ 0 & 2 \end{bmatrix} = \begin{bmatrix} 1 & 2 \\ 2 & 8 \end{bmatrix}.$

5 (b) The top row of R is $R_{11} = \sqrt{a_{11}} = 2$, followed by $R_{12} = u = \dfrac{[-2]}{\sqrt{a_{11}}} = -1$. Subtracting the outer product uu^T from the lower principal submatrix $[5/4]$ leaves $5/4 - 1 = 1/4$. Repeating the factorization step for the remaining 1×1 matrix yields $R_{22} = \sqrt{1/4} = 1/2$. Therefore

$$R = \begin{bmatrix} 2 & -1 \\ 0 & 1/2 \end{bmatrix} \text{ satisfies } R^T R = \begin{bmatrix} 2 & 0 \\ -1 & 1/2 \end{bmatrix} \begin{bmatrix} 2 & -1 \\ 0 & 1/2 \end{bmatrix} = \begin{bmatrix} 4 & -2 \\ -2 & 5/4 \end{bmatrix}.$$

5 (c) The top row of R is $R_{11} = \sqrt{a_{11}} = 5$, followed by $R_{12} = u = \dfrac{[5]}{\sqrt{a_{11}}} = 1$. Subtracting

the outer product uu^T from the lower principal submatrix $[26]$ leaves $26 - 1 = 25$. Repeating the factorization step for the remaining 1×1 matrix yields $R_{22} = \sqrt{25} = 5$. Therefore

$$R = \begin{bmatrix} 5 & 1 \\ 0 & 5 \end{bmatrix} \text{ satisfies } R^T R = \begin{bmatrix} 5 & 0 \\ 1 & 5 \end{bmatrix} \begin{bmatrix} 5 & 1 \\ 0 & 5 \end{bmatrix} = \begin{bmatrix} 25 & 5 \\ 5 & 26 \end{bmatrix}.$$

5 (d) The top row of R is $R_{11} = \sqrt{a_{11}} = 1$, followed by $R_{12} = u = \dfrac{[-2]}{\sqrt{a_{11}}} = -2$. Subtracting

the outer product uu^T from the lower principal submatrix $[8]$ leaves $5 - (-2)(-2) = 1$. Repeating the factorization step for the remaining 1×1 matrix yields $R_{22} = \sqrt{1} = 1$. Therefore

$$R = \begin{bmatrix} 1 & -2 \\ 0 & 1 \end{bmatrix} \text{ satisfies } R^T R = \begin{bmatrix} 1 & 0 \\ -2 & 1 \end{bmatrix} \begin{bmatrix} 1 & -2 \\ 0 & 1 \end{bmatrix} = \begin{bmatrix} 1 & -2 \\ -2 & 5 \end{bmatrix}.$$

7 (a) The Cholesky factorization is $R^T R = \begin{bmatrix} 1 & 0 \\ -1 & 2 \end{bmatrix} \begin{bmatrix} 1 & -1 \\ 0 & 2 \end{bmatrix}$.

The two-part back substitution is $R^T c = b$ followed by $Rx = c$.

The solution of $\begin{bmatrix} 1 & 0 \\ -1 & 2 \end{bmatrix} \begin{bmatrix} c_1 \\ c_2 \end{bmatrix} = \begin{bmatrix} 3 \\ -7 \end{bmatrix}$ is $c = \begin{bmatrix} 3 \\ -2 \end{bmatrix}$,

and the solution of $\begin{bmatrix} 1 & -1 \\ 0 & 2 \end{bmatrix} \begin{bmatrix} x_1 \\ x_2 \end{bmatrix} = \begin{bmatrix} 3 \\ -2 \end{bmatrix}$ is $x = \begin{bmatrix} 2 \\ -1 \end{bmatrix}$.

7 (b) The Cholesky factorization is $R^T R = \begin{bmatrix} 2 & 0 \\ -1 & 3 \end{bmatrix} \begin{bmatrix} 2 & -1 \\ 0 & 3 \end{bmatrix}$.

The two-part back substitution is $R^T c = b$ followed by $Rx = c$.

The solution of $\begin{bmatrix} 2 & 0 \\ -1 & 3 \end{bmatrix} \begin{bmatrix} c_1 \\ c_2 \end{bmatrix} = \begin{bmatrix} 10 \\ 4 \end{bmatrix}$ is $c = \begin{bmatrix} 5 \\ 3 \end{bmatrix}$,

and the solution of $\begin{bmatrix} 2 & -1 \\ 0 & 3 \end{bmatrix} \begin{bmatrix} x_1 \\ x_2 \end{bmatrix} = \begin{bmatrix} 5 \\ 3 \end{bmatrix}$ is $x = \begin{bmatrix} 3 \\ 1 \end{bmatrix}$.

9 Multiply out $x^T A x = \begin{bmatrix} x_1 & x_2 \end{bmatrix} \begin{bmatrix} 1 & 2 \\ 2 & d \end{bmatrix} \begin{bmatrix} x_1 \\ x_2 \end{bmatrix} = x_1^2 + 4x_1 x_2 + d x_2^2 > 0$ and complete the

square as $(x_1 + 2x_2)^2 + (d - 4)x_2^2$. If $d > 4$, then $x^T A x$ is expressed as a sum of squares and is positive for all $x \neq 0$.

11 We attempt to find the Cholesky factorization. The matrix A is positive-definite exactly when the diagonal entries of R are positive. The top row of R is $R_{11} = \sqrt{a_{11}} = 1$, followed by

$[R_{12} \ R_{13}] = u = \dfrac{[-1 \ 0]}{\sqrt{a_{11}}} = [-1 \ 0]$. Subtracting the outer product $uu^T = \begin{bmatrix} 1 & 0 \\ 0 & 0 \end{bmatrix}$ from the lower principal submatrix $uu^T = \begin{bmatrix} 2 & 1 \\ 1 & d \end{bmatrix}$ leaves $uu^T = \begin{bmatrix} 1 & 1 \\ 1 & d \end{bmatrix}$. Repeating the factoriza-

tion step for the remaining 2×2 matrix yields $R_{22} = \sqrt{1} = 1$, followed by $R_{23} = u = \dfrac{[1]}{\sqrt{a_{22}}} = 1$.

Subtracting the outer product uu^T from the lower principal submatrix $[d]$ leaves $d - 1$. The R_{33} entry will be the square root of $d - 1$. The matrix is positive-definite if and only if $d > 1$.

13 (a)   Following the Conjugate Gradient Method pseudocode:

$$x_0 = \begin{bmatrix} 0 \\ 0 \end{bmatrix}, r_0 = d_0 = \begin{bmatrix} 1 \\ 1 \end{bmatrix}$$

$$\alpha_0 = \frac{\begin{bmatrix} 1 \\ 1 \end{bmatrix}^T \begin{bmatrix} 1 \\ 1 \end{bmatrix}}{\begin{bmatrix} 1 \\ 1 \end{bmatrix}^T \begin{bmatrix} 2 & 2 \\ 2 & 5 \end{bmatrix} \begin{bmatrix} 1 \\ 1 \end{bmatrix}} = \frac{2}{10} = \frac{1}{5}$$

$$x_1 = \begin{bmatrix} 0 \\ 0 \end{bmatrix} + \frac{1}{5} \begin{bmatrix} 1 \\ 1 \end{bmatrix} = \begin{bmatrix} 1/5 \\ 1/5 \end{bmatrix}$$

$$r_1 = \begin{bmatrix} 1 \\ 1 \end{bmatrix} - \frac{1}{5} \begin{bmatrix} 3 \\ 7 \end{bmatrix} = \begin{bmatrix} 0.4 \\ -0.4 \end{bmatrix}$$

$$\beta_0 = \frac{r_1^T r_1}{r_0^T r_0} = 0.16$$

$$d_1 = 12 \begin{bmatrix} 0.4 \\ -0.4 \end{bmatrix} + 0.16 \begin{bmatrix} 1 \\ 1 \end{bmatrix} = \begin{bmatrix} 0.56 \\ -0.24 \end{bmatrix}$$

$$\alpha_1 = \frac{\begin{bmatrix} 0.4 \\ -0.4 \end{bmatrix}^T \begin{bmatrix} 0.4 \\ -0.4 \end{bmatrix}}{\begin{bmatrix} 0.56 \\ -0.24 \end{bmatrix}^T \begin{bmatrix} 1 & 2 \\ 2 & 5 \end{bmatrix} \begin{bmatrix} 0.56 \\ -0.24 \end{bmatrix}} = 5$$

$$x_2 = \begin{bmatrix} 1/5 \\ 1/5 \end{bmatrix} + 5 \begin{bmatrix} 0.56 \\ -0.24 \end{bmatrix} = \begin{bmatrix} 3 \\ -1 \end{bmatrix}$$

$$r_2 = \begin{bmatrix} 0.4 \\ -0.4 \end{bmatrix} - 5 \begin{bmatrix} 1 & 2 \\ 2 & 5 \end{bmatrix} \begin{bmatrix} 0.56 \\ -0.24 \end{bmatrix} = \begin{bmatrix} 0 \\ 0 \end{bmatrix}$$

13 (b)

$$x_0 = \begin{bmatrix} 0 \\ 0 \end{bmatrix}, r_0 = d_0 = \begin{bmatrix} 1 \\ 3 \end{bmatrix}$$

$$\alpha_0 = \frac{\begin{bmatrix} 1 \\ 3 \end{bmatrix}^T \begin{bmatrix} 1 \\ 3 \end{bmatrix}}{\begin{bmatrix} 1 \\ 3 \end{bmatrix}^T \begin{bmatrix} 1 & 2 \\ 2 & 5 \end{bmatrix} \begin{bmatrix} 1 \\ 3 \end{bmatrix}} = \frac{10}{58} = \frac{5}{29}$$

$$x_1 = \begin{bmatrix} 0 \\ 0 \end{bmatrix} + \frac{5}{29} \begin{bmatrix} 1 \\ 3 \end{bmatrix} = \begin{bmatrix} 5/29 \\ 15/29 \end{bmatrix}$$

$$r_1 = \begin{bmatrix} 1 \\ 3 \end{bmatrix} - \frac{5}{29} \begin{bmatrix} 7 \\ 17 \end{bmatrix} = \begin{bmatrix} -6/29 \\ 2/29 \end{bmatrix}$$

$$\beta_0 = \frac{r_1^T r_1}{r_0^T r_0} = \frac{4}{(29)^2}$$

$$d_1 = 12 \begin{bmatrix} -6/29 \\ 2/29 \end{bmatrix} + \frac{4}{(29)^2} \begin{bmatrix} 1 \\ 3 \end{bmatrix} = \begin{bmatrix} -\frac{170}{(29)^2} \\ \frac{70}{(29)^2} \end{bmatrix}$$

$$\alpha_1 = \frac{\begin{bmatrix} -6/29 \\ 2/29 \end{bmatrix}^T \begin{bmatrix} -6/29 \\ 2/29 \end{bmatrix}}{\frac{1}{(29)^4} \begin{bmatrix} -170 \\ 70 \end{bmatrix}^T \begin{bmatrix} 1 & 2 \\ 2 & 5 \end{bmatrix} \begin{bmatrix} -170 \\ 70 \end{bmatrix}} = 5.8$$

$$x_2 = \begin{bmatrix} 5/29 \\ 15/29 \end{bmatrix} + 5.8 \begin{bmatrix} -170/(29)^2 \\ 70/(29)^2 \end{bmatrix} = \begin{bmatrix} -1 \\ 1 \end{bmatrix}$$

$$r_2 = \begin{bmatrix} -6/29 \\ 2/29 \end{bmatrix} - 5.8 \begin{bmatrix} 1 & 2 \\ 2 & 5 \end{bmatrix} \begin{bmatrix} -170/(29)^2 \\ 70/(29)^2 \end{bmatrix} = \begin{bmatrix} 0 \\ 0 \end{bmatrix}$$

15 $\alpha_0 = 1/A, x_1 = b/A, r_1 = b - Ab/A = 0$

COMPUTER PROBLEMS 2.6

1 (a) The Conjugate Gradient loop written in pseudocode in the textbook can be coded as follows.

```
function x=cg(a,b,n)
% Inputs: symm. pos. def. matrix a, right-hand side b, number of steps n
% Output: solution x
x=zeros(n,1);
r=b-a*x;
d=r;d1(:,1)=d;r1(:,1)=r;
for i=1:n
    if max(abs(r))<eps break; end
    alf=d'*r/(d'*a*d);
    x=x+alf*d;
    rold=r;
    r=rold-alf*a*d;
    beta=r'*r/(rold'*rold);
    d=r+beta*d;d1(:,i+1)=d;r1(:,i+1)=r;
end
```

The test for r equal to zero uses `eps`, the machine epsilon. The MATLAB command

```
>> x=cg([1 0;0 2],[2;4],2)
```

returns the solution $x = [2, 2]$.

1 (b) Applying the code from part (a) returns the solution $x = [3, -1]$.

3 (a) The Conjugate Gradient code from Computer Problem 1 can be used with `a = hilb(4)` and `b = ones(4,1)` to yield the solution $x = [-4, 60, -180, 140]$ after 4 steps.

3 (b) The exact solution $x = [-8, 504, -7560, 46200, -138600, 216216, -168168, 51480]$. is approached after more than 20 steps of Conjugate Gradient.

5 Use Program 2.1, `sparsesetup.m` to define the matrix a and right-hand side (b). For $n = 100$, Conjugate Gradient runs 34 steps before the residual r is smaller than machine epsilon in the infinity norm. The final residual is $r \approx 9.76 \times 10^{-17}$. For $n = 1000$, only 35 steps are needed to make the residual $r \approx 7.12 \times 10^{-17}$. For $n = 10000$, 35 steps are needed to make the residual $r \approx 7.17 \times 10^{-17}$.

7 Part (a) shows the output of MATLAB `spy` command on the matrix A. The code shown in the answer to Computer Problem 1(a) above can be slightly modified to carry out the Preconditioned Conjugate Gradient Method outlined in pseudocode in the textbook. Applying this code to the A and b defined in the problem result in Part (b), showing the error as a function of step number for no preconditioner (circles), Jacobi preconditioner (squares), and Gauss-Seidel preconditioner (diamonds).

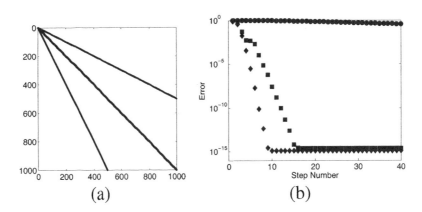

9 Part (a) shows the output of MATLAB spy command on the matrix A. Applying the code as described in the answer to Computer Problem 7 to the A and b defined in the problem result in Part (b), showing the error as a function of step number for no preconditioner (circles), Jacobi preconditioner (squares), and Gauss-Seidel preconditioner (diamonds).

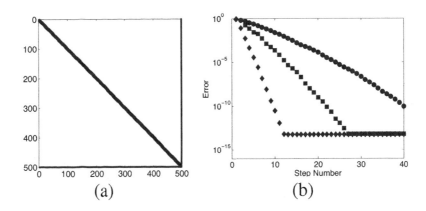

EXERCISES 2.7   Nonlinear Systems of Equations

1 (a) $DF(u,v) = \begin{bmatrix} 3u^2 & 0 \\ v^3 & 3uv^2 \end{bmatrix}$

1 (b) $DF(u,v) = \begin{bmatrix} v\cos uv & u\cos uv \\ ve^{uv} & ue^{uv} \end{bmatrix}$

1 (c) $DF(u,v) = \begin{bmatrix} 2u & 2v \\ 2(u-1) & 2v \end{bmatrix}$

1 (d) $DF(u,v,w) = \begin{bmatrix} 2u & 1 & -2w \\ vw\cos uvw & uw\cos uvw & uv\cos uvw \\ vw^4 & uw^4 & 4uvw^3 \end{bmatrix}$

3 (a)   The curves are circles with radius 1 centered at $(u, v) = (0, 0)$ and $(1, 0)$, respectively. Solving the first equation for v^2 and substituting into the second yields $(u - 1)^2 + 1 - u^2 = 1$ or $-2u + 1 = 0$, so $u = \frac{1}{2}$. The two solutions are $(u, v) = (\frac{1}{2}, \frac{\sqrt{3}}{2})$ and $(\frac{1}{2}, -\frac{\sqrt{3}}{2})$.

3 (b)   The curves are ellipses with semimajor axes 1 and 2 centered at zero and aligned with the x and y axes. Solving by substitution gives the four solutions $(u, v) = (\pm\frac{2}{\sqrt{5}}, \pm\frac{2}{\sqrt{5}})$.

3 (c)   The curves are a hyperbola and a circle that intersects one half of the hyperbola in two points. Solving by substitution gives the two solutions $(u, v) = (\frac{4}{5}(1 + \sqrt{6}), \pm\frac{1}{5}\sqrt{3 + 8\sqrt{6}})$.

5 (a)   Given initial values $A_0 = I$ and $x_0 = [1, 1]^T$, set $F\begin{bmatrix} u \\ v \end{bmatrix} = \begin{bmatrix} u^2 + v^2 - 1 \\ (u - 1)^2 + v^2 - 1 \end{bmatrix}$.

According to Broyden's Method,

$$x_1 = x_0 - A_0^{-1}F(x_0) = \begin{bmatrix} 1 \\ 1 \end{bmatrix} - \begin{bmatrix} 1 \\ 0 \end{bmatrix} = \begin{bmatrix} 0 \\ 1 \end{bmatrix}$$

$$\Delta_1 = F(x_1) - F(x_0) = F\begin{bmatrix} 0 \\ 1 \end{bmatrix} - F\begin{bmatrix} 1 \\ 1 \end{bmatrix} = \begin{bmatrix} 0 \\ 1 \end{bmatrix} - \begin{bmatrix} 1 \\ 0 \end{bmatrix}\begin{bmatrix} -1 \\ 1 \end{bmatrix}$$

$$\delta_1 = x_1 - x_0 = \begin{bmatrix} -1 \\ 0 \end{bmatrix}$$

$$A_1 = A_0 + \frac{(\Delta_1 - A_0\delta_1)\delta_1^T}{\delta_1^T\delta_1} = \begin{bmatrix} 1 & 0 \\ 0 & 1 \end{bmatrix} + \frac{\begin{bmatrix} 0 \\ 1 \end{bmatrix}\begin{bmatrix} -1 & 0 \end{bmatrix}}{\begin{bmatrix} -1 & 0 \end{bmatrix}\begin{bmatrix} -1 \\ 0 \end{bmatrix}} = \begin{bmatrix} 1 & 0 \\ 0 & 1 \end{bmatrix}$$

$$x_2 = x_1 - A_1^{-1}F(x_1) = \begin{bmatrix} 0 \\ 1 \end{bmatrix} - \begin{bmatrix} 0 \\ 1 \end{bmatrix} = \begin{bmatrix} 0 \\ 0 \end{bmatrix}$$

5 (b)   Proceed as in (a), with $F\begin{bmatrix} u \\ v \end{bmatrix} = \begin{bmatrix} u^2 + 4v^2 - 4 \\ 4u^2 + v^2 - 4 \end{bmatrix}$. According to Broyden's Method,

$$x_1 = x_0 - A_0^{-1}F(x_0) = \begin{bmatrix} 1 \\ 1 \end{bmatrix} - \begin{bmatrix} 1 \\ 1 \end{bmatrix} = \begin{bmatrix} 0 \\ 0 \end{bmatrix}$$

$$\Delta_1 = F(x_1) - F(x_0) = F\begin{bmatrix} 0 \\ 0 \end{bmatrix} - F\begin{bmatrix} 1 \\ 1 \end{bmatrix} = \begin{bmatrix} -4 \\ -4 \end{bmatrix} - \begin{bmatrix} 1 \\ 1 \end{bmatrix} = \begin{bmatrix} -5 \\ -5 \end{bmatrix}$$

$$\delta_1 = x_1 - x_0 = \begin{bmatrix} -1 \\ -1 \end{bmatrix}$$

$$A_1 = A_0 + \frac{(\Delta_1 - A_0\delta_1)\delta_1^T}{\delta_1^T\delta_1} = \begin{bmatrix} 1 & 0 \\ 0 & 1 \end{bmatrix} + \frac{\begin{bmatrix} -4 \\ -4 \end{bmatrix}\begin{bmatrix} -1 & -1 \end{bmatrix}}{\begin{bmatrix} -1 & -1 \end{bmatrix}\begin{bmatrix} -1 \\ -1 \end{bmatrix}} = \begin{bmatrix} 3 & 2 \\ 2 & 3 \end{bmatrix}$$

$$x_2 = x_1 - A_1^{-1}F(x_1) = \begin{bmatrix} 0 \\ 0 \end{bmatrix} - \begin{bmatrix} 3 & 2 \\ 2 & 3 \end{bmatrix}^{-1}\begin{bmatrix} -4 \\ -4 \end{bmatrix} = \begin{bmatrix} 0.8 \\ 0.8 \end{bmatrix}$$

5 (c) Proceed as in (a), with $F\begin{bmatrix} u \\ v \end{bmatrix} = \begin{bmatrix} u^2 - 4v^2 - 4 \\ (u-1)^2 + v^2 - 4 \end{bmatrix}$. According to Broyden's Method,

$$x_1 = x_0 - A_0^{-1}F(x_0) = \begin{bmatrix} 1 \\ 1 \end{bmatrix} - \begin{bmatrix} -7 \\ -3 \end{bmatrix} = \begin{bmatrix} 8 \\ 4 \end{bmatrix}$$

$$\Delta_1 = F(x_1) - F(x_0) = F\begin{bmatrix} 8 \\ 4 \end{bmatrix} - F\begin{bmatrix} 1 \\ 1 \end{bmatrix} = \begin{bmatrix} -4 \\ 61 \end{bmatrix} - \begin{bmatrix} -7 \\ -3 \end{bmatrix} = \begin{bmatrix} 3 \\ 64 \end{bmatrix}$$

$$\delta_1 = x_1 - x_0 = \begin{bmatrix} 7 \\ 3 \end{bmatrix}$$

$$A_1 = A_0 + \frac{(\Delta_1 - A_0\delta_1)\delta_1^T}{\delta_1^T\delta_1} = \begin{bmatrix} 1 & 0 \\ 0 & 1 \end{bmatrix} + \frac{\begin{bmatrix} -4 \\ 61 \end{bmatrix}\begin{bmatrix} 7 & 3 \end{bmatrix}}{\begin{bmatrix} 7 & 3 \end{bmatrix}\begin{bmatrix} 7 \\ 3 \end{bmatrix}} = \begin{bmatrix} 0.5172 & -0.2069 \\ 7.3621 & 4.1552 \end{bmatrix}$$

$$x_2 = x_1 - A_1^{-1}F(x_1) = \begin{bmatrix} 8 \\ 4 \end{bmatrix} - A_1^{-1}\begin{bmatrix} -4 \\ 61 \end{bmatrix} = \begin{bmatrix} 9.0892 \\ -12.6103 \end{bmatrix}$$

COMPUTER PROBLEMS 2.7

1 (a) For the function $F\begin{pmatrix} u \\ v \end{pmatrix} = \begin{bmatrix} u^2 + v^2 - 1 \\ (u-1)^2 + v^2 - 1 \end{bmatrix}$,

the Jacobian is $DF(u,v) = \begin{bmatrix} 2u & 2v \\ 2(u-1) & 2v \end{bmatrix}$.

Multivariate Newton's Method from p. 131 of the textbook with appropriate initial vectors converges to the roots shown in the Exercise 3(a) solution above.

1 (b) Similar to (a); check solutions with Exercise 3(b).

1 (c) Similar to (a); check solutions with Exercise 3(c).

3 Given the multivariate function $F\begin{pmatrix} u \\ v \end{pmatrix} = \begin{bmatrix} u^3 - v^3 + u \\ u^2 + v^2 - 1 \end{bmatrix}$,

the Jacobian is $DF(u,v) = \begin{bmatrix} 3u^2 + 1 & -3v^2 \\ 2u & 2v \end{bmatrix}$.

Using the initial vector $[1,1]$, Newton's Method converges to $[0.50799200, 0.86136179]$. Using the initial vector $[-1,-1]$, Newton's Method converges to root $[-0.50799200, -0.86136179]$.

5 (a) Points that lie on all three spheres satisfy

$$(u-1)^2 + (v-1)^2 + w^2 - 1 = 0$$
$$(u-1)^2 + v^2 + (w-1)^2 - 1 = 0$$
$$u^2 + (v-1)^2 + (w-1)^2 - 1 = 0.$$

The Jacobian is $DF = \begin{bmatrix} 2(u-1) & 2(v-1) & 2w \\ 2(u-1) & 2v & 2(w-1) \\ 2u & 2(v-1) & 2(w-1) \end{bmatrix}$. Under the Newton iteration, ini-

tial guesses near each of the roots $[1,1,1]$ and $[1/3, 1/3, 1/3]$ converge to them.

5 (b) Points that lie on all three spheres satisfy

$$(u-1)^2 + (v+2)^2 + w^2 - 25 = 0$$
$$(u+2)^2 + (v-2)^2 + (w+1)^2 - 25 = 0$$
$$(u-4)^2 + (v+2)^2 + (w-3)^2 - 25 = 0.$$

The Jacobian is $DF = \begin{bmatrix} 2(u-1) & 2(v+2) & 2w \\ 2(u+2) & 2(v-2) & 2(w+1) \\ 2(u-4) & 2(v+2) & 2(w-3) \end{bmatrix}$. Under the Newton iteration, ini-

tial guesses near each of the roots $[17/9, 22/9, 19/9]$ and $[1,2,3]$ converge to them.

7 (a) Broyden I can be used to compute the root with initial vector $[1,1]$. Convergence occurs within 15 decimal places to the root $(1/2, \sqrt{3}/2)$ after about 11 steps.

7 (b) Similar to (a). Broyden I converges within 15 decimal places to the root $(2/\sqrt{5}, 2/\sqrt{5})$ after about 13 steps.

7 (c) Similar to (a). Broyden I converges to the root $(4(1+\sqrt{6})/5, \sqrt{3+8\sqrt{6}}/5)$ within 15 decimal places after about 14 steps.

9 (a) Applying Broyden I with initial matrix $A_0 = I$ and initial guesses near each of the roots $[1,1,1]$ and $[1/3, 1/3, 1/3]$ converge to them.

9 (b) Applying Broyden I with initial matrix $A_0 = I$ and initial guesses near each of the roots $[17/9, 22/9, 19/9]$ and $[1,2,3]$ converge to them.

11 (a) Broyden II with initial matrix $B_0 = I$ converges to each of the roots $[1,1,1]$ and $[\frac{1}{3}, \frac{1}{3}, \frac{1}{3}]$.

11 (b) Broyden II with initial matrix $B_0 = I$ converges to each of the roots $[17/9, 22/9, 19/9]$ and $[1,2,3]$.

CHAPTER 3
Interpolation

EXERCISES 3.1   Data and Interpolating Functions

1 (a) The Lagrange interpolating polynomial through the points $(0, 1), (2, 3), (3, 0)$ is

$$P(x) = 1\frac{(x-2)(x-3)}{(0-2)(0-3)} + 3\frac{(x-0)(x-3)}{(2-0)(2-3)} + 0\frac{(x-0)(x-2)}{(3-0)(3-2)}$$

1 (b) The Lagrange interpolating polynomial is

$$P(x) = 1\frac{(x+1)(x-3)(x-5)}{(2+1)(2-3)(2-5)} + 1\frac{(x+1)(x-2)(x-5)}{(3+1)(3-2)(3-5)} + 2\frac{(x+1)(x-2)(x-3)}{(5+1)(5-2)(5-3)}$$

1 (c) The Lagrange interpolating polynomial is

$$P(x) = -2\frac{(x-2)(x-4)}{(0-2)(0-4)} + 1\frac{(x-0)(x-4)}{(2-0)(2-4)} + 4\frac{(x-0)(x-2)}{(4-0)(4-2)}$$

3 (a) Compute the Newton's divided differences of the data points:

$$
\begin{array}{r|lllll}
-1 & 3 \\
   &   & -1 \\
 1 & 1 &   & 1 \\
   &   & 2 &   & 0 \\
 2 & 3 &   & 1 \\
   &   & 4 \\
 3 & 7 \\
\end{array}
$$

The interpolating polynomial is given by $P(x) = 3 - (x+1) + (x+1)(x-1)$.

3 (b) By Theorem 3.2, there is exactly one polynomial of degree ≤ 3 that passes through all four points. This is the degree 2 polynomial in (a). No degree 3 polynomial exists.

3 (c) Infinitely many of degree 6; the following works for any nonzero degree 2 polynomial $Q(x)$:

$$P(x) = 3 - (x+1) + (x+1)(x-1) + (x+1)(x-1)(x-2)(x-3)Q(x)$$

5 (a)　Compute the Newton's divided differences of the data points:

$$
\begin{array}{r|rccc}
-2 & 8 \\
   &   & -2 \\
0 & 4 &   & 0 \\
   &   & -2 &   & 0 \\
1 & 2 &   & 0 \\
   &   & -2 \\
3 & -2
\end{array}
$$

The polynomial $P(x) = 8 - 2(x + 2)$ passes through the four data points.

5 (b)　According to Theorem 3.2, there are no other degree ≤ 3 polynomials through the four data points, but $P_4(x) = 8 - 2(x+2) + c(x+2)x(x-1)(x-3)$ interpolates for all c.

7　By definition, $P(x)$ passes through the points $(1,0), ..., (10,0), (12,44)$. In Lagrange form, the interpolating polynomial can be written

$$
P(x) = 44\frac{(x-1)\cdots(x-10)}{(12-1)\cdots(12-10)}
$$

Substituting $x = 0$ gives $P(x) = 44\dfrac{(0-1)\cdots(0-10)}{(12-1)\cdots(12-10)} = 44\dfrac{1\times2\times\cdots\times10}{11\times10\times\cdots\times2} = 4.$

9 (a)　For the data points $(1,0),(2,0),(3,0),(4,0),(5,0),(6,0),(7,10)$, the Lagrange interpolating polynomial is

$$
L(x) = 10\frac{(x-1)(x-2)\cdots(x-6)}{(7-1)(7-2)\cdots(7-6)}
$$

9 (b)　The degree 6 polynomial asked for contains the seven data points in (a). According to Theorem 3.2, there is only one polynomial that does so, the one computed above. Therefore it suffices to check whether the $L(x)$ from part (a) passes through $(8,70)$. Since

$$
L(8) = 10\frac{7\times6\times\cdots\times2}{6\times5\times\cdots\times1} = 70
$$

the polynomial $L(x)$ from part (a) also works for part (b).

11　Since the four points have distinct x-coordinates, Theorem 3.2 implies that only one polynomial of degree ≤ 3 passes through them. This polynomial is obviously the parabola $y = ax^2 + bx + c$. Therefore no cubic polynomials pass through the four points.

13　The polynomial $Q(x) = P(x) - 5$ passes through the points
$(-5,0),(-4,0),(-3,0),(-2,0),(-1,0),(0,0),(1,0),(2,0),(3,0),(4,0),(5,37)$.
The Lagrange form of the interpolating polynomial is

$$
Q(x) = 37\frac{(x+5)(x+4)(x+3)(x+2)(x+1)(x)(x-1)(x-2)(x-3)(x-4)}{(5+5)(5+4)(5+3)(5+2)(5+1)(5)(5-1)(5-2)(5-3)(5-4)}.
$$

Then

$$P(6) = Q(6) + 5 = 37\frac{(11)(10)(9)(8)(7)(6)(5)(4)(3)(2)}{(10)(9)(8)(7)(6)(5)(4)(3)(2)(1)} + 5 = 412.$$

15 The constant term of a polynomial $P(x)$ is $P(0)$. Therefore we require the polynomial $P(x)$ to pass through $(0, 25), (1, -1), (2, -2), \ldots, (25, -25)$. Define $Q(x) = P(x) + x$. The polynomial $Q(x)$ passes through $(0, 25), (1, 0), (2, 0), \ldots, (25, 0)$. The Lagrange form is

$$Q(x) = 25\frac{(x-1)(x-2)\cdots(x-25)}{(0-1)(0-2)\cdots(0-25)}.$$

Thus $P(x) = -x - \dfrac{25}{25!}(x-1)(x-2)\cdots(x-25) = -x - (x-1)(x-2)\cdots(x-25)/24!$

17 (a) The Newton's divided difference triangle follows:

1800	280			
		0.06		
1850	283		0.0010	
		0.16		0.000016
1900	291		0.0042	
		0.79		
2000	370			

The interpolating polynomial is

$$P(x) = 280 + 0.06(x - 1800) + 0.001(x - 1800)(x - 1850)$$
$$+ 0.000016(x - 1800)(x - 1850)(x - 1900)$$

Estimate the 1950 carbon dioxide concentration by
$$P(1950) = 280 + 0.06(150) + 0.001(150)(100) + 0.000016(150)(100)(50) = 316$$
17 (b) Estimate the 2050 concentration by
$$P(2050) = 280 + 0.06(250) + 0.001(250)(200) + 0.000016(250)(200)(150) = 465$$

COMPUTER PROBLEMS 3.1

1 (a) The `newtdd` MATLAB code can be used to construct the coefficients of the degree one interpolating polynomial. The commands

```
>> x=[1970 1990];y=[3707475887 5281653820];
>> c=newtdd(x,y,2);
>> nest(1,c,1980,x)
```

return 4494564853.5 as the 1980 population linear estimate, compared to the actual 4452584502, a difference of only 400 million.

1 (b) Follow the steps in (a), but use the three data points and construct a degree two interpolating polynomial. The resulting 1980 estimate is 4454831983.7, differing by only 2 million or so from the actual population.

1 (c) Following the steps in (a) for all four data points results in an estimate of 4472888287.8, about 20 million more than the actual population.

3 The MATLAB function could have the form:

```
function y0=polyinterp(x,y,x0)
len=length(x);
c=newtdd(x,y,len);
y0=nest(len-1,c,x0,x);
```

5 (a) $\tan(\frac{\pi}{2} - x) = \dfrac{\sin(\frac{\pi}{2} - x)}{\cos(\frac{\pi}{2} - x)} = \dfrac{\sin\frac{\pi}{2}\cos x - \cos\frac{\pi}{2}\sin x}{\cos\frac{\pi}{2}\cos x + \sin\frac{\pi}{2}\sin x} = \dfrac{\cos x}{\sin x}.$

5 (b) The $\tan x$ function is periodic with period π, or in other words, $\tan(x + \pi) = \tan x$. Therefore if we can compute $\tan x$ on the domain $[-\frac{\pi}{2}, \frac{\pi}{2})$, all other x can be referred to this interval by subtracting integer multiples of π.

Likewise, the identity $\tan(\frac{\pi}{2} - x) = 1/\tan x$ shows that for x satisfying $\frac{\pi}{4} < x < \frac{\pi}{2}$, $\tan x = 1/\tan(\frac{\pi}{2} - x)$ where $\frac{\pi}{2} - x$ lies in $[0, \frac{\pi}{4}]$. Furthermore, $\tan x$ for x in $[-\frac{\pi}{2}, 0]$ is the negative of $\tan |x|$.

Summarizing, given any real number, first subtract enough integer multiples of π to locate a corresponding x in $[-\frac{\pi}{2}, \frac{\pi}{2}]$. If $x < 0$, replace x by $|x|$ and remember to attach a minus sign at the final step. If the positive x is less than $\frac{\pi}{4}$, compute $\tan$ from the fundamental domain, and if $x > \frac{\pi}{4}$, set $\tan x = 1/\tan(\frac{\pi}{2} - x)$.

5 (c) The following MATLAB code moves the input x to the fundamental domain $[0, \pi/4]$ and carries out the evaluation of the interpolating polynomial.

```
function y=tan1(x)
b=pi*(0:3)/12;yb=tan(b);
c=newtdd(b,yb,4);
s=1;d=1;
x=mod(x+pi/2,pi)-pi/2;
if x < 0
    s=-1;x=abs(x);
end
if x > pi/4
    d=-1; x=pi/2-x;
end
y=s*nest(3,c,x,b)^d;
nest(3,c,x,b)
```

5 (d) The maximum error in the interval $[0, \pi/4]$ is approximately 0.003.

EXERCISES 3.2 Interpolation Error

1 (a) The Newton divided difference triangle is

$$
\begin{array}{c|c}
0 & 0 \\
& & \dfrac{2}{\pi} \\
\dfrac{\pi}{2} & 1 & & -\dfrac{4}{\pi^2} \\
& & -\dfrac{2}{\pi} & & \dfrac{?}{?} \\
\pi & 0
\end{array}
$$

The degree 2 interpolating polynomial is $P_2(x) = \dfrac{2}{\pi}x - \dfrac{4}{\pi^2}x(x - \dfrac{\pi}{2})$.

1 (b) $P_2(\dfrac{\pi}{4}) = \dfrac{2}{\pi}\dfrac{\pi}{4} - \dfrac{4}{\pi^2}\dfrac{\pi}{4}(-\dfrac{\pi}{4}) = \dfrac{1}{2} + \dfrac{1}{4} = \dfrac{3}{4}$

1 (c) The interpolation error formula in Theorem 3.4 applies to give

$$\left|\sin\dfrac{\pi}{4} - P_2\left(\dfrac{\pi}{4}\right)\right| \le \dfrac{\frac{\pi}{4}\frac{\pi}{4}\frac{3\pi}{4}}{6} = \dfrac{\pi^3}{128} \approx 0.242.$$

1 (d) The error is $\left|\sin\dfrac{\pi}{4} - P_2\left(\dfrac{\pi}{4}\right)\right| = \left|\dfrac{\sqrt{2}}{2} - \dfrac{3}{4}\right| \approx 0.043$, less than the error bound in (c).

3 (a) According to Theorem 3.4,

$$|f(x) - P_9(x)| = \left|\dfrac{(x-0)(x-\frac{1}{9})\cdots(x-1)}{10!}\right|2^{10}e^{-2c}$$

where c is between 0 and 1. At $x = \frac{1}{2}$, the error is

$$\left|f\left(\dfrac{1}{2}\right) - P_9\left(\dfrac{1}{2}\right)\right| \le \dfrac{\frac{9}{18}\frac{7}{18}\frac{5}{18}\frac{3}{18}\frac{1}{18}\frac{1}{18}\frac{3}{18}\frac{5}{18}\frac{7}{18}\frac{9}{18}}{10!}2^{10} \times 1 \approx 7.06 \times 10^{-11}.$$

3 (b) Since $f(\frac{1}{2}) = 1/e$, we can use $P_9(\frac{1}{2})$ as an approximation for $1/e$. According to (a), since $7.06 \times 10^{-11} \le 0.5 \times 10^{-9}$, the approximation will have at least 9 correct decimal places.

5 By Theorem 3.4, the interpolation error at x is

$$|f(x) - P(x)| \le \left|\dfrac{(x-0.1)(x-0.2)\cdots(x-0.6)}{6!}\right||f^{(6)}(c)|$$

when c is between the smallest and largest of $0.1, 0.2, \ldots, 0.6$, and x. We are given no information about $f^{(6)}(c)$. All things being equal, the ratio of the errors at $x = 0.55$ and $x = 0.35$ is

$$\dfrac{|(0.55-0.1)(0.55-0.2)\cdots(0.55-0.6)|}{|(0.35-0.1)(0.35-0.2)\cdots(0.35-0.6)|} = \dfrac{(0.45)(0.35)(0.25)(0.15)(0.05)(0.05)}{(0.25)(0.15)(0.05)(0.05)(0.15)(0.25)} = 4.2.$$

COMPUTER PROBLEMS 3.2

1 (a)   Using the MATLAB program `newtdd` to generate the coefficients of the interpolating polynomial results in

$$P_4(x) = 1.433329 + 1.989870(x - 0.6) + 3.258900(x - 0.6)(x - 0.7)$$
$$+ 3.680667(x - 0.6)(x - 0.7)(x - 0.8)$$
$$+ 4.0000417(x - 0.6)(x - 0.7)(x - 0.8)(x - 0.9),$$

or in nested form,

$$P_4(x) = 1.433329 + (x - 0.6)(1.989870 + (x - 0.7)(3.258900$$
$$+ (x - 0.8)(3.680667 + (x - 0.9)4.0000417))).$$

1 (b)   Substitute into $P_4(x)$ to get $P_4(0.82) = 1.958910$ and $P_4(0.98) = 2.612848$.

1 (c)   According to Theorem 3.4, the interpolation error satisfies

$$|e^{x^2} - P_4(x)| = \frac{|(x - 0.6)(x - 0.7)(x - 0.8)(x - 0.9)(x - 1)|}{5!}|f^{(v)}(c)|$$

where $f^{(v)}(x) = (32x^5 + 160x^3 + 120x)e^{x^2}$.

For $c \leq 1$, an upper bound for $f^{(v)}(c)$ is $|f^{(v)}(c)| \leq (32 + 160 + 120)e^1 = 312e \approx 848.1$.

Substituting into the error formula gives the error bounds

$|e^{(0.82)^2} - P_4(0.82)| \leq 0.0000537$ and $|e^{(0.98)^2} - P_4(0.98)| \leq 0.000217$.

The actual errors, using the results of part (b), are

$|e^{(0.82)^2} - P_4(0.82)| \approx 0.0000234$ and $|e^{(0.98)^2} - P_4(0.98)| \approx 0.000107$.

1 (d)

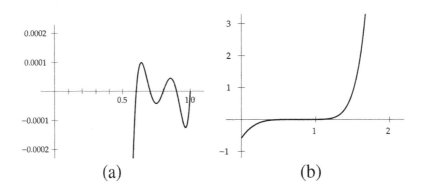

(a)   (b)

3 The degree 9 interpolating polynomial from Newton's divided differences, written in nested form, is

$$P_9(x) = 67.052 + (x - 1994)(0.9556 + (x - 1995)(0.4195$$
$$+ (x - 1996)(-0.6883 + (x - 1997)(-0.03575 + (x - 1998)(0.002175$$
$$+ (x - 1999)(0.0123056 + (x - 2000)(-0.007915$$
$$+ (x - 2001)(0.0028646 + (x - 2002)(-0.0007352))))))))))$$

and is plotted below.

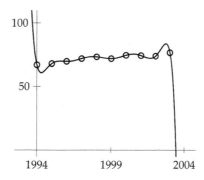

Substituting $x = 2010$ gives $P_9(2010) \approx -1.952 \times 10^{12}$ barrels, which is mathematically correct but nonsensical, and not consistent with the data shown. This is a typical example of the Runge phenomenon, which prevents the degree-9 interpolating polynomial from being a usable model for extrapolating this data

EXERCISES 3.3   Chebyshev Interpolation

1 (a) Using the formula $x = \cos(2i - 1)\pi/(2n)$ for $i = 1, \ldots, n$, the interpolation nodes are

$$\cos\frac{\pi}{12}, \cos\frac{3\pi}{12}, \cos\frac{5\pi}{12}, \cos\frac{7\pi}{12}, \cos\frac{9\pi}{12}, \cos\frac{11\pi}{12}.$$

1 (b) The general formula for Chebyshev nodes on $[a, b]$ is $(a+b)/2 + ((b-a)/2)\cos(2i-1)\pi/n$ for $i = 1, \ldots, n$. The 4 nodes on $[-2, 2]$ are therefore $2\cos(2i - 1)\pi/8$ for $i = 1, \ldots, 4$ or

$$2\cos\frac{\pi}{8}, 2\cos\frac{3\pi}{8}, 2\cos\frac{5\pi}{8}, 2\cos\frac{7\pi}{8}.$$

1 (c) Using the general formula from (b), the 6 nodes in $[4, 12]$ are

$$8 + 4\cos\frac{\pi}{12}, 8 + 4\cos\frac{3\pi}{12}, 8 + 4\cos\frac{5\pi}{12}, 8 + 4\cos\frac{7\pi}{12}, 8 + 4\cos\frac{9\pi}{12}, 8 + 4\cos\frac{11\pi}{12}.$$

1 (d) Using the general formula from (b), the 5 nodes in $[-0.3, 0.7]$ are

$$0.2 + 0.5\cos\frac{\pi}{10}, \ 0.2 + 0.5\cos\frac{3\pi}{10}, \ 0.2 + 0.5\cos\frac{5\pi}{10}, \ 0.2 + 0.5\cos\frac{7\pi}{10}, \ 0.2 + 0.5\cos\frac{9\pi}{10}.$$

3 To find a degree 5 interpolating polynomial, we need $n = 6$ nodes. By Theorem 3.4, the interpolation error is

$$e^x - Q_5(x) = \frac{(x - x_1)\cdots(x - x_6)}{6!}f^{(vi)}(c)$$

where $-1 \le c \le 1$. Using (3.14), $|e^x - Q_5(x)| \le \dfrac{|f^{(vi)}(c)|}{2^5 6!} = \dfrac{e^c}{2^5 6!} \le \dfrac{e}{2^5 6!} \approx 1.1798 \times 10^{-4}$. Since $0.11798 \times 10^{-3} < 0.5 \times 10^{-3}$, $Q_5(x)$ and e^x will agree to 3 decimal places for $-1 \le x \le 1$.

5 To find a degree 3 interpolating polynomial $P_3(x)$, $n = 4$ nodes are needed. By Theorem 3.4 and (3.14),

$$|\sin x - P_3(x)| = \frac{(x - x_1)(x - x_2)(x - x_3)(x - x_4)}{4!}|f^{(iv)}(c)| \le \frac{1}{2^3 4!} \approx 0.0052.$$

7 To get 6 correct digits we want to control the interpolation error to less than 0.5×10^{-6}. Using Theorem 3.4 and (3.14), the error for the degree d interpolation polynomial is

$$|\ln x - P_d(x)| = \frac{|(x - x_1)\cdots(x - x_{d+1})|}{(d + 1)!}|f^{(d+1)}(c)| \le \frac{(\frac{e-1}{2})^{d+1}}{2^d(d + 1)!}d!c^{-d-1} \le \frac{(e - 1)^{d+1}}{2^{2d+1}(d + 1)}$$

where $1 \le c \le e$. This expression is less than 0.5×10^{-6} when $d = 14$.

9 (a) Using the recursion relation (3.13) with $x = -1$, we find $T_{n+1}(-1) = -2T_n(-1) - T_{n-1}(-1)$. Since $T_0(-1) = 1$ and $T_1(-1) = -1$, this implies $T_2(-1) = 1$, $T_3(-1) = -1$, $T_4(-1) = 1$, and in general $T_n(-1) = (-1)^n$. Therefore $T_{999}(-1) = -1$.

9 (b) $T_{1000}(-1) = 1$, from the discussion in (a).

9 (c) Using (3.13), $T_{n+1}(0) = -T_{n-1}(0)$. We know $T_0(0) = 1$ and $T_1(0) = 0$, so $T_n(0) = 0$ for n odd, $T_n(0) = 1$ if 4 divides evenly into n, and $T_n(0) = -1$ if n is even and not a multiple of 4. Therefore $T_{999}(0) = 0$.

9 (d) $T_{1000}(0) = 1$, from the discussion in (c).

9 (e) Using (3.13), $T_{n+1}(-\frac{1}{2}) = -T_n(-\frac{1}{2}) - T_{n-1}(-\frac{1}{2})$, and $T_0(-\frac{1}{2}) = 1$, $T_1(-\frac{1}{2}) = -\frac{1}{2}$. Note that $T_2(-\frac{1}{2}) = -\frac{1}{2}$, $T_3(-\frac{1}{2}) = 1$, $T_4(-\frac{1}{2}) = -\frac{1}{2}$, $T_5(-\frac{1}{2}) = -\frac{1}{2}$ establishes the pattern: $T_n(-\frac{1}{2}) - 1$ if 3 divides n and $T_n(-\frac{1}{2}) = -\frac{1}{2}$ otherwise. Thus $T_{999}(-\frac{1}{2}) = 1$.

9 (f) $T_{1000}(-\frac{1}{2}) = -\frac{1}{2}$, from the discussion in (e).

COMPUTER PROBLEMS 3.3

1 The base points in Program 3.3 must be changed to be the Chebyshev nodes, using for example the MATLAB code

```
>> b=pi/4+(pi/4)*cos((1:2:7)*pi/8);
```

Then evaluating the degree 3 interpolating polynomial at a grid of points in the interval $[-2, 2]$ gives the following plot, where the interpolating polynomial is the thick curve and $y = \sin x$ is the thin curve.

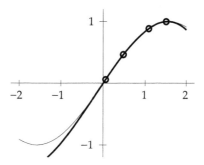

3   According to Theorem 3.4 and formula (3.14), the interpolation error of the degree $n - 1$ interpolation polynomial on the fundamental domain $[1, e]$ is at most

$$\frac{\left(\frac{e-1}{2}\right) |f^{(n)}(c)|}{2^{n-1} n!}$$

where $|f^{(n)}(x)| = (n - 1)! |x^{-n}|$ and $1 \leq c \leq e$. The maximum value of $|f(n)(c)|$ for $1 \leq c \leq e$ is $(n - 1)!$, so the interpolation error is bounded above by $(e - 1)^n / 2^{2n-1} n$. Checking shows that this expression is less than 0.5×10^{-10} for $n = 26$. Program 3.4 can be adapted to find the degree 25 interpolating polynomial at 26 Chebyshev nodes in $[1, e]$.

   The part of Program 3.4 that moves any input between 10^{-4} and 10^4 into the fundamental domain must also be changed. Since $e^{10} > 10^4$, the exponent k satisfying $e^k \leq x < e^{k+1}$ can be found using MATLAB code

```
k = 10;
while exp(k)>x
  k = k-1;
end
```

Now that xe^{-k} is in $[1, e]$, it can be substituted into the interpolation polynomial, and the result is added to k to get the approximate natural logarithm.

5 The MATLAB commands

```
>> b=2*(0:(n-1))/(n-1)-1;
```

or

```
>> b=cos((1:2:2*n-1)*pi/(2*n));
```

together with

```
>> yb=exp(-b.^2);
>> c=newtdd(b,yb,n);
```

define the coefficients of the degree $n - 1$ interpolating polynomial for evenly-spaced or Chebyshev nodes, respectively. Setting (a) $n = 10$ or (b) $n = 20$ gives the interpolation curves below. For both $n = 10$ and 20, the evenly-spaced and Chebyshev interpolants are indistinguishable in the plot. In (a), the 10 evenly-spaced interpolation points are plotted and in (b), the Chebyshev nodes are shown. The reason the curves are indistinguishable is clear when

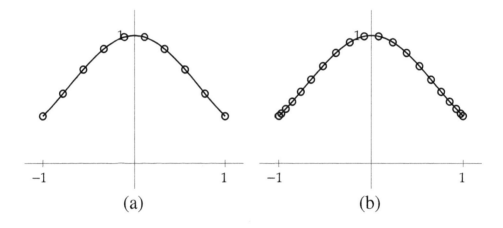

(a)   (b)

the empirical interpolation errors are plotted, in (c) $n = 10$ and (d) $n = 20$. The dashed curve is the interpolation error for evenly-spaced interpolation, and the solid curve is the Chebyshev interpolation error. There is a small hint of Runge phenomenon at the ends of the interval.

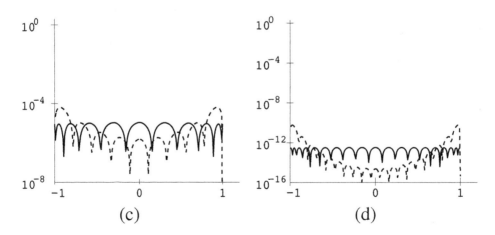

(c)   (d)

EXERCISES 3.4   Cubic Splines

1 (a) Calculating $S_1'(x) = 3x^2 + 1$ and $S_2'(x) = -3(x-1)^2 + 6(x-1) + 3$, note that $S_1'(1) = 4$ and $S_2'(1) = 3$, so that $S(x)$ is not a cubic spline.

1 (b) The derivatives are

$$S_1'(x) = 6x^2 + 2x + 4$$
$$S_1''(x) = 12x + 2$$
$$S_2'(x) = 3(x-1)^2 + 4(x-1) + 12$$
$$S_2''(x) = 6(x-1) + 14$$

Calculating $S_1(1) = 12$, $S_1'(1) = 12$, $S_1''(1) = 14$, and $S_2(1) = 12$, $S_2'(1) = 12$, $S_2''(1) = 14$, we conclude that $S(x)$ is a cubic spline.

3 (a) The second derivatives $S_1''(x) = \frac{9}{2}x$ and $S_2''(x) = -\frac{9}{2}(x-1) + 2c$ must agree at $x = 1$, implying that $\frac{9}{2} = 2c$, or $c = \frac{9}{4}$. Since $S_1''(0) = 0$ and $S_2''(2) = -\frac{9}{2} + \frac{9}{2} = 0$, the spline is natural. The spline fails the not-a-knot condition because $S_1'''(1) = \frac{9}{2} \neq -\frac{9}{2} = S_2'''(1)$, and is not parabolically terminated because of the degree 3 terms.

3 (b) The second derivatives $S_1''(x) = 8$ and $S_2''(x) = 2c$ must agree at $x = 1$, thus $c = 4$. The spline is parabolically terminated because of the absence of degree 3 terms, and is not-a-knot because $S_1'''(1) = 0 = S_2'''(1)$. It fails to be natural because $S_1''(0) = 8 \neq 0$.

3 (c) The first derivatives $S_1'(x) = -\frac{3}{2} + 7x - 3x^2$ and $S_2'(x) = c + (x-1) - 3(x-1)^2$ must agree at $x = 1$, so $c = \frac{5}{2}$. Since $S_1''(0) = 7 - 6(0) = 7 \neq 0$, the spline is not natural. It is not parabolically terminated because of the nonzero degree 3 terms. The spline is not-a-knot because $S_1'''(1) = S_2'''(1) = -6$ and $S_2'''(2) = S_3'''(2) = -6$.

5 By Theorem 3.9, there is exactly one natural cubic spline through any three points with distinct x coordinates. The cubic spline $S_1(x) = S_2(x) = x$ on $[0, 1]$ and $[1, 2]$, respectively, satisfies the conditions.

7 (a) There are $n = 3$ given data points. First calculate $\delta_1 = x_2 - x_1 = 1 - 0 = 1$, $\delta_2 = x_3 - x_2 = 2 - 1 = 1$, $\Delta_1 = y_2 - y_1 = 1 - 0 = 1$, $\Delta_2 = y_3 - y_2 = 4 - 1 = 3$. Equation (3.30) has the form

$$\begin{bmatrix} 1 & 0 & 0 \\ 1 & 4 & 1 \\ 0 & 0 & 1 \end{bmatrix} \begin{bmatrix} c_1 \\ c_2 \\ c_3 \end{bmatrix} = \begin{bmatrix} 0 \\ 6 \\ 0 \end{bmatrix}$$

with solutions $c_1 = 0$, $c_2 = \frac{3}{2}$, $c_3 = 0$. Equation (3.28) yields

$$d_1 = \frac{c_2 - c_1}{3\delta_1} = \frac{\frac{3}{2} - 0}{3(1)} = \frac{1}{2}$$

$$d_2 = \frac{c_3 - c_2}{3\delta_2} = \frac{0 - \frac{3}{2}}{3(1)} = -\frac{1}{2}$$

and equation (3.29) gives

$$b_1 = \frac{\Delta_1}{\delta_1} - \frac{\delta_1}{3}(2c_1 + c_2) = \frac{1}{2}$$

$$b_2 = \frac{\Delta_2}{\delta_2} - \frac{\delta_2}{3}(2c_2 + c_3) = 2$$

The cubic spline is therefore

$$S_1(x) = 0 + \frac{1}{2}x + 0x^2 + \frac{1}{2}x^3 \qquad \text{on} \quad [0,1]$$

$$S_2(x) = 1 + 2(x-1) + \frac{3}{2}(x-1)^2 - \frac{1}{2}(x-1)^3 \quad \text{on} \quad [1,2].$$

7 (b)   There are $n = 3$ data points. Calculate $\delta_1 = 2$, $\delta_2 = 1$, $\Delta_1 = 0$, $\Delta_2 = 3$. System (3.30) is

$$\begin{bmatrix} 1 & 0 & 0 \\ 2 & 6 & 1 \\ 0 & 0 & 1 \end{bmatrix} \begin{bmatrix} c_1 \\ c_2 \\ c_3 \end{bmatrix} = \begin{bmatrix} 0 \\ 9 \\ 0 \end{bmatrix}$$

with solutions $c_1 = 0$, $c_2 = \frac{3}{2}$, $c_3 = 0$. Equation (3.28) implies $d_1 = \frac{1}{4}$, $d_2 = -\frac{1}{2}$ and equation (3.29) implies $b_1 = -1$, $b_2 = 2$. The cubic spline is therefore

$$S_1(x) = 1 - (x+1) \qquad\qquad + \frac{1}{4}(x+1)^3 \quad \text{on} \quad [-1,1]$$

$$S_2(x) = 1 + 2(x-1) + \frac{3}{2}(x-1)^2 - \frac{1}{2}(x-1)^3 \quad \text{on} \quad [1,2].$$

9   Setting $S_1(1) = S_2(1)$ implies $4 + b_1 = 1$, or $b_1 = -3$. Setting $S_1'(1) = S_2'(1)$ implies $b_1 + 3 = b_2$, or $b_2 = 0$. Therefore $S_1'(0) = b_1 + 3(0)^2 = -3$, and $S_2'(3) = b_2 + 6(3-1) - 6(3-1)^2 = -12$.

11 (a)   By Theorem 3.10, there is exactly one parabolically terminated cubic spline through the three points. The parabola passing through the three points, used on both intervals $[0,1]$ and $[1,2]$, will be the unique spline. By Newton divided differences:

$$\begin{array}{c|ccc} 0 & 2 & & \\ & & -2 & \\ 1 & 0 & & 2 \\ & & 2 & \\ 2 & 2 & & \end{array}$$

The parabola is $S(x) = 2 - 2x + 2x(x-1) = 2x^2 - 4x + 2$.

11 (b)   We know from Section 3.1 that there are infinitely many degree 3 polynomials through the three points. Each can be used as a not-a-knot spline. The cubic polynomials are $S(x) = 2x^2 - 4x + 2 + cx(x-1)(x-2)$ for arbitrary $c \neq 0$.

13 (a) The coefficient b_1 can be found from the spline property $S_1'(1) = S_2'(1)$, or $b_1 - \frac{10}{9}x + \frac{5}{3}x^2 = \frac{14}{9}$, which implies $b_1 = 1$. Similarly, c_3 is found from $S_2''(2) = S_3''(2)$, or $\frac{20}{9} - 4 = 2c_3$, which implies $c_3 = -8/9$.

13 (b) A spline is natural if $0 = S''(0) = S''(3)$. Neither is true, since $S''(0) = -10/9$ and $S''(3) = -\frac{16}{9} - \frac{2}{3} = -22/9$.

13 (c) The clamps are $S_1'(0) = b_1 = 1$ and $S_3'(3) = \frac{16}{9} + 2(-\frac{8}{9}) - \frac{1}{3} = -1/3$.

15 If a cubic spline is natural and parabolically terminated, then $S_1(x) = a_1 + b_1(x - x_1) + c_1(x - x_1)^2$ and $S_1''(x_1) = 0$. Differentiating gives $S_1''(x) = 2c_1$, implying $c_1 = 0$, and $S_1(x)$ is linear. The same argument applies to show that $S_{n-1}(x)$ is linear.

17 We have $S_1(x) = 1$, $S_2(x) = 1 + b_2x + c_2x^2 + d_2x^3$. Differentiating, $S_2'(x) = b_2 + 2c_2x + 3d_2x^2$ and $S_2''(x) = 2c_2 + 6d_2x$. The spline conditions imply $0 = S_1'(0) = S_2'(0) = b_2$ and $0 = S_1''(0) = S_2''(0) = 2c_2$; in other words, the conditions are satisfied provided that $0 = b_2 = c_2$, for arbitrary d_2. Thus $S_2(x) = 1 + d_2x^3$ works for any d_2.

19 Since there are infinitely many parabolas through $n = 2$ data points with distinct x coordinates, there are infinitely many parabolically terminated cubic splines. Thus existence holds but uniqueness fails.

21 (a) Infinitely many. For a three point spline, not-a-knot implies $S_1(x) = S_2(x)$. We know from Section 3.1 that there are infinitely many degree 3 polynomials $S(x)$ through the three points.

21 (b) Choose $S_1(x) = S_2(x)$ to be any degree three polynomial through $(0,0)$, $(1,1)$, and $(2,4)$, for example $S(x) = x^2 + cx(x-1)(x-2)$ for any nonzero c.

COMPUTER PROBLEMS 3.4

1 (a) Programs 3.5 and 3.6 can be used to compute the spline coefficients and plot the spline, respectively. The command

```
>> c=splinecoeff([0 1 2 3],[3 5 4 1])
```

returns the spline coefficients

$$\begin{cases} S_1(x) = 3 + \frac{8}{3}x - \frac{2}{3}x^3 & \text{on } [0,1] \\ S_2(x) = 5 + \frac{2}{3}(x-1) - 2(x-1)^2 + \frac{1}{3}(x-1)^3 & \text{on } [1,2] \\ S_3(x) = 4 - \frac{7}{3}(x-2) - (x-2)^2 + \frac{1}{3}(x-2)^3 & \text{on } [2,3] \end{cases}.$$

The plot from

```
>> [x1,y1]=splineplot([0 1 2 3],[3 5 4 1]);
```

is shown as (a) below.

1 (b)   Programs 3.5 and 3.6 can be used as in (a) to compute the spline coefficients and plot the spline. The result is

$$\begin{cases} S_1(x) = 3 + 2.5629(x+1) - 0.5629(x+1)^3 & \text{on } [-1,0] \\ S_2(x) = 5 + 0.8742x - 1.6887x^2 + 0.3176x^3 & \text{on } [0,3] \\ S_3(x) = 1 - 0.6824(x-3) + 1.1698(x-3)^2 - 0.4874(x-3)^3 & \text{on } [3,4] \\ S_4(x) = 1 + 0.1950(x-4) - 0.2925(x-4)^2 + 0.0975(x-4)^3 & \text{on } [4,5] \end{cases}$$

The plot of the natural cubic spline is shown in (b) below.

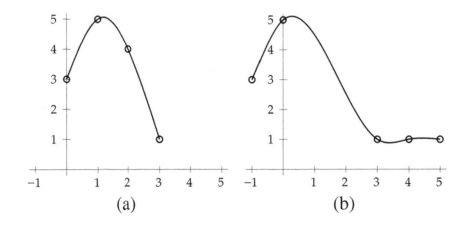

(a)   (b)

3   The spline is natural, and Programs 3.5 and 3.6 calculate

$$\begin{cases} S_1(x) = 1 + 2.6607x - 0.6607x^3 & \text{on } [0,1] \\ S_2(x) = 3 + 0.6786(x-1) - 1.9821(x-1)^2 + 1.3036(x-1)^3 & \text{on } [1,2] \\ S_3(x) = 3 + 0.6250(x-2) + 1.9286(x-2)^2 - 1.5536(x-2)^3 & \text{on } [2,3] \\ S_4(x) = 4 - 0.1786(x-3) - 2.7321(x-3)^2 + 0.9107(x-3)^3 & \text{on } [3,4] \end{cases}$$

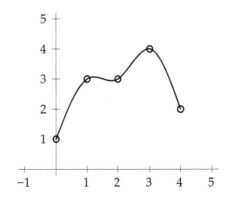

5 The cubic spline is clamped, and can be found by Programs 3.5 and 3.6 with the clamped conditions enabled and variables v1 = 0 and vn = 1.

$$\begin{cases} S_1(x) = 1 + 4.6786x^2 - 2.6786x^3 & \text{on } [0,1] \\ S_2(x) = 3 + 1.3214(x-1) - 3.3571(x-1)^2 + 2.0357(x-1)^3 & \text{on } [1,2] \\ S_3(x) = 3 + 0.7143(x-2) + 2.7500(x-2)^2 - 2.4643(x-2)^3 & \text{on } [2,3] \\ S_4(x) = 4 - 1.1786(x-3) - 4.6429(x-3)^2 + 3.8214(x-3)^3 & \text{on } [3,4] \end{cases}$$

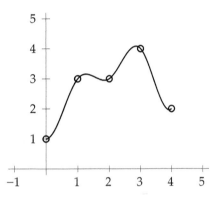

7 Program 3.5 can be used to find the cubic spline, using input vectors

```
>> x=pi*(0:4)/8;
>> y=cos(x);
```

The clamps v1 and vn should be chosen to match the derivatives at the endpoints, namely $S'(0) = -\sin 0 = 0$ and $S'(\pi/2) = -\sin \pi/2 = -1$, respectively. The cubic spline is plotted below along with the cosine curve, although they are indistinguishable at this resolution.

$$\begin{cases} S_1(x) = 1 - 0.5065x^2 + 0.0327x^3 & \text{on } [0, \tfrac{\pi}{8}] \\ S_2(x) = 0.9239 - 0.3826(x - \tfrac{\pi}{8}) - 0.4679(x - \tfrac{\pi}{8})^2 + 0.0931(x - \tfrac{\pi}{8})^3 & \text{on } [\tfrac{\pi}{8}, \tfrac{\pi}{4}] \\ S_3(x) = 0.7071 - 0.7070(x - \tfrac{\pi}{4}) - 0.3582(x - \tfrac{\pi}{4})^2 + 0.1396(x - \tfrac{\pi}{4})^3 & \text{on } [\tfrac{\pi}{4}, \tfrac{3\pi}{8}] \\ S_4(x) = 0.3827 - 0.9237(x - \tfrac{3\pi}{4}) - 0.1937(x - \tfrac{3\pi}{4})^2 + 0.1639(x - \tfrac{3\pi}{4})^3 & \text{on } [\tfrac{3\pi}{8}, \tfrac{\pi}{2}] \end{cases}$$

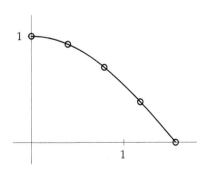

9 The clamped cubic spline can be calculated from Program 3.5 after setting the clamps $S'(1) = f'(1) = 1$ and $S'(3) = f'(3) = 1/3$. The spline is

$$
\begin{cases}
S_1(x) = (x-1) - 0.4638(x-1)^2 + 0.1713(x-1)^3 & \text{on } [1, \tfrac{3}{2}] \\
S_2(x) = 0.4055 + 0.6647(x - \tfrac{3}{2}) - 0.2068(x - \tfrac{3}{2})^2 + 0.0563(x - \tfrac{3}{2})^3 & \text{on } [\tfrac{3}{2}, 2] \\
S_3(x) = 0.6931 + 0.5001(x-2) - 0.1224(x-2)^2 + 0.0295(x-2)^3 & \text{on } [2, \tfrac{5}{2}] \\
S_4(x) = 0.9163 + 0.3998(x - \tfrac{5}{2}) - 0.0782(x - \tfrac{5}{2})^2 + 0.0155(x - \tfrac{5}{2})^3 & \text{on } [\tfrac{5}{2}, 3]
\end{cases}
$$

The maximum difference between the spline and the function $f(x) = \ln x$ can be determined by a slight modification of Program 3.5. The maximum interpolation error on $[1, 3]$ is approximately 0.0005464.

11 (a) The natural cubic spline through the four data points is

$$
\begin{cases}
S_1(x) = 3039585530 + 64621942(x - 1960) + 21671(x - 1960)^3 \\
S_2(x) = 3707475887 + 71123224(x - 1970) + 650128(x - 1970)^2 - 13542(x - 1970)^3 \\
S_3(x) = 5281653820 + 80877678(x - 1990) - 162405(x - 1990)^2 + 5414(x - 1990)^3
\end{cases}
$$

on $[1960, 1970], [1970, 1990]$ and $[1990, 2000]$ respectively. Substituting $x = 1980$ gives the estimate 4470178717.

11 (b) Using the data points, we can estimate the derivatives at the left and right endpoints as $(3707475887 - 3039585530)/10 = 66789036$ and $(6079603571 - 5281653820)/10 = 79794975$, respectively. The clamped cubic spline through the four points is

$$
\begin{cases}
S_1(x) = 3039585530 + 66789036(x - 1960) - 362212(x - 1960)^2 + 36221(x - 1960)^3 \\
S_2(x) = 3707475887 + 70411154(x - 1970) + 724424(x - 1970)^2 - 15477(x - 1970)^3 \\
S_3(x) = 5281653820 + 80815906(x - 1990) - 204186(x - 1990)^2 + 10209(x - 1990)^3
\end{cases}
$$

on $[1960, 1970], [1970, 1990]$ and $[1990, 2000]$ respectively. Substituting $x = 1980$ gives the estimate 4468552974. The natural cubic spline estimate misses the actual 1980 population by 17.6 million, while the clamped spline misses by 16 million, and is slightly closer.

13 Program 3.6 can be adapted to plot the three different cubic splines. They are barely distinguishable in the following plot; the solid curve is natural, the dashed curve is not-a-knot, and the dotted curve is parabolically-terminated.

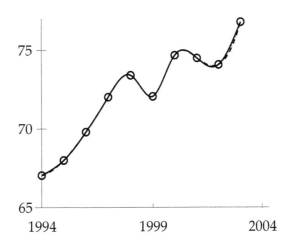

EXERCISES 3.5   Bézier Curves

1 (a)   Using the Bézier curve equations on page 164, one calculates $b_x = 3(0) = 0, c_x = 3(2-0) - 0 = 6, d_x = 1 - 0 - 0 - 6 = -5, b_y = 3(2-0) = 6, c_y = 3(0-2) - 6 = -12, d_y = 0 - 0 - 6 + 12 = 6$. The Bézier curve is

$$\begin{cases} x(t) = x_1 + b_x t + c_x t^2 + d_x t^3 = 6t^2 - 5t^3 \\ y(t) = y_1 + b_y t + c_y t^2 + d_y t^3 = 6t - 12t^2 + 6t^3 \end{cases}.$$

1 (b)   Similar to (a). One calculates $b_x = -3, c_x = -3, d_x = 3$ and $b_y = -3, c_y = 3, d_y = 0$. The Bézier curve is

$$\begin{cases} x(t) = 1 - 3t - 3t^2 + 3t^3 \\ y(t) = 1 - 3t + 3t^2 \end{cases}.$$

1 (c)   Similar to (a). One calculates $b_x = 0, c_x = 3, d_x = -2$ and $b_y = 3, c_y = -3, d_y = 0$. The Bézier curve is

$$\begin{cases} x(t) = 1 + 3t^2 - 2t^3 \\ y(t) = 2 + 3t - 3t^2 \end{cases}.$$

3   We use Example 3.16 to draw three line segments as a three-piece Bézier curve. Each piece is characterized by four two-dimensional points:

$$\begin{array}{cccc} (1,2) & (1,2) & (3,4) & (3,4) \\ (3,4) & (3,4) & (5,1) & (5,1) \\ (5,1) & (5,1) & (1,2) & (1,2) \end{array}$$

Translating to Bézier curves yields

$$\begin{cases} x(t) = 1 + 2t^2(3-2t) \\ y(t) = 2 + 2t^2(3-2t) \end{cases} \quad \begin{cases} x(t) = 3 + 2t^2(3-2t) \\ y(t) = 4 - 3t^2(3-2t) \end{cases} \quad \begin{cases} x(t) = 5 - 4t^2(3-2t) \\ y(t) = 1 + t^2(3-2t) \end{cases}$$

5 The number 3:

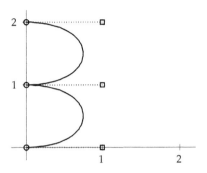

7   There are infinitely many Bézier curves satisfying the requirements. The data points are $(-1, 0), (-1, y_2), (1, y_3), (1, 0)$ which generate the Bézier curve

$$\begin{cases} x(t) = -1 + 6t^2 - 4t^3 \\ y(t) = 3y_2 t + (3y_3 - 6y_2)t^2 + (3y_2 - 3y_3)t^3 \end{cases}.$$

At $t = \frac{1}{2}, x(\frac{1}{2}) = 0$, so we must solve $1 = y(\frac{1}{2}) = \frac{3}{8}(y_2 + y_3)$. Any combination of y_2 and $y_3 = \frac{8}{3} - y_2$ satisfies the requirements. The solutions are

$$\begin{cases} x(t) = -1 + 6t^2 - 4t^3 \\ y(t) = 3y_2 t + (8 - 9y_2)t^2 + (6y_2 - 8)t^3 \end{cases}.$$

for arbitrary y_2. A particularly symmetric Bézier curve is given by setting $y_2 = y_3 = \frac{4}{3}$, or $y(t) = 4t - 4t^2$.

9 (a)   For a space curve, the Bézier equations are applied to the x, y and z coordinates. Therefore $b_x = 3, c_x = -9, d_x = 5, b_y = 0, c_y = 6, d_y = -5$, and $b_z = 0, c_z = 3, d_z = -3$. The Bézier space curve is

$$\begin{cases} x(t) = 1 + 3t - 9t^2 + 5t^3 \\ y(t) = 6t^2 - 5t^3 \\ z(t) = 3t^2 - 3t^3 \end{cases}.$$

9 (b)   Similar to (a). Calculate $b_x = 0, c_x = -6, d_x = 6, b_y = 3, c_y = -9, d_y = 6$, and $b_z = 3, c_z = -12, d_z = 8$. The Bézier space curve is

$$\begin{cases} x(t) = 1 - 6t^2 + 6t^3 \\ y(t) = 1 + 3t - 9t^2 + 6t^3 \\ z(t) = 2 + 3t - 12t^2 + 8t^3 \end{cases}.$$

9 (c) Similar to (a). Calculate $b_x = 3, c_x = -12, d_x = 10, b_y = c_y = d_y = 0$, and $b_z = 0, c_z = 6, d_z = -4$. The Bézier space curve is

$$\begin{cases} x(t) = 2 + 3t - 12t^2 + 10t^3 \\ y(t) = 1 \\ z(t) = 1 + 6t^2 - 4t^3 \end{cases}.$$

11 Differentiating the Bézier formula $x(t) = x_1 + b_x t + c_x t^2 + d_x t^3$ gives $x'(t) = b_x + 2c_x t + 3d_x t^2$. Substituting yields $x'(0) = b_x = 3(x_2 - x_1)$ and

$$\begin{aligned} x'(1) &= b_x + 2c_x + 3d_x \\ &= b_x + 2c_x + 3(x_4 - x_1 - b_x - c_x) \\ &= -3(x_1 - x_1) - 3(x_2 - x_2) + 3(x_4 - x_1) \\ &= 4(x_4 - x_3). \end{aligned}$$

Similarly, $y'(0) = 3(y_2 - y_1)$ and $y'(1) = 3(y_4 - y_3)$. Therefore the direction vector of the parametric curve at $t = 0$ is $3(x_2 - x_1, y_2 - y_1)$, the direction from the first endpoint to the first control point. The direction vector at $t = 1$ is $3(x_4 - x_3, y_4 - y_3)$, the direction from the second control point to the second endpoint. Therefore the Bézier equations are designed to allow the control points to control the tangent directions at the endpoints.

COMPUTER PROBLEMS 3.5

1 A Bézier spline from Exercise 5 that satisfies the requirements is

$$\begin{cases} x(t) = -1 + 6t^2 - 4t^3 \\ y(t) = 4t - 4t^2 \end{cases}.$$

A parametric plot of the spline is shown below.

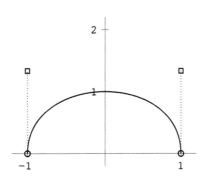

3 Examples of Bezier splines for the four letters are shown. Program 3.7 can be adapted to accept, instead of input data from the mouse, $n \times 4$ arrays xlist and ylist holding rows of four x and y data points, respectively. For example, in (b) below we defined

```
>> xlist=[1 1 1 1;1 3 3 1;1 3 3 1];
>> ylist=[1 1 5 5;5 5 3 3;3 3 1 1];
```

to represent the three splines defined by the four point groups

$$(1,1) \quad (1,1) \quad (1,5) \quad (1,5)$$
$$(1,5) \quad (3,5) \quad (3,3) \quad (1,3)$$
$$(1,3) \quad (3,3) \quad (3,1) \quad (1,1)$$

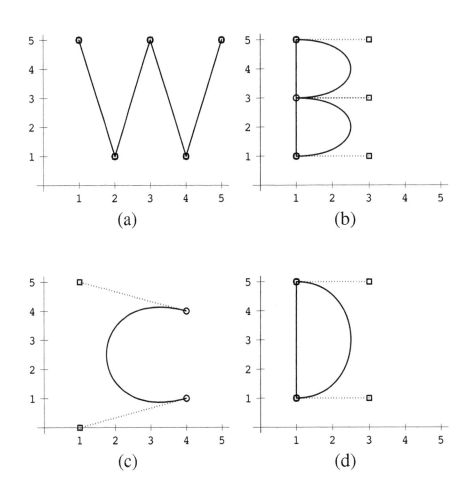

CHAPTER 4
Least Squares

EXERCISES 4.1 Least Squares and the Normal Equations

1 (a) To solve the normal equations we first calculate

$$A^T A = \begin{bmatrix} 5 & 4 \\ 4 & 6 \end{bmatrix} \text{ and } A^T b = \begin{bmatrix} 5 \\ 8 \end{bmatrix}.$$

Solving $A^T A x = A^T b$ yields the least squares solution $\overline{x} = [-1/7, 10/7]^T$. The residual error is $e = b - Ax = [2/7, -3/7, 1/7]$ with 2-norm $||e||_2 = \sqrt{\frac{4}{49} + \frac{9}{49} + \frac{1}{49}} = \sqrt{14}/7$.

1 (b) The normal equations are $A^T A x = A^T b$ where

$$A^T A = \begin{bmatrix} 14 & 6 \\ 6 & 3 \end{bmatrix} \text{ and } A^T b = \begin{bmatrix} 5 \\ 3 \end{bmatrix}.$$

Solving the normal equations gives the least squares solution $\overline{x} = [-1/2, 2]^T$. The residual error is $e = b - Ax = [-1/2, 1, -1/2]$ with 2-norm $||e||_2 = \sqrt{\frac{1}{4} + 1 + \frac{1}{4}} = \sqrt{6}/2$.

1 (c) The normal equations are $A^T A x = A^T b$ where

$$A^T A = \begin{bmatrix} 10 & 9 \\ 9 & 10 \end{bmatrix} \text{ and } A^T b = \begin{bmatrix} 16 \\ 16 \end{bmatrix}.$$

The normal equations give $\overline{x} = [16/19, 16/19]^T$. The residual error is $e = b - Ax = [9/19, 25/19, 9/19, -26/19]$ with 2-norm $||e||_2 \approx 2.013$.

3 The normal equations are $A^T A x = A^T b$, or

$$\begin{bmatrix} 3 & 0 \\ 0 & 0 \end{bmatrix} \begin{bmatrix} x_1 \\ x_2 \end{bmatrix} = \begin{bmatrix} 12 \\ 0 \end{bmatrix}.$$

Solving the normal equations gives $x_1 = 4$ and x_2 arbitrary. Therefore there are infinitely many least squares solutions $\overline{x} = [4, x_2]$.

5 The three properties:
(i) $||x||_2 \geq 0$ is guaranteed by the definition $||x||_2 = \sqrt{x_1^2 + \ldots + x_n^2}$, and if $||x||_2 = 0$, all components x_i must be zero.
(ii) For a scalar α,

$$\begin{aligned} ||\alpha x||_2 &= \sqrt{\alpha^2 x_1^2 + \ldots + \alpha^2 x_n^2} \\ &= |\alpha| \sqrt{x_1^2 + \ldots + x_n^2} \\ &= |\alpha| \cdot ||x||_2 \end{aligned}$$

(iii) Given two vectors x and y,

$$
\begin{aligned}
\|x + y\|_2^2 &= (x_1 + y_1)^2 + \ldots + (x_n + y_n)^2 \\
&= x_1^2 + \ldots + x_n^2 + y_1^2 + \ldots + y_n^2 + 2(x_1 y_1 + \ldots + x_n y_n) \\
&\leq \|x\|_2^2 + \|y\|_2^2 + 2\|x\|_2 \|y\|_2 = (\|x\|_2 + \|y\|_2)^2
\end{aligned}
$$

where the Cauchy-Schwarz inequality was used to obtain the last line. Taking square roots proves the triangle inequality for the 2-norm.

7 (a)   Substituting the data points (t, y) into the model $y = c_1 + c_2 t$ gives the five equations

$$
\begin{aligned}
c_1 + c_2(-3) &= 3 \\
c_1 + c_2(-1) &= 2 \\
c_1 + c_2(0) &= 1 \\
c_1 + c_2(1) &= -1 \\
c_1 + c_2(3) &= -4.
\end{aligned}
$$

Converting to matrix form,

$$
Ax = \begin{bmatrix} 1 & -3 \\ 1 & -1 \\ 1 & 0 \\ 1 & 1 \\ 1 & 3 \end{bmatrix} \begin{bmatrix} c_1 \\ c_2 \end{bmatrix} = \begin{bmatrix} 3 \\ 2 \\ 1 \\ -1 \\ -4 \end{bmatrix} = b.
$$

The normal equations are

$$
\begin{bmatrix} 5 & 0 \\ 0 & 20 \end{bmatrix} \begin{bmatrix} c_1 \\ c_2 \end{bmatrix} = \begin{bmatrix} 1 \\ -24 \end{bmatrix}
$$

and the least squares solution is $\bar{c} = [1/5, -6/5]^T$, corresponding to the line $y = \frac{1}{5} - \frac{6}{5}t$. The residual error is $e = [-4/5, 3/5, 4/5, 0, -3/5]^T$, which has RMSE

$$
\frac{\sqrt{(-\frac{4}{5})^2 + (\frac{3}{5})^2 + (\frac{4}{5})^2 + (-\frac{3}{5})^2}}{\sqrt{5}} = \sqrt{\frac{2}{5}}.
$$

7 (b)   Similar to (a). The model $y = c_1 + c_2 t$ leads to the system

$$
Ax = \begin{bmatrix} 1 & 1 \\ 1 & 1 \\ 1 & 2 \\ 1 & 2 \\ 1 & 4 \end{bmatrix} \begin{bmatrix} c_1 \\ c_2 \end{bmatrix} = \begin{bmatrix} 1 \\ 2 \\ 2 \\ 3 \\ 3 \end{bmatrix} = b.
$$

The normal equations are

$$\begin{bmatrix} 5 & 10 \\ 10 & 26 \end{bmatrix} \begin{bmatrix} c_1 \\ c_2 \end{bmatrix} = \begin{bmatrix} 11 \\ 25 \end{bmatrix}$$

and the least squares solution is $\bar{c} = [6/5, 1/2]^T$, corresponding to the line $y = 6/5 + t/2$. The residual error is $e = [-0.7, 0.3, -0.2, 0.8, -0.2]^T$, which has RMSE $= \sqrt{26}/10$.

9 (a)   Substituting the four data points into the model $y = c_1 + c_2 t + c_3 t^2$ results in the system of equations

$$\begin{bmatrix} 1 & 0 & 0 \\ 1 & 1 & 1 \\ 1 & 2 & 4 \\ 1 & 5 & 25 \end{bmatrix} \begin{bmatrix} c_1 \\ c_2 \\ c_3 \end{bmatrix} = \begin{bmatrix} 0 \\ 3 \\ 3 \\ 6 \end{bmatrix}$$

The normal equations are

$$\begin{bmatrix} 4 & 8 & 30 \\ 8 & 30 & 134 \\ 30 & 134 & 642 \end{bmatrix} \begin{bmatrix} c_1 \\ c_2 \\ c_3 \end{bmatrix} = \begin{bmatrix} 12 \\ 39 \\ 165 \end{bmatrix}.$$

Solving for c_1, c_2, c_3 leads to the least squares parabola $y = 0.3481 + 1.9475t - 0.1657t^2$. The RMSE is 0.5519, compared to 0.6944 for the least squares line fit in Exercise 8(a).

9 (b)   Substituting the four data points into the model $y = c_1 + c_2 t + c_3 t^2$ results in the system of equations

$$\begin{bmatrix} 1 & 1 & 1 \\ 1 & 3 & 9 \\ 1 & 4 & 16 \\ 1 & 6 & 36 \end{bmatrix} \begin{bmatrix} c_1 \\ c_2 \\ c_3 \end{bmatrix} = \begin{bmatrix} 2 \\ 2 \\ 1 \\ 3 \end{bmatrix}$$

Solving the normal equations for c_1, c_2, c_3 yields the best parabola $y = 2.9615 - 1.0128t + 0.1667t^2$. The RMSE is 0.4160, compared to 0.6504 for the best line in Exercise 8(b).

9 (c)   Substituting into the model parabola gives the system of equations

$$\begin{bmatrix} 1 & 0 & 0 \\ 1 & 1 & 1 \\ 1 & 2 & 4 \\ 1 & 3 & 9 \end{bmatrix} \begin{bmatrix} c_1 \\ c_2 \\ c_3 \end{bmatrix} = \begin{bmatrix} 5 \\ 3 \\ 3 \\ 1 \end{bmatrix}$$

The normal equations are

$$\begin{bmatrix} 4 & 6 & 14 \\ 6 & 14 & 36 \\ 14 & 36 & 98 \end{bmatrix} \begin{bmatrix} c_1 \\ c_2 \\ c_3 \end{bmatrix} = \begin{bmatrix} 12 \\ 12 \\ 24 \end{bmatrix}$$

Solving the normal equations gives $c_1 = 4.8, c_2 = -1.2, c_3 = 0$. Therefore the best fit polynomial of degree two or less is the line $y = 4.8 - 1.2t$. The RMSE is 0.4472.

11 Substituting the data points into the given model $h = a + bt - 4.905t^2$ results in the system

$$
\begin{aligned}
a + b(1) - 4.905(1)^2 &= 135 \\
a + b(2) - 4.905(2)^2 &= 265 \\
a + b(3) - 4.905(3)^2 &= 385 \\
a + b(4) - 4.905(4)^2 &= 485
\end{aligned}
$$

which leads to the inconsistent system

$$
\begin{bmatrix} 1 & 1 \\ 1 & 2 \\ 1 & 3 \\ 1 & 4 \end{bmatrix}
\begin{bmatrix} a \\ b \end{bmatrix} =
\begin{bmatrix} 135 + 4.905 \\ 265 + (4)4.905 \\ 385 + (9)4.905 \\ 485 + (16)4.905 \end{bmatrix}
$$

Solving the normal equations for a, b yields $a = 0.475, b = 141.525$. The best model is the height $h(t) = 0.475 + 141.525t - 4.905t^2$. The maximum height occurs when $0 = h'(t) = 141.525 - 9.1t$, or approximately $t = 14.4$ seconds. The corresponding height is 1021 meters. The rocket returns to earth at time 28.9 seconds, found from the quadratic formula.

COMPUTER PROBLEMS 4.1

1 (a) Computing the normal equations $A^T A x = A^T b$ gives

$$
\begin{bmatrix} 39 & -4 & 2 \\ -4 & 7 & 5 \\ 2 & 5 & 39 \end{bmatrix}
\begin{bmatrix} x_1 \\ x_2 \\ x_3 \end{bmatrix} =
\begin{bmatrix} 100 \\ 5 \\ 90 \end{bmatrix}
$$

which has solution $\overline{x} = [2.5246, 0.6616, 2.0934]$. The 2-norm error is $||A\overline{x} - b||_2 \approx 2.4135$.

1 (b) The calculation is similar to (a). The normal equations are

$$
\begin{bmatrix} 31 & 8 & 20 & -7 \\ 8 & 23 & -6 & 7 \\ 20 & -6 & 36 & -16 \\ -7 & 7 & -16 & 10 \end{bmatrix}
\begin{bmatrix} x_1 \\ x_2 \\ x_3 \\ x_4 \end{bmatrix} =
\begin{bmatrix} 57 \\ 31 \\ 37 \\ -6 \end{bmatrix}
$$

The least squares solution is $\overline{x} = [1.2379, 0.6885, 1.2124, 1.7497]$ and the 2-norm error is $||e||_2 = 0.8256$.

3 (a) We choose the model $y = a + b(t - 1960)$. Putting the data into this model yields the inconsistent system

$$
\begin{bmatrix} 1 & 0 \\ 1 & 10 \\ 1 & 30 \\ 1 & 40 \end{bmatrix}
\begin{bmatrix} a \\ b \end{bmatrix} =
\begin{bmatrix} 3039585530 \\ 3707475887 \\ 5281653820 \\ 6079603571 \end{bmatrix}
$$

Solving the normal equations gives the best least squares line $2996236899 + 76542140(t - 1960)$, with RMSE $= 36751088$. The 1980 population estimate from this model is 4527079702.

3 (b)   Choosing a second-degree model $y = a + b(t - 1960) + c(t - 1960)^2$, and inserting the data yields the inconsistent system

$$\begin{bmatrix} 1 & 0 & 0 \\ 1 & 10 & 100 \\ 1 & 30 & 900 \\ 1 & 40 & 1600 \end{bmatrix} \begin{bmatrix} a \\ b \\ c \end{bmatrix} = \begin{bmatrix} 3039585530 \\ 3707475887 \\ 5281653820 \\ 6079603571 \end{bmatrix}$$

Solving the normal equations gives the best least squares parabola $3028751748 + 67871514(t - 1960) + 216766(t - 1960)^2$ and RMSE $= 17129714$. The lower RMSE shows the parabola is a superior fit at the four data points. In addition, the parabola'a estimate of the 1980 population is 4472888288, closer to the actual 1980 population than the linear approximation.

5 (a)   The normal equations are $A^T A x = A^T b$, where A is the 22×2 matrix whose first column consists of ones and second column consists of the 22 prices, and where b is the list of sales/week. Calculating the 2×2 normal equations results in

$$\begin{bmatrix} 22.0000 & 16.9300 \\ 16.9300 & 13.7127 \end{bmatrix} \begin{bmatrix} c_1 \\ c_2 \end{bmatrix} = \begin{bmatrix} 68460 \\ 46994 \end{bmatrix},$$

with solution $c_1 = 9510, c_2 = -8314$. The best line is $S = 9510 - 8314P$, plotted below. The RMSE is 518.3.

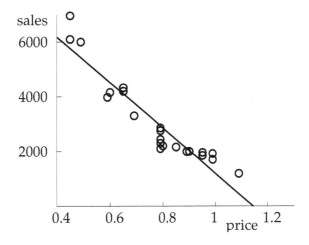

5 (b)   The profit is given by $F(P) = S(P - 0.23) = (c_1 + c_2 P)(P - 0.23)$, when the model is substituted for the sales. To find the maximum of the second-degree polynomial $F(P)$, differentiate and set to zero: $0 = F'(P) = c_2(P - 0.23) + c_1 + c_2 P = 2c_2 P + c_1 - 0.23c_2$ implies $P = (0.23c_2 - c_1)/(2c_2) = ((0.23)(-8314) - 9510)/((2)(-8314)) \approx 68.7$. The company's profit will be maximized for a selling price near 69 cents.

7 (a)   Fitting the model $y = c_1 + c_2 t$ leads to minimizing $||Ac - b||_2$ where

$$A = \begin{bmatrix} 1 & -3.0 \\ 1 & -2.5 \\ 1 & -2.0 \\ 1 & -1.5 \\ 1 & -1.0 \\ 1 & -0.5 \\ 1 & 0.0 \\ 1 & 0.5 \\ 1 & 1.0 \\ 1 & 1.5 \\ 1 & 2.0 \\ 1 & 2.5 \\ 1 & 3.0 \end{bmatrix} \quad \text{and} \quad b = \begin{bmatrix} 0 \\ 0 \\ 0 \\ 0 \\ 0 \\ 0 \\ 1 \\ 0 \\ 0 \\ 0 \\ 0 \\ 0 \\ 0 \end{bmatrix}$$

The normal equations are

$$\begin{bmatrix} 13 & 0 \\ 0 & 45.5 \end{bmatrix} \begin{bmatrix} c_1 \\ c_2 \end{bmatrix} = \begin{bmatrix} 1 \\ 0 \end{bmatrix}$$

which have solution $c_1 = 1/13, c_2 = 0$, with RMSE ≈ 0.2665. The best line is $y = 1/13$.

7 (b)   Similar to (a), but the model is $y = c_1 + c_2 t + c_3 t^2$, leading to

$$A = \begin{bmatrix} 1 & -3.0 & 9.00 \\ 1 & -2.5 & 6.25 \\ 1 & -2.0 & 4.00 \\ 1 & -1.5 & 2.25 \\ 1 & -1.0 & 1.00 \\ 1 & -0.5 & 0.25 \\ 1 & 0.0 & 0.00 \\ 1 & 0.5 & 0.25 \\ 1 & 1.0 & 1.00 \\ 1 & 1.5 & 2.25 \\ 1 & 2.0 & 4.00 \\ 1 & 2.5 & 6.25 \\ 1 & 3.0 & 9.00 \end{bmatrix} \quad \text{and} \quad b = \begin{bmatrix} 0 \\ 0 \\ 0 \\ 0 \\ 0 \\ 0 \\ 1 \\ 0 \\ 0 \\ 0 \\ 0 \\ 0 \\ 0 \end{bmatrix}$$

The normal equations are

$$\begin{bmatrix} 13 & 0 & 45.5 \\ 0 & 45.5 & 0 \\ 45.5 & 0 & 284.375 \end{bmatrix} \begin{bmatrix} c_1 \\ c_2 \\ c_3 \end{bmatrix} = \begin{bmatrix} 1 \\ 0 \\ 0 \end{bmatrix}$$

which have solution $c_1 = 0.1748, c_2 = 0, c_3 = -0.02797$, with RMSE ≈ 0.2519. The best parabola is $y = 0.1748 - 0.02797t^2$.

9 (a) The MATLAB code in Example 4.5 can be adapted to solve for the coefficients. For $d = 5$, the commands are

```
>> x = (2+(0:10)/5)';
>> y = 1+x+x.^2+x.^3+x.^4+x.^5;
>> A = [x.^0 x x.^2 x.^3 x.^4 x.^5];
>> c = (A'*A)\(A'*y)
```

The best degree 5 polynomial is $y = 1.000009 + 0.999983x + 1.000012x^2 + 0.999996x^3 + 1.000000x^4 + 1.000000x^5$. The coefficients have at least 4 correct places. The condition number of $A^T A$ is approximately 2.72×10^{13}.

9 (b) Similar to (a), but with $d = 6$. The best degree 6 polynomial is $y = 0.99 + 1.02x + 0.98x^2 + 1.01x^3 + 0.998x^4 + 1.00029x^5 + 0.99998x^6$. The coefficients have one decimal place accuracy, and the condition number of $A^T A$ is approximately 2.55×10^{16}.

9 (c) Similar to (a), but with $d = 8$. The resulting coefficients have no decimal places of accuracy, due to the condition number $\approx 1.41 \times 10^{19}$.

EXERCISES 4.2   A Survey of Models

1 (a) Substituting the data into the periodic model yields the four equations

$$
\begin{aligned}
c_1 + c_2 \cos 2\pi(0) + c_3 \sin 2\pi(0) &= 1 \\
c_1 + c_2 \cos 2\pi\left(\frac{1}{4}\right) + c_3 \sin 2\pi\left(\frac{1}{4}\right) &= 3 \\
c_1 + c_2 \cos 2\pi\left(\frac{1}{2}\right) + c_3 \sin 2\pi\left(\frac{1}{2}\right) &= 2 \\
c_1 + c_2 \cos 2\pi\left(\frac{3}{4}\right) + c_3 \sin 2\pi\left(\frac{3}{4}\right) &= 0
\end{aligned}
$$

The matrix form of the equations is

$$
Ac = \begin{bmatrix} 1 & 1 & 0 \\ 1 & 0 & 1 \\ 1 & -1 & 0 \\ 1 & 0 & -1 \end{bmatrix} \begin{bmatrix} c_1 \\ c_2 \\ c_3 \end{bmatrix} = \begin{bmatrix} 1 \\ 3 \\ 2 \\ 0 \end{bmatrix} = b.
$$

The normal equations $A^T Ac = A^T b$ are

$$
\begin{bmatrix} 4 & 0 & 0 \\ 0 & 2 & 0 \\ 0 & 0 & 2 \end{bmatrix} \begin{bmatrix} c_1 \\ c_2 \\ c_3 \end{bmatrix} = \begin{bmatrix} 6 \\ -1 \\ 3 \end{bmatrix}
$$

with solution $c = [3/2, -1/2, 3/2]$. The best fit model is

$$F_3(t) = \frac{3}{2} - \frac{1}{2}\cos 2\pi t + \frac{3}{2}\sin 2\pi t.$$

The errors of the fit are $e = b - Ac$, or

$$e = \begin{bmatrix} 1 \\ 3 \\ 2 \\ 0 \end{bmatrix} - \begin{bmatrix} 1 & 1 & 0 \\ 1 & 0 & 1 \\ 1 & -1 & 0 \\ 1 & 0 & -1 \end{bmatrix} \begin{bmatrix} \frac{3}{2} \\ -\frac{1}{2} \\ \frac{3}{2} \end{bmatrix} = \begin{bmatrix} 0 \\ 0 \\ 0 \\ 0 \end{bmatrix},$$

so $\|e\|_2 = 0$ and RMSE $= 0$.

1 (b)   Similar to (a). The normal equations are

$$\begin{bmatrix} 4 & 0 & 0 \\ 0 & 2 & 0 \\ 0 & 0 & 2 \end{bmatrix} \begin{bmatrix} c_1 \\ c_2 \\ c_3 \end{bmatrix} = \begin{bmatrix} 7 \\ -1 \\ 2 \end{bmatrix}$$

with solution $c = [7/4, -1/2, 1]$. The best fit model is $F_3(t) = \frac{7}{4} - \frac{1}{2}\cos 2\pi t + \sin 2\pi t$. The errors of the fit are $e = b - Ac$, or

$$e = \begin{bmatrix} 1 \\ 3 \\ 2 \\ 1 \end{bmatrix} - \begin{bmatrix} 1 & 1 & 0 \\ 1 & 0 & 1 \\ 1 & -1 & 0 \\ 1 & 0 & -1 \end{bmatrix} \begin{bmatrix} 7/4 \\ -1/2 \\ 1 \end{bmatrix} = \begin{bmatrix} -1/4 \\ 1/4 \\ -1/4 \\ 1/4 \end{bmatrix},$$

so $\|e\|_2 = \sqrt{(\frac{1}{4})^2 + (\frac{1}{4})^2 + (\frac{1}{4})^2 + (\frac{1}{4})^2} = \frac{1}{2}$ and RMSE $= \|e\|_2/\sqrt{4} = \frac{1}{4}$.

1 (c)   Similar to (a). The normal equations are

$$\begin{bmatrix} 4 & 0 & 0 \\ 0 & 4 & 0 \\ 0 & 0 & 0 \end{bmatrix} \begin{bmatrix} c_1 \\ c_2 \\ c_3 \end{bmatrix} = \begin{bmatrix} 9 \\ 3 \\ 0 \end{bmatrix}$$

with solution $c = [9/4, 3/4, 0]$. The best fit model is $F_3(t) = \frac{9}{4} + \frac{3}{4}\cos 2\pi t$. The errors of the fit are $e = [0, -1/2, 0, 1/2]$ and so $\|e\|_2 = 1/\sqrt{2}$, RMSE $= \sqrt{2}/4$.

3 (a)   Fitting to the model $y = c_1 e^{c_2 t}$ by linearization means finding the best least squares model $\ln y = \ln c_1 + c_2 t$ for the data. Setting $k = \ln c_1$ and substituting data into the model gives the matrix equation

$$Ac = \begin{bmatrix} 1 & -2 \\ 1 & 0 \\ 1 & 1 \\ 1 & 2 \end{bmatrix} \begin{bmatrix} k \\ c_2 \end{bmatrix} = \begin{bmatrix} 0 \\ \ln 2 \\ \ln 2 \\ \ln 5 \end{bmatrix}.$$

The normal equations $A^T Ac = A^T b$ are

$$\begin{bmatrix} 4 & 1 \\ 1 & 9 \end{bmatrix} \begin{bmatrix} k \\ c_2 \end{bmatrix} = \begin{bmatrix} \ln 20 \\ \ln 50 \end{bmatrix}$$

with solution $k = 0.6586, c_2 = 0.3615$. Since $c_1 = e^k \approx 1.932$, the best fit model is $y = 1.932e^{0.3615t}$. The errors of the exponential fit are

$$e = \begin{bmatrix} 1 \\ 2 \\ 2 \\ 5 \end{bmatrix} - \begin{bmatrix} c_1 e^{c_2(-2)} \\ c_1 e^{c_2(0)} \\ c_1 e^{c_2(1)} \\ c_1 e^{c_2(2)} \end{bmatrix}$$

which has 2-norm $\|e\|_2 \approx 1.2825$. Note that the 2-norm error of the exponential model fit is not minimized by linearized least squares. Instead, the 2-norm difference of the logs of the above vectors have been minimized. (This minimum is 0.4052.)

3 (b) Similar to (a). Substituting data into the linearized model gives the matrix equation

$$Ac = \begin{bmatrix} 1 & 0 \\ 1 & 1 \\ 1 & 1 \\ 1 & 2 \end{bmatrix} \begin{bmatrix} k \\ c_2 \end{bmatrix} = \begin{bmatrix} 0 \\ 0 \\ \ln 2 \\ \ln 4 \end{bmatrix}.$$

The normal equations are

$$\begin{bmatrix} 4 & 4 \\ 4 & 6 \end{bmatrix} \begin{bmatrix} k \\ c_2 \end{bmatrix} = \begin{bmatrix} \ln 8 \\ \ln 32 \end{bmatrix}$$

with solution $k = -(\ln 2)/4, c_2 = \ln 2$. Therefore $c_1 = e^{-\frac{1}{4}\ln 2} = 2^{-\frac{1}{4}}$ and the best fit model is $y = 2^{-\frac{1}{4}}e^{(\ln 2)t} = 2^{t-1/4}$. The 2-norm of the fit errors is $\|e\|_2 \approx 0.9982$.

5 (a) Fitting to the power law model $y = c_1 t^{c_2}$ by linearization means finding the best least squares model $\ln y = \ln c_1 + c_2 \ln t$ for the data. Setting $k = \ln c_1$ and substituting data into the model gives the matrix equation

$$Ac = \begin{bmatrix} 1 & 0 \\ 1 & \ln 2 \\ 1 & \ln 3 \\ 1 & \ln 4 \end{bmatrix} \begin{bmatrix} k \\ c_2 \end{bmatrix} = \begin{bmatrix} \ln 6 \\ \ln 2 \\ 0 \\ 0 \end{bmatrix}.$$

The solution of the normal equations is $k = 1.7159, c_2 = -1.3778$. Since $c_1 = e^k \approx 5.5618$, the best fit model is $y = 5.5618 t^{-1.3778t}$. The errors of the fit are

$$e = \begin{bmatrix} 1 \\ 2 \\ 3 \\ 4 \end{bmatrix} - \begin{bmatrix} c_1(1)^{c_2} \\ c_1(2)^{c_2} \\ c_1(3)^{c_2} \\ c_1(4)^{c_2} \end{bmatrix}$$

which has RMSE ≈ 0.2707.

5 (b) Fitting the least squares model $\ln y = \ln c_1 + c_2 \ln t$ gives the matrix equation

$$Ac = \begin{bmatrix} 1 & 0 \\ 1 & 0 \\ 1 & \ln 2 \\ 1 & \ln 3 \\ 1 & \ln 5 \end{bmatrix} \begin{bmatrix} k \\ c_2 \end{bmatrix} = \begin{bmatrix} \ln 2 \\ \ln 4 \\ \ln 5 \\ \ln 6 \\ \ln 10 \end{bmatrix}.$$

The solution of the normal equations is $k = 1.0387, c_2 = 0.7614$. Since $c_1 = e^k \approx 2.8256$, the best fit model is $y = 2.8256 t^{0.7614}$. The RMSE of the fit is ≈ 0.7099.

COMPUTER PROBLEMS 4.2

1 Each of the 12 data points (t_i, y_i) leads to an equation

$$c_1 + c_2 \cos 2\pi t_i + c_3 \sin 2\pi t_i + c_4 \cos 4\pi t_i = y_i$$

in the coefficients c_j. The t_i are evenly-spaced from 0 to $11/12$, using years as the time unit. The matrix form of the equations is

$$\begin{bmatrix} 1 & \cos 2\pi(0) & \sin 2\pi(0) & \cos 4\pi(0) \\ 1 & \cos 2\pi(\frac{1}{12}) & \sin 2\pi(\frac{1}{12}) & \cos 4\pi(\frac{1}{12}) \\ \vdots & \vdots & \vdots & \vdots \\ 1 & \cos 2\pi(\frac{11}{12}) & \sin 2\pi(\frac{11}{12}) & \cos 4\pi(\frac{11}{12}) \end{bmatrix} \begin{bmatrix} c_1 \\ c_2 \\ c_3 \\ c_4 \end{bmatrix} = \begin{bmatrix} 6.224 \\ 6.665 \\ \vdots \\ 6.372 \end{bmatrix}.$$

Computing the normal equations yields

$$\begin{bmatrix} 12 & 0 & 0 & 0 \\ 0 & 6 & 0 & 0 \\ 0 & 0 & 6 & 0 \\ 0 & 0 & 0 & 6 \end{bmatrix} \begin{bmatrix} c_1 \\ c_2 \\ c_3 \\ c_4 \end{bmatrix} = \begin{bmatrix} 67.0050 \\ 4.5247 \\ 0.7318 \\ 1.1610 \end{bmatrix},$$

and the least squares solution is

$$c = \begin{bmatrix} 5.5837 \\ 0.7541 \\ 0.1220 \\ 0.1935 \end{bmatrix}.$$

The best least squares periodic model of form (4.9) is $5.5837 + 0.7541 \cos 2\pi t + 0.1220 \sin 2\pi t + 0.1935 \cos 4\pi t$. The RMSE of the fit is $\|b - Ax\|_2/\sqrt{12} \approx 0.1836$.

3 Substituting the data into the linearized model $\ln y = k + c_2 t$ results in

$$
\begin{bmatrix} 1 & 0 \\ 1 & 10 \\ 1 & 30 \\ 1 & 40 \end{bmatrix}
\begin{bmatrix} k \\ c_2 \end{bmatrix} =
\begin{bmatrix} \ln 3039585530 \\ \ln 3707475887 \\ \ln 5281653820 \\ \ln 6079603571 \end{bmatrix}
$$

where we are using years after 1960 as the time variable. The normal equations are

$$
\begin{bmatrix} 4 & 80 \\ 80 & 2600 \end{bmatrix}
\begin{bmatrix} k \\ c_2 \end{bmatrix} =
\begin{bmatrix} 88.784 \\ 1793.1 \end{bmatrix}.
$$

Solving for the coefficients yields $k \approx 21.848$, $c_2 \approx 0.0174$, and $c_1 = e^k \approx 3079440361$. The best model through linearization is

$$
y = c_1 e^{c_2 t} = 3079440361 e^{0.0174(t-1960)}.
$$

Substituting $t = 1980$ yields the estimate 4361485000, which differs from the actual 1980 population by 91 million.

5 (a) Differentiating the model $y = c_1 t e^{c_2 t}$ and setting the result to zero gives the equation $0 = c_1 e^{c_2 t}(1 + c_2 t)$, whose solution is $t = -1/c_2$, the maximum.

5 (b) Starting with the model $y = 9.77 t e^{-0.215t}$, the maximum occurs at $t_{\max} \approx 4.65$ hours, according to (a). The maximum value is $y_{\max} = 16.72$. To find the half-life, we must solve the equation

$$
\frac{16.72}{2} = 9.77 t e^{-0.215t}
$$

for $t_{\text{half}} = 12.456$, using an equation solver from Chapter 1. The time needed to reduce from the maximum to half of the maximum concentration is $t_{\max} - t_{\text{half}} = 7.81$ hours.

7 (a) The coefficients c_1, c_2, c_3, c_4 are obtained by solving the normal equations for the system $Ac = b$:

$$
\begin{bmatrix}
1 & \cos 2\pi t_1 & \sin 2\pi t_1 & \cos 4\pi t_1 \\
\vdots & \vdots & \vdots & \vdots \\
1 & \cos 2\pi t_n & \sin 2\pi t_n & \cos 4\pi t_n
\end{bmatrix}
\begin{bmatrix} c_1 \\ c_2 \\ c_3 \\ c_4 \end{bmatrix} =
\begin{bmatrix} x_1 \\ \vdots \\ x_n \end{bmatrix}
$$

where $x_1, \ldots, x_n$ denotes the monthly wind turbine output in MWh. The solution of the normal equations give the least squares trigonometric polynomial
$P(t) = 229.9 + 26.8160 \cos 2\pi t + 32.2504 \sin 2\pi t - 8.8833 \cos 4\pi t$.

7 (b) The least squares curve, shown below, captures the seasonal variation (high production in early spring, low production in early fall) of wind power.

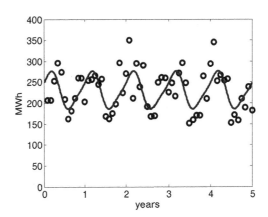

9 (a) The coefficients c_1, c_2, c_3, c_4 are obtained by solving the normal equations for the system $Ac = b$:

$$\begin{bmatrix} 1 & t_1 & \cos 2\pi t_1 & \sin 2\pi t_1 \\ \vdots & \vdots & \vdots & \vdots \\ 1 & t_n & \cos 2\pi t_n & \sin 2\pi t_n \end{bmatrix} \begin{bmatrix} c_1 \\ c_2 \\ c_3 \\ c_4 \end{bmatrix} = \begin{bmatrix} x_1 \\ \vdots \\ x_n \end{bmatrix}$$

where $x_1, \ldots, x_n$ denotes the monthly CO_2 measurement. The solution of the normal equations give the least squares trigonometric polynomial

$P(t) = 360.9977 + 1.9507(t - 1996) - 1.6669 \cos 2\pi(t - 1996) + 2.4359 \sin 2\pi(t - 1996)$, with RMSE $= 0.8015$.

9 (b) Substituting into the model and comparing with the four data points (numbers 101, 105, 113, 117 respectively) yields $0.533, 1.580, 0.212$, and 1.181 for the errors.

9 (c) The solution of the normal equations give the least squares trigonometric polynomial

$P(t) = 361.0121 + 1.9488(t - 1996) - 1.6668 \cos 2\pi(t - 1996) + 2.4353 \sin 2\pi(t - 1996) + 0.8595 \cos 2\pi(t - 1996)$, with RMSE $= 0.5225$. Substituting into the model and comparing with the four data points yields $0.105, 0.719, 0.214$, and 0.318 for the errors. The best fit curves from 9(a) and 9(c) are shown below in figures (a) and (b) below:

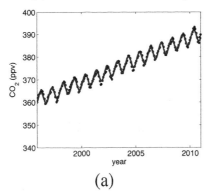

(a)

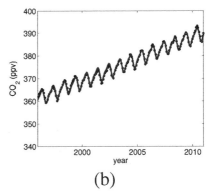

(b)

9 (d)   The solution of the normal equations give the least squares trigonometric polynomial
$P(t) = 361.5409 + 1.7358(t - 1996) + 0.0142(t - 1996)^2 - 1.6683 \cos 2\pi(t - 1996) + 2.4355 \sin 2\pi(t - 1996)$, with RMSE $= 0.7650$. The four errors are $0.788, 1.334, 0.428$, and 0.984. This fit is inferior to part (c).

9 (e)   The solution of the normal equations give the least squares trigonometric polynomial
$P(t) = 361.5541 + 1.7343(t - 1996) + 0.0142(t - 1996)^2 - 1.6681 \cos 2\pi(t - 1996) + 2.4348 \sin 2\pi(t - 1996) + 0.8593 \sin 4\pi(t - 1996)$, with RMSE $= 0.4649$. This fit gives the smallest RMSE. The four errors for this fit are $0.360, 0.474, 0.002$, and 0.121.

EXERCISES 4.3   QR Factorization

1 (a)   We follow the Gram-Schmidt procedure as outlined in Section 4.3. Starting with the first column of the matrix A,

$$y_1 = A_1 = \begin{bmatrix} 4 \\ 3 \end{bmatrix} \text{ and } r_{11} = ||y_1||_2 = \sqrt{4^2 + 3^2} = 5.$$

The first unit vector is

$$q_1 = \frac{A_1}{||A_1||_2} = \begin{bmatrix} 4/5 \\ 3/5 \end{bmatrix}.$$

Then

$$y_2 = A_2 - q_1 q_1^T A_2 = \begin{bmatrix} 0 \\ 1 \end{bmatrix} - \begin{bmatrix} 4/5 \\ 3/5 \end{bmatrix} \frac{3}{5} = \begin{bmatrix} -12/25 \\ 16/25 \end{bmatrix},$$

$r_{12} = q_1^T A_2 = 3/5, r_{22} = ||y_2||_2 = 4/5$, and

$$q_2 = \frac{y_2}{||y_2||_2} = \begin{bmatrix} -3/5 \\ 4/5 \end{bmatrix}.$$

Putting the columns q_1, q_2 together and filling in the matrix R with r_{11}, r_{12}, r_{22}, we have

$$A = \begin{bmatrix} 4 & 0 \\ 3 & 1 \end{bmatrix} = \begin{bmatrix} 4/5 & -3/5 \\ 3/5 & 4/5 \end{bmatrix} \begin{bmatrix} 5 & 3/5 \\ 0 & 4/5 \end{bmatrix} = QR.$$

1 (b)   Starting with the first column of $A = \begin{bmatrix} 1 & 2 \\ 1 & 1 \end{bmatrix}$,

$$y_1 = A_1 = \begin{bmatrix} 1 \\ 1 \end{bmatrix} \text{ and } r_{11} = ||y_1||_2 = \sqrt{1^2 + 1^2} = \sqrt{2}.$$

The first column of Q is $q_1 = A_1/||A_1||_2 = [1/\sqrt{2}, 1/\sqrt{2}]^T$. Then

$$y_2 = A_2 - q_1 q_1^T A_2 = \begin{bmatrix} 2 \\ 1 \end{bmatrix} - \begin{bmatrix} 1/\sqrt{2} \\ 1/\sqrt{2} \end{bmatrix} \frac{3}{\sqrt{2}} = \begin{bmatrix} 1/2 \\ -1/2 \end{bmatrix},$$

$r_{12} = 3/\sqrt{2}, r_{22} = \|y_2\|_2 = 1/\sqrt{2}, q_2 = [1/\sqrt{2}, -1/\sqrt{2}]^T$, and the QR factorization is

$$A = \begin{bmatrix} 1 & 2 \\ 1 & 1 \end{bmatrix} = \begin{bmatrix} 1/\sqrt{2} & 1/\sqrt{2} \\ 1/\sqrt{2} & -1/\sqrt{2} \end{bmatrix} \begin{bmatrix} \sqrt{2} & 3/\sqrt{2} \\ 0 & 1/\sqrt{2} \end{bmatrix} = QR.$$

1 (c)   Starting with the first column of $A = \begin{bmatrix} 2 & 1 \\ 1 & -1 \\ 2 & 1 \end{bmatrix}$,

$$y_1 = A_1 = \begin{bmatrix} 2 \\ 1 \\ 2 \end{bmatrix} \text{ and } r_{11} = \|y_1\|_2 = \sqrt{2^2 + 1^2 + 2^2} = 3.$$

The first column of Q is $q_1 = A_1/\|A_1\|_2 = [2/3, 1/3, 2/3]^T$. Then

$$y_2 = A_2 - q_1 q_1^T A_2 = \begin{bmatrix} 1 \\ -1 \\ 1 \end{bmatrix} - \begin{bmatrix} 2/3 \\ 1/3 \\ 2/3 \end{bmatrix} 1 = \begin{bmatrix} 1/3 \\ -4/3 \\ 1/3 \end{bmatrix},$$

$r_{12} = 1, r_{22} = \|y_2\|_2 = \sqrt{2}, q_2 = y_2/r_{22} = [\sqrt{2}/6, 2\sqrt{2}/3, \sqrt{2}/6]^T$. In order to make Q square, we need a third column. To orthogonalize a "random" vector $[1, 0, 0]$, we compute

$$y_3 = A_3 - q_1 q_1^T A_3 - q_2 q_2^T A_3 = \begin{bmatrix} 1 \\ 0 \\ 0 \end{bmatrix} - \frac{2}{3} \begin{bmatrix} 2/3 \\ 1/3 \\ 2/3 \end{bmatrix} - \frac{\sqrt{2}}{6} \begin{bmatrix} \sqrt{2}/6 \\ 2\sqrt{2}/3 \\ \sqrt{2}/6 \end{bmatrix} = \begin{bmatrix} 1/2 \\ 0 \\ -1/2 \end{bmatrix},$$

while $q_3 = [1/2, 0, -1/2]^T/\|q_3\|_2 = [\sqrt{2}/2, 0, -\sqrt{2}/2]^T$. The QR factorization is

$$A = \begin{bmatrix} 2 & 1 \\ 1 & -1 \\ 2 & 1 \end{bmatrix} = \begin{bmatrix} 2/3 & \sqrt{2}/6 & \sqrt{2}/2 \\ 1/3 & -4\sqrt{2}/6 & 0 \\ 2/3 & \sqrt{2}/6 & -\sqrt{2}/2 \end{bmatrix} \begin{bmatrix} 3 & 1 \\ 0 & \sqrt{2} \\ 0 & 0 \end{bmatrix} = QR.$$

1 (d)   Starting with the first column of $A = \begin{bmatrix} 4 & 8 & 1 \\ 0 & 2 & -2 \\ 3 & 6 & 7 \end{bmatrix}$,

$$y_1 = A_1 = \begin{bmatrix} 4 \\ 0 \\ 3 \end{bmatrix} \text{ and } r_{11} = \|y_1\|_2 = 5.$$

The first column of Q is $q_1 = A_1/\|A_1\|_2 = [4/5, 0, 3/5]^T$. Then

$$y_2 = A_2 - q_1 q_1^T A_2 = \begin{bmatrix} 8 \\ 2 \\ 6 \end{bmatrix} - \begin{bmatrix} 4/5 \\ 0 \\ 3/5 \end{bmatrix} 10 = \begin{bmatrix} 0 \\ 2 \\ 0 \end{bmatrix},$$

$r_{12} = 10, r_{22} = ||y_2||_2 = 2, q_2 = y_2/r_{22} = [0, 1, 0]^T$. The third column of A is orthogonalized by

$$y_3 = A_3 - q_1 q_1^T A_3 - q_2 q_2^T A_3 = \begin{bmatrix} 1 \\ -2 \\ 7 \end{bmatrix} - \begin{bmatrix} 4/5 \\ 0 \\ 3/5 \end{bmatrix} 5 - \begin{bmatrix} 0 \\ 1 \\ 0 \end{bmatrix} (-2) = \begin{bmatrix} -3 \\ 0 \\ 4 \end{bmatrix},$$

while $q_3 = [-3, 0, 4]^T/||q_3||_2 = [-3/5, 0, 4/5]^T$, and $r_{33} = 5$. The QR factorization is

$$A = \begin{bmatrix} 4 & 8 & 1 \\ 0 & 2 & -2 \\ 3 & 6 & 7 \end{bmatrix} = \begin{bmatrix} 4/5 & 0 & -3/5 \\ 0 & 1 & 0 \\ 3/5 & 0 & 4/5 \end{bmatrix} \begin{bmatrix} 5 & 10 & 5 \\ 0 & 2 & -2 \\ 0 & 0 & 5 \end{bmatrix} = QR.$$

3   The Modified Gram-Schmidt is different than the classical version only for part (d), and in exact arithmetic, the difference is only in the order of operations. In 3(d), the first two columns of Q are carried out the same as the classical version. The first column of Q is $q_1 = A_1/||A_1||_2 = [4/5, 0, 3/5]^T$ with $r_{11} = ||y_1||_2 = 5$, and the second column is calculated as

$$y_2 = A_2 - q_1 q_1^T A_2 = \begin{bmatrix} 8 \\ 2 \\ 6 \end{bmatrix} - \begin{bmatrix} 4/5 \\ 0 \\ 3/5 \end{bmatrix} 10 = \begin{bmatrix} 0 \\ 2 \\ 0 \end{bmatrix},$$

$r_{12} = 10, r_{22} = ||y_2||_2 = 2, q_2 = y_2/r_{22} = [0, 1, 0]^T$. While the Classical Gram-Schmidt would orthogonalize the third column of A by $y_3 = A_3 - q_1 q_1^T A_3 - q_2 q_2^T A_3$, Modified Gram-Schmidt orthogonalizes by

$$\begin{aligned} y_3 &= A_3 - q_1 q_1^T A_3 - q_2 q_2^T (A_3 - q_1 q_1^T A_3) \\ &= \begin{bmatrix} 1 \\ -2 \\ 7 \end{bmatrix} - \begin{bmatrix} 4/5 \\ 0 \\ 3/5 \end{bmatrix} 5 - \begin{bmatrix} 0 \\ 1 \\ 0 \end{bmatrix} \left(\begin{bmatrix} 0 & 1 & 0 \end{bmatrix} \begin{bmatrix} -3 \\ -2 \\ 4 \end{bmatrix} \right) = \begin{bmatrix} -3 \\ 0 \\ 4 \end{bmatrix}, \end{aligned}$$

and thus $q_3 = [-3, 0, 4]^T/||q_3||_2 = [-3/5, 0, 4/5]^T$, and $r_{33} = 5$. The QR factorization is

$$A = \begin{bmatrix} 4 & 8 & 1 \\ 0 & 2 & -2 \\ 3 & 6 & 7 \end{bmatrix} = \begin{bmatrix} 4/5 & 0 & -3/5 \\ 0 & 1 & 0 \\ 3/5 & 0 & 4/5 \end{bmatrix} \begin{bmatrix} 5 & 10 & 5 \\ 0 & 2 & -2 \\ 0 & 0 & 5 \end{bmatrix} = QR.$$

5 (a)   We begin by applying a Householder reflector to transform the first column to the x-axis. Set $x = [4, 3]^T$ and $w = [||x||_2, 0]^T = [5, 0]^T$. (An alternative, and often preferred choice, is $w = -[||x||_2, 0]^T$.) Define $v = w - x = [1, -3]^T$. The reflector is

$$H = I - \frac{2vv^T}{v^T v} = \begin{bmatrix} 1 & 0 \\ 0 & 1 \end{bmatrix} - \frac{2}{10} \begin{bmatrix} 1 & -3 \\ -3 & 9 \end{bmatrix} = \begin{bmatrix} 0.8 & 0.6 \\ 0.6 & -0.8 \end{bmatrix}.$$

Multiplying the matrix on the left by H yields

$$HA = \begin{bmatrix} 0.8 & 0.6 \\ 0.6 & -0.8 \end{bmatrix} \begin{bmatrix} 4 & 0 \\ 3 & 1 \end{bmatrix} = \begin{bmatrix} 5 & 0.6 \\ 0 & -0.8 \end{bmatrix} = R.$$

Multiplying by H on the left,

$$A = \begin{bmatrix} 4 & 0 \\ 3 & 1 \end{bmatrix} = \begin{bmatrix} 0.8 & 0.6 \\ 0.6 & -0.8 \end{bmatrix} \begin{bmatrix} 5 & 0.6 \\ 0 & -0.8 \end{bmatrix} = QR,$$

where Q is defined to be the orthogonal matrix H.

5 (b)   Let $x = [1,1]^T$ be the first column, and set $w = [\sqrt{2}, 0]^T$. The Householder reflector for $v = w - x = [\sqrt{2} - 1, -1]$ is

$$H = I - \frac{2vv^T}{v^T v} = \begin{bmatrix} 1 & 0 \\ 0 & 1 \end{bmatrix} - \frac{2}{4 - 2\sqrt{2}} \begin{bmatrix} 3 - 2\sqrt{2} & 1 - \sqrt{2} \\ 1 - \sqrt{2} & 1 \end{bmatrix} = \begin{bmatrix} 1/\sqrt{2} & 1/\sqrt{2} \\ 1/\sqrt{2} & -1/\sqrt{2} \end{bmatrix}.$$

Multiplying by A yields

$$HA = \begin{bmatrix} 1/\sqrt{2} & 1/\sqrt{2} \\ 1/\sqrt{2} & -1/\sqrt{2} \end{bmatrix} \begin{bmatrix} 1 & 2 \\ 1 & 1 \end{bmatrix} = \begin{bmatrix} \sqrt{2} & 3/\sqrt{2} \\ 0 & 1/\sqrt{2} \end{bmatrix}.$$

Multiplying by H on the left and setting $Q = H$ reveals the QR factorization

$$A = \begin{bmatrix} 1 & 2 \\ 1 & 1 \end{bmatrix} = \begin{bmatrix} 1/\sqrt{2} & 1/\sqrt{2} \\ 1/\sqrt{2} & -1/\sqrt{2} \end{bmatrix} \begin{bmatrix} \sqrt{2} & 3/\sqrt{2} \\ 0 & 1/\sqrt{2} \end{bmatrix} = QR.$$

5 (c)   Denote by $x = [2,1,2]^T$ the first column and set $w = [\|x\|_2, 0, 0]^T = [3, 0, 0]^T$, and $v = w - x = [1, -1, -2]^T$. The first Householder reflector is

$$H_1 = I - \frac{2vv^T}{v^T v} = \begin{bmatrix} 1 & 0 & 0 \\ 0 & 1 & 0 \\ 0 & 0 & 1 \end{bmatrix} - \frac{2}{6} \begin{bmatrix} 1 & -1 & -2 \\ -1 & 1 & 2 \\ -2 & 2 & 4 \end{bmatrix} = \begin{bmatrix} 2/3 & 1/3 & 2/3 \\ 1/3 & 2/3 & -2/3 \\ 2/3 & -2/3 & -1/3 \end{bmatrix}.$$

Multiplying the matrix A on the left by H_1 yields

$$H_1 A = \begin{bmatrix} 2/3 & 1/3 & 2/3 \\ 1/3 & 2/3 & -2/3 \\ 2/3 & -2/3 & -1/3 \end{bmatrix} \begin{bmatrix} 2 & 1 \\ 1 & -1 \\ 2 & 1 \end{bmatrix} = \begin{bmatrix} 3 & 1 \\ 0 & -1 \\ 0 & 1 \end{bmatrix}.$$

To finish, we need to find a 2×2 matrix $\hat{H}_2$ that moves the vector $x_2 = [-1, 1]^T$ to the x-axis. Set $w_2 = [\|x_2\|_2, 0]^T$ and $v_2 = w_2 - x_2 = [\sqrt{2} + 1, -1]^T$. Then

$$\hat{H}_2 = I - \frac{2v_2 v_2^T}{v_2^T v_2} = \begin{bmatrix} 1 & 0 \\ 0 & 1 \end{bmatrix} - \frac{2}{4 + \sqrt{2}} \begin{bmatrix} 3 + 2\sqrt{2} & -\sqrt{2} - 1 \\ -\sqrt{2} - 1 & 1 \end{bmatrix} = \begin{bmatrix} -1\sqrt{2} & 1/\sqrt{2} \\ 1/\sqrt{2} & 1/\sqrt{2} \end{bmatrix},$$

and

$$H_2 H_1 A = \begin{bmatrix} 1 & 0 & 0 \\ 0 & -1\sqrt{2} & 1/\sqrt{2} \\ 0 & 1/\sqrt{2} & 1/\sqrt{2} \end{bmatrix} \begin{bmatrix} 3 & 1 \\ 0 & -1 \\ 0 & 1 \end{bmatrix} = \begin{bmatrix} 3 & 1 \\ 0 & \sqrt{2} \\ 0 & 0 \end{bmatrix}.$$

Multiplying on the left by $H_1 H_2$ yields

$$A = \begin{bmatrix} 2 & 1 \\ 1 & -1 \\ 2 & 1 \end{bmatrix} = \begin{bmatrix} 2/3 & 1/3 & 2/3 \\ 1/3 & 2/3 & -2/3 \\ 2/3 & -2/3 & -1/3 \end{bmatrix} \begin{bmatrix} 1 & 0 & 0 \\ 0 & -1\sqrt{2} & 1/\sqrt{2} \\ 0 & 1/\sqrt{2} & 1/\sqrt{2} \end{bmatrix} \begin{bmatrix} 3 & 1 \\ 0 & \sqrt{2} \\ 0 & 0 \end{bmatrix}$$

$$= \begin{bmatrix} 2/3 & \sqrt{2}/6 & 1/\sqrt{2} \\ 1/3 & -2\sqrt{2}/3 & 0 \\ 2/3 & \sqrt{2}/6 & -1/\sqrt{2} \end{bmatrix} \begin{bmatrix} 3 & 1 \\ 0 & \sqrt{2} \\ 0 & 0 \end{bmatrix} = QR.$$

5 (d) Let $x = [4, 0, 3]^T$ denote the first column, $w = [5, 0, 0]^T$, and $v = w - x = [1, 0, -3]^T$. The Householder reflector is

$$H = I - \frac{2vv^T}{v^T v} = \begin{bmatrix} 1 & 0 & 0 \\ 0 & 1 & 0 \\ 0 & 0 & 1 \end{bmatrix} - \frac{2}{10} \begin{bmatrix} 1 & 0 & -3 \\ 0 & 0 & 0 \\ -3 & 0 & 9 \end{bmatrix} = \begin{bmatrix} 0.8 & 0.0 & 0.6 \\ 0.0 & 1.0 & 0.0 \\ 0.6 & 0.0 & -0.8 \end{bmatrix}.$$

Multiplying the matrix A on the left by H yields

$$HA = \begin{bmatrix} 0.8 & 0.0 & 0.6 \\ 0.0 & 1.0 & 0.0 \\ 0.6 & 0.0 & -0.8 \end{bmatrix} \begin{bmatrix} 4 & 8 & 1 \\ 0 & 2 & -2 \\ 3 & 6 & 7 \end{bmatrix} = \begin{bmatrix} 5 & 10 & 5 \\ 0 & 2 & -2 \\ 0 & 0 & -5 \end{bmatrix},$$

and multiplying by H on the left gives

$$A = \begin{bmatrix} 4 & 8 & 1 \\ 0 & 2 & -2 \\ 3 & 6 & 7 \end{bmatrix} = \begin{bmatrix} 0.8 & 0.0 & 0.6 \\ 0.0 & 1.0 & 0.0 \\ 0.6 & 0.0 & -0.8 \end{bmatrix} \begin{bmatrix} 5 & 10 & 5 \\ 0 & 2 & -2 \\ 0 & 0 & -5 \end{bmatrix} = QR.$$

7 (a) Using the QR factorization

$$A = \begin{bmatrix} 2 & 3 \\ -2 & -6 \\ 1 & 0 \end{bmatrix} = \begin{bmatrix} 2/3 & 1/3 & 2/3 \\ -2/3 & 2/3 & 1/3 \\ 1/3 & 2/3 & -2/3 \end{bmatrix} \begin{bmatrix} 3 & 6 \\ 0 & -3 \\ 0 & 0 \end{bmatrix} = QR,$$

we proceed as in Example 4.14. The system $Rx = Q^T b$ is

$$\begin{bmatrix} 3 & 6 \\ 0 & -3 \\ 0 & 0 \end{bmatrix} \begin{bmatrix} x_1 \\ x_2 \end{bmatrix} = \begin{bmatrix} 2/3 & -2/3 & 1/3 \\ 1/3 & 2/3 & 2/3 \\ 2/3 & 1/3 & -2/3 \end{bmatrix} \begin{bmatrix} 3 \\ -3 \\ 6 \end{bmatrix} = \begin{bmatrix} 6 \\ 3 \\ -3 \end{bmatrix}.$$

The top two equations

$$
\begin{aligned}
3x_1 + 6x_2 &= 6 \\
-3x_2 &= 3
\end{aligned}
$$

have solutions $x_2 = -1, x_1 = 4$. The least squares solution is $\bar{x} = [4, -1]^T$.

7 (b) Similar to (a). Using the QR factorization

$$
A = \begin{bmatrix} -4 & -4 \\ -2 & 7 \\ 4 & -5 \end{bmatrix} = \begin{bmatrix} 2/3 & 2/3 & 1/3 \\ 1/3 & -2/3 & 2/3 \\ -2/3 & 1/3 & 2/3 \end{bmatrix} \begin{bmatrix} -6 & 3 \\ 0 & -9 \\ 0 & 0 \end{bmatrix} = QR,
$$

the system $Rx = Q^T b$ is

$$
\begin{bmatrix} -6 & 3 \\ 0 & -9 \\ 0 & 0 \end{bmatrix} \begin{bmatrix} x_1 \\ x_2 \end{bmatrix} = \begin{bmatrix} 2/3 & 1/3 & -2/3 \\ 2/3 & -2/3 & 1/3 \\ 1/3 & 2/3 & 2/3 \end{bmatrix} \begin{bmatrix} 3 \\ 9 \\ 0 \end{bmatrix} = \begin{bmatrix} 5 \\ -4 \\ 7 \end{bmatrix}.
$$

The top two equations $-6x_1 + 3x_2 = 5$ and $-9x_2 = -4$ have solutions $x_2 = 4/9, x_1 = -11/18$. The least squares solution is $\bar{x} = [-11/18, 4/9]^T$.

9 By definition, a matrix Q is orthogonal if $Q^{-1} = Q^T$. Note that the (i, j)th entry of the product $Q^T Q$ is the dot product $q_i^T q_j$. If Q is orthogonal, $q_i^T q_j = 1$ if $i = j$ and 0 if $i \neq j$, showing that the columns are pairwise orthogonal unit vectors. Conversely, if the latter holds, $Q^T Q = I$ and since Q is square, $Q^T = Q^{-1}$.

11 Each dot product $q_k^T v_i$ in equation (4.25) together with a scalar multiplication of the result with q_k requires $2n$ multiplications and $n - 1$ additions. There are $i - 1$ of these in (4.25), for a total of $2n(i - 1)$ multiplications and $(i - 1)(n - 1)$ additions. Computing the sum of the i vectors in (4.23) requires $(i - 1)n$ more additions. Making the unit vector q_i requires n multiplications, n divisions, and $n - 1$ additions. Therefore the total operation count of multiplication/divisions is

$$
\sum_{i=1}^{n} 2ni = 2n \frac{n(n+1)}{2} = n^3 + n^2
$$

and of additions is

$$
\begin{aligned}
\sum_{i=1}^{n} (i-1)(2n-1) + n - 1 &= (2n-1) \sum_{i=1}^{n} (i-1) + (n-1)n \\
&= \frac{(2n-1)(n-1)n}{2} + n(n-1) \\
&= n(n-1)(n + \frac{1}{2}) \\
&= n^3 - \frac{1}{2}n^2 - \frac{1}{2}n.
\end{aligned}
$$

13 $(I - 2\dfrac{vv^T}{v^Tv})^T = I - 2\dfrac{(vv^T)^T}{v^Tv} = I - 2\dfrac{vv^T}{v^Tv}$

COMPUTER PROBLEMS 4.3

1 The pseudocode for Classical Gram-Schmidt orthogonalization can be translated directly into a MATLAB program, as follows.

```
function [q,r]=mycgs(A)
[m,n]=size(A);
for j=1:n
  y=A(:,j);
  for i=1:j-1
    r(i,j)=q(:,i)'*A(:,j);
    y=y-r(i,j)*q(:,i);
  end
  r(j,j)=norm(y);
  q(:,j)=y/r(j,j);
end
```

3 The description following Example 4.17 of factoring a general $m \times n$ matrix using Householder reflections can be converted into a MATLAB program. An example implementation follows. Note that we have made the choice $w = -[\|x\|_2, 0, \ldots, 0]$, which helps avoid subtracting nearly equal numbers in the construction of $v = w - x$.

```
function [Q,R]=myqr(A)
[m,n]=size(A);
Q=eye(m,m);
for i=1:min(n,m-1)
  x=A(i:m,i);
  w=[-norm(x);zeros(m-i,1)];
  v=w-x;
  H=eye(m,m);
  H(i:m,i:m)=eye(m-i+1,m-i+1)-2*v*v'/(v'*v);
  Q=Q*H;
  A=H*A;
end
R=A;
```

5 (a) The full $A = QR$ factorization of the $m \times n$ matrix A is

$$\begin{bmatrix} 1 & 1 \\ 2 & 1 \\ 1 & 2 \\ 0 & 3 \end{bmatrix} = \begin{bmatrix} 0.4082 & 0.0506 & 0.8597 & 0.3029 \\ 0.8165 & -0.2025 & -0.1987 & -0.5028 \\ 0.4082 & 0.3545 & -0.4624 & 0.7028 \\ 0.0000 & 0.9115 & 0.0879 & -0.4019 \end{bmatrix} \begin{bmatrix} 2.4495 & 2.0412 \\ 0.0000 & 3.2914 \\ 0.0000 & 0.0000 \\ 0.0000 & 0.0000 \end{bmatrix}.$$

The upper n entries of $d = Q^T b = \begin{bmatrix} -7.3485 \\ 5.4688 \\ 0.2158 \\ 0.2139 \end{bmatrix}$ are $\hat{d} = \begin{bmatrix} -7.3485 \\ 5.4688 \end{bmatrix}$.

Solving $\hat{R}\overline{x} = \hat{d}$, or $\begin{bmatrix} 2.4495 & 2.0412 \\ 0.0000 & 3.2914 \end{bmatrix} \begin{bmatrix} x_1 \\ x_2 \end{bmatrix} = \begin{bmatrix} -7.3485 \\ 5.4688 \end{bmatrix}$, yields $\overline{x} = \begin{bmatrix} 1.6154 \\ 1.6615 \end{bmatrix}$.

5 (b) The full $A = QR$ factorization of the $m \times n$ matrix A is

$$\begin{bmatrix} 1 & 2 & 2 \\ 2 & -1 & 2 \\ 3 & 1 & 1 \\ 1 & 1 & -1 \end{bmatrix} = \begin{bmatrix} 0.2582 & 0.7116 & 0.6290 & 0.1771 \\ 0.5164 & -0.6295 & 0.3755 & 0.4428 \\ 0.7746 & 0.0821 & -0.2488 & -0.5756 \\ 0.2582 & 0.3011 & -0.6337 & 0.6642 \end{bmatrix} \begin{bmatrix} 3.8730 & 1.0328 & 2.0656 \\ 0.0000 & 2.4358 & -0.0547 \\ 0.0000 & 0.0000 & 2.3938 \\ 0.0000 & 0.0000 & 0.0000 \end{bmatrix}.$$

The upper n entries of $d = Q^T b = \begin{bmatrix} 13.6845 \\ 5.6928 \\ 3.7785 \\ 0.2214 \end{bmatrix}$ are $\hat{d} = \begin{bmatrix} 13.6845 \\ 5.6928 \\ 3.7785 \end{bmatrix}$. Solving $\hat{R}\overline{x} = \hat{d}$,

or $\begin{bmatrix} 3.8730 & 1.0328 & 2.0656 \\ 0.0000 & 2.4358 & -0.0547 \\ 0.0000 & 0.0000 & 2.3938 \end{bmatrix} \begin{bmatrix} x_1 \\ x_2 \\ x_3 \end{bmatrix} = \begin{bmatrix} 13.6845 \\ 5.6928 \\ 3.7785 \end{bmatrix}$, yields $\overline{x} = \begin{bmatrix} 2.0588 \\ 2.3725 \\ 1.5784 \end{bmatrix}$.

7 (a) The matrix can be formed in MATLAB by the commands

```
>> a=hilb(10);a=a(:,1:n);
```

The correct solution $\overline{x} = [1, \dots, 1]$ can be computed to about 10 correct decimal places.

7 (b) Similar to (a), but with $n = 8$. The correct $\overline{x} = [1, \dots, 1]$ can be computed to about 6 correct places.

EXERCISES 4.4 GMRES Method

1 (a) The residual is $r = b - Ax_0 = \begin{bmatrix} 1 \\ 0 \\ 0 \end{bmatrix} = q_1 = r.$

$y = Aq_1 = \begin{bmatrix} 1 \\ 0 \\ 1 \end{bmatrix}$ and we orthogonalize by $y' = y - q_1 q_1^T y = y - h_{11}q_1 = \begin{bmatrix} 0 \\ 0 \\ 1 \end{bmatrix}, h_{11} = 1,$

and so $q_2 = \begin{bmatrix} 0 \\ 0 \\ 1 \end{bmatrix}$ and $h_{21} = 1$. The first estimate x_1 is found by finding the number c_1

that best fits $\begin{bmatrix} 1 \\ 1 \end{bmatrix} c_1 = \begin{bmatrix} 1 \\ 0 \end{bmatrix}$, which from the normal equations is $c_1 = 1/2$. Therefore

$$x_1 = Q_1 c_1 + x_0 = \begin{bmatrix} 1 \\ 0 \\ 0 \end{bmatrix} (1/2) + \begin{bmatrix} 0 \\ 0 \\ 0 \end{bmatrix} = \begin{bmatrix} 1/2 \\ 0 \\ 0 \end{bmatrix}.$$

In step two, we find $y = Aq_2 = \begin{bmatrix} 0 \\ 0 \\ 1 \end{bmatrix}$ and orthogonalize by

$$y' = y - q_1 q_1^T y = y - h_{12} q_1 = \begin{bmatrix} 0 \\ 0 \\ 1 \end{bmatrix}, h_{12} = 0$$

$$y'' = y' - q_2 q_2^T y = y - h_{22} q_1 = \begin{bmatrix} 0 \\ 0 \\ 0 \end{bmatrix}, h_{22} = 1.$$

Therefore $h_{32} = 0$, terminating the iteration. The second and final estimate x_2 is found by finding the 2-vector c_2 that best fits $\begin{bmatrix} 1 & 0 \\ 1 & 1 \\ 0 & 0 \end{bmatrix} c_2 = \begin{bmatrix} 1 \\ 0 \\ 0 \end{bmatrix}$, which from the normal equations

is $c_2 = [1, -1]^T$. Finally $x_2 = Q_2 c_2 + x_0 = \begin{bmatrix} 1 & 0 \\ 0 & 0 \\ 0 & 1 \end{bmatrix} \begin{bmatrix} 1 \\ -1 \end{bmatrix} + \begin{bmatrix} 0 \\ 0 \\ 0 \end{bmatrix} = \begin{bmatrix} 1 \\ 0 \\ -1 \end{bmatrix}.$

1 (b) The residual is $r = b - Ax_0 = \begin{bmatrix} 1 \\ 0 \\ 0 \end{bmatrix} = q_1 = r.$

$y = Aq_1 = \begin{bmatrix} 1 \\ -1 \\ 0 \end{bmatrix}$ and we orthogonalize by $y' = y - q_1 q_1^T y = y - h_{11} q_1 = \begin{bmatrix} 0 \\ -1 \\ 0 \end{bmatrix}, h_{11} = 1,$

and so $q_2 = \begin{bmatrix} 0 \\ -1 \\ 0 \end{bmatrix}$ and $h_{21} = 1$. The first estimate x_1 is found by finding the number c_1

that best fits $\begin{bmatrix} 1 \\ 1 \end{bmatrix} c_1 = \begin{bmatrix} 1 \\ 0 \end{bmatrix}$, which from the normal equations is $c_1 = 1/2$. Therefore

$$x_1 = Q_1 c_1 + x_0 = \begin{bmatrix} 1 \\ 0 \\ 0 \end{bmatrix} (1/2) + \begin{bmatrix} 0 \\ 0 \\ 0 \end{bmatrix} = \begin{bmatrix} 1/2 \\ 0 \\ 0 \end{bmatrix}.$$

In step two, we find $y = Aq_2 = \begin{bmatrix} -1 \\ -1 \\ 0 \end{bmatrix}$ and orthogonalize by

$$y' = y - q_1 q_1^T y = y - h_{12} q_1 = \begin{bmatrix} 0 \\ -1 \\ 0 \end{bmatrix}, h_{12} = -1$$

$$y'' = y' - q_2 q_2^T y = y - h_{22} q_1 = \begin{bmatrix} 0 \\ 0 \\ 0 \end{bmatrix}, h_{22} = 1.$$

Therefore $h_{32} = 0$, terminating the iteration. The second and final estimate x_2 is found by finding the 2-vector c_2 that best fits $\begin{bmatrix} 1 & -1 \\ 1 & 1 \\ 0 & 0 \end{bmatrix} c_2 = \begin{bmatrix} 1 \\ 0 \\ 0 \end{bmatrix}$, which from the normal equations is

$$c_2 = [1/2, -1/2]^T. \text{ Finally } x_2 = Q_2 c_2 + x_0 = \begin{bmatrix} 1 & 0 \\ 0 & -1 \\ 0 & 0 \end{bmatrix} \begin{bmatrix} 1/2 \\ -1/2 \end{bmatrix} + \begin{bmatrix} 0 \\ 0 \\ 0 \end{bmatrix} = \begin{bmatrix} 1/2 \\ 1/2 \\ 0 \end{bmatrix}.$$

1 (c) The residual is $r = b - Ax_0 = \begin{bmatrix} 1 \\ 0 \\ 0 \end{bmatrix} = q_1 = r.$

$y = Aq_1 = \begin{bmatrix} 0 \\ 1 \\ 0 \end{bmatrix}$ and we orthogonalize by $y' = y - q_1 q_1^T y = y - h_{11} q_1 = \begin{bmatrix} 0 \\ 1 \\ 0 \end{bmatrix}, h_{11} = 0,$

and so $q_2 = \begin{bmatrix} 0 \\ 1 \\ 0 \end{bmatrix}$ and $h_{21} = 1$. The first estimate x_1 is found by finding the number

c_1 that best fits $\begin{bmatrix} 0 \\ 1 \end{bmatrix} c_1 = \begin{bmatrix} 1 \\ 0 \end{bmatrix}$, which from the normal equations is $c_1 = 0$. Therefore

$x_1 = Q_1 c_1 + x_0 = \begin{bmatrix} 0 \\ 0 \\ 0 \end{bmatrix}.$

In step two, we find $y = Aq_2 = \begin{bmatrix} 0 \\ 0 \\ 1 \end{bmatrix}$ and orthogonalize by

$$y' = y - q_1 q_1^T y = y - h_{12} q_1 = \begin{bmatrix} 0 \\ 0 \\ 1 \end{bmatrix}, h_{12} = 0$$

$$y'' = y' - q_2 q_2^T y = y - h_{22} q_1 = \begin{bmatrix} 0 \\ 0 \\ 1 \end{bmatrix}, h_{22} = 0.$$

Therefore $h_{32} = 1$. The second estimate x_2 is found by finding the vector c_2 that best fits
$\begin{bmatrix} 0 & 0 \\ 1 & 0 \\ 0 & 1 \end{bmatrix} c_2 = \begin{bmatrix} 1 \\ 0 \\ 0 \end{bmatrix}$, which from the normal equations is $c_2 = \begin{bmatrix} 0 \\ 0 \end{bmatrix}$.

Therefore $x_2 = Q_2 c_2 + x_0 = \begin{bmatrix} 0 \\ 0 \\ 0 \end{bmatrix}$.

In step three, we find $y = Aq_3 = \begin{bmatrix} 1 \\ 0 \\ 0 \end{bmatrix}$ and orthogonalize by

$$y' = y - q_1 q_1^T y = y - h_{12} q_1 = \begin{bmatrix} 0 \\ 0 \\ 0 \end{bmatrix}, h_{13} = 1$$

and $h_{23} = h_{33} = h_{43} = 0$. The third and final estimate x_3 is found by finding the 3-vector c_3
that best fits $\begin{bmatrix} 0 & 0 & 1 \\ 1 & 0 & 0 \\ 0 & 1 & 0 \\ 0 & 0 & 0 \end{bmatrix} c_3 = \begin{bmatrix} 1 \\ 0 \\ 0 \\ 0 \end{bmatrix}$, which from the normal equations is $c_3 = \begin{bmatrix} 0 \\ 0 \\ 1 \end{bmatrix}$.

Finally $x_3 = Q_3 c_3 + x_0 = \begin{bmatrix} 1 & 0 & 0 \\ 0 & 1 & 0 \\ 0 & 0 & 1 \end{bmatrix} \begin{bmatrix} 0 \\ 0 \\ 1 \end{bmatrix} + \begin{bmatrix} 0 \\ 0 \\ 0 \end{bmatrix} = \begin{bmatrix} 0 \\ 0 \\ 1 \end{bmatrix}$.

3 GMRES terminates at the correct solution after two steps because $h_{32} = 0$ in the $k = 2$ step, since the Modified Gram Schmidt orthogonalization in the inner loop results in $y = 0$. To show this, it suffices to prove that $A^2 r$ belongs to span $\langle r, Ar \rangle$. Write the matrix

$$A = \begin{bmatrix} 1 & 0 & a_{13} \\ 0 & 1 & a_{23} \\ 0 & 0 & 1 \end{bmatrix} = \begin{bmatrix} I & a \\ 0 & I \end{bmatrix}$$

in block form where $a = \begin{bmatrix} a_{13} \\ a_{23} \end{bmatrix}$, and the residual as $r = \begin{bmatrix} r_1 \\ r_2 \end{bmatrix}$ where r_1 is a 2-vector and r_2 is a scalar. In block form we can multiply

$$Ar = \begin{bmatrix} I & a \\ 0 & I \end{bmatrix} \begin{bmatrix} r_1 \\ r_2 \end{bmatrix} = \begin{bmatrix} r_1 + ar_2 \\ r_2 \end{bmatrix} = r + \begin{bmatrix} ar_2 \\ 0 \end{bmatrix},$$

and

$$A^2 r = Ar + A \begin{bmatrix} ar_2 \\ 0 \end{bmatrix} = r + \begin{bmatrix} ar_2 \\ 0 \end{bmatrix} + \begin{bmatrix} ar_2 \\ 0 \end{bmatrix} = r + 2 \begin{bmatrix} ar_2 \\ 0 \end{bmatrix},$$

showing that $A^2 r$ belongs to span $\langle r, Ar \rangle$.

COMPUTER PROBLEMS 4.4

1 Part (a) shows the output of MATLAB spy command on the matrix A. The Preconditioned GMRES Method outlined in pseudocode can be applied to the A and b defined in the problem, resulting in Part (b), showing the error as a function of step number or no preconditioner and Gauss-Seidel preconditioner (circles), and Jacobi preconditioner (squares).

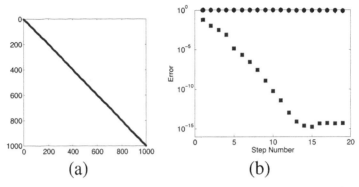

(a)   (b)

3 Part (a) shows the MATLAB spy command. Applying the code to the A and b defined in the problem result in Part (b), showing the error as a function of step number for no preconditioner and Jacobi preconditioner (circles), and Gauss-Seidel preconditioner (diamonds).

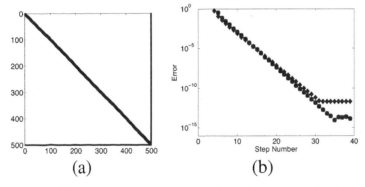

(a)   (b)

5 Part (a) shows the output of MATLAB spy command on the matrix A. Part (b) shows the error for no preconditioner and Jacobi (circles), and Gauss-Seidel (diamonds).

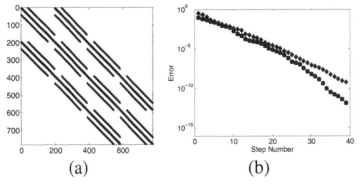

(a)   (b)

EXERCISES 4.5   Nonlinear Least Squares

1 (a) As in Example 4.21, we seek the point $(\overline{x}, \overline{y})$ that minimizes the sum of the squared distances to the three circles. The distance to the ith circle is $r_i = \sqrt{(x - x_i)^2 + (y - y_i)^2} - R_i$, where (x_i, y_i) is the center and R_i the radius. Therefore

$$Dr = \begin{bmatrix} \frac{x-x_1}{S_1} & \frac{y-y_1}{S_1} \\ \frac{x-x_2}{S_2} & \frac{y-y_2}{S_2} \\ \frac{x-x_3}{S_3} & \frac{y-y_3}{S_3} \end{bmatrix} = \begin{bmatrix} 0 & -1 \\ -1/\sqrt{2} & -1/\sqrt{2} \\ 0 & 1 \end{bmatrix}$$

where $S_i = \sqrt{(x - x_i)^2 + (y - y_i)^2}$. To take a Gauss-Newton step, start with $x^0 = [0, 0]$ and compute

$$Dr^T Dr = \begin{bmatrix} 1/2 & 1/2 \\ 1/2 & 5/2 \end{bmatrix} \text{ and } Dr^T r \begin{bmatrix} 1/\sqrt{2} - 1 \\ 1/\sqrt{2} - 1 \end{bmatrix}.$$

Solving $Dr^T Dr v = -Dr^T r$ yields $v = (2 - \sqrt{2}, 0)$, and $x^1 = x^0 + v = (2 - \sqrt{2}, 0)$.

1 (b) Similar to (a).

$$Dr = \begin{bmatrix} 1 & 0 \\ -1/\sqrt{2} & -1/\sqrt{2} \\ -1/\sqrt{2} & 1/\sqrt{2} \end{bmatrix}$$

and so

$$Dr^T Dr = \begin{bmatrix} 2 & 0 \\ 0 & 1 \end{bmatrix} \text{ and } Dr^T r = \begin{bmatrix} \sqrt{2} - 2 \\ 0 \end{bmatrix}.$$

Solving $(Dr^T Dr)v = -Dr^T r$ yields $v = (1 - \sqrt{2}/2, 0)$, and $x^1 = x^0 + v = (1 - \sqrt{2}/2, 0)$.

3 The distance from (x, y) to the circle occurs along a line segment connecting (x, y) to the center of the circle. If (x, y) lies outside the circle, the distance to the circle equals the distance to the center, $\sqrt{(x - x_1)^2 + (y - y_1)^2}$, minus the radius R_1. If (x, y) lies inside the circle, the distance to the circle is the radius R_1 minus the distance to the center. In either case, the distance is $|\sqrt{(x - x_1)^2 + (y - y_1)^2} - R_1|$.

5 (a) The functions to be minimized are $r_1(c_1, c_2) = c_1 t_1^{c_2} - y_1, r_2(c_1, c_2) = c_1 t_2^{c_2} - y_2$, and $r_3(c_1, c_2) = c_1 t_3^{c_2} - y_3$. The Jacobian is $Dr = \begin{bmatrix} t_1^{c_2} & c_1 t_1^{c_2} \ln t_1 \\ t_2^{c_2} & c_1 t_2^{c_2} \ln t_2 \\ t_3^{c_2} & c_1 t_3^{c_2} \ln t_3 \end{bmatrix}$

5 (b) The functions to be minimized are $r_1(c_1, c_2) = c_1 t_1 e^{c_2 t_1} - y_1, r_2(c_1, c_2) = c_1 t_2 e^{c_2 t_2} - y_2$, and $r_3(c_1, c_2) = c_1 t_3 e^{c_2 t_3} - y_3$. The Jacobian is

$$Dr = \begin{bmatrix} t_1 e^{c_2 t_1} & c_1 t_1^2 e^{c_2 t_1} \\ t_2 e^{c_2 t_2} & c_1 t_2^2 e^{c_2 t_2} \\ t_3 e^{c_2 t_3} & c_1 t_3^2 e^{c_2 t_3} \end{bmatrix}$$

7 The solutions correspond to the common intersection of three circles. If the three circles coincide, there are infinitely many solutions. In any other configuration, the common intersection will be two or fewer points.

COMPUTER PROBLEMS 4.5

1 (a) Each Gauss-Newton step is $x^{k+1} = x^k + v^k$, where $Dr^T Dr v^k = -Dr^T r$. The definition of r and Dr are given in the solution of Exercise 4.4.1(a). The iteration converges to $(\overline{x}, \overline{y}) = (0.4106, 0.0555)$ after about 15 steps.

1 (b) Similar to (a). The definition of r and Dr are given in the solution of Exercise 4.4.1(b). The iteration converges to $(\overline{x}, \overline{y}) = (0.2755, 0.0000)$ after about 10 steps.

3 (a) We apply the Gauss-Newton Method to minimize the sum of the squares of the residuals

$$
\begin{aligned}
r_1(x, y, K) &= \sqrt{(x - x_1)^2 + (y - y_1)^2} - (R_1 + K) \\
r_2(x, y, K) &= \sqrt{(x - x_2)^2 + (y - y_2)^2} - (R_2 + K) \\
r_3(x, y, K) &= \sqrt{(x - x_3)^2 + (y - y_3)^2} - (R_3 + K) \\
r_4(x, y, K) &= \sqrt{(x - x_4)^2 + (y - y_4)^2} - (R_4 + K).
\end{aligned}
$$

The derivative is

$$
Dr = \begin{bmatrix}
\frac{x - x_1}{S_1} & \frac{y - y_1}{S_1} & -1 \\
\frac{x - x_2}{S_2} & \frac{y - y_2}{S_2} & -1 \\
\frac{x - x_3}{S_3} & \frac{y - y_3}{S_3} & -1 \\
\frac{x - x_4}{S_4} & \frac{y - y_4}{S_4} & -1
\end{bmatrix}
$$

where $S_i = \sqrt{(x - x_i)^2 + (y - y_i)^2}$. From initial guess $(x, y, K) = (0, 0, 0)$, Gauss-Newton converges within about five steps to $x = 0, y = -0.5862$ and $K = 0.3296$.

3 (b) Similar to (a). The Gauss-Newton method converges within about five steps to $x = 0.5569, y = 0$, and $K = 1.2880$.

5 We fit a power law $W = c_1 H^{c_2}$ to the 10 height/weight data points $(H_1, W_1), \ldots, (H_{10}, W_{10})$ from Example 4.10. To solve the true least squares problem, we avoid linearizing the model and apply the Gauss-Newton method to minimize the sum of the squares of

$$
\begin{aligned}
r_1(c_1, c_2) &= W_1 - c_1 H_1^{c_2} \\
&\vdots \\
r_{10}(c_1, c_2) &= W_{10} - c_1 H_{10}^{c_2}
\end{aligned}
$$

The Jacobian is

$$Dr = \begin{bmatrix} H_1^{c_2} & c_1 H_1^{c_2} \ln H_1 \\ \vdots & \vdots \\ H_{10}^{c_2} & c_1 H_{10}^{c_2} \ln H_{10} \end{bmatrix}.$$

Using initial guess $(c_1, c_2) = (10, 4)$, the Gauss-Newton Method converges to the solution $c_1 = 15.9$ and $c_2 = 2.53$ after about 5 steps. The RMSE is 0.755. The best fit solution $W = c_1 H^{c_2}$ is plotted below.

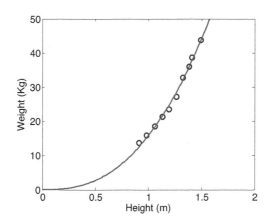

7 Levenberg-Marquardt is applied to the residuals $r = \begin{bmatrix} c_1 H_1^{c_2} - W_1 \\ \vdots \\ c_1 H_{10}^{c_2} - W_{10} \end{bmatrix}$ with Jacobian matrix

$Dr = \begin{bmatrix} H_1^{c_2} & c_1 H_1^{c_2} \ln H_1 \\ \vdots & \vdots \\ H_{10}^{c_2} & c_1 H_{10}^{c_2} \ln H_{10} \end{bmatrix}$. For example, using starting guess $c_1 = 10, c_2 = 2$ and fixed $\lambda = 1$, Levenberg-Marquardt converges to the solution $c_1 = 15.9, c_2 = 2.53$. The RMSE is 0.755. The best fit curve is shown above in Computer Problem 5.

9 (a) Levenberg-Marquardt with initial guess $c_1 = 5, c_2 = 0.5, c_3 = 1$ and fixed $\lambda = 1$ converges to parameters $c_1 = 11.9935, c_2 = 0.2796, c_3 = 1.8023$. The best fit curve $y = c_1 e^{c_2(t-c_3)^2}$ is plotted below. The RMSE $= 0.4413$.

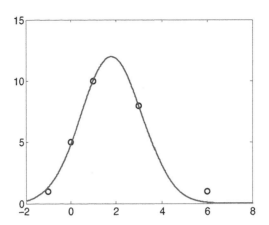

9 (b) Levenberg-Marquardt with initial guess $c_1 = 5, c_2 = 0.5, c_3 = 1$ and fixed $\lambda = 1$ converges to parameters $c_1 = 12.7028, c_2 = 0.1596, c_3 = 5.6828$. The best fit curve $y = c_1 e^{c_2(t-c_3)^2}$ is plotted below. The RMSE $= 0.8028$.

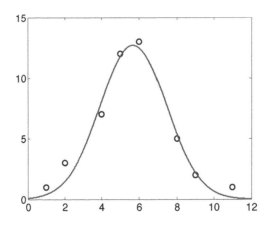

11 (a) Levenberg-Marquardt is applied to the residuals $r = \begin{bmatrix} c_1 e^{-c_2 t_1} \cos(c_3 t_1 + c_4) - y_1 \\ \vdots \\ c_1 e^{-c_2 t_7} \cos(c_3 t_7 + c_4) - y_7 \end{bmatrix}$

with Jacobian matrix $Dr = \begin{bmatrix} e^{-c_2 t_1} C_1 & -c_1 t_1 e^{-c_2 t_1} C_1 & -c_1 t_1 e^{-c_2 t_1} S_1 & -c_1 e^{-c_2 t_1} S_1 \\ \vdots & \vdots & \vdots & \vdots \\ e^{-c_2 t_7} C_7 & -c_1 t_7 e^{-c_2 t_7} C_7 & -c_1 t_7 e^{-c_2 t_7} S_7 & -c_1 e^{-c_2 t_7} S_7 \end{bmatrix}$

where C_i and S_i represent $\cos(c_3 t_i + c_4)$ and $\sin(c_3 t_i + c_4)$, respectively. For example, using starting guess $c_1 = 1, c_2 = 0, c_3 = c_4 = 1$ and fixed $\lambda = 0.01$, Levenberg-Marquardt converges to the solution $c_1 = 8.67, c_2 = 0.27, c_3 = 0.98, c_4 = 1.23$. The RMSE is 0.1027. The best fit curve is shown below.

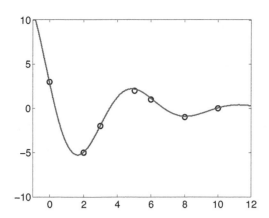

11 (b) Levenberg-Marquardt is applied to the residuals as in part (a). For example, using starting guess $c_1 = 10, c_2 = 0, c_3 = c_4 = 1$ and fixed $\lambda = 0.01$, Levenberg-Marquardt converges to the solution $c_1 = -8.68, c_2 = 0.13, c_3 = 0.62, c_4 = 1.22$. The RMSE is 0.1998. The best fit curve is shown below.

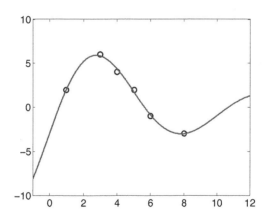

CHAPTER 5
Numerical Differentiation and Integration

EXERCISES 5.1   Numerical Differentiation

1 (a)   The two-point forward-difference formula is

$$\frac{f(x+h) - f(x)}{h} = \frac{\ln(1 + 0.1) - \ln 1}{0.1} = 0.9531.$$

The correct value is $f'(1) = 1$, so the approximation error is the difference 0.0469.

1 (b) $\dfrac{\ln(1 + 0.01) - \ln 1}{0.01} = 0.9950$, approximation error 0.0050.

1 (c) $\dfrac{\ln(1 + 0.001) - \ln 1}{0.001} = 0.9995$, approximation error 0.0005.

3 (a)   The two-point forward-difference formula is

$$\frac{f(x+h) - f(x)}{h} = \frac{\sin(\frac{\pi}{3} + 0.1) - \sin\frac{\pi}{3}}{0.1} = 0.455901.$$

Comparing with the correct answer $\cos\dfrac{\pi}{3} = \dfrac{1}{2}$, the approximation error is 0.044098. The error term of the formula (5.3) is $-\dfrac{h}{2}f''(c) = \dfrac{0.1}{2}\sin c$, where $\dfrac{\pi}{3} < c < \dfrac{\pi}{3} + 0.1$, which covers the range from $0.05 \sin \pi/3 \approx 0.0433$ to $0.05 \sin(\pi/3 + 0.1) \approx 0.0456$, containing the actual approximation error as expected.

3 (b)   The two-point forward-difference formula gives $\dfrac{\sin(\frac{\pi}{3} + 0.01) - \sin\frac{\pi}{3}}{0.01} = 0.495662$. Comparing with the correct answer $\dfrac{1}{2}$, the approximation error is 0.004338. The error term is $-\dfrac{h}{2}f''(c) = \dfrac{0.01}{2}\sin c$, where $\dfrac{\pi}{3} < c < \dfrac{\pi}{3} + 0.01$, implying that the error must lie between $0.005 \sin \pi/3 \approx 0.004330$ and $0.005 \sin(\pi/3 + 0.01) \approx 0.004355$.

3 (c)   The two-point forward-difference formula gives $\dfrac{\sin(\frac{\pi}{3} + 0.001) - \sin\frac{\pi}{3}}{0.001} = 0.499567$. Comparing with the correct answer $\dfrac{1}{2}$, the approximation error is 0.000433. The error term is $-\dfrac{h}{2}f''(c) = \dfrac{0.001}{2}\sin c$, where $\dfrac{\pi}{3} < c < \dfrac{\pi}{3} + 0.001$, implying that the error must lie between $0.0005 \sin \pi/3 \approx 0.0004330$ and $0.0005 \sin(\pi/3 + 0.001) \approx 0.0004333$.

5 (a) The three-point centered-difference formula for the second derivative is

$$\frac{f(x-h) - 2f(x) + f(x+h)}{h^2} = \frac{\frac{1}{0.9} - 2 + \frac{1}{1.1}}{(0.1)^2} \approx 2.02020202$$

for $f(x) = 1/x$. Comparing with the correct answer $f''(1) = 2$, the approximation error is 0.02020202.

5 (b) Using $h = 0.01$, the second derivative approximation is

$$\frac{f(x-h) - 2f(x) + f(x+h)}{h^2} = \frac{\frac{1}{0.99} - 2 + \frac{1}{1.01}}{(0.01)^2} \approx 2.00020002,$$

with approximation error 0.00020002.

5 (c) Using $h = 0.001$, the second derivative approximation is

$$\frac{f(x-h) - 2f(x) + f(x+h)}{h^2} = \frac{\frac{1}{0.999} - 2 + \frac{1}{1.001}}{(0.001)^2} \approx 2.00000200,$$

with approximation error 0.00000200.

7 According to Taylor's Theorem, if f is twice continuously differentiable, then

$$f(x-h) = f(x) - hf'(x) + \frac{h^2 f''(c)}{2},$$

where $x - h < c < x$. Solving for $f'(x)$ gives the formula

$$f'(x) = \frac{f(x) - f(x-h)}{h} + \frac{h}{2}f''(c).$$

9 According to Taylor's Theorem, if f is three times continuously differentiable, then

$$f(x - 2h) = f(x) - 2hf'(x) + \frac{4}{2}h^2 f''(x) + O(h^3)$$

$$f(x - h) = f(x) - hf'(x) + \frac{1}{2}h^2 f''(x) + O(h^3).$$

Subtracting 4 times the second equation from the first eliminates the $f''(x)$ term and results in

$$f(x - 2h) - 4f(x - h) + 3f(x) = 2hf'(x) + O(h^3).$$

Solving for $f'(x)$ gives the second order formula

$$f'(x) = \frac{f(x - 2h) - 4f(x - h) + 3f(x)}{2h} + O(h^2).$$

11 Extrapolation for the first-order formula $K(h) = (f(x+h) - f(x))/h$ is

$$\frac{2K(\frac{h}{2}) - K(h)}{2 - 1} = \frac{2[f(x + \frac{h}{2}) - f(x)]}{h/2} - \frac{f(x+h) - f(x)}{h}.$$

Therefore

$$f'(x) \approx \frac{4f(x + \frac{h}{2}) - 3f(x) - f(x+h)}{h}.$$

13 According to Taylor's Theorem, if f is three times continuously differentiable, then

$$f(x + 3h) = f(x) + 3hf'(x) + \frac{9}{2}h^2 f''(x) + \frac{27}{6}h^3 f'''(c_1)$$

$$f(x - h) = f(x) - hf'(x) + \frac{1}{2}h^2 f''(x) - \frac{1}{6}h^3 f'''(c_2)$$

where c_1 and c_2 lie between $x - h$ and $x + 3h$. Subtracting 9 times the second equation from the first eliminates the $f''(x)$ term and results in

$$f(x + 3h) - 9f(x - h) + 8f(x) = 12hf'(x) + \frac{9}{2}h^3 f'''(c_1) + \frac{3}{2}h^3 f'''(c_2)$$

$$= 12hf'(x) + 6h^3 f'''(c)$$

where Theorem 5.1 has been used to combine the f''' terms. Solving for $f'(x)$ gives the formula with error term

$$f'(x) = \frac{f(x + 3h) - 9f(x - h) + 8f(x)}{12h} - \frac{1}{2}h^2 f'''(c),$$

where c lies between $x - h$ and $x + 3h$.

15 If f is four times continuously differentiable, then Taylor's Theorem implies the expansions

$$f(x + 3h) = f(x) + 3hf'(x) + \frac{9}{2}h^2 f''(x) + \frac{27}{6}h^3 f'''(x) + \frac{27}{8}h^4 f^{(iv)}(c_1)$$

$$f(x - h) = f(x) - hf'(x) + \frac{1}{2}h^2 f''(x) - \frac{1}{6}h^3 f'''(x) + \frac{1}{24}h^4 f^{(iv)}(c_2)$$

where c_1 and c_2 lie between $x - h$ and $x + 3h$. Adding $\frac{1}{3}$ times the first equation to the second equation eliminates the $f'(x)$ term and results in

$$\frac{1}{3}f(x + 3h) + f(x - h) - \frac{4}{3}f(x) = 2h^2 f''(x) + \frac{4}{3}h^3 f'''(x) + \frac{7}{12}h^4 f^{(iv)}(c)$$

where Theorem 5.1 has been used to combine the fourth derivative terms. Solving for $f''(x)$ gives the first order formula

$$f''(x) = \frac{\frac{1}{6}f(x + 3h) + \frac{1}{2}f(x - h) - \frac{2}{3}f(x)}{h^2} - \frac{2}{3}hf'''(x) - \frac{7}{12}h^2 f^{(iv)}(c).$$

17 Using Taylor's Theorem, if f is three times continuously differentiable, then

$$f(x + 3h) = f(x) + 3hf'(x) + \frac{9}{2}h^2 f''(x) + \frac{27}{6}h^3 f'''(c_1)$$

$$f(x - 2h) = f(x) - 2hf'(x) + 2h^2 f''(x) - \frac{4}{3}h^3 f'''(c_2)$$

where c_1 and c_2 lie between $x - 2h$ and $x + 3h$. Subtracting $9/4$ times the second equation from the first eliminates the $f''(x)$ term and results in

$$f(x + 3h) - \frac{9}{4}f(x - 2h) + \frac{5}{4}f(x) = \frac{15}{2}hf'(x) + \frac{9}{2}h^3 f'''(c_1) + 3h^3 f'''(c_2)$$

$$= \frac{15}{2}hf'(x) + \frac{15}{2}h^3 f'''(c)$$

for $x - 2h < c < x + 3h$, where Theorem 5.1 has been used to combine the f''' terms. Solving for $f'(x)$ gives the following formula with error term, where c lies between $x - 2h$ and $x + 3h$:

$$f'(x) = \frac{4f(x + 3h) - 9f(x - 2h) + 5f(x)}{30h} - h^2 f'''(c).$$

19 Using Taylor's Theorem, if f is five times continuously differentiable, then

$$f(x + 2h) = f(x) + 2hf'(x) + 2h^2 f''(x) + \frac{4}{3}h^3 f'''(x) + \frac{2}{3}h^4 f^{(iv)}(x) + O(h^5)$$

$$f(x + h) = f(x) + hf'(x) + \frac{1}{2}h^2 f''(x) + \frac{1}{6}h^3 f'''(x) + \frac{1}{24}h^4 f^{(iv)}(x) + O(h^5)$$

$$f(x - h) = f(x) - hf'(x) + \frac{1}{2}h^2 f''(x) - \frac{1}{6}h^3 f'''(x) + \frac{1}{24}h^4 f^{(iv)}(x) + O(h^5)$$

$$f(x - 2h) = f(x) - 2hf'(x) + 2h^2 f''(x) - \frac{4}{3}h^3 f'''(x) + \frac{2}{3}h^4 f^{(iv)}(x) + O(h^5)$$

Then

$$-f(x - 2h) + 2f(x - h) - 2f(x + h) + f(x + 2h) = 2h^3 f'''(x) + O(h^5)$$

and the result follows.

21 Using the Taylor expansions from Exercise 17, notice that

$$f(x - 2h) - 4f(x - h) - 4f(x + h) + f(x + 2h) = -6f(x) + h^4 f^{(iv)}(x) + O(h^6)$$

since the $h^5 f^{(v)}(x)$ terms cancel. Solving for $f^{(iv)}$ gives the result.

23 Using Taylor's Theorem, if f is five times continuously differentiable, then

$$f(x+h) = \ f(x) \quad +hf'(x) \ +\frac{1}{2}h^2f''(x) \ +\frac{1}{6}h^3f'''(x) \ +\frac{1}{24}h^4f^{(iv)}(x)+O(h^5)$$

$$f(x+h/2) = \ f(x) \ +\frac{1}{2}hf'(x) \ +\frac{1}{8}h^2f''(x) \ +\frac{1}{48}h^3f'''(x) \ +\frac{1}{384}h^4f^{(iv)}(x)+O(h^5)$$

$$f(x-h/2) = \ f(x) \ -\frac{1}{2}hf'(x) \ +\frac{1}{8}h^2f''(x) \ -\frac{1}{48}h^3f'''(x) \ +\frac{1}{384}h^4f^{(iv)}(x)+O(h^5)$$

$$f(x-h) = \ f(x) \quad -hf'(x) \ +\frac{1}{2}h^2f''(x) \ -\frac{1}{6}h^3f'''(x) \ +\frac{1}{24}h^4f^{(iv)}(x)+O(h^5).$$

Then $f(x-h) - 8f(x-h/2) + 8f(x+h/2) - f(x+h) = 6hf'(x) + O(h^5)$ and

$$f'(x) = \frac{f(x-h) - 8f(x-h/2) + 8f(x+h/2) - f(x+h)}{6h} + O(h^4).$$

25 The y-intercept of the line through the two points $(Kh^n, F(h))$ and $(K(h/2)^n, F(h/2))$ represents the value of the linear interpolant of the two points when the x-coordinate, or error, is zero. The y-intercept is easily computed to be

$$\frac{2^n F(\frac{h}{2}) - F(h)}{2^n - 1},$$

in agreement with the extrapolation formula (5.15).

COMPUTER PROBLEMS 5.1

1 Double precision floating-point computation of the quotient

$$\frac{\sin h - \cos h - (\sin(-h) - \cos(-h))}{2h}$$

for $h = 10^{-1}, \ldots, 10^{-12}$, yields the table

h	error
0.10000000000000	0.00166583353172
0.01000000000000	0.00001666658333
0.00100000000000	0.00000016666662
0.00010000000000	0.00000000166711
0.00001000000000	0.00000000001565
0.00000100000000	0.00000000002676
0.00000010000000	0.00000000052636
0.00000001000000	0.00000000052636
0.00000000100000	0.00000002722922
0.00000000010000	0.0000008274037
0.00000000001000	0.0000008274037
0.00000000000100	0.00003338943111

The same data is plotted below. Note that the minimum occurs at $h = 10^{-5}$, in rough agreement with the theory in Section 5.1.2.

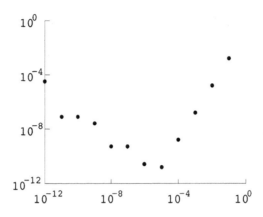

3 Double precision floating-point computation of the quotient

$$\frac{\sin h - \cos h - (\sin(0) - \cos(0))}{2h}$$

for $h = 10^{-1}, \ldots, 10^{-12}$, yields the table

h	error
0.10000000000000	0.04829251368803
0.01000000000000	0.00498329175014
0.00100000000000	0.00049983329165
0.00010000000000	0.00004999833314
0.00001000000000	0.00000499998476
0.00000100000000	0.00000050007321
0.00000010000000	0.00000004943368
0.00000001000000	0.00000000502476
0.00000000100000	0.00000002828193
0.00000000010000	0.00000008274037
0.00000000001000	0.00000008274037
0.00000000000100	0.00002212172012

The data is plotted below. Note that the minimum occurs at $h = 10^{-8}$, in rough agreement with the predicted $\sqrt{\epsilon_{\text{mach}}}$ from Exercise 16.

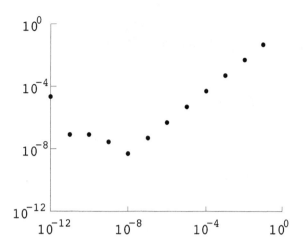

5 The quotient

$$\frac{\cos h - 2 + \cos(-h)}{h^2}$$

for $h = 10^{-1}, \ldots, 10^{-12}$ was calculated and compared with the correct second derivative $-\cos(0) = -1$. The error is plotted below. Note that the minimum occurs at $h = 10^{-4} \approx \epsilon_{mach}^{1/4}$.

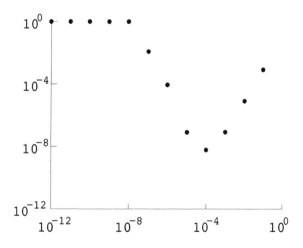

EXERCISES 5.2   Newton-Cotes Formulas for Numerical Integration

1 (a)   The composite Trapezoid Rule with $m = 1$ is the original Trapezoid Rule

$$\int_0^1 x^2 \, dx \approx \frac{h}{2}(y_0 + y_1).$$

Since $a = 0, b = 1, h = (b-a)/m = 1$, the approximation evaluates to $\frac{1}{2}(0^2 + 1^2) = \frac{1}{2}$. The correct integral is $\frac{1}{3}$, so the approximation error is $|\frac{1}{3} - \frac{1}{2}| = \frac{1}{6}$. For $m = 2$, the Composite Trapezoid Rule approximation is

$$\frac{h}{2}(y_0 + y_2 + 2y_1) = \frac{1}{4}(0^2 + 1^2 + 2(\tfrac{1}{2})^2) = \frac{3}{8},$$

and error $= |\frac{1}{3} - \frac{3}{8}| = \frac{1}{24}$. For $m = 4$, the approximation is

$$\frac{h}{2}(y_0 + y_4 + 2(y_1 + y_2 + y_3)) = \tfrac{1}{8}(0^2 + 1^2 + 2((\tfrac{1}{4})^2 + (\tfrac{1}{2})^2 + (\tfrac{3}{4})^2)) = \frac{11}{32},$$

and error $= |\frac{1}{3} - \frac{11}{32}| = \frac{1}{96}$.

1 (b)   The Composite Trapezoid Rule approximations are

$$m = 1 \; : \; \frac{\pi/2}{2}(\cos 0 + \cos \frac{\pi}{2}) = \frac{\pi}{4}, \qquad\qquad\qquad \text{error} = |1 - \frac{\pi}{4}| \approx 0.214602$$

$$m = 2 \; : \; \frac{\pi/4}{2}(\cos 0 + \cos \frac{\pi}{2} + 2\cos \frac{\pi}{4}) = \frac{\pi(1 + \sqrt{2})}{8}, \qquad\qquad \text{error} \approx 0.051941$$

$$m = 4 \; : \; \frac{\pi/8}{2}(\cos 0 + \cos \frac{\pi}{2} + 2(\cos \frac{\pi}{8} + \cos \frac{\pi}{4} + \cos \frac{3\pi}{8})) \approx 0.987116, \; \text{error} \approx 0.012884.$$

1 (c)   The Composite Trapezoid Rule approximations are

$$m = 1 \; : \; \frac{1}{2}(e^0 + e^1) = \frac{1 + e}{2}, \qquad \text{error} = |e - 1 - (1 + e)/2| = \frac{3 - e}{2} \approx 0.140859$$

$$m = 2 \; : \; \frac{1/2}{2}(e^0 + e^1 + 2e^{1/2}) \approx 1.753931, \qquad\qquad\qquad\qquad \text{error} \approx 0.035649$$

$$m = 4 \; : \; \frac{1/4}{2}(e^0 + e^1 + 2(e^{1/4} + e^{1/2} + e^{3/4})) \approx 1.727222, \qquad\qquad \text{error} \approx 0.008940.$$

3 (a)   Composite Simpson's Rule with $m = 1$ is

$$\int_0^1 x^2 \, dx \approx \frac{h}{3}(y_0 + y_2 + 4y_1).$$

Since $a = 0, b = 1, h = (b-a)/(2m) = 1/2$, the approximation evaluates to

$$\frac{1}{6}(0^2 + 1^2 + 4(1/2)^2) = \frac{1}{3},$$

in exact agreement with the correct integral. The approximation error is zero. For $m = 2$ and $m = 4$, Composite Simpson's Rule approximation is again exact:

$$m = 2 \; : \; \frac{1/4}{3}(y_0 + y_4 + 4(y_1 + y_3) + 2y_2) = \frac{1}{12}(0 + 1 + 4(\tfrac{1}{16} + \tfrac{9}{16}) + 2\tfrac{1}{4}) = \tfrac{1}{3}$$

$$m = 4 \; : \; \frac{1/8}{3}(y_0 + y_8 + 4(y_1 + y_3 + y_5 + y_7) + 2(y_2 + y_4 + y_6)) = \frac{1}{3}.$$

3 (b) Composite Simpson's Rule approximations are:

$$m = 1 \quad : \quad \frac{\pi/4}{3}(y_0 + y_2 + 4y_1) = \frac{\pi}{12}(1 + 0 + 4\cos\frac{\pi}{4}) \approx 1.002280, \quad \text{error} = 0.002280$$

$$m = 2 \quad : \quad \frac{\pi/8}{3}(y_0 + y_4 + 4(y_1 + y_3) + 2y_2) \approx 1.000135, \quad \text{error} = 0.000135$$

$$m = 4 \quad : \quad \frac{\pi/16}{3}(y_0 + y_8 + 4(y_1 + y_3 + y_5 + y_7) + 2(y_2 + y_4 + y_6))$$
$$\approx 1.000008, \quad \text{error} = 0.000008$$

3 (c) Composite Simpson's Rule approximations are:

$$m = 1 \quad : \quad \frac{1/2}{3}(y_0 + y_2 + 4y_1) = \frac{1}{6}(e^0 + e^1 + 4e^{1/2}) \approx 1.718861, \quad \text{error} = 0.000579$$

$$m = 2 \quad : \quad \frac{1/4}{3}(y_0 + y_4 + 4(y_1 + y_3) + 2y_2) \approx 1.718319, \quad \text{error} = 0.000037$$

$$m = 4 \quad : \quad \frac{1/8}{3}(y_0 + y_8 + 4(y_1 + y_3 + y_5 + y_7) + 2(y_2 + y_4 + y_6))$$
$$\approx 1.718284, \quad \text{error} = 0.000002$$

5 (a) The exact value is $\int_0^1 \frac{1}{\sqrt{x}} \, dx = 2$. The Composite Midpoint Rule with $m = 1$ is

$\int_0^1 f(x) \, dx \approx h w_1 = (1)f(1/2)$. Since $a = 0, b = 1, h = (b - a)/m = 1$, the approximation evaluates to $(1)(1/\sqrt{1/2}) = \sqrt{2}$. The approximation error is $|\sqrt{2} - 2| \approx 0.5858$. For $m = 2$ and $m = 4$, the Composite Midpoint Rule approximation is

$$m = 2 \quad : \quad \frac{1}{2}[f(1/4) + f(3/4)] = \frac{1}{2}[2 + 2/\sqrt{3}] = 1.5774, \quad \text{error} = 0.4226$$

$$m = 4 \quad : \quad \frac{1}{4}[f(1/8) + f(3/8) + f(5/8) + f(7/8)] = 1.6988, \quad \text{error} = 0.3012.$$

5 (b) The exact value is $\int_0^1 x^{-1/3} \, dx = 3/2$. Composite Midpoint Rule approximations are:

$$m = 1 \quad : \quad (1)f(1/2) = 2^{1/3} = 1.2599, \quad \text{error} = 0.2401$$

$$m = 2 \quad : \quad \frac{1}{2}[f(1/4) + f(3/4)] = 1.3440, \quad \text{error} = 0.1560$$

$$m = 4 \quad : \quad \frac{1}{4}[f(1/8) + f(3/8) + f(5/8) + f(7/8)] = 1.4005, \quad \text{error} = 0.0995.$$

5 (c) The exact value is $\int_0^2 \dfrac{dx}{\sqrt{2-x}} = 2\sqrt{2} \approx 2.8284$. Composite Midpoint Rule approximations are:

$$m = 1 \ : \ (2)f(1) = 2^1 = 2, \quad \text{error} = 0.8284$$
$$m = 2 \ : \ (1)[f(1/2) + f(3/2)] = 2.2307, \quad \text{error} = 0.5977$$
$$m = 4 \ : \ \frac{1}{2}[f(1/4) + f(3/4) + f(5/4) + f(7/4)] = 2.4025, \quad \text{error} = 0.4259.$$

7 (a) The exact value is $\int_0^1 \dfrac{1}{\sqrt{x}} \, dx = 2$. The Open Newton-Cotes Method (5.28) is

$\int_a^b f(x) \, dx \approx \dfrac{4h}{3}[2f(x_1) - f(x_2) + 2f(x_3)]$. Since $a = 0, b = 1, h = (b-a)/4 = 1/4$, the approximation evaluates to $\dfrac{1}{3}[2f(1/4) - f(1/2) + 2f(3/4)] = 1.6317$. The approximation error is 0.3683.

7 (b) The exact value is $\int_0^1 x^{-1/3} \, dx = 3/2$. The Open Newton-Cotes Method yields

$\dfrac{1}{3}[2f(1/4) - f(1/2) + 2f(3/4)] = 1.3721$, with error 0.1279.

7 (c) The exact value is $\int_0^2 \dfrac{dx}{\sqrt{2-x}} = 2\sqrt{2} \approx 2.8284$. The Open Newton-Cotes Method yields

$\dfrac{2}{3}[2f(1/4) - f(1/2) + 2f(3/4)] = 2.3076$, with error 0.5208.

9 Simpson's Rule applied to the integral is

$$\int_0^1 x^4 \, dx \approx \frac{1/2}{3}(y_0 + 4y_1 + y_2) = \frac{1}{6}\left(0^4 + 4\left(\frac{1}{2}\right)^4 + 1^4\right) = \frac{5}{24},$$

where $h = (b-a)/2 = 1/2$. The correct value of the integral is $\frac{1}{5}$, for an error of $\left|\frac{1}{5} - \frac{5}{24}\right| = \frac{5}{600} = \frac{1}{120}$. The error term of Simpson's Rule can be computed exactly since $f^{(iv)}(x) = 24$, and is

$$\frac{h^5}{90}f^{(iv)}(c) = \frac{(1/2)^5}{90}24 = \frac{1}{120},$$

agreeing with the actual error.

11 (a) We must test polynomials of increasing degree for the exactness of the approximation

$$\int_{-1}^1 f(x) \, dx = f(1) + f(-1).$$

$$\text{degree} = 0 \quad : \quad \int_{-1}^{1} 1 \, dx = 2 \quad \text{and} \quad f(1) + f(-1) = 1 + 1 = 2$$

$$\text{degree} = 1 \quad : \quad \int_{-1}^{1} x \, dx = 0 \quad \text{and} \quad f(1) + f(-1) = 1 + (-1) = 0$$

$$\text{degree} = 2 \quad : \quad \int_{-1}^{1} x^2 \, dx = \frac{2}{3} \quad \text{and} \quad f(1) + f(-1) = 1 + 1 = 2$$

Since the approximation is exact up to degree one polynomials, the degree of precision is one.

11 (b) Proceeding as in part (a), we find that the degree of precision is one:

$$\text{degree} = 0 \quad : \quad \int_{-1}^{1} 1 \, dx = 2 \quad \text{and} \quad \frac{2}{3}[f(-1) + f(0) + f(1)] = \frac{2}{3}[1 + 1 + 1] = 2$$

$$\text{degree} = 1 \quad : \quad \int_{-1}^{1} x \, dx = 0 \quad \text{and} \quad \frac{2}{3}[f(-1) + f(0) + f(1)] = \frac{2}{3}[(-1) + 0 + 1] = 0$$

$$\text{degree} = 2 \quad : \quad \int_{-1}^{1} x^2 \, dx = \frac{2}{3} \quad \text{and} \quad \frac{2}{3}[f(-1) + f(0) + f(1)] = \frac{2}{3}[1 + 0 + 1] = \frac{4}{3}$$

11 (c) Proceeding as in part (a), we find that the degree of precision is three:

$$\text{degree} = 0 \quad : \quad \int_{-1}^{1} 1 \, dx = 2 \quad \text{and} \quad [f(-1/\sqrt{3}) + f(1/\sqrt{3})] = 1 + 1 = 2$$

$$\text{degree} = 1 \quad : \quad \int_{-1}^{1} x \, dx = 0 \quad \text{and} \quad [f(-1/\sqrt{3}) + f(1/\sqrt{3})] = -1/\sqrt{3} + 1/\sqrt{3} = 0$$

$$\text{degree} = 2 \quad : \quad \int_{-1}^{1} x^2 \, dx = \frac{2}{3} \quad \text{and} \quad [f(-1/\sqrt{3}) + f(1/\sqrt{3})] = \frac{1}{3} + \frac{1}{3} = \frac{2}{3}$$

$$\text{degree} = 3 \quad : \quad \int_{-1}^{1} x^3 \, dx = 0 \quad \text{and} \quad [f(-1/\sqrt{3}) + f(1/\sqrt{3})] = -\frac{1}{3\sqrt{3}} + \frac{1}{3\sqrt{3}} = 0$$

$$\text{degree} = 4 \quad : \quad \int_{-1}^{1} x^4 \, dx = \frac{2}{5} \quad \text{and} \quad [f(-1/\sqrt{3}) + f(1/\sqrt{3})] = \frac{1}{9} + \frac{1}{9} = \frac{2}{9}$$

13 For a composite open Newton-Cotes rule, the terms never overlap. On the interval $[a, b]$, set $x_0 = a$ and $x_{4m} = b$ for an m-panel composite rule. Define $h = (b - a)/(4m) = x_1 - x_0$.

$$\int_{x_0}^{x_{4m}} f(x) \, dx \;\approx\; \frac{4h}{3}[2f(x_1) - f(x_2) + 2f(x_3) + 2f(x_5) - f(x_6) + 2f(x_7) + \ldots$$

$$+ \; 2f(x_{4m-3}) - f(x_{4m-2}) + 2f(x_{4m-1})] + \frac{14}{45}h^5[f^{(iv)}(c_1) + \ldots + f^{(iv)}(c_m)]$$

$$= \; \frac{4h}{3}\sum_{i=1}^{m}(2y_{4i-1} + 2y_{4i-3} - y_{4i-2}) + \frac{7}{90}(b - a)h^4 f^{(iv)}(c)$$

where c lies between a and b. Here we have used Theorem 5.1 and the fact that $4hm = b - a$ to simplify the error term.

15 It is easiest to simplify in terms of the midpoint x_2. Sample computations:

$$d = 2 \quad : \quad \int_{x_0}^{x_4} x^2 \, dx = \frac{(x_2 + h)^3}{3} - \frac{(x_2 - h)^3)}{3} = 4hx_2^2 + \frac{16}{3}h^3$$

$$\text{and} \quad \frac{2}{45}h[7(x_2 - 2h)^2 + 32(x_2 - h)^2 + 12x_2^2 + 32(x_2 + h)^2 + 7(x_2 + 2h)^2]$$

$$= 4hx_2^2 + \frac{16}{3}h^3$$

$$d = 5 \quad : \quad \int_{x_0}^{x_4} x^5 \, dx = \frac{(x_2 + 2h)^6}{6} - \frac{(x_2 - 2h)^6}{6} = 4hx_2^5 + \frac{160}{3}x_2^3h^3 + 64x_2h^5$$

$$\text{and} \quad \frac{2}{45}h[7(x_2 - 2h)^5 + 32(x_2 - h)^5 + 12x_2^5 + 32(x_2 + h)^5 + 7(x_2 + 2h)^5]$$

$$= \quad 4hx_2^5 + \frac{160}{3}x_2^3h^3 + 64x_2h^5$$

The degree of precision is five.

17 Let $P_3(x) = a_0 + a_1x + a_2x^2 + a_3x^3$. From Newton's divided differences, the interpolating polynomial $P_2(x)$ is found to be $P_2(x) = a_0 + (a_1 + a_3h^2)x + a_2x^2$. Integrating shows that

$$\int_{-h}^{h} P_2(x) \, dx = 2ha_0 + \frac{2}{3}h^3a_2 = \int_{-h}^{h} P_3(x) \, dx.$$

Simpson's Rule approximates a definite integral by integrating the interpolating polynomial of the integrand at three evenly-spaced points. The result shows that this approximation is exact for integrands that are degree 3 polynomials. This explains why Simpson's Rule has degree of precision three.

COMPUTER PROBLEMS 5.2

1 Compute the Composite Trapezoid Rule sum

$$\frac{h}{2}\left(y_0 + y_m + 2\sum_{i=1}^{m-1} y_i\right)$$

for $m = 16$ and $m = 32$, where $h = (b - a)/m$. The results are shown in the table.

	exact	$m = 16$	error	$m = 32$	error
(a)	2.000000	1.998638	0.001362	1.999660	0.000340
(b)	$(1 - \ln 2)/2 \approx 0.153426$	0.153752	0.000326	0.153508	0.000082
(c)	1.000000	1.001444	0.001444	1.000361	0.000361
(d)	$9 \ln 3 - 26/9 \approx 6.998622$	7.009809	0.011187	7.001419	0.002797
(e)	$\pi^2 - 4 \approx 5.869604$	5.837900	0.031704	5.861678	0.007926
(f)	$2\sqrt{5} - \sqrt{15}/2 \approx 2.535644$	2.535672	0.000028	2.535651	0.000007
(g)	$\ln(\sqrt{3} + 2) \approx 1.316958$	1.316746	0.000212	1.316905	0.000053
(h)	$\ln(\sqrt{2} + 1)/2 \approx 0.440687$	0.440361	0.000326	0.440605	0.000082

3 Compute the Composite Trapezoid Rule for $m = 16$ and $m = 32$, as in Computer Problem 1.

	$m = 16$	$m = 32$
(a)	1.464420	1.463094
(b)	0.891197	0.893925
(c)	3.977463	3.977463
(d)	0.264269	0.264025
(e)	0.160686	0.160936
(f)	−0.278013	−0.356790
(g)	0.785276	0.783951
(h)	0.369964	0.371168

5 Compute the Composite Midpoint Rule $h \sum\limits_{i=1}^{m} f(w_i)$ for $m = 10, 100$ and 1000.

	$m = 10$	error	$m = 100$	error	$m = 1000$	error
(a)	1.8089	0.1911	1.9395	0.0605	1.9809	0.0191
(b)	1.4456	0.0544	1.4883	0.0117	1.4975	0.0025
(c)	2.5582	0.2702	2.7429	0.0855	2.8014	0.0271

7 Compute the Composite Midpoint Rule for $m = 16$ and $m = 32$. Results are shown below.

(a)	1.83152990	1.83183081
(b)	2.99986658	3.00116293
(c)	0.91601205	0.91597721

9 We compute the Composite Trapezoid Rule approximations and find the difference from the correct integrals, given in Computer Problem 1(a)-(d). Plots of h versus the error are below. The log-log plots show an approximate slope of 2, confirming the fact that error $\propto h^2$.

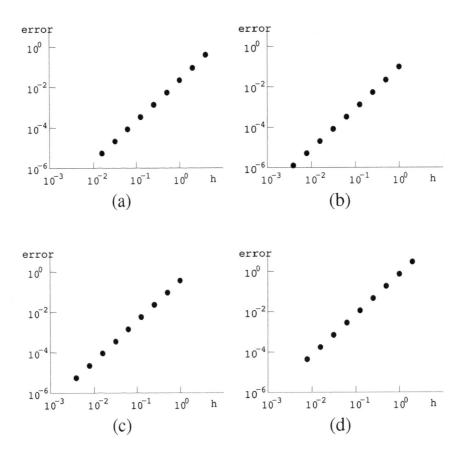

EXERCISES 5.3   Romberg Integration

1 (a)   Let $f(x) = x^2, a = 0, b = 1$. Following the definition of Romberg Integration,

$$R_{11} = (b - a)\frac{f(a) + f(b)}{2} = \frac{0^2 + 1^2}{2} = \frac{1}{2}.$$

The remainder of the first column is computed from the Composite Trapezoid Rule with $h_2 = (b - a)/2 = 1/2$,

$$R_{21} = \frac{1}{2}R_{11} + h_2 f(a + h_2) = \frac{1}{2} \cdot \frac{1}{2} + \frac{1}{2} \cdot \frac{1}{4} = \frac{3}{8}$$

and $h_3 = (b - a)/4 = 1/4$,

$$R_{31} = \frac{1}{2}R_{21} + h_3[f(a + h_3) + f(a + 3h_3)] = \frac{1}{2} \cdot \frac{3}{8} + \frac{1}{4}\left(\frac{1}{4}\right)^2 + \frac{1}{4}\left(\frac{3}{4}\right)^2 = \frac{11}{32}.$$

The second column consists of extrapolations of the first column

$$R_{22} = \frac{4R_{21} - R_{11}}{4 - 1} = \frac{4(\frac{3}{8}) - \frac{1}{2}}{3} = \frac{1}{3}$$

$$R_{32} = \frac{4R_{31} - R_{21}}{4 - 1} = \frac{4(\frac{11}{32}) - \frac{3}{8}}{3} = \frac{1}{3},$$

and the third column extrapolates the second column

$$R_{33} = \frac{4^2 R_{32} - R_{22}}{4^2 - 1} = \frac{16(\frac{1}{3}) - \frac{1}{3}}{15} = \frac{1}{3}$$

The Romberg triangle is

$$R_{11} = \tfrac{1}{2}$$

$$R_{21} = \tfrac{3}{8} \quad R_{22} = \tfrac{1}{3}$$

$$R_{31} = \tfrac{11}{32} \quad R_{32} = \tfrac{1}{3} \quad R_{33} = \tfrac{1}{3}$$

1 (b) Let $f(x) = \cos x, a = 0, b = \pi/2$. Set $h_2 = \pi/4, h_3 = \pi/8$. Then the first column of the Romberg triangle is

$$
\begin{aligned}
R_{11} &= (b-a)\frac{f(a)+f(b)}{2} = \frac{\pi}{2}\frac{1}{2} = \frac{\pi}{4} \approx 0.785398 \\
R_{21} &= \tfrac{1}{2}R_{11} + h_2 f(a + h_2) = \frac{\pi}{8} + \frac{\pi}{4}\frac{\sqrt{2}}{2} = \frac{\pi}{8}(1 + \sqrt{2}) = 0.948059 \\
R_{31} &= \tfrac{1}{2}R_{21} + h_3[f(a + h_3) + f(a + 3h_3)] = \frac{\pi}{16}(a + \sqrt{2}) + \frac{\pi}{8}[\cos\frac{\pi}{8} + \cos\frac{3\pi}{8}] \approx 0.987116
\end{aligned}
$$

The second column is

$$R_{22} = \frac{4R_{21} - R_{11}}{4 - 1} \approx 1.002280$$

$$R_{32} = \frac{4R_{31} - R_{21}}{4 - 1} \approx 1.000135$$

and the third column extrapolates the second column

$$R_{33} = \frac{4^2 R_{32} - R_{22}}{4^2 - 1} = 0.999992$$

The Romberg triangle is

$$R_{11} = 0.785398$$

$$R_{21} = 0.948059 \quad R_{22} = 1.002280$$

$$R_{31} = 0.987116 \quad R_{32} = 1.000135 \quad R_{33} = 0.999992$$

1 (c)   Similar to (a) and (b). Set $f(x) = e^x, a = 0, b = 1$. The Romberg triangle is

$$R_{11} = 1.859141$$

$$R_{21} = 1.753931 \quad R_{22} = 1.718861$$

$$R_{31} = 1.727222 \quad R_{32} = 1.718319 \quad R_{33} = 1.718283$$

3   Notice that $R_{11} = (b - a)(f(a) + f(b))/2 = h_2(f(a) + f(b))$. Then

$$
\begin{aligned}
R_{22} &= \frac{4R_{21} - R_{11}}{4 - 1} \\
&= \frac{4(\frac{1}{2}R_{11} + h_2 f(a + h_2)) - R_{11}}{3} \\
&= \frac{R_{11} + 4h_2 f(a + h_2)}{3} \\
&= \frac{h_2(f(a) + f(b)) + 4h_2 f(a + h_2)}{3} \\
&= \frac{h_2}{3}[f(a) + 4f(a + h_2) + f(b)]
\end{aligned}
$$

is Simpson's Rule on $[a, b]$.

5   We prove (5.31) by induction. For $j = 2$, the definition of R_{21} is from the Composite Trapezoid Rule

$$
\begin{aligned}
R_{21} &= \frac{h_2}{2}[f(a) + 2f(\frac{a+b}{2}) + f(b)] \\
&= \frac{1}{2}[h_2 f(a) + h_2 f(b)] + h_2 f(a + \frac{b-a}{2}) \\
&= \frac{1}{2}R_{11} + h_2 f(a + h_2)
\end{aligned}
$$

where we have used the fact that $h_2 = (b - a)/2$. For $j > 2$, we assume (5.31) is true for j, namely

$$R_{j1} = \frac{h_j}{2}[f(a) + f(b) + 2\sum_{i=1}^{m-1} y_{2i}],$$

where $m = 2^{j-1}$. Since the Composite Trapezoid Rule with $h_{j+1} = (b-a)/2^j$ is

$$
\begin{aligned}
R_{j+1,1} &= \frac{h_{j+1}}{2}[f(a) + f(b) + 2\sum_{i=1}^{2m-1} y_i] \\
&= \frac{1}{2}\frac{h_j}{2}[f(a) + f(b) + 2\sum_{i=1}^{m-1} y_{2i} + 2\sum_{i=1}^{m} y_{2i-1}] \\
&= \frac{1}{2}R_{j1} + \frac{h_j}{2}\sum_{i=1}^{m} y_{2i-1} \\
&= \frac{1}{2}R_{j1} + h_{j+1}\sum_{i=1}^{m} f(a + (2i-1)h_{j+1}).
\end{aligned}
$$

COMPUTER PROBLEMS 5.3

1 Compute the Romberg triangle, using for example the MATLAB program `romberg.m`. The result R_{55} is given in the table.

	exact	R_{55}	error
(a)	2.00000000	2.00000010	1.00×10^{-7}
(b)	$(1 - \ln 2)/2 \approx 0.15342641$	0.15342640	1.23×10^{-8}
(c)	1.00000000	1.00000000	3.50×10^{-13}
(d)	$9 \ln 3 - 26/9 \approx 6.99862171$	6.99862171	3.00×10^{-9}
(e)	$\pi^2 - 4 \approx 5.86960440$	5.86960486	4.56×10^{-7}
(f)	$2\sqrt{5} - \sqrt{15}/2 \approx 2.53564428$	2.53564428	1.21×10^{-10}
(g)	$\ln(\sqrt{3} + 2) \approx 1.31695790$	1.31695765	2.46×10^{-7}
(h)	$\ln(\sqrt{2} + 1)/2 \approx 0.44068679$	0.44068686	6.98×10^{-8}

3 (a) The errors of the Romberg triangle can be determined from the MATLAB code `romberg.m` as follows.

```
>> (2*log(2)-1)-romberg(inline('log(x)'),1,2,6)

ans =

    0.03972077083992    0.38629436111989    0.38629436111989
    0.01027501192582    0.00045975895446    0.38629436111989
    0.00259485171045    0.00003479830532    0.00000646759538
    0.00065045116780    0.00000231765358    0.00000015227679
    0.00016272337502    0.00000014744410    0.00000000276347
    0.00004068778692    0.00000000925756    0.00000000004512
```

The errors of the second column $R_{22}, \ldots, R_{62}$ are plotted in (a) below versus the values of $h = 2^{-1}, \ldots, 2^{-5}$. The slope is approximately 4, showing that the error $\propto h^4$ as expected.

3 (b) We use the data from part (a). The errors of the third column of the Romberg triangle are plotted in (b). The slope is approximately 6, consistent with the error $\propto h^6$ in the third column.

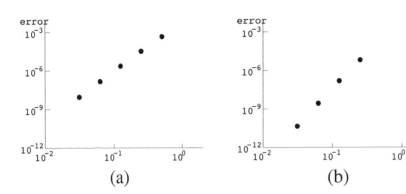

(a)   (b)

EXERCISES 5.4 Adaptive Quadrature

1 (a) For $f(x) = x^2$, the Trapezoid Rule is $S_{[a,b]} = (b-a)(a^2+b^2)/2$. Begin with one interval $S_{[0,1]} = 1/2$. Checking the interval $[0,1]$,

$$S_{[0,\frac{1}{2}]} = \frac{1}{16}, \qquad S_{[\frac{1}{2},1]} = \frac{5}{16}, \qquad \left| S_{[0,1]} - S_{[0,\frac{1}{2}]} - S_{[\frac{1}{2},1]} \right| = \frac{1}{8} < 3\,\text{TOL} = 0.15,$$

therefore the estimate

$$S_{[0,\frac{1}{2}]} + S_{[\frac{1}{2},1]} = \frac{3}{8}$$

is accepted for the integral. The error is $\left| \frac{3}{8} - \frac{1}{3} \right| = \frac{1}{24} \approx 0.0417 < 0.05$ as required.

1 (b) For $f(x) = \cos x$, the Trapezoid Rule is $S_{[a,b]} = (b-a)(\cos a + \cos b)/2$. Begin with one interval $S_{[0,\frac{\pi}{2}]} = 0.7854$. Checking the interval $[0, \frac{\pi}{2}]$,

$$S_{[0,\frac{\pi}{4}]} \approx 0.6704, \quad S_{[\frac{\pi}{4},\frac{\pi}{2}]} \approx 0.2777, \quad \left| S_{[0,\frac{\pi}{2}]} - S_{[0,\frac{\pi}{4}]} - S_{[\frac{\pi}{4},\frac{\pi}{2}]} \right| \approx 0.1627 > 3\,\text{TOL} = 0.15,$$

therefore $S_{[0,\frac{\pi}{2}]}$ is rejected and $[0, \frac{\pi}{4}], [\frac{\pi}{4}, \frac{\pi}{2}]$ are added to the list of intervals.
    Checking the interval $[0, \frac{\pi}{4}]$,

$$S_{[0,\frac{\pi}{8}]} \approx 0.3778, \quad S_{[\frac{\pi}{8},\frac{\pi}{4}]} \approx 0.3202, \quad \left| S_{[0,\frac{\pi}{4}]} - S_{[0,\frac{\pi}{8}]} - S_{[\frac{\pi}{8},\frac{\pi}{4}]} \right| \approx 0.0275 < \frac{3}{2}\text{TOL} = 0.075,$$

therefore the estimate $S_{[0,\frac{\pi}{8}]} + S_{[\frac{\pi}{8},\frac{\pi}{4}]} = 0.6980$ is accepted for $[0, \pi/4]$.
    Checking the interval $[\frac{\pi}{4}, \frac{\pi}{2}]$,

$$S_{[\frac{\pi}{4},\frac{3\pi}{8}]} \approx 0.2140,\ S_{[\frac{3\pi}{8},\frac{\pi}{2}]} \approx 0.0751,\ \left| S_{[\frac{\pi}{4},\frac{\pi}{2}]} - S_{[\frac{\pi}{4},\frac{3\pi}{8}]} - S_{[\frac{3\pi}{8},\frac{\pi}{2}]} \right| \approx 0.0114 < \frac{3}{2}\text{TOL} = 0.075,$$

therefore the estimate $S_{[\frac{\pi}{4},\frac{3\pi}{8}]} + S_{[\frac{3\pi}{8},\frac{\pi}{2}]} = 0.2891$ is accepted for $[\pi/4, \pi/2]$. Adding the accepted estimates above, the approximate integral is $0.6980 + 0.2891 = 0.9871$. Compared to the correct value 1 of the integral, the error is $0.0129 < 0.05$ as required.

1 (c) For $f(x) = e^x$, the Trapezoid Rule is $S_{[a,b]} = (b-a)(e^a + e^b)/2$. Begin with one interval $S_{[0,1]} = (1+e)/2 \approx 1.8591$. Checking the interval $[0, 1]$,

$$S_{[0,\frac{1}{2}]} \approx 0.6622, \qquad S_{[\frac{1}{2},1]} \approx 1.0917, \qquad |S_{[0,1]} - S_{[0,\frac{1}{2}]} - S_{[\frac{1}{2},1]}| \approx 0.1051 < 3\,\text{TOL} = 0.15,$$

therefore the estimate

$$S_{[0,\frac{1}{2}]} + S_{[\frac{1}{2},1]} = 1.7539$$

is accepted for the integral. The error is $|(e-1) - 1.7539| \approx 0.0356 < 0.05$ as required.

3 To construct an Adaptive Midpoint Method we define $S_{[a,b]} = (b-a)f(\frac{a+b}{2})$. Then (5.26) implies that

$$\int_a^b f(x)\, dx = S_{[a,b]} + \frac{h^3}{3}f''(c_1),$$

where $h = (b-a)/2$, and applying the Midpoint Method to both $[a, c]$ and $[c, b]$ where c is the midpoint of $[a, b]$,

$$\begin{aligned}
\int_a^b f(x)\, dx &= S_{[a,c]} + \frac{h^3}{8}\frac{f''(c_2)}{3} + S_{[c,b]} + \frac{h^3}{8}\frac{f''(c_3)}{3} \\
&= S_{[a,c]} + S_{[c,b]} + \frac{h^3}{12}f''(c_4).
\end{aligned}$$

Theorem 5.1 has been used to consolidate the error terms. Subtracting the two equations yields

$$S_{[a,b]} - (S_{[a,c]} + S_{[c,b]}) = \frac{h^3}{12}f''(c_4) - \frac{h^3}{3}f''(c_1) \approx -\frac{h^3}{4}f''(c_4),$$

assuming $f''(c_1) \approx f''(c_4)$. Comparing the previous two equations, we conclude that

$$|S_{[a,b]} - (S_{[a,c]} + S_{[c,b]})| \approx 3\left|\int_a^b f(x)\, dx - (S_{[a,c]} + S_{[c,b]})\right|$$

so we will need to require

$$|S_{[a,b]} - (S_{[a,c]} + S_{[c,b]})| < 3\,\text{TOL},$$

which is the same error tolerance criterion used for Adaptive Trapezoid Rule Quadrature.

COMPUTER PROBLEMS 5.4

1   The MATLAB program `adapquad` can be used with error tolerance set to be 0.5×10^{-8}. The number of intervals needed in the adaptive procedure are given in the table.

	approximation	intervals
(a)	2.00000000	12606
(b)	0.15342641	6204
(c)	1.00000000	12424
(d)	6.99862171	32768
(e)	5.86960440	73322
(f)	2.53564428	1568
(g)	1.31695790	7146
(h)	0.44068679	5308

3   Adaptive Simpson's Rule Quadrature should be used with error tolerance set to be 0.5×10^{-8}. The results are shown in the table.

	approximation	intervals
(a)	2.00000000	56
(b)	0.15342641	46
(c)	1.00000000	40
(d)	6.99862171	56
(e)	5.86960440	206
(f)	2.53564428	22
(g)	1.31695790	54
(h)	0.44068679	52

5   Adaptive quadrature with the open Newton-Cotes rule from (5.28) was developed in Exercise 4. When used with error tolerance 0.5×10^{-8}, the results are as shown in the table.

	approximation	intervals
(a)	2.00000000	50
(b)	0.15342641	44
(c)	1.00000000	36
(d)	6.99862171	54
(e)	5.86960440	198
(f)	2.53564428	22
(g)	1.31695790	50
(h)	0.44068679	52

7 Same as answers to Computer Problem 6.

9 Assuming you have written a MATLAB program `adapsimp.m`, similar to `adapquad.m`, but using Simpson's Rule, the `myerf` function can be written in two lines:

```
function y=myerf(x)
y=2*adapsimp(@(x) exp(-x^2),0,x,0.5e-8)/sqrt(pi);
```

Then `myerf(1)` returns 0.84270079 and `myerf(3)` returns 0.99997791 rounded to 8 decimal places, in agreement with the MATLAB "error function" `erf`.

EXERCISES 5.5   Gaussian Quadrature

1 (a) $f(-\frac{1}{\sqrt{3}}) + f(\frac{1}{\sqrt{3}}) = 0$, which agrees with the correct value of the integral. Error $= 0$.

1 (b) $f(-\frac{1}{\sqrt{3}}) + f(\frac{1}{\sqrt{3}}) = \frac{1}{9} + \frac{1}{9} = \frac{2}{9}$. Correct value is $2/5$, and the error $= 8/45 \approx 0.177778$.

1 (c) $f(-\frac{1}{\sqrt{3}}) + f(\frac{1}{\sqrt{3}}) = e^{-1/\sqrt{3}} + e^{1/\sqrt{3}} \approx 2.342696$. Compared to the correct value $e - 1/e$, the error $= 0.007706$.

1 (d) $f(-\frac{1}{\sqrt{3}}) + f(\frac{1}{\sqrt{3}}) = \cos -\pi/\sqrt{3} + \cos \pi/\sqrt{3} \approx -0.481237$. Compared to the correct value 0, the error $= 0.481237$.

3 (a) Use roots x_1, x_2, x_3, x_4 and coefficients c_1, c_2, c_3, c_4 from Table 5.1. For $f(x) = x^3 + 2x$, the Gaussian quadrature estimate $c_1 f(x_1) + c_2 f(x_2) + c_3 f(x_3) + c_4 f(x_4)$ is zero, in agreement with the correct value. Error $= 0$.

3 (b) Similar to (a). For $f(x) = x^4$, the Gaussian quadrature estimate is 0.4, equal to the correct value. Error $= 0$.

3 (c) Similar to (a). For $f(x) = e^x$, the Gaussian quadrature estimate is 2.350402, differing from the correct value by error 2.95×10^{-7}.

3 (d) Similar to (a). For $f(x) = \cos \pi x$, the Gaussian quadrature estimate is -0.002136, differing from the correct value zero by error 0.002136.

5 (a) By change of interval,

$$\int_0^4 \frac{x}{\sqrt{x^2+9}}\, dx = \int_{-1}^1 \frac{4t+4}{\sqrt{4(t+1)^2+9}}\, dt.$$

Calculating the $n = 3$ Gaussian quadrature approximation

$$\frac{5}{9}f(-\sqrt{3/5}) + \frac{8}{9}f(0) + \frac{5}{9}f(\sqrt{3/5})$$

with $f(t) = (4t+4)/\sqrt{4(t+1)^2+9}$ yields 1.999825.

5 (b) By change of interval,

$$\int_0^1 \frac{x^3}{x^2+1} \, dx = \int_{-1}^1 \frac{(t+1)^3}{4((t+1)^2+4)} \, dt.$$

The $n = 3$ Gaussian quadrature approximation yields 0.15340700.

5 (c) By change of interval,

$$\int_0^1 xe^x \, dx = \int_{-1}^1 \frac{t+1}{4} e^{(t+1)/2} \, dt.$$

The $n = 3$ Gaussian quadrature approximation yields 0.99999463.

5 (d) By change of interval,

$$\int_1^3 x^2 \ln x \, dx = \int_{-1}^1 (t+2)^2 \ln(t+2) \, dt.$$

The $n = 3$ Gaussian quadrature approximation yields 6.99867782.

7 The functions are orthogonal on the interval $[-1, 1]$ because

$$\int_{-1}^1 x\left(x^2 - \frac{1}{3}\right) dx = \int_{-1}^1 x^3 - \frac{1}{3}x \, dx = (1)^4 - \frac{(1)^2}{6} - \left((-1)^4 - \frac{(-1)^2}{6}\right) = 0.$$

9 The third Legendre polynomial is calculated from the formula in Example 5.14 as

$$p_3(x) \;=\; \frac{1}{2^3 3!} \frac{d^3}{dx^3}[(x^2-1)^3] = \frac{1}{48}(120x^3 - 72x) = \frac{5}{2}x^3 - \frac{3}{2}x.$$

By factoring $p_3(x) = \frac{1}{2}x(5x^2 - 3)$, the three roots $x_1 = -\sqrt{5/3}, x_2 = 0, x_3 = \sqrt{5/3}$ are found. The corresponding coefficients for Gaussian Quadrature are the integrals of the Lagrange interpolating functions

$$c_i = \int_{-1}^1 L_i(x) \, dx.$$

For example, $c_1 = \displaystyle\int_{-1}^1 \frac{(x - \sqrt{\frac{3}{5}})x}{2\sqrt{\frac{3}{5}}\sqrt{\frac{3}{5}}} \, dx = \frac{5}{6}\left[\frac{x^3}{3} - \frac{\sqrt{\frac{3}{5}}x^2}{2}\right]_{-1}^1 = \frac{5}{6}\left[\frac{2}{3}\right] = \frac{5}{9}$ and

$$c_2 = \int_{-1}^1 \frac{(x + \sqrt{\frac{3}{5}})(x - \sqrt{\frac{3}{5}})}{-\sqrt{\frac{3}{5}}\sqrt{\frac{3}{5}}} \, dx = -\frac{5}{3}\left[\frac{x^3}{3} - \frac{3}{5}x\right]_{-1}^1 = -\frac{5}{3}\left[-\frac{8}{15}\right] = \frac{8}{9}.$$

The third coefficient $c_3 = 5/9$ is equal to c_1 by symmetry.

CHAPTER 6
Ordinary Differential Equations

EXERCISES 6.1 Initial Value Problems

1 (a) Since $y'(t) = \sin t + t \cos t$, the right-hand side of the differential equation is $ty' = t \sin t + t^2 \cos t = y + t^2 \cos t$, agreeing with the left-hand side.

1 (b) Since $y''(t) = 2 \cos t - t \sin t = 2 \cos t - y$, the differential equation is satisfied.

1 (c) Using the second derivative from (b), the left-hand side is $t(y'' + y) = t(2 \cos t - t \sin t + t \sin t) = 2t \cos t = 2(t \cos t + \sin t) - 2 \sin t = 2y' - 2 \sin t$.

3 (a) Separation of variables leads to

$$\int dy = \int t \, dt$$
$$y = \frac{1}{2}t^2 + C$$

The initial condition is $1 = y(0) = \frac{1}{2}(0)^2 + C$, so $C = 1$. The solution is $y(t) = \frac{1}{2}t^2 + 1$.

3 (b)

$$\int \frac{dy}{y} = \int t^2 \, dt$$
$$\ln |y| = \frac{1}{3}t^3 + C_1$$
$$y = C_2 e^{t^3/3}$$

The initial condition is $1 = y(0) = C_2$, so $C_2 = 1$. The solution is $y(t) = e^{t^3/3}$.

3 (c)

$$\int \frac{dy}{y} = \int 2(t + 1) \, dt$$
$$\ln |y| = (t + 1)^2 + C_1$$
$$y = C_2 e^{(t+1)^2}$$

The initial condition $1 = y(0) = C_2 e$ shows $C_2 = 1/e$. Solution is $y(t) = \frac{1}{e}e^{(t+1)^2} = e^{t^2+2t}$.

3 (d)

$$\int \frac{dy}{y} = \int 5t^4 \, dt$$
$$\ln |y| = t^5 + C_1$$
$$y = C_2 e^{t^5}$$

The initial condition is $1 = y(0) = C_2$, so $C_2 = 1$. The solution is $y(t) = e^{t^5}$.

3 (e)

$$\int y^2 \, dy = \int 1 \, dt$$

$$\frac{y^3}{3} = t + C_1$$

$$y = (3t + C_2)^{1/3}$$

The initial condition is $1 = y(0) = C_2^{1/3}$, so $C_2 = 1$. The solution is $y(t) = (3t + 1)^{1/3}$.

3 (f)

$$\int y^2 \, dy = \int t^3 \, dt$$

$$\frac{y^3}{3} = \frac{1}{4}t^4 + C_1$$

$$y = \left(\frac{3}{4}t^4 + C_2\right)^{1/3}$$

The initial condition is $1 = y(0) = C_2^{1/3}$, so $C_2 = 1$. The solution is $y(t) = \left(\frac{3}{4}t^4 + 1\right)^{1/3}$.

5 (a) For the step size $h = 1/4$ on $[0, 1]$, the grid is $t_0 = 0, t_1 = 1/4, t_2 = 1/2, t_3 = 3/4, t_4 = 1$. Applying Euler's Method to $y' = t$ gives the formula $w_{i+1} = w_i + hf(t_i, w_i) = w_i + ht_i$. The approximate solution values are

$$w_0 = y_0 = 1$$

$$w_1 = w_0 + ht_0 = 1 + \frac{1}{4}(0) = 1$$

$$w_2 = w_1 + ht_1 = 1 + \frac{1}{4}\left(\frac{1}{4}\right) = \frac{17}{16}$$

$$w_3 = w_2 + ht_2 = \frac{17}{16} + \frac{1}{4}\left(\frac{1}{2}\right) = \frac{19}{16}$$

$$w_4 = w_3 + ht_3 = \frac{19}{16} + \frac{1}{4}\left(\frac{3}{4}\right) = \frac{22}{16} = \frac{11}{8}$$

Compared with the correct solution $y(1) = \frac{1}{2}(1)^2 + 1 = \frac{3}{2}$, the approximate solution $w(1) = w_4 = \frac{11}{8}$ has error $\left|\frac{3}{2} - \frac{11}{8}\right| = \frac{1}{8}$.

5 (b) Applying Euler's Method to $y' = t^2 y$ gives the formula

$$w_{i+1} = w_i + h t_i^2 w_i.$$

The Euler steps are

$$
\begin{aligned}
w_0 &= y_0 = 1 \\
w_1 &= w_0 + h t_0^2 w_0 = 1.0000 \\
w_2 &= w_1 + h t_1^2 w_1 \approx 1.0156 \\
w_3 &= w_2 + h t_2^2 w_2 \approx 1.0791 \\
w_4 &= w_3 + h t_3^2 w_3 \approx 1.2309
\end{aligned}
$$

Comparing with the correct solution $y(1) = e^{1/3}$, the error is $|y(1) - w(1)| \approx 0.1648$.

5 (c) Applying Euler's Method to $y' = 2(t+1)y$ gives the formula

$$w_{i+1} = w_i + 2h(t_i + 1)w_i.$$

The Euler steps are

$$
\begin{aligned}
w_0 &= y_0 = 1 \\
w_1 &= w_0 + 2h(t_0 + 1)w_0 = 1.5000 \\
w_2 &= w_1 + 2h(t_1 + 1)w_1 \approx 2.4375 \\
w_3 &= w_2 + 2h(t_2 + 1)w_2 \approx 4.2656 \\
w_4 &= w_3 + 2h(t_3 + 1)w_3 \approx 7.9980
\end{aligned}
$$

Comparing with the correct solution $y(1) = e^3$, the error is $|y(1) - w(1)| \approx 12.0875$.

5 (d) Applying Euler's Method to $y' = 5t^4 y$ gives the formula

$$w_{i+1} = w_i + 5h t_i^4 w_i.$$

The Euler steps are

$$
\begin{aligned}
w_0 &= y_0 = 1 \\
w_1 &= w_0 + 5h t_0^4 w_0 = 1.0000 \\
w_2 &= w_1 + 5h t_1^4 w_1 \approx 1.0049 \\
w_3 &= w_2 + 5h t_2^4 w_2 \approx 1.0834 \\
w_4 &= w_3 + 5h t_3^4 w_3 \approx 1.5119
\end{aligned}
$$

Comparing with the correct solution $y(1) = e$, the error is $|y(1) - w(1)| \approx 1.2064$.

5 (e)   Applying Euler's Method to $y' = 1/y^2$ gives the formula

$$w_{i+1} = w_i + \frac{h}{w_i^2}.$$

The Euler steps are

$$
\begin{aligned}
w_0 &= y_0 = 1 \\
w_1 &= w_0 + \frac{h}{w_0^2} = 1.2500 \\
w_2 &= w_1 + \frac{h}{w_1^2} \approx 1.4100 \\
w_3 &= w_2 + \frac{h}{w_2^2} \approx 1.5357 \\
w_4 &= w_3 + \frac{h}{w_3^2} \approx 1.6417
\end{aligned}
$$

Comparing with the correct solution $y(1) = 4^{1/3} \approx 1.5874$, the error is $|y(1) - w(1)| \approx 0.0543$.

5 (f)   Applying Euler's Method to $y' = t^3/y^2$ gives the formula

$$w_{i+1} = w_i + h\frac{t_i^3}{w_i^2}.$$

The Euler steps are

$$
\begin{aligned}
w_0 &= y_0 = 1 \\
w_1 &= w_0 + h\frac{t_0^3}{w_0^2} = 1.0000 \\
w_2 &= w_1 + h\frac{t_1^3}{w_1^2} \approx 1.0039 \\
w_3 &= w_2 + h\frac{t_2^3}{w_2^2} \approx 1.0349 \\
w_4 &= w_3 + h\frac{t_3^3}{w_3^2} \approx 1.1334
\end{aligned}
$$

Comparing with the correct solution $y(1) = (7/4)^{1/3} \approx 1.2051$, the error is $|y(1) - w(1)| \approx 0.0717$.

7 (a)   Check the solution $y = \tan(t + c)$ by differentiating:
$y'(t) = \sec^2(t + c) = 1 + \tan^2(t + c) = 1 + y^2.$

7 (b) $y_0 = y(0) = \tan(0 + c) \Rightarrow c = \arctan y_0.$
Therefore $y(t) = \tan(t + \arctan y_0)$ solves the initial value problem $y' = 1 + y^2, y(0) = y_0.$

9 (a) The Lipschitz constant $L = 0$ holds for $f(t, y) = t$ on the rectangle $[0, 1] \times (-\infty, \infty)$. By Theorem 6.2, there exists exactly one solution to the IVP on $[0, 1]$.

9 (b) The Lipschitz constant $L = 1$ holds for $f(t, y) = y$ on the rectangle $[0, 1] \times (-\infty, \infty)$. By Theorem 6.2, there exists exactly one solution to the IVP on $[0, 1]$.

9 (c) Similar to (b). The Lipschitz constant $L = 1$ holds for $f(t, y) = -y$, and there exists exactly one solution to the IVP on $[0, 1]$.

9 (d) The partial derivative $\dfrac{\partial f}{\partial y} = -3y^2$ is unbounded on the rectangle $[0, 1] \times (-\infty, \infty)$, showing that the Lipschitz condition fails on the rectangle. Theorem 6.2 does not guarantee a solution for t in $[0, 1]$.

11 (a) The solution is $y(t) = \frac{1}{2}t^2 + C$. For initial conditions $y(0) = 0$ and $y(0) = 1$, respectively, the solutions are $Y(t) = \frac{1}{2}t^2$ and $Z(t) = \frac{1}{2}t^2 + 1$. The Lipschitz constant is $L = 0$, and Theorem 6.3 implies $|Y(t) - Z(t)| \leq |Y(0) - Z(0)|$. In this example, $|Y(t) - Z(t)| = |Y(0) - Z(0)| = 1$, consistent with the theory.

11 (b) The solution is $y(t) = Ce^t$. The pair of solutions is $Y(t) = 0$ and $Z(t) = e^t$, so that $|Y(t) - Z(t)| = e^t$. The Lipschitz constant is $L = 1$. The inequality from Theorem 6.3 is

$$|Y(t) - Z(t)| \leq e^{(t-0)}|Y(0) - Z(0)| = e^t,$$

which holds for $t \geq 0$.

11 (c) The solution is $y(t) = Ce^{-t}$. The pair of solutions is $Y(t) = 0$ and $Z(t) = e^{-t}$, so that $|Y(t) - Z(t)| = e^{-t}$. The Lipschitz constant is $L = 1$. The inequality from Theorem 6.3 is

$$|Y(t) - Z(t)| \leq e^{(t-0)}|Y(0) - Z(0)| = e^t,$$

which holds for $t \geq 0$.

11 (d) No Lipschitz constant exists on the rectangle $[0, 1] \times (-\infty, \infty)$. However, the solutions $y(t) = 0$ and $y(t) = (1 + 2t)^{-1/2}$ exist for initial conditions $y(0) = 0$ and $y(0) = 1$, respectively.

13

$$\int \frac{dy}{y^2} = \int dt$$
$$\frac{y^{-1}}{-1} = t + C$$
$$y = -\frac{1}{t + C}$$

The initial condition is $1 = y(0) = -1/(0 + C)$, implying $C = -1$, and $y(t) = 1/(1 - t)$.

15 (a) Since $f(t, y) = \sin y$ has Lipschitz constant $L = 1$ for all (t, y), Theorem 6.2 guarantees a unique solution on the entire interval $[a, b]$ (and moreover, on $[a, \infty)$).

15 (b)   Check the solution $y(t) = 2\arctan(e^{t-a}\tan\frac{y_a}{2}) + 2\pi \lfloor (y_a + \pi)/2\pi \rfloor$, where $\lfloor\ \rfloor$ denotes the greatest integer function, by differentiating: $y'(t) = \dfrac{2e^{t-a}\tan\frac{y_a}{2}}{1 + e^{2(t-a)}\tan^2\frac{y_a}{2}}$. To simplify this expression, notice that $\tan\left(\dfrac{y}{2} - \pi k\right) = e^{t-a}\tan\dfrac{y_a}{2}$ where k is the greatest integer $\lfloor (y_a + \pi)/2\pi \rfloor$, and so one can rewrite

$$y'(t) = \frac{2\tan(\frac{y}{2} - \pi k)}{1 + \tan^2(\frac{y}{2} - \pi k)} = 2\sin\left(\frac{y}{2} - \pi k\right)\cos\left(\frac{y}{2} - \pi k\right) = \sin(y - 2\pi k) = \sin y.$$

Second, the initial condition must be checked. Since $\arctan(\tan x) = x - \left\lfloor \dfrac{x + \frac{\pi}{2}}{\pi} \right\rfloor \pi$,

$$\begin{aligned} y_a &= y(a) = 2\arctan(e^{a-a}\tan\frac{y_a}{2}) + 2\pi\left\lfloor \frac{y_a + \pi}{2\pi} \right\rfloor \\ &= 2\left(\frac{y_a}{2} - \left\lfloor \frac{\frac{y_a}{2} + \frac{\pi}{2}}{\pi} \right\rfloor \pi\right) + 2\pi\left\lfloor \frac{y_a + \pi}{2\pi} \right\rfloor = y_a \end{aligned}$$

COMPUTER PROBLEMS 6.1

1   The Euler's Method approximations can be calculated with Program 6.1, after placing the right-hand side $f(t, y)$ of the differential equations into the `ydot` function of the code.

t_i	w_i	error	t_i	w_i	error	t_i	w_i	error
0.0	1.0000	0.0000	0.0	1.0000	0.0000	0.0	1.0000	0.0000
0.1	1.0000	0.0050	0.1	1.0000	0.0003	0.1	1.2000	0.0337
0.2	1.0100	0.0100	0.2	1.0010	0.0017	0.2	1.4640	0.0887
0.3	1.0300	0.0150	0.3	1.0050	0.0040	0.3	1.8154	0.1784
0.4	1.0600	0.0200	0.4	1.0140	0.0075	0.4	2.2874	0.3243
0.5	1.1000	0.0250	0.5	1.0303	0.0123	0.5	2.9278	0.5625
0.6	1.1500	0.0300	0.6	1.0560	0.0186	0.6	3.8062	0.9527
0.7	1.2100	0.0350	0.7	1.0940	0.0271	0.7	5.0241	1.5952
0.8	1.2800	0.0400	0.8	1.1477	0.0384	0.8	6.7323	2.6610
0.9	1.3600	0.0450	0.9	1.2211	0.0540	0.9	9.1560	4.4431
1.0	1.4500	0.0500	1.0	1.3200	0.0756	1.0	12.6352	7.4503

(a)   (b)   (c)

	t_i	w_i	error		t_i	w_i	error		t_i	w_i	error
	0.0	1.0000	0.0000		0.0	1.0000	0.0000		0.0	1.0000	0.0000
	0.1	1.0000	0.0000		0.1	1.1000	0.0086		0.1	1.0000	0.0000
	0.2	1.0001	0.0003		0.2	1.1826	0.0130		0.2	1.0001	0.0003
	0.3	1.0009	0.0016		0.3	1.2541	0.0156		0.3	1.0009	0.0011
(d)	0.4	1.0049	0.0054	**(e)**	0.4	1.3177	0.0181	**(f)**	0.4	1.0036	0.0028
	0.5	1.0178	0.0140		0.5	1.3753	0.0181		0.5	1.0099	0.0054
	0.6	1.0496	0.0313		0.6	1.4282	0.0187		0.6	1.0222	0.0092
	0.7	1.1176	0.0654		0.7	1.4772	0.0191		0.7	1.0429	0.0139
	0.8	1.2517	0.1360		0.8	1.5230	0.0193		0.8	1.0744	0.0190
	0.9	1.5081	0.2968		0.9	1.5661	0.0195		0.9	1.1188	0.0239
	1.0	2.0028	0.7154		1.0	1.6069	0.0195		1.0	1.1770	0.0281

3 Program 6.1 can be used to generate the plots. The correct solution from Exercise 4 must be added. The solutions are shown below.

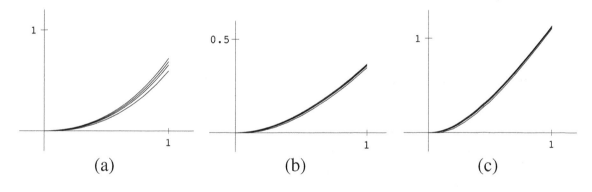

(a)   (b)   (c)

5 Euler's Method is run for the six step sizes h, and the error is plotted on a loglog graph.

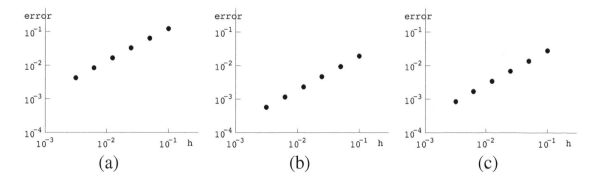

(a)   (b)   (c)

7 Program 6.1 can be used to generate the plots, with initial conditions (a) $y_0 = 0$ and (b) $y_0 = 1/2$. The correct solution from Exercise 6.1.7 is added (thicker curve). The solutions are shown below.

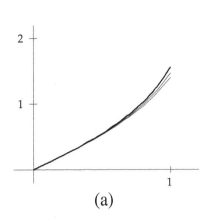

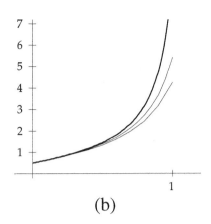

(a)   (b)

EXERCISES 6.2   Analysis of IVP Solvers

1 (a)   The Explicit Trapezoid Method is

$$w_{i+1} = w_i + \frac{h}{2}[f(t_i, w_i) + f(t_i + h, w_i + hf(t_i, w_i))].$$

Applied to the differential equation $y' = f(t, y) = t$, the method is

$$w_{i+1} = w_i + \frac{h}{2}[t_i + t_i + h] = w_i h[t_i + \frac{h}{2}].$$

With $y(0) = 1$ and $h = 1/4$, we calculate

$$
\begin{aligned}
w_0 &= y(0) = 1 \\
w_1 &= 1 + \frac{1}{4}(0) + \frac{1}{2}\left(\frac{1}{4}\right)^2 = \frac{33}{32} \\
w_2 &= \frac{33}{32} + \frac{1}{4}\left(\frac{1}{4}\right) + \frac{1}{32} = \frac{9}{8} \\
w_3 &= \frac{9}{8} + \frac{1}{4}\left(\frac{5}{2}\right) + \frac{1}{32} = \frac{41}{32} \\
w_4 &= \frac{41}{32} + \frac{1}{4}\left(\frac{3}{4}\right) + \frac{1}{32} = \frac{3}{2}
\end{aligned}
$$

Global error at $t = 1$ is 0.

1 (b)   The Explicit Trapezoid Method applied to $y' = f(t, y) = t^2 y$ is

$$w_{i+1} = w_i + \frac{h}{2}[t_i^2 w_i + (t_i + h)^2(w_i + h(t_i^2 w_i))].$$

Starting with $y(0) = 1$ we calculate

t_i	w_i
0	1.0000
1/4	1.0078
1/2	1.0477
3/4	1.1587
1	1.4054

Global error at $t = 1$ is 0.0097.

1 (c) The Explicit Trapezoid Method applied to $y' = f(t, y) = 2(t + 1)y$ is

$$w_{i+1} = w_i + \frac{h}{2}[2(t_i + 1)w_i + 2(t_i + h + 1)(w_i + 2h(t_i + 1)w_i)].$$

t_i	w_i
0	1.0000
1/4	1.7188
1/2	3.3032
3/4	7.0710
1	16.7935

Global error at $t = 1$ is 3.2920.

1 (d) The Explicit Trapezoid Method applied to $y' = f(t, y) = 5t^4 y$ is

$$w_{i+1} = w_i + \frac{h}{2}[5t_i^4 w_i + 5(t_i + h)^4(w_i + 5h(t_i^4 w_i))].$$

t_i	w_i
0	1.0000
1/4	1.0024
1/2	1.0442
3/4	1.3077
1	2.7068

Global error at $t = 1$ is 0.0115.

1 (e) The Explicit Trapezoid Method applied to $y' = f(t, y) = 1/y^2$ is

$$w_{i+1} = w_i + \frac{h}{2}\left[\frac{1}{w_i^2} + \frac{1}{(w_i + h/w_i^2)^2}\right].$$

t_i	w_i
0	1.0000
1/4	1.2050
1/2	1.3570
3/4	1.4810
1	1.5871

Global error at $t = 1$ is 0.0003.

1 (f)   The Explicit Trapezoid Method applied to $y' = f(t, y) = t^3/y^2$ is

$$w_{i+1} = w_i + \frac{h}{2}\left[\frac{t_i^3}{w_i^2} + \frac{(t_i + h)^3}{(w_i + ht_i^3/w_i^2)^2}\right].$$

t_i	w_i
0	1.0000
1/4	1.0020
1/2	1.0193
3/4	1.0823
1	1.2182

Global error at $t = 1$ is 0.0132.

3 (a)   The second-order Taylor Method is

$$w_{i+1} = w_i + hf(t_i, w_i) + \frac{h^2}{2}[f_t(t_i, w_i) + f_y(t_i, y_i)f(t_i, w_i)].$$

For $f(t, y) = ty$, the partial derivatives are $f_t = y$ and $f_y = t$, so the Taylor Method step is

$$\begin{aligned} w_{i+1} &= w_i + ht_iw_i + \frac{h^2}{2}[w_i + t_i(t_iw_i)] \\ &= w_i + ht_iw_i + \frac{h^2}{2}[w_i + t_i^2w_i] \end{aligned}$$

3 (b)   Since the partial derivatives are $f_t = y^2$ and $f_y = 2ty + 3y^2$, the second-order Taylor Method is

$$w_{i+1} = w_i + h(t_iw_i^2 + w_i^3) + \frac{h^2}{2}[w_i^2 + (2t_iw_i + 3w_i^2)(t_iw_i^2 + w_i^3)].$$

3 (c)   The partial derivatives are $f_t = 0$ and $f_y = \sin y + y\cos y$. The second-order Taylor Method is

$$w_{i+1} = w_i + hw_i\sin w_i + \frac{h^2}{2}(\sin w_i + w_i\cos w_i)w_i\sin w_i.$$

3 (d)   The partial derivatives are $f_t = 2tye^{yt^2}$ and $f_y = t^2e^{yt^2}$. The second-order Taylor Method is

$$w_{i+1} = w_i + he^{w_it_i^2} + \frac{h^2}{2}[2t_iw_ie^{w_it_i^2} + t_i^2e^{2w_it_i^2}].$$

5 (a)   At step 3, the global error satisfies

$$g_3 = |w_3 - y_3| \leq |w_3 - z(t_3)| + |z_1(t_3) - y_3|,$$

where $z_1(t_3)$ is the solution of the differential equation on $[t_2, t_3]$ with initial condition $z_1(t_2) = w_2$. By definition, $e_3 = |w_3 - z_1(t_3)|$ is less than the local truncation error, and

$$|z_1(t_3) - y_3| \le |z_1(t_2) - y_2|e^{Lh} = |w_2 - y_2|e^{Lh} = g_2 e^{Lh}.$$

Therefore

$$g_3 \le e_3 + g_2 e^{Lh} \le e_3 + (e_2 + e^{Lh}e_1)e^{Lh} = e_3 + e^{Lh}e_2 + e^{2Lh}e_1,$$

as required.

5 (b)   The argument in part (a) can be continued to prove $g_i \le e_i + g_{i-1}e^{Lh}$. Then, using the same fact for g_{i-1} we can write

$$\begin{aligned} g_i &\le e_i + g_{i-1}e^{Lh} \\ &\le e_i + e^{Lh}(e_{i-1} + g_{i-2}e^{Lh}) \\ &\le e_i + e^{Lh}e_{i-1} + e^{2Lh}e_{i-2} + \ldots + e^{(i-1)Lh}e_1 \end{aligned}$$

COMPUTER PROBLEMS 6.2

1 (a)   The Explicit Trapezoid Rule is run with interval $[0, 1]$ and step size $h = 0.1$. The resulting approximations are

	t_i	w_i	error		t_i	w_i	error
	0.0	1.00000000	0.00000000		0.0	1.00000000	0.00000000
	0.1	1.00500000	0.00000000		0.1	1.00050000	0.00016661
	0.2	1.02000000	0.00000000		0.2	1.00300325	0.00033303
	0.3	1.04500000	0.00000000		0.3	1.00954083	0.00050020
(a)	0.4	1.08000000	0.00000000	**(b)**	0.4	1.02223277	0.00067026
	0.5	1.12500000	0.00000000		0.5	1.04339299	0.00084609
	0.6	1.18000000	0.00000000		0.6	1.07568600	0.00103066
	0.7	1.24500000	0.00000000		0.7	1.12235142	0.00122564
	0.8	1.32000000	0.00000000		0.8	1.18752412	0.00142880
	0.9	1.40500000	0.00000000		0.9	1.27669768	0.00162905
	1.0	1.50000000	0.00000000		1.0	1.39740944	0.00179702

(c)

t_i	w_i	error
0.0	1.00000000	0.00000000
0.1	1.23200000	0.00167806
0.2	1.54788480	0.00482242
0.3	1.98315001	0.01056553
0.4	2.59078717	0.02090931
0.5	3.45092851	0.03941445
0.6	4.68636091	0.07246033
0.7	6.48779805	0.13157063
0.8	9.15558060	0.23775068
0.9	13.16938714	0.42966371
1.0	19.30632155	0.77921537

(d)

t_i	w_i	error
0.0	1.00000000	0.00000000
0.1	1.00002500	0.00001500
0.2	1.00045003	0.00012998
0.3	1.00287774	0.00044479
0.4	1.01135298	0.00106037
0.5	1.03383030	0.00208689
0.6	1.08452676	0.00366354
0.7	1.18898254	0.00596312
0.8	1.39671933	0.00897451
0.9	1.81575932	0.01088674
1.0	2.71644404	0.00183779

(e)

t_i	w_i	error
0.0	1.00000000	0.00000000
0.1	1.09132231	0.00007057
0.2	1.16950222	0.00010487
0.3	1.23844045	0.00012188
0.4	1.30046139	0.00013006
0.5	1.35707533	0.00013347
0.6	1.40932553	0.00013421
0.7	1.45796632	0.00013341
0.8	1.50356287	0.00013173
0.9	1.54655084	0.00012953
1.0	1.58727399	0.00012706

(f)

t_i	w_i	error
0.0	1.00000000	0.00000000
0.1	1.00005000	0.00002500
0.2	1.00049988	0.00010003
0.3	1.00224597	0.00022506
0.4	1.00675859	0.00039911
0.5	1.01600550	0.00061848
0.6	1.03227754	0.00087404
0.7	1.05789304	0.00114885
0.8	1.09482212	0.00141807
0.9	1.14434840	0.00165369
1.0	1.20690398	0.00183285

3 The Explicit Trapezoid Method is run for the six step sizes h, and the error is plotted on a loglog graph. For differential equation (a), the Trapezoid Method integrates exactly, and the error is zero for all steps sizes. Some of the remaining plots are shown below.

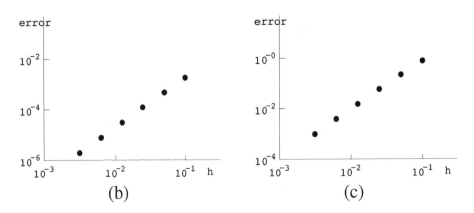

(b)   (c)

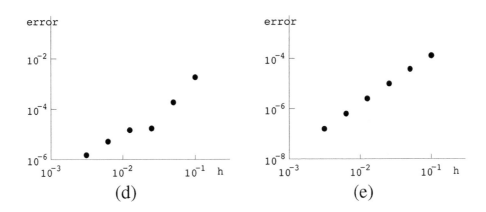

(d) (e)

5 Trapezoid Method output with initial conditions (a) $y_0 = 0$ and (b) $y_0 = 1/2$. The correct solution from Exercise 6.1.7 is added (thicker curve). In some cases, the approximate solutions are covered by the exact solutions.

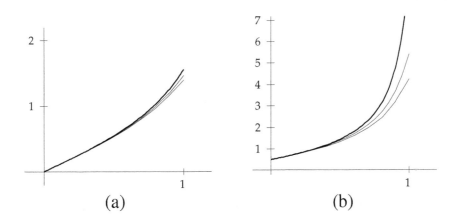

(a) (b)

EXERCISES 6.3 Systems of Ordinary Differential Equations

1 (a) Euler's Method generates w_{i1} and w_{i2}, $i = 1, 2, 3, 4$, to approximate y_1 and y_2, respectively. For step size $h = 1/4$, the formulas are

$$w_{i+1,1} = w_{i1} + h(w_{i1} + w_{i2}) \quad \text{and} \quad w_{i+1,2} = w_{i2} + h(-w_{i1} + w_{i2}).$$

Starting with the initial conditions $w_{01} = y_1(0) = 1$ and $w_{02} = y_2(0) = 0$, the approximate solutions are

$$w_{01} = 1 \qquad\qquad\qquad w_{02} = 0$$

$$w_{11} = 1 + \tfrac{1}{4}(1 + 0) = \tfrac{5}{4} \qquad\qquad w_{12} = 0 + \tfrac{1}{4}(-1 + 0) = -\tfrac{1}{4}$$

$$w_{21} = \tfrac{5}{4} + \tfrac{1}{4}\left(\tfrac{5}{4} - \tfrac{1}{4}\right) = \tfrac{3}{2} \qquad\qquad w_{22} = -\tfrac{1}{4} + \tfrac{1}{4}\left(-\tfrac{5}{4} - \tfrac{1}{4}\right) = -\tfrac{5}{8}$$

$$w_{31} = \tfrac{3}{2} + \tfrac{1}{4}\left(\tfrac{3}{2} - \tfrac{5}{8}\right) = \tfrac{55}{32} \qquad\qquad w_{32} = -\tfrac{5}{8} + \tfrac{1}{4}\left(-\tfrac{3}{2} - \tfrac{5}{8}\right) = -\tfrac{37}{32}$$

$$w_{41} = \tfrac{55}{32} + \tfrac{1}{4}\left(\tfrac{55}{32} - \tfrac{37}{32}\right) = \tfrac{119}{64} \qquad\qquad w_{42} = -\tfrac{37}{32} + \tfrac{1}{4}\left(-\tfrac{55}{32} - \tfrac{37}{32}\right) = -\tfrac{15}{8}$$

The correct solutions can be used to find the global truncation errors of the approximations. The global error of w_{41} is $|y_1(1) - w_{41}| \approx 0.3907$. The global error of w_{42} is $|y_2(1) - w_{42}| \approx 0.4124.$

1 (b) The Euler's Method formulas are

$$w_{i+1,1} = w_{i1} + h(-w_{i1} - w_{i2}) \quad \text{and} \quad w_{i+1,2} = w_{i2} + h(w_{i1} - w_{i2}).$$

The approximate solutions are

$$\begin{aligned}
w_{01} &= 1.0000 & w_{02} &= 0.0000 \\
w_{11} &= 0.7500 & w_{12} &= 0.2500 \\
w_{21} &= 0.5000 & w_{22} &= 0.3750 \\
w_{31} &= 0.2813 & w_{32} &= 0.4063 \\
w_{41} &= 0.1094 & w_{42} &= 0.3750
\end{aligned}$$

The global error of w_{41} is $|y_1(1) - w_{41}| \approx 0.0894$, and of w_{42} is $|y_2(1) - w_{42}| \approx 0.0654$.

1 (c) The Euler's Method formulas are

$$w_{i+1,1} = w_{i1} + h(-w_{i2}) \qquad \text{and} \qquad w_{i+1,2} = w_{i2} + h(w_{i1}).$$

The approximate solutions are

$$\begin{aligned}
w_{01} &= 1.0000 & w_{02} &= 0.0000 \\
w_{11} &= 1.0000 & w_{12} &= 0.2500 \\
w_{21} &= 0.9375 & w_{22} &= 0.5000 \\
w_{31} &= 0.8125 & w_{32} &= 0.7344 \\
w_{41} &= 0.6289 & w_{42} &= 0.9375
\end{aligned}$$

The global error of w_{41} is $|y_1(1) - w_{41}| \approx 0.0886$, and of w_{42} is $|y_2(1) - w_{42}| \approx 0.0960$.

1 (d) The Euler's Method formulas are

$$w_{i+1,1} = w_{i1} + h(w_{i1} + 3w_{i2}) \qquad \text{and} \qquad w_{i+1,2} = w_{i2} + h(2w_{i1} + 2w_{i2}).$$

The approximate solutions are

$$w_{01} = 5.0000 \quad w_{02} = 0.0000$$
$$w_{11} = 6.2500 \quad w_{12} = 2.5000$$
$$w_{21} = 9.6875 \quad w_{22} = 6.8750$$
$$w_{31} = 17.2656 \quad w_{32} = 15.1563$$
$$w_{41} = 32.9492 \quad w_{42} = 31.3672$$

The global error of w_{41} is $|y_1(1) - w_{41}| \approx 77.3507$, and of w_{42} is $|y_2(1) - w_{42}| \approx 77.0934$.

3 (a)   Set $y_1(t) = y(t)$ and $y_2(t) = y'(t)$. Then by differentiating the latter, $y_2'(t) = y''(t) = ty_1$ from the differential equation, and $y_1'(t) = y_2$ by definition. Therefore the first-order system equivalent to Airy's equation is $y_1' = y_2, y_2' = ty_1$.

3 (b)   Set $y_1(t) = y(t)$ and $y_2(t) = y'(t)$. Then by differentiating the latter, $y_2'(t) = y''(t) = 2ty_1'(t) - 2y_1(t)$ from the differential equation. The equivalent first order system is $y_1' = y_2, y_2' = 2ty_2 - 2y_1$.

3 (c)   Set $y_1(t) = y(t)$ and $y_2(t) = y'(t)$. Then by differentiating the latter, $y_2'(t) = y''(t) = ty_1'(t) + y_1(t)$ from the differential equation. The equivalent first order system is $y_1' = y_2, y_2' = ty_2 + y_1$.

5 (a)   Since $y'(t) = (e^t - e^{-t} - 2t)/2$ and $y'''(t) = (e^t - e^{-t})/2$, it follows that $y''' - y' = t$. The initial conditions $y(0) = y'(0) = y''(0) = 0$ are easily checked.

5 (b)   Set $y_1 = y, y_2 = y', y_3 = y''$. Then $y_3' = y''' = y' + t = y_2 + t$, so the equivalent first-order system is $y_1' = y_2, y_2' = y_3, y_3' = t + y_2$.

5 (c)   Euler's Method generates w_{i1}, w_{i2} and $w_{i3}, i = 1, 2, 3, 4$, to approximate y_1, y_2 and y_3, respectively. The formulas are

$$w_{i+1,1} = w_{i1} + hw_{i2} \quad w_{i+1,2} = w_{i2} + hw_{i3} \quad w_{i+1,3} = w_{i3} + h(t_i + w_{i2}).$$

Starting with the initial conditions $w_{01} = w_{02} = w_{03} = 0$, the approximate solutions are

$$w_{01} = 0 \qquad\qquad w_{02} = 0 \qquad\qquad w_{03} = 0$$

$$w_{11} = 0 + \tfrac{1}{4}(0) = 0 \qquad w_{12} = 0 + \tfrac{1}{4}(0) = 0 \qquad w_{13} = 0 + \tfrac{1}{4}(0 + 0) = 0$$

$$w_{21} = 0 + \tfrac{1}{4}(0) = 0 \qquad w_{22} = 0 + \tfrac{1}{4}(0) = 0 \qquad w_{23} = 0 + \tfrac{1}{4}(\tfrac{1}{4} + 0) = \tfrac{1}{16}$$

$$w_{31} = 0 + \tfrac{1}{4}(0) = 0 \qquad w_{32} = 0 + \tfrac{1}{4}(\tfrac{1}{16}) = \tfrac{1}{64} \quad w_{33} = \tfrac{1}{16} + \tfrac{1}{4}(\tfrac{1}{2} + 0) = \tfrac{3}{16}$$

$$w_{41} = 0 + \tfrac{1}{4}(\tfrac{1}{64}) = \tfrac{1}{256} \quad w_{42} = \tfrac{1}{64} + \tfrac{1}{4}\tfrac{3}{16} = \tfrac{1}{16} \quad w_{43} = \tfrac{3}{16} + \tfrac{1}{4}(\tfrac{3}{4} + \tfrac{1}{64}) = \tfrac{97}{256}$$

The solution $y(t)$ is approximated by w_{i1}, so $y(1) \approx w_{41} = 1/256 \approx 0.0039$.

5 (d)   The global truncation error is $|y(1) - w_{41}| = |(e + e^{-1} - 1)/2 - 1 - 1/256| \approx 0.0392$.

COMPUTER PROBLEMS 6.3

1 (a)   The MATLAB code `euler2` in Program 6.2 can be used to calculate the two approximations, for step sizes $h = 0.1$ and $h = 0.01$. For $h = 0.1$, the global truncation errors are $[0.1973, 0.1592]$ for w_{n1} and w_{n2}, $n = 10$. For $h = 0.01$, the global truncation errors are $[0.0226, 0.0149]$ for w_{n1} and w_{n2}, $n = 100$. The errors decrease by roughly a factor of 10 for the smaller step size, as expected for a first order method. The plots of the two approximations and the correct solution (dashed) are below.

1 (b)   Similar to (a). The global truncation errors are $[0.0328, 0.0219]$ for step size $h = 0.1$, and $[0.0031, 0.0020]$ for $h = 0.01$.

1 (c)   Similar to (a). The global truncation errors are $[0.0305, 0.0410]$ for step size $h = 0.1$, and $[0.0027, 0.0042]$ for $h = 0.01$.

1 (d)   Similar to (a). The global truncation errors are $[51.4030, 51.3070]$ for step size $h = 0.1$, and $[8.1919, 8.1827]$ for $h = 0.01$.

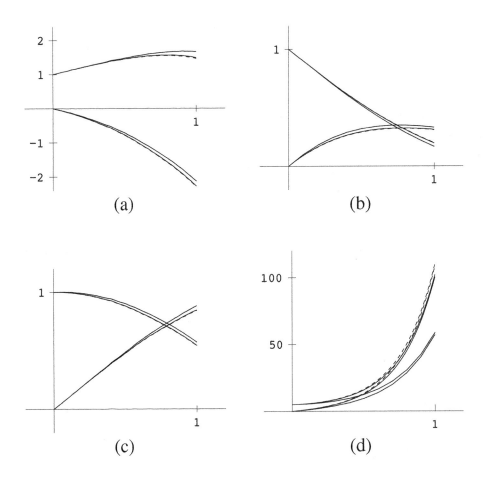

(a)   (b)

(c)   (d)

3   To modify `pend` to exhibit damping, add the term $-dy_2$ to the y_2' equation in the `ydot` function, where $d = 0.1$. All initial conditions lead toward the straight-down position of the pendulum, except for the straight-up position $y_1(0) = \pi, y_2(0) = 0$. In theory, this position is an unstable steady-state, meaning that it will never move unless there is a small outside perturbation. For a physical pendulum, small perturbations will occur, and the pendulum will fall from the up position. The outcome of the simulation with pend depends on the step size and the fact that in current versions of MATLAB , $\sin \pi$ is not exactly zero. It differs on the order of machine epsilon, providing the perturbation needed, at least when step size $h = 0.05$ is used, to cause the pendulum to fall and eventually move to the straight-down position as a physical pendulum would.

5 To modify pend to exhibit periodic forcing and damping, add the term $-dy_2 + A \sin t$ to the y_2' equation in the ydot function, where $d = 1$ and $A = 12$. After waiting for transient effects to die down, the pendulum will settle into one of two stable trajectories. One of them makes three and one-half clockwise revolutions followed by two and one-half counterclockwise revolutions, and repeats. The other does the same, replacing clockwise with counterclockwise. For example, the initial condition $(y_1, y_2) = (0.2, 0)$ settles into the first motion, and the initial condition $(y_1, y_2) = (0.15, 0)$ converges to the second.

7 The ydot function in pend.m must be modified to solve the system

$$\begin{aligned} y_1' &= y_2 \\ y_2' &= (-\frac{g}{l} + A \cos 2\pi t) \sin y_1 - dy_2 \end{aligned}$$

where $g = 9.81, l = 2.5$. Starting with an initial position that is close to, but not exactly, zero (for example, $(y_1, y_2) = (0.01, 0)$), one finds that for A above 14.7, the downward position is unstable as defined in the Computer Problem, in that the pendulum travels through the upward position.

9 To adjust orbit.m to solve the two-body problem, we must change the stationary sun into a moving body. Eliminate the line

```
sun=line('color','y','Marker','.','markersize',25,...
  'xdata',0,'ydata',0);
```

and replace with

```
head2=line('color','g','Marker','.','markersize',25,...
  'erase','xor','xdata',[],'ydata',[]);
tail2=line('color','b','LineStyle','-','erase','none',...
  'xdata',[],'ydata',[]);
```

Two new set commands must be added, one each for head2 and tail2. Notice that y is now an eight-dimensional vector, requiring additions to the initial conditions and to the differential equation. The formulas of type (6.45) should be added to ydot:

```
function z = ydot(t,x)
m2=0.3;g=1;mg2=m2*g;m1=0.03;mg1=m1*g;
px1=x(1);py1=x(3);vx1=x(2);vy1=x(4);
px2=x(5);py2=x(7);vx2=x(6);vy2=x(8);
dist=sqrt((px2-px1)^2+(py2-py1)^2);
z=zeros(1,8);
z(1)=vx1;
z(2)=(mg2*(px2-px1))/(dist^3);
z(3)=vy1;
z(4)=(mg2*(py2-py1))/(dist^3);
z(5)=vx2;
z(6)=(mg1*(px1-px2))/(dist^3);
z(7)=vy2;
z(8)=(mg1*(py1-py2))/(dist^3);
```

EXERCISES 6.4   Runge-Kutta Methods and Applications

1 (a)   The Midpoint Method is

$$w_{i+1} = w_i + hf(t_i + \frac{h}{2}, w_i + \frac{h}{2}f(t_i, w_i)).$$

Applied to the differential equation $y' = f(t, y) = t$, the method is $w_{i+1} = w_i + h(t_i + \frac{h}{2})$.
With $y(0) = 1$ and $h = 1/4$, we calculate

$$
\begin{aligned}
w_0 &= y(0) = 1 \\
w_1 &= 1 + \frac{1}{4} \cdot \frac{1}{8} = \frac{33}{32} \\
w_2 &= \frac{33}{32} + \frac{1}{4} \cdot \frac{3}{8} = \frac{9}{8} \\
w_3 &= \frac{9}{8} + \frac{1}{4} \cdot \frac{5}{8} = \frac{41}{32} \\
w_4 &= \frac{41}{32} + \frac{1}{4} \cdot \frac{7}{8} = \frac{3}{2}
\end{aligned}
$$

Global error at $t = 1$ is 0.

1 (b)   The Midpoint Method applied to $y' = f(t, y) = t^2 y$ is

$$w_{i+1} = w_i + h(t_i + \frac{1}{8})^2(w_i + \frac{1}{8}t_i^2 w_i).$$

Starting with $y(0) = 1$ we calculate

t_i	w_i
0	1.0000
1/4	1.0039
1/2	1.0395
3/4	1.1442
1	1.3786

Global error at $t = 1$ is 0.0171.

1 (c)   The Midpoint Method applied to $y' = f(t, y) = 2(t + 1)y$ is

$$w_{i+1} = w_i + h2(t_i + \frac{1}{8} + 1)(w_i + \frac{1}{8}2(t_i + 1)w_i).$$

t_i	w_i
0	1.0000
1/4	1.7031
1/2	3.2399
3/4	6.8595
1	16.1038

Global error at $t = 1$ is 3.9817.

1 (d)   The Midpoint Method applied to $y' = f(t, y) = 5t^4 y$ is

$$w_{i+1} = w_i + h5(t_i + \frac{1}{8})^4(w_i + \frac{1}{8}5t_i^4 w_i).$$

t_i	w_i
0	1.0000
1/4	1.0003
1/2	1.0251
3/4	1.2283
1	2.3062

Global error at $t = 1$ is 0.4121.

1 (e)   The Midpoint Method applied to $y' = f(t, y) = 1/y^2$ is $w_{i+1} = w_i + \dfrac{h}{(w_i + \frac{1}{8}\frac{1}{w_i^2})^2}$.

t_i	w_i
0	1.0000
1/4	1.1975
1/2	1.3490
3/4	1.4734
1	1.5801

Global error at $t = 1$ is 0.0073.

1 (f) The Midpoint Method applied to $y' = f(t, y) = t^3/y^2$ is $w_{i+1} = w_i + h\dfrac{(t_i + \frac{1}{8})^3}{(w_i + \frac{1}{8}\frac{t_i^3}{w_i^2})}$.

t_i	w_i
0	1.0000
1/4	1.0005
1/2	1.0136
3/4	1.0713
1	1.2055

Global error at $t = 1$ is 0.0004.

3 (a) The fourth-order Runge-Kutta Method applied to the differential equation $y' = f(t, y) = t$ yields

$$
\begin{aligned}
w_0 &= y(0) = 1 \\
s_1 &= f(t_0, w_0) = t_0 = 0 \\
s_2 &= f(t_0 + h/2, w_0 + hs_1/2) = 1/8 \\
s_3 &= f(t_0 + h/2, w_0 + hs_2/2) = 1/8 \\
s_4 &= f(t_0 + h, w_0 + hs_3) = 1/4
\end{aligned}
$$

$$
\begin{aligned}
w_1 &= w_0 + \frac{h}{6}(s_1 + 2s_2 + 2s_3 + s_4) = 1 + \frac{1}{24}(0 + \frac{1}{4} + \frac{1}{4} + \frac{1}{4}) = \frac{33}{32} \\
w_2 &= 1.1250 \\
w_3 &= 1.2813 \\
w_4 &= 1.5000
\end{aligned}
$$

Global error at $t = 1$ is 0.

3 (b) RK4 applied to $y' = f(t, y) = t^2 y$ yields

$$
\begin{aligned}
w_0 &= y(0) = 1 \\
s_1 &= f(t_0, w_0) = t_0^2 w_0 = 0 \\
s_2 &= f(t_0 + h/2, w_0 + hs_1/2) = (\frac{1}{8})^2(1) = \frac{1}{64} \\
s_3 &= f(t_0 + h/2, w_0 + hs_2/2) = (\frac{1}{8})^2(1 + \frac{1}{4}\frac{1}{128}) = \frac{513}{2^{15}} \approx 0.0157 \\
s_4 &= f(t_0 + h, w_0 + hs_3) = (\frac{1}{4})^2(1 + \frac{1}{4}\frac{513}{2^{15}}) \approx 0.0627
\end{aligned}
$$

$$w_1 = w_0 + \frac{h}{6}(s_1 + 2s_2 + 2s_3 + s_4) \approx 1.0052$$
$$w_2 = 1.0425$$
$$w_3 = 1.1510$$
$$w_4 = 1.3956$$

Global error at $t = 1$ is 1.2476×10^{-5}.

3 (c) RK4 applied to $y' = f(t, y) = 2(t + 1)y$ gives

t_i	w_i
0	1.0000
1/4	1.7545
1/2	3.4865
3/4	7.8448
1	19.975

Global error at $t = 1$ is 0.11007.

3 (d) RK4 applied to $y' = f(t, y) = 5t^4 y$ yields

t_i	w_i
0	1.0000
1/4	1.0010
1/2	1.0318
3/4	1.2678
1	2.7103

Global error at $t = 1$ is 7.9505×10^{-3}.

3 (e) RK4 applied to $y' = f(t, y) = 1/y^2$ gives

t_i	w_i
0	1.0000
1/4	1.2051
1/2	1.3573
3/4	1.4813
1	1.5874

Global error at $t = 1$ is 4.1996×10^{-5}.

3 (f) RK4 applied to $y' = f(t, y) = t^3/y^2$ gives

t_i	w_i
0	1.0000
1/4	1.0010
1/2	1.0154
3/4	1.0736
1	1.2051

Global error at $t = 1$ is 6.0464×10^{-5}.

5 To compute the local truncation error of the ODE solver (6.49), assume that $w_i = y_i$ and calculate $y_{i+1} - w_{i+1}$. Using the Taylor expansion,

$$
\begin{aligned}
w_{i+1} &= y_i + h(1 - \tfrac{1}{2\alpha})f(t_i, y_i) + \tfrac{h}{2\alpha}f(t_i + \alpha h, y_i + \alpha h f(t_i, y_i)) \\
&= y_i + h(\tfrac{2\alpha-1}{2\alpha})f(t_i, y_i) + \tfrac{h}{2\alpha}[f(t_i, y_i) + \alpha h f_t(t_i, y_i) + \alpha h f(t_i, y_i)f_y(t_i, y_i) + O(h^2)] \\
&= y_i + hf(t_i, y_i) + \tfrac{1}{2}h^2[f_t(t_i, y_i) + f(t_i, y_i)f_y(t_i, y_i)] + O(h^3)
\end{aligned}
$$

Comparing with (6.47), we conclude that $y_{i+1} - w_{i+1} = O(h^3)$. Therefore Theorem 6.4 implies that (6.49) is an order two ODE solver.

7 Assume that $f(t, y) = f(t)$ does not depend on y. Using the Runge-Kutta order four formula, $s_1 = f(t_i)$, and $s_2 = s_3 = f(t_i + h/2)$. Also, $s_4 = f(t_i + h)$, so that

$$
w_{i+1} = w_i + \frac{h}{6}[s_1 + 2s_2 + 2s_3 + s_4] = w_i + \frac{h}{6}[f(t_i) + 4f(t_i + h/2) + f(t_i + h)]
$$

which increments the solution with Simpson's Rule on the interval $[t_i, t_i + h]$.

COMPUTER PROBLEMS 6.4

1 The Midpoint Rule is run with interval $[0, 1]$ and step size $h = 0.1$. The resulting approximations are

(a)

t_i	w_i	error
0.0	1.0000	0
0.1	1.0050	0
0.2	1.0200	0
0.3	1.0450	0
0.4	1.0800	0
0.5	1.1250	0
0.6	1.1800	0
0.7	1.2450	0
0.8	1.3200	0
0.9	1.4050	0
1.0	1.5000	0

(b)

t_i	w_i	error
0.0	1.0000	0.0000
0.1	1.0003	0.0001
0.2	1.0025	0.0002
0.3	1.0088	0.0003
0.4	1.0212	0.0004
0.5	1.0420	0.0005
0.6	1.0740	0.0007
0.7	1.1201	0.0010
0.8	1.1847	0.0014
0.9	1.2730	0.0020
1.0	1.3926	0.0030

(c)

t_i	w_i	error
0.0	1.0000	0.0000
0.1	1.2310	0.0027
0.2	1.5453	0.0074
0.3	1.9780	0.0158
0.4	2.5814	0.0303
0.5	3.4348	0.0555
0.6	4.6594	0.0995
0.7	6.4430	0.1764
0.8	9.0814	0.3120
0.9	13.0463	0.5528
1.0	19.1011	0.9845

	t_i	w_i	error		t_i	w_i	error		t_i	w_i	error
	0.0	1.0000	0.0000		0.0	1.0000	0.0000		0.0	1.0000	0.0000
	0.1	1.0000	0.0000		0.1	1.0907	0.0007		0.1	1.0000	0.0000
	0.2	1.0003	0.0001		0.2	1.1686	0.0010		0.2	1.0003	0.0000
	0.3	1.0022	0.0002		0.3	1.2375	0.0011		0.3	1.0019	0.0001
(d)	0.4	1.0097	0.0005	(e)	0.4	1.2995	0.0011	(f)	0.4	1.0062	0.0002
	0.5	1.0306	0.0012		0.5	1.3561	0.0011		0.5	1.0151	0.0003
	0.6	1.0785	0.0024		0.6	1.4083	0.0011		0.6	1.0311	0.0003
	0.7	1.1778	0.0052		0.7	1.4570	0.0011		0.7	1.0564	0.0003
	0.8	1.3754	0.0124		0.8	1.5026	0.0011		0.8	1.0931	0.0003
	0.9	1.7711	0.0338		0.9	1.5456	0.0010		0.9	1.1426	0.0001
	1.0	2.6107	0.1076		1.0	1.5864	0.0010		1.0	1.2051	0.0001

3 Solving the equations with order four Runge Kutta for the three step sizes $h = 0.1, 0.05$ and 0.025 are shown below:

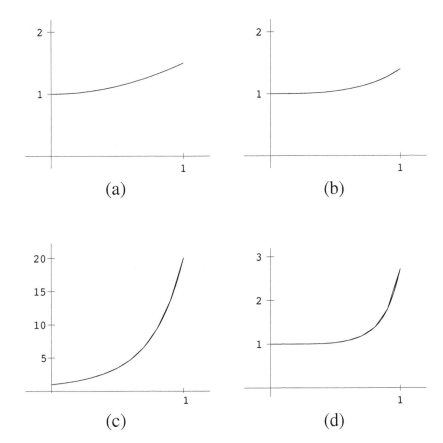

(a)

(b)

(c)

(d)

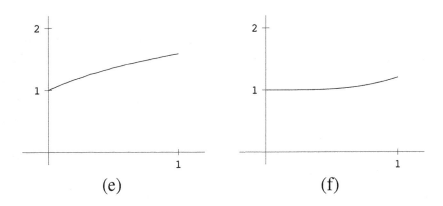

(e)   (f)

5 Runge-Kutta order 4 output with initial conditions (a) $y_0 = 0$ and (b) $y_0 = 1/2$. The correct solution from Exercise 6.1.7 is added (thicker curve). In (a), the approximate solution is covered by the exact solution.

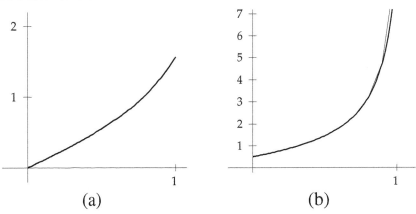

(a)   (b)

9 The fourth order Runge Kutta method approximates equation (a) without error. Applying RK4 to the other IVPs in Exercise 6.4.1 gives errors as shown below.

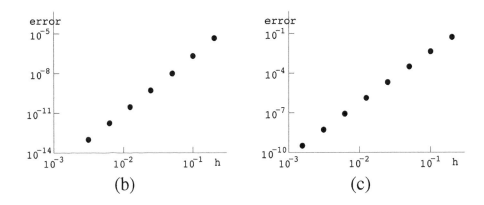

(b)   (c)

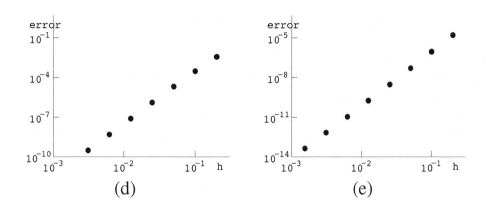

(d)   (e)

11 The `ydot` function for the Lorenz system on page 326 can be used with the order four Runge Kutta code to plot the attractor with initial condition $(x_0, y_0, z_0) = (5, 5, 5)$. The `orbit` program can be adapted by changing from four to three initial conditions, eliminating the sun, and changing the axis limits. Plotting the x and z coordinates of the Lorenz system gives the plot below.

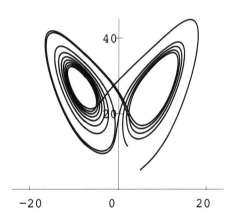

13 As an example we follow two trajectories of the Lorenz equations, one with initial condition $(x, y, z) = (5, 5, 5)$ and the other with initial condition $(5.00001, 5, 5)$. The x-coordinate is plotted as a function of time below, the former as a solid curve and the latter as a dashed curve. They agree on the symbol sequence 100000000110111001010 during the first 15 time units, and then disagree.

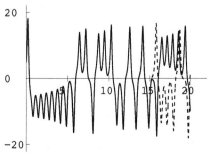

COMPUTER PROBLEMS 6.5　Variable Step-Size Methods

1　The MATLAB program should compute at each step the estimated error e_i (from s_1, s_2, s_3) and check the relative tolerance $e_i <$ TOL$|w_i|$. If satisfied, update $t_{i+1} = t_i + h$ and $w_{i+1} = w_i + z$, update the step size from (6.57), and start the next step. If not satisfied, revise the step size using (6.57), and repeat the current step. To stop the approximation exactly at the end of the time interval $[0, 1]$, after computing the step size h, replace it with $\min\{h, 1 - t_i\}$. The number of steps and maximum step size is as follows:

	steps	max step size
(a)	1	1.000000
(b)	280	0.011245
(c)	1116	0.001057
(d)	751	0.001978
(e)	144	0.012470
(f)	416	0.002711

3　The logic of the program is identical to Computer Problem 1, but using the Runge Kutta Fehlberg formulas. The number of steps and the maximum step size h needed are given below.

	steps	max step size
(a)	1	1.000000
(b)	11	0.111363
(c)	39	0.033592
(d)	36	0.036331
(e)	9	0.183837
(f)	13	0.113143

5　Similar to Computer Problem 3, except that the solution is a two-dimensional vector function of time. Using the Runge Kutta Fehlberg formulas, the number of steps and the maximum step size h needed are given below.

	steps	max step size
(a)	7	0.149366
(b)	8	0.135138
(c)	6	0.191209
(d)	19	0.068005

EXERCISES 6.6　Implicit Methods and Stiff Equations

1 (a)　The Backward Euler method applied to $y' = t + y$ is

$$w_{i+1} = w_i + hf(t_{i+1}, w_{i+1}) = w_i + h(t_{i+1} + w_{i+1}),$$

which can be simplified to

$$w_{i+1} = \frac{w_i + ht_{i+1}}{1 - h} = \frac{4w_i + t_{i+1}}{3}$$

for step size $h = 1/4$. In this explicit formulation, we compute

$$
\begin{aligned}
w_0 &= y_0 = 0 \\
w_1 &= \frac{4w_0 + t_1}{3} = \frac{1}{12} \approx 0.0833 \\
w_2 &= \frac{4w_1 + t_2}{3} = \frac{\frac{1}{3} + \frac{1}{2}}{3} = \frac{5}{18} \approx 0.2778 \\
w_3 &= \frac{4w_2 + t_3}{3} = \frac{\frac{10}{9} + \frac{3}{4}}{3} = \frac{67}{108} \approx 0.6204 \\
w_4 &= \frac{4w_3 + t_4}{3} = \frac{\frac{67}{27} + 1}{3} = \frac{94}{81} \approx 1.1605
\end{aligned}
$$

The correct solution at $t = 1$ is $e - 2$. The global error is 0.4422.

1 (b) The Backward Euler method applied to $y' = t - y$ is

$$w_{i+1} = w_i + hf(t_{i+1}, w_{i+1}) = w_i + h(t_{i+1} - w_{i+1}),$$

which can be simplified to

$$w_{i+1} = \frac{4w_i + t_{i+1}}{5}$$

for step size $h = 1/4$. We compute

$$
\begin{aligned}
w_0 &= y_0 = 0 \\
w_1 &= \frac{4w_0 + t_1}{5} = 0.05 \\
w_2 &= \frac{4w_1 + t_2}{5} = 0.14 \\
w_3 &= \frac{4w_2 + t_3}{5} = 0.262 \\
w_4 &= \frac{4w_3 + t_4}{5} = 0.4096
\end{aligned}
$$

The global error is 0.0417.

1 (c) The Backward Euler method applied to $y' = 4t - 2y$ is

$$w_{i+1} = w_i + hf(t_{i+1}, w_{i+1}) = w_i + h(4t_{i+1} - 2w_{i+1}),$$

which can be simplified to

$$w_{i+1} = \frac{2w_i + 2t_{i+1}}{3}$$

for step size $h = 1/4$. We compute

$$
\begin{aligned}
w_0 &= y_0 = 0 \\
w_1 &= \frac{2w_0 + 2t_1}{3} = \frac{1}{6} \\
w_2 &= \frac{2w_1 + 2t_2}{3} = \frac{4}{9} \\
w_3 &= \frac{2w_2 + 2t_3}{3} = \frac{43}{54} \\
w_4 &= \frac{2w_3 + 2t_4}{3} = \frac{97}{81}
\end{aligned}
$$

The global error is 0.0622.

3 The Backward Euler method for $y' = 10(1 - y)$ gives $w_{i+1} = (w_i + 10h)/(1 + 10h)$. This is the Fixed Point Iteration for the equation $w = g(w) = (w + 10h)/(1 + 10h)$ for a fixed h. Check that $w = 1$ is a fixed point, and $|g'(1)| = 1/(1 + 10h) < 1$ for any step size $h > 0$, implying that w_i tends to 1 as $i \to \infty$ as required.

COMPUTER PROBLEMS 6.6

1 (a) The differential equation has equilibrium solutions, corresponding to $0 = f(t, y) = y^2 - y^3$, at $y = 0$ and 1. The Backward Euler method applied to the equation is

$$w_{i+1} = w_i + h(w_{i+1}^2 - w_{i+1}^3).$$

To solve for w_{i+1} at each step, we use the Newton's Method iteration

$$
\begin{aligned}
z_0 &= w_i \\
z_{j+1} &= z_j - \frac{z_j - w_i - hz_j^2 + hz_j^3}{1 - 2hz_j + 3hz_j^2},
\end{aligned}
$$

setting w_{i+1} to be the last z_j. The Euler method roughly approaches the equilibrium at $y = 1$ for step sizes $h \leq 1.8$. For $h = 2.5$, the results of Backward Euler (solid curve) and Euler (dashed curve) are directly compared in the plots below.

1 (b) Similar to (a). The equilibrium solutions are $y = 0$ and 1. The Backward Euler method gives

$$w_{i+1} = w_i + 6h(w_{i+1} - w_{i+1}^2).$$

The Newton iteration is

$$z_0 = w_i$$

$$z_{j+1} = z_j - \frac{z_j - w_i - 6hz_j + 6hz_j^2}{1 - 6h + 12hz_j}.$$

The Euler method roughly approaches the equilibrium at $y = 1$ for step sizes $h \leq 1/3$. For $h = 1/2$, the results of Backward Euler (solid curve) and Euler (dashed curve) are directly compared in the plot.

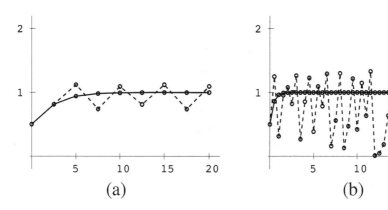

(a)   (b)

EXERCISES 6.7   Multistep Methods

1 (a) Using the Explicit Trapezoid Method with $y(0) = 1$ and $h = 1/4$, we calculate

$$w_1 = w_0 + \frac{h}{2}[f(t_0, w_0) + f(t_0 + h, w_0 + hf(t_0, w_0))]$$

$$= 1 + \frac{1}{8}[t_0 + t_1] = 1 + \frac{1}{8}\left[\frac{1}{4}\right] = \frac{33}{32}.$$

For the remainder of the steps, we apply the Adams-Bashforth Two-Step Method, which is

$$w_{i+1} = w_i + h\left[\frac{3}{2}f(t_i, w_i) - \frac{1}{2}f(t_{i-1}, w_{i-1})\right] = w_i + h\left[\frac{3}{2}t_i - \frac{1}{2}t_{i-1}\right].$$

Therefore

$$w_2 = \frac{33}{32} + \frac{1}{4}\left[\frac{3}{2} \cdot \frac{1}{4}\right] = \frac{9}{8}$$

$$w_3 = \frac{9}{8} + \frac{1}{4}\left[\frac{3}{2} \cdot \frac{1}{2} - \frac{1}{2} \cdot \frac{1}{4}\right] = \frac{41}{32}$$

$$w_4 = \frac{41}{32} + \frac{1}{4}\left[\frac{3}{2} \cdot \frac{3}{4} - \frac{1}{2} \cdot \frac{1}{2}\right] = \frac{3}{2}$$

Global error at $t = 1$ is 0.

1 (b)　Using the Explicit Trapezoid Method with $y(0) = 1$ and $h = 1/4$, we calculate $w_1 \approx 1.0078$, as in Exercise 6.2.1(b). The Adams-Bashforth Two-Step Method is

$$
\begin{aligned}
w_{i+1} &= w_i + h[\frac{3}{2}f(t_i, w_i) - \frac{1}{2}f(t_{i-1}, w_{i-1})] \\
&= w_i + h\left[\frac{3}{2}t_i^2 w_i - \frac{1}{2}t_{i-1}^2 w_{i-1}\right].
\end{aligned}
$$

Completing the last three steps results in the following table:

t_i	w_i
0	1.0000
1/4	1.0078
1/2	1.0314
3/4	1.1203
1	1.3243

Global error at $t = 1$ is 0.0713.

1 (c)　The Explicit Trapezoid Method gives $w_1 \approx 1.7188$. The Adams-Bashforth Two-Step Method for the equation is

$$
\begin{aligned}
w_{i+1} &= w_i + h[\frac{3}{2}f(t_i, w_i) - \frac{1}{2}f(t_{i-1}, w_{i-1})] \\
&= w_i + h\left[\frac{3}{2}2(t_i + 1)w_i - \frac{1}{2}2(t_{i-1} + 1)w_{i-1}\right].
\end{aligned}
$$

The Adams-Bashforth approximation is

t_i	w_i
0	1.0000
1/4	1.7188
1/2	3.0801
3/4	6.0081
1	12.7386

Global error at $t = 1$ is 7.3469.

1 (d)　The Explicit Trapezoid Method gives $w_1 \approx 1.0024$. The Adams-Bashforth Two-Step Method for the equation is

$$
\begin{aligned}
w_{i+1} &= w_i + h[\frac{3}{2}f(t_i, w_i) - \frac{1}{2}f(t_{i-1}, w_{i-1})] \\
&= w_i + h\left[\frac{3}{2}5t_i^4 w_i - \frac{1}{2}5t_{i-1}^4 w_{i-1}\right].
\end{aligned}
$$

The Adams-Bashforth approximation is

t_i	w_i
0	1.0000
1/4	1.0024
1/2	1.0098
3/4	1.1257
1	1.7540

Global error at $t = 1$ is 0.9642.

1 (e)   The Explicit Trapezoid Method gives $w_1 \approx 1.2050$. The Adams-Bashforth Two-Step Method for the equation is

$$
\begin{aligned}
w_{i+1} &= w_i + h[\frac{3}{2}f(t_i, w_i) - \frac{1}{2}f(t_{i-1}, w_{i-1})] \\
&= w_i + h\left[\frac{3}{2}\frac{1}{w_i^2} - \frac{1}{2}\frac{1}{w_{i-1}^2}\right].
\end{aligned}
$$

The Adams-Bashforth approximation is

t_i	w_i
0	1.0000
1/4	1.2050
1/2	1.3383
3/4	1.4616
1	1.5673

Global error at $t = 1$ is 0.0201.

1 (f)   The Explicit Trapezoid Method gives $w_1 \approx 1.0020$. The Adams-Bashforth Two-Step Method for the equation is

$$
w_{i+1} = w_i + h[\frac{3}{2}f(t_i, w_i) - \frac{1}{2}f(t_{i-1}, w_{i-1})] = w_i + h\left[\frac{3}{2}\frac{t_i^3}{w_i^2} - \frac{1}{2}\frac{t_{i-1}^3}{w_{i-1}^2}\right].
$$

The Adams-Bashforth approximation is

t_i	w_i
0	1.0000
1/4	1.0020
1/2	1.0078
3/4	1.0520
1	1.1796

Global error at $t = 1$ is 0.0255.

3 The local truncation error of a two-step explicit method is

$$\frac{4+a_1}{12}h^3 y_i''' + O(h^4)$$

according to (6.79). Setting $a_1 = -4$ makes the local truncation error of order four, and the resulting method of order three. From (6.78), we calculate $a_2 = 5, b_1 = 4, b_2 = 2$. Referring to the definition (6.74), the third-order two-step explicit method is

$$w_{i+1} = -4w_i + 5w_{i-1} + h[4f_i + 2f_{i-1}].$$

Stability is checked from the roots of the polynomial

$$P(x) = x^2 - a_1 x - a_2 = x^2 + 4x - 5 = (x+5)(x-1).$$

The root -5 causes the method to fail Definition 6.6 of stability.

5 From (6.75) and (6.76), we need to check the requirements

$$
\begin{aligned}
a_1 + a_2 &= 1 \\
b_0 + b_1 + b_2 - a_2 &= 1 \\
a_2 - 2b_2 + 2b_0 &= 1
\end{aligned}
$$

If so, then the local truncation error is $O(h^3)$ and the method is second order. For the Implicit Trapezoidal Method (6.89), $a_1 = 1, a_2 = 0, b_0 = 1/2, b_1 = 1/2, b_2 = 0$, and it is easy to check that the requirements are satisfied.

7 (a) The second-order two-step methods are those that satisfy (6.77). The characteristic polynomial is

$$P(x) = x^2 - a_1 x - a_2 = x^2 - a_1 x - (1 - a_1) = (x-1)(x+1-a_1).$$

The roots are 1 and $a_1 - 1$. The method is stable if $|a_1 - 1| \leq 1$ and $a_1 \neq 2$, true for $0 \leq a_1 < 2$. If $0 < a_1 < 2$, there is only one root of absolute value one, and the method is strongly stable.

7 (b) From Exercise 7(a), the method is weakly stable if $a_1 = 0$.

9 (a) The coefficients of the method are $a_1 = 3, a_2 = -2, b_0 = 13/12, b_1 = -5/3, b_2 = -5/12$. The first three equations of (6.91) are satisfied:

$$
\begin{aligned}
a_1 + a_2 &= 3 - 2 = 1 \\
-a_2 + b_0 + b_1 + b_2 &= 2 + \frac{13}{12} - \frac{5}{3} - \frac{5}{12} = 1 \\
a_2 + 2b_0 - 2b_2 &= -2 + \frac{13}{6} + \frac{5}{6} = 1,
\end{aligned}
$$

implying that the method is at least second-order. It will be third order if and only if it satisfies the fourth equation of (6.91):

$$-a_2 + 3b_0 + 3b_2 = 2 + \frac{13}{4} - \frac{5}{4} = 0 \neq 1.$$

Therefore the method is second order. The characteristic polynomial is

$$P(x) = x^2 - 3x + 2 = (x-2)(x-1).$$

Since there is a root of absolute value greater than 1, the method is unstable.

9 (b)   The coefficients are $a_1 = 4/3, a_2 = -1/3, b_0 = 2/3, b_1 = b_2 = 0$. The first three equations of (6.91) are satisfied but the fourth equation fails:

$$-a_2 + 3b_0 + 3b_2 = \frac{1}{3} + 2 \neq 1.$$

The method is second order. The characteristic polynomial is

$$P(x) = x^2 - \frac{4}{3}x + \frac{1}{3} = (x-1)(x - \frac{1}{3})$$

with all roots less than one in absolute value and only one root of absolute value one. Therefore the method is strongly stable.

9 (c)   The coefficients are $a_1 = 4/3, a_2 = -1/3, b_0 = b_1 = 4/9, b_2 = -2/9$. The first three equations of (6.91) are satisfied, and the fourth equation is satisfied as well:

$$-a_2 + 3b_0 + 3b_2 = \frac{1}{3} + \frac{4}{3} - \frac{2}{3} = 1.$$

Therefore the method is third order. The characteristic polynomial is

$$P(x) = x^2 - \frac{4}{3}x + \frac{1}{3} = (x-1)(x - \frac{1}{3}).$$

Since all roots are less than one in absolute value and only one root has absolute value one, the method is strongly stable.

9 (d)   The coefficients are $a_1 = 3, a_2 = -2, b_0 = 7/12, b_1 = -2/3, b_2 = -11/12$. The first three equations of (6.91) are satisfied, and the fourth equation is satisfied as well:

$$-a_2 + 3b_0 + 3b_2 = 2 + \frac{7}{4} - \frac{11}{4} = 1.$$

The method is third order, with characteristic polynomial $P(x) = x^2 - 3x + 2 = (x-1)(x-2)$. Because the roots are 1 and 2, the method is unstable.

9 (e)   The coefficients are $a_1 = 2, a_2 = -1, b_0 = 1/2, b_1 = 0, b_2 = -1/2$. The first three equations of (6.91) are satisfied, and the fourth equation is satisfied as well:

$$-a_2 + 3b_0 + 3b_2 = 1 + \frac{3}{2} - \frac{3}{2} = 1.$$

Therefore the method is third order. The characteristic polynomial is $P(x) = x^2 - 2x + 1 = (x-1)^2$. Because of the double root, the method is unstable.

11 A second-order implicit method must satisfy $b_0 \neq 0$ and the first two equations of (6.91), and fail to satisfy the third. The characteristic polynomial is

$$P(x) = x^2 - a_1 x - (1 - a_1) = (x-1)(x - (a_1 - 1))$$

with roots 1 and $a_1 - 1$. To be weakly stable, a_1 must be 0. If $a_1 = 0$, then $a_2 = 1$, and $b_0 + b_1 + b_2 = 2$. For example, $a_1 = 0, a_2 = 1, b_0 = 1, b_1 = -1, b_2 = 2$ satisfy the requirements.

13 (a) We mimic the development on pages 338-9. Assume that all previous w_i are correct, i.e. $w_i = y_i$ and $w_{i-1} = y_{i-1}$. Assume that $b_0 = 0$ for an explicit method. The differential equation says that $y_i' = f_i$, so that all terms can be expanded in a Taylor expansion as follows:

$$
\begin{aligned}
w_{i+1} &= a_1 w_i + a_2 w_{i-1} + a_3 w_{i-2} + h[b_0 f_{i+1} + b_1 f_i + b_2 f_{i-1} + b_3 f_{i-2}] \\
&= a_1 [y_i] \\
&\quad + a_2 [y_i - hy_i' + \tfrac{h^2}{2}y_i'' - \tfrac{h^3}{6}y_i''' + \tfrac{h^4}{24}y_i'''' - \ldots] \\
&\quad + a_3 [y_i - 2hy_i' + \tfrac{4h^2}{2}y_i'' - \tfrac{8h^3}{6}y_i''' + \tfrac{16h^4}{24}y_i'''' - \ldots] \\
&\quad + b_1 [\quad hy_i'] \\
&\quad + b_2 [\quad hy_i' - h^2 y_i'' + \tfrac{h^3}{2}y_i''' - \tfrac{h^4}{6}y_i'''' + \ldots] \\
&\quad + b_3 [\quad hy_i' - 2h^2 y_i'' + \tfrac{4h^3}{2}y_i''' - \tfrac{8h^4}{6}y_i'''' + \ldots]
\end{aligned}
$$

Adding up the terms gives

$$
\begin{aligned}
w_{i+1} &= (a_1 + a_2 + a_3)y_i \\
&\quad + (-a_2 - 2a_3 + b_1 + b_2 + b_3)hy_i' + (a_2 + 4a_3 - 2b_2 - 4b_3)\tfrac{h^2}{2}y_i'' \\
&\quad + (-a_2 - 8a_3 + 3b_2 + 12b_3)\tfrac{h^3}{6}y_i''' + (a_2 + 16a_3 - 4b_2 - 32b_3)\tfrac{h^4}{24}y_i'''' + \ldots
\end{aligned}
$$

By choosing the a_i and b_i appropriately, the local truncation error $y_{i+1} - w_{i+1}$, where

$$y_{i+1} = y_i + hy_i' + \frac{h^2}{2}y_i'' + \frac{h^3}{6}y_i''' + \ldots$$

can be made as small as possible. Matching terms up to a fourth order local truncation error yields the system

$$
\begin{aligned}
a_1 + a_2 + a_3 &= 1 \\
-a_2 - 2a_3 + b_1 + b_2 + b_3 &= 1 \\
a_2 + 4a_3 - 2b_2 - 4b_3 &= 1 \\
-a_2 - 8a_3 + 3b_2 + 12b_3 &= 1.
\end{aligned}
$$

A three-step explicit method is third order if and only if these equations hold.

13 (b)   For the Adams-Bashforth Three-Step Method, the coefficients are $a_1 = 1, a_2 = a_3 = 0, b_1 = 23/12, b_2 = -4/3, b_3 = 5/12$, which satisfy the four equations above.

13 (c)   The characteristic polynomial for the Adams-Bashforth Three-Step Method is

$$P(x) = x^3 - a_1 x^2 - a_2 x - a_3 = x^3 - x^2 = x^2(x - 1),$$

with a double root at 0 and a simple root at 1. The method is stable.

13 (d)   To make the method weakly stable, we could require $P(x) = x(x + 1)(x - 1) = x^3 - x$, or $a_1 = a_3 = 0$ and $a_2 = 1$. Then the first of the above four equations is satisfied, and the three remaining equations are

$$
\begin{aligned}
-1 + b_1 + b_2 + b_3 &= 1 \\
1 - 2b_2 - 4b_3 &= 1 \\
-1 + 3b_2 + 12b_3 &= 1.
\end{aligned}
$$

Solving the three equations yields $b_1 = 7/3, b_2 = -2/3$, and $b_3 = 1/3$. Therefore

$$w_{i+1} = w_{i-1} + h\left[\frac{7}{3} - \frac{2}{3}f_{i-1} + \frac{1}{3}f_{i-2}\right]$$

is a weakly stable third-order three-step method.

15 (a)   Similar to Exercise 13(a), except that b_0 is allowed to be nonzero. Assume that all previous w_i are correct, i.e. $w_i = y_i$ and $w_{i-1} = y_{i-1}$. The differential equation says that $y_i' = f_i$, so that all terms can be expanded in a Taylor expansion as follows:

$$
\begin{aligned}
w_{i+1} &= a_1 w_i + a_2 w_{i-1} + a_3 w_{i-2} + h[b_0 f_{i+1} + b_1 f_i + b_2 f_{i-1} + b_3 f_{i-2}] \\
&= a_1[y_i] \\
&\quad + a_2[y_i \quad - hy_i' \quad + \frac{h^2}{2}y_i'' \quad - \frac{h^3}{6}y_i''' \quad + \frac{h^4}{24}y_i'''' - \ldots] \\
&\quad + a_3[y_i \quad - 2hy_i' \quad + \frac{4h^2}{2}y_i'' \quad - \frac{8h^3}{6}y_i''' \quad + \frac{16h^4}{24}y_i'''' - \ldots] \\
&\quad + b_0[\qquad\quad hy_i' \quad + h^2 y_i'' \quad + \frac{h^3}{2}y_i''' \quad + \frac{h^4}{6}y_i'''' + \ldots] \\
&\quad + b_1[\qquad\quad hy_i'] \\
&\quad + b_2[\qquad\quad hy_i' \quad - h^2 y_i'' \quad + \frac{h^3}{2}y_i''' \quad - \frac{h^4}{6}y_i'''' + \ldots] \\
&\quad + b_3[\qquad\quad hy_i' \quad - 2h^2 y_i'' \quad + \frac{4h^3}{2}y_i''' \quad - \frac{8h^4}{6}y_i'''' + \ldots]
\end{aligned}
$$

Adding up the terms gives

$$
\begin{aligned}
w_{i+1} &= (a_1 + a_2 + a_3)y_i \\
&\quad + (-a_2 - 2a_3 + b_0 + b_1 + b_2 + b_3)hy_i' + (a_2 + 4a_3 + 2b_0 - 2b_2 - 4b_3)\frac{h^2}{2}y_i'' \\
&\quad + (-a_2 - 8a_3 + 3b_0 + 3b_2 + 12b_3)\frac{h^3}{6}y_i''' + (a_2 + 16a_3 + 4b_0 - 4b_2 - 32b_3)\frac{h^4}{24}y_i'''' \\
&\quad + \ldots
\end{aligned}
$$

By choosing the a_i and b_i appropriately, the local truncation error $y_{i+1} - w_{i+1}$, where

$$y_{i+1} = y_i + hy_i' + \frac{h^2}{2}y_i'' + \frac{h^3}{6}y_i''' + \frac{h^4}{24}y_i'''' + \dots$$

can be made as small as possible. Matching terms up to a fourth order local truncation error yields the system

$$
\begin{aligned}
a_1 + a_2 + a_3 &= 1 \\
-a_2 - 2a_3 + b_0 + b_1 + b_2 + b_3 &= 1 \\
a_2 + 4a_3 + 2b_0 - 2b_2 - 4b_3 &= 1 \\
-a_2 - 8a_3 + 3b_0 + 3b_2 + 12b_3 &= 1 \\
a_2 + 16a_3 + 4b_0 - 4b_2 - 32b_3 &= 1.
\end{aligned}
$$

A three-step implicit method is fourth order if and only if these equations hold.

15 (b)   For the Adams-Moulton Three-Step Method, the coefficients are $a_1 = 1, a_2 = a_3 = 0, b_0 = 9/24, b_1 = 19/24, b_2 = -5/24, b_3 = 1/24$, which satisfy the five equations above.

15 (c)   The characteristic polynomial for the Adams-Bashforth Three-Step Method is

$$P(x) = x^3 - a_1 x^2 - a_2 x - a_3 = x^3 - x^2 = x^2(x - 1),$$

with a double root at 0 and a simple root at 1. The method is stable.

COMPUTER PROBLEMS 6.7

1   The MATLAB program `exmultistep` is run with step size $h = 0.1$ and with the differential equation in `ydot`. The results are as follows.

	t_i	w_i	error		t_i	w_i	error		t_i	w_i	error
	0.0	1.0000	0		0.0	1.0000	0.0000		0.0	1.0000	0.0000
	0.1	1.0050	0		0.1	1.0005	0.0002		0.1	1.2320	0.0017
	0.2	1.0200	0		0.2	1.0020	0.0007		0.2	1.5386	0.0141
	0.3	1.0450	0		0.3	1.0075	0.0015		0.3	1.9569	0.0368
(a)	0.4	1.0800	0	**(b)**	0.4	1.0191	0.0025	**(c)**	0.4	2.5355	0.0762
	0.5	1.1250	0		0.5	1.0390	0.0035		0.5	3.3460	0.1443
	0.6	1.1800	0		0.6	1.0698	0.0048		0.6	4.4967	0.2621
	0.7	1.2450	0		0.7	1.1146	0.0065		0.7	6.1533	0.4661
	0.8	1.3200	0		0.8	1.1773	0.0088		0.8	8.5720	0.8214
	0.9	1.4050	0		0.9	1.2630	0.0121		0.9	12.1548	1.4443
	1.0	1.5000	0		1.0	1.3788	0.0168		1.0	17.5400	2.5455

(d)

t_i	w_i	error
0.0	1.0000	0.0000
0.1	1.0000	0.0000
0.2	1.0001	0.0002
0.3	1.0013	0.0012
0.4	1.0070	0.0033
0.5	1.0243	0.0075
0.6	1.0658	0.0150
0.7	1.1534	0.0296
0.8	1.3266	0.0611
0.9	1.6649	0.1400
1.0	2.3483	0.3700

(e)

t_i	w_i	error
0.0	1.0000	0.0000
0.1	1.0913	0.0001
0.2	1.1673	0.0023
0.3	1.2354	0.0032
0.4	1.2970	0.0036
0.5	1.3534	0.0038
0.6	1.4055	0.0039
0.7	1.4542	0.0039
0.8	1.4998	0.0039
0.9	1.5428	0.0038
1.0	1.5836	0.0038

(f)

t_i	w_i	error
0.0	1.0000	0.0000
0.1	1.0001	0.0000
0.2	1.0002	0.0002
0.3	1.0013	0.0007
0.4	1.0050	0.0014
0.5	1.0131	0.0022
0.6	1.0282	0.0032
0.7	1.0528	0.0039
0.8	1.0890	0.0044
0.9	1.1383	0.0044
1.0	1.2011	0.0040

3 The MATLAB program `exmultistep` can be run with the `ab2step` function replaced by the unstable two-step method. The resulting approximations follow:

(a)

t_i	w_i	error
0.0	0.0000	0.0000
0.1	0.0050	0.0002
0.2	0.0213	0.0002
0.3	0.0493	0.0005
0.4	0.0916	0.0002
0.5	0.1474	0.0013
0.6	0.2222	0.0001
0.7	0.3105	0.0032
0.8	0.4276	0.0020
0.9	0.5510	0.0086
1.0	0.7283	0.0100

(b)

t_i	w_i	error
0.0	0.0000	0.0000
0.1	0.0050	0.0002
0.2	0.0187	0.0000
0.3	0.0413	0.0005
0.4	0.0699	0.0004
0.5	0.1082	0.0016
0.6	0.1462	0.0027
0.7	0.2032	0.0066
0.8	0.2360	0.0134
0.9	0.3363	0.0297
1.0	0.3048	0.0631

(c)

t_i	w_i	error
0.0	0.0000	0.0000
0.1	0.0200	0.0013
0.2	0.0700	0.0003
0.3	0.1530	0.0042
0.4	0.2435	0.0058
0.5	0.3855	0.0176
0.6	0.4645	0.0367
0.7	0.7356	0.0890
0.8	0.5990	0.2029
0.9	1.4392	0.4739
1.0	0.0394	1.0959

9 To plot the solution, the `predcorr` program can be altered slightly as follows: Replace the Adams-Bashforth Two-Step Method with the Three-Step Method, and replace the Adams-Moulton One-Step Method with the Two-Step Method. In addition, order-four Runge-Kutta should be used as a startup method. The approximate solution on $[0, 2]$ is indistinguishable from the correct solution in the plot below.

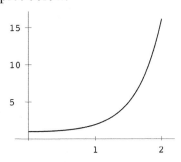

CHAPTER 7
Boundary Value Problems

EXERCISES 7.1 Shooting Method

1 (a) The derivatives of $y(t) = te^t$ are $y'(t) = (t+1)e^t$ and $y''(t) = (t+2)e^t$. Thus $y + 2e^t = te^t 2e^t = (t+2)e^t = y''(t)$ as required. The boundary conditions are easily checked.

1 (b) The derivatives of $y(t) = e^{t^2}$ are $y'(t) = 2te^{t^2}$ and $y''(t) = (2+4t^2)e^{t^2}$. Thus $(2+4t^2)y = y''$ as required. The boundary conditions are $y(0) = e^0 = 1$ and $y(1) = e^1$.

1 (c) The derivatives of $y(t) = t \sin t$ are $y'(t) = \sin t + t \cos t$ and $y''(t) = 2 \cos t - t \sin t$. Thus $-y + 2 \cos t = -t \sin t + 2 \cos t = y''$ as required. The boundary conditions are $y(0) = 0$ and $y(\pi/2) = (\pi/2) \sin \pi/2 = \pi/2$.

1 (d) The derivatives of $y(t) = \sin^2 t$ are $y'(t) = 2 \sin t \cos t$ and $y''(t) = -2 \sin^2 t + 2 \cos^2 t = 2 - 4 \sin^2 t$. Thus $2 - 4y = 2 - 4 \sin^2 t = y''$ as required. The boundary conditions are $y(0) = \sin^2 0 = 0$ and $y(\pi/2) = \sin^2 \pi/2 = 1$.

3 (a) The linearly independent solutions of $y'' = -4y$ are $y_1(t) = \cos 2t$ and $y_2(t) = \sin 2t$.

3 (b) All solutions of the differential equation have form $y(t) = c_1 \cos 2t + c_2 \sin 2t$. Substituting the boundary conditions gives

$$y_a = y(0) = c_1 \cos 0 + c_2 \sin 0 = c_1$$

and

$$y_b = y(\pi) = c_1 \cos 2\pi + c_2 \sin 2\pi = c_1.$$

Therefore a solution to the boundary value problem exists if and only if $y_a = y_b$.

3 (c) From part (b), $y_a = y(0) = c_1$. Additionally,

$$y_b = y(\pi/2) = c_1 \cos \pi + c_2 \sin \pi = -c_1.$$

Therefore a solution to the BVP problem exists if and only if $y_a + y_b = 0$.

3 (d) From part (b), $y_a = c_1$. Additionally,

$$y_b = y\left(\frac{\pi}{4}\right) = c_1 \cos \frac{\pi}{2} + c_2 \sin \frac{\pi}{2} = c_2.$$

Therefore the solution $y(t) = y_a \cos 2t + y_b \sin 2t$ exists for arbitrary y_a, y_b.

5 Two linearly independent solutions of the differential equations are $e^{\sqrt{k}t}$ and $e^{-\sqrt{k}t}$. The general solution is

$$y(t) = c_1 e^{\sqrt{k}t} + c_2 e^{-\sqrt{k}t}.$$

Substituting the boundary conditions gives $y_0 = y(0) = c_1 + c_2$ and $y_1 = y(1) = c_1 e^{\sqrt{k}} + c_2 e^{-\sqrt{k}}$. Solving for c_1 and c_2 yields the solution

$$y(t) = \frac{y_1 - y_0 e^{-\sqrt{k}}}{e^{\sqrt{k}} - e^{-\sqrt{k}}} e^{\sqrt{k}t} + \frac{y_0 e^{\sqrt{k}} - y_1}{e^{\sqrt{k}} - e^{-\sqrt{k}}} e^{-\sqrt{k}t}.$$

COMPUTER PROBLEMS 7.1

1 (a)   As a first-order system, the differential equation is

$$\begin{aligned} y_1' &= y_2 \\ y_2' &= y_1 + \frac{2}{3}e^t \end{aligned}$$

Write a MATLAB function file de.m for the differential equation:

```
function ydot=de(t,y)
ydot=[0;0];
ydot(1)=y(2);
ydot(2)=y(1)+2*exp(t)/3;
```

and a function file F.m to represent the shooting method problem, as in (7.5).

```
function z=F(s);
a=0;b=1;yb=exp(1)/3;
[t,y]=ode45('de',[a,b],[0,s]);
z=y(end,1)-yb;
```

By trial and error, we find that $F(0.2) = -0.1567$ and $F(0.4) = 0.0783$. The interval $0.2 < s < 0.4$ is a bracketing interval, and we can apply the Bisection Method to find a root of F. The MATLAB commands

```
>> F=inline('F(x)','x');
>> s=bisect(F,0.2,0.4,0.5e-6);
```

make the MATLAB function F available as in inline function, and use the program bisect.m to calculate s to within 6 decimal places. The result is $s = 0.333333$. Finally, the MATLAB command ode45 can be used to plot the solution in (a):

```
>> [t,y]=ode45('de',[0,1],[0,s]);
>> plot(t,y(:,1))
```

1 (b)   As a first-order system, the differential equation is

$$\begin{aligned} y_1' &= y_2 \\ y_2' &= (2 + 4t^2)y_1 \end{aligned}$$

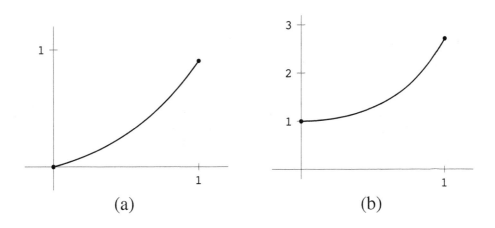

(a)   (b)

Write function files for the differential equation and F as in part (a). Note that $F(-1)F(2) < 0$, so there is a root s in $[-1, 2]$. The Bisection Method converges to $s = 0$. The solution is plotted in (b) above.

3 (a) Proceed as in Computer Problem 1, replacing the Bisection Method with the Secant Method from Chapter 1. Note that $F(-1)F(0) < 0$. Applying the Secant Method, we calculate $s = -0.666667$ to six correct places. The solution is plotted in (a) below.

3 (b) Proceed as in Computer Problem 1. Note that $F(-1)F(1) < 0$. The Secant Method converges to $s = 0$. The solution is plotted in (b) below.

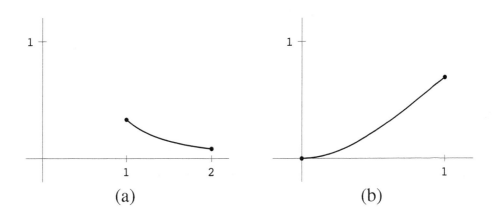

(a)   (b)

5 (a) Write a MATLAB function file de.m for the differential equation:

```
function ydot=de(t,y)
ydot=[0;0];
ydot(1)=1/y(2);
ydot(2)=t+tan(y(1));
```

and a function file F.m to represent the shooting method problem, as in (7.5).

```
function z=F(s);
a=0;b=1;yb=2;
[t,y]=ode45('de',[a,b],[0,s]);
z=y(end,2)-yb;
```

By trial and error, we find that $F(3/4) = -0.0622$ and $F(2) = 0.7452$. The interval $3/4 < s < 2$ is a bracketing interval, and either the Bisection Method or Secant Method can be applied to converge to the root $s = y_2(0) = 1$. The MATLAB command `ode45` can be used to plot the solution:

```
>> [t,y]=ode45('de',[0,1],[0,s]);
>> plot(t,y)
```

The solutions $y_1(t)$ and $y_2(t)$ are plotted in (a) below.

5 (b) Similar to part (a). There will be convergence to the root $s = y_2(0) = 1/3$, and the solutions $y_1(t)$ and $y_2(t)$ are plotted in (b) below.

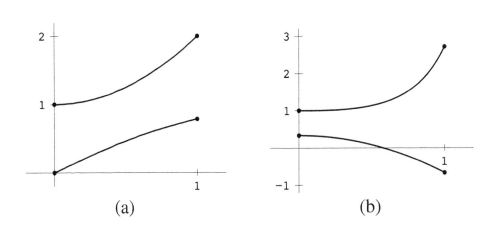

(a)   (b)

COMPUTER PROBLEMS 7.2   Finite Difference Methods

1 (a)   Substituting the finite difference approximation (7.12) for y'' results in the equation

$$\frac{w_{i+1} - 2w_i + w_{i-1}}{h^2} = w_i + \frac{2}{3}e^{t_i},$$

or

$$w_{i+1} - 2w_i + w_{i-1} - h^2 w_i - \frac{2}{3}h^2 e^{t_i} = 0$$

at t_i, where $h = 1/(n + 1), w_0 = y(0) = 0$, and $w_{n+1} = y(1) = e/3$. Evaluating at $t_1, \ldots, t_n$

leads to the system of n linear equations in n unknowns

$$
\begin{bmatrix}
-2-h^2 & 1 & & & & \\
1 & -2-h^2 & 1 & & & \\
& \ddots & \ddots & \ddots & & \\
& & 1 & -2-h^2 & 1 & \\
& & & 1 & -2-h^2
\end{bmatrix}
\begin{bmatrix}
w_1 \\
\vdots \\
\vdots \\
\vdots \\
w_n
\end{bmatrix}
=
\begin{bmatrix}
\frac{2}{3}h^2 e^{t_1} - 0 \\
\vdots \\
\frac{2}{3}h^2 e^{t_i} \\
\vdots \\
\frac{2}{3}h^2 e^{t_n} - \frac{e}{3}
\end{bmatrix}.
$$

Solving for w_i with $n = 9, 19$, and 39 gives the approximate solutions in (a), which are indistinguishable at the resolution shown. In (b) we have plotted the errors at each t_i, for $n = 9, 19$ and 39, by comparing with the correct solution.

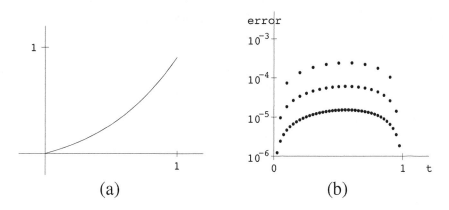

(a)   (b)

1 (b) Similar to (a). Substituting the finite difference approximation results in

$$
\frac{w_{i+1} - 2w_i + w_{i-1}}{h^2} = (2 + 4t_i^2)w_i
$$

or

$$
w_{i+1} + (-2 - h^2(2 + 4t_i^2))w_i + w_{i-1} = 0
$$

at t_i, where $h = 1/(n+1)$, $w_0 = y(0) = 1$, and $w_{n+1} = y(1) = e$. Evaluating at $t_1, \ldots, t_n$ leads to the system of n linear equations in n unknowns

$$
\begin{bmatrix}
A_{11} & 1 & & & & \\
1 & A_{22} & 1 & & & \\
& \ddots & \ddots & \ddots & & \\
& & 1 & A_{n-1,n-1} & 1 & \\
& & & 1 & A_{nn}
\end{bmatrix}
\begin{bmatrix}
w_1 \\
\vdots \\
\vdots \\
\vdots \\
w_n
\end{bmatrix}
=
\begin{bmatrix}
-1 \\
\vdots \\
0 \\
\vdots \\
-e
\end{bmatrix}
$$

where $A_{ii} = -2 - 2h^2 - 4t_i^2 h^2$. Solving for w_i gives the approximate solutions in (a), and the errors for $n = 9, 19$ and 39 in (b).

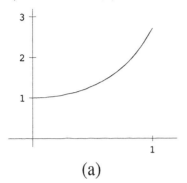

(a)

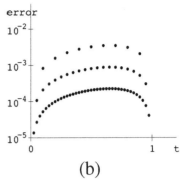

(b)

3 (a)   The MATLAB program nlbvpfd can be adapted to apply to the equation. The function that the w_i must satisfy is $F(w) = 0$, where the ith component of F is $w_{i-1} - 2w_i - 18h^2 w_i^2 + w_{i+1}$. The Jacobian is

$$DF = \begin{bmatrix} -2 - 36h^2 w_1 & 1 & & & & \\ 1 & -2 - 36h^2 w_2 & 1 & & & \\ & \ddots & \ddots & \ddots & & \\ & & 1 & -2 - 36h^2 w_{n-1} & 1 \\ & & & 1 & -2 - 36h^2 w_n \end{bmatrix}.$$

Applying 20 Newton's Method iterations determines the approximation w_i, which is plotted below along with the errors for $n = 9, 19$, and 39.

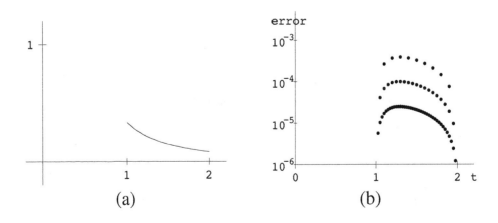

(a)   (b)

3 (b)   The MATLAB program nlbvpfd can be adapted to apply to the equation. The solution function is $F(w) = 0$, where the ith component of F is $w_{i-1} - 2w_i - 2h^2 e^{-2w_i}(1 - t_i^2) + w_{i+1}$.

The Jacobian is

$$DF = \begin{bmatrix} A_{11} & 1 & & & & \\ 1 & A_{22} & 1 & & & \\ & & \ddots & \ddots & \ddots & \\ & & & 1 & A_{n-1,n-1} & 1 \\ & & & & 1 & A_{nn} \end{bmatrix}$$

where $A_{ii} = -2 + 4h^2 e^{-2w_1}(1 - t_i^2)$. Applying 20 Newton's Method iterations determines the approximation w_i, which is plotted below along with the errors for $n = 9, 19$, and 39.

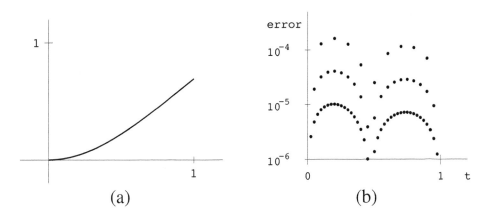

(a)   (b)

5 (a)   The two linearly independent solutions of the differential equation $y'' = y$ are e^t and e^{-t}. By fitting coefficients to the boundary values, the solution of the boundary value problem is found to be $y(t) = (e^{1+t} - e^{1-t})/(e^2 - 1)$.

5 (b)   Using the second-order finite difference expression for y'', the equations

$$\frac{w_{i+1} - 2w_i + w_{i-1}}{h^2} - w_i = 0$$

can be written in matrix form as

$$\begin{bmatrix} -2-h^2 & 1 & & & & \\ 1 & -2-h^2 & 1 & & & \\ & & \ddots & \ddots & \ddots & \\ & & & 1-h & -2-h^2 & 1 \\ & & & & 1 & -2-h^2 \end{bmatrix} \begin{bmatrix} w_1 \\ \vdots \\ \vdots \\ w_n \end{bmatrix} = \begin{bmatrix} 0 \\ \vdots \\ 0 \\ \vdots \\ -1 \end{bmatrix}.$$

Solving the system of equations for $n = 15$ results in the solution shown in (b) below.

5 (c)   We repeat the solutions in (b) for $n = 2^p - 1, p = 2, \ldots, 7$, and compute the errors at $t = 1/2$. The plot in (c) shows that the errors are inversely proportional to n^2, as the theory predicts.

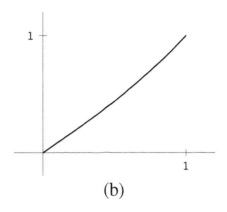

(b)

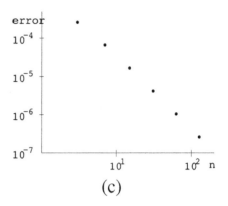

(c)

7   The approximation $w_h(3/2) = w_{2^{p-1}}$ for $y(1/2)$ in Computer Problem 5, where $n = 2^p - 1$, is second order, meaning that the error is proportional to h^2. Define $N_1(h) = w_{2^{p-1}}$. The extrapolation formula from Section 5.1 gives a new formula

$$N_2(h) = \frac{2^2 N_1(\frac{h}{2}) - N_1(h)}{2^2 - 1}$$

that turns out to be a fourth order formula for $y(1/2)$. Extrapolating again gives the sixth order formula

$$N_3(h) = \frac{2^4 N_2(\frac{h}{2}) - N_2(h)}{2^4 - 1}.$$

Using the approximations from the finite difference method as the entries in $N_1(h)$, we can build the following triangle.

$N_1(2^{-2}) = 0.443674176776$ $N_2(2^{-2}) = 0.443409958575$ $N_3(2^{-2}) = 0.443409442296$
$N_1(2^{-3}) = 0.443476013126$ $N_2(2^{-3}) = 0.443409474564$
$N_1(2^{-4}) = 0.443426109204$
$N_1(2^{-5}) = 0.443413610320$
$N_1(2^{-6}) = 0.443410484165$
$N_1(2^{-7}) = 0.443409702536$

Comparing with the correct value $y(1/2) = \dfrac{e^{3/2} - e^{1/2}}{e^2 - 1} \approx 0.443409441985$, we find the errors

2.65×10^{-4} 5.17×10^{-7} 3.11×10^{-10}

6.66×10^{-5} 3.26×10^{-8}

1.67×10^{-5}

4.17×10^{-6}

1.04×10^{-6}

2.61×10^{-7}

Note that $N_3(2^{-2})$, built only from information given by $N_1(2^{-2})$, $N_1(2^{-3})$, and $N_1(2^{-4})$, is orders of magnitude more accurate than $N_1(2^{-7})$.

9 Newton's Method is used to solve the nonlinear finite difference method equations $w_{i-1} - 2w_i - h^2 \sin w_i + w_{i+1} = 0$. The Jacobian is

$$DF = \begin{bmatrix} -2 - h^2 \cos w_1 & 1 & & & & \\ 1 & -2 - h^2 \cos w_2 & 1 & & & \\ & & \ddots & \ddots & \ddots & \\ & & & 1 & -2 - h^2 \cos w_{n-1} & 1 \\ & & & & 1 & -2 - h^2 \cos w_n \end{bmatrix}.$$

Newton's Method yields the approximation w_i, which is plotted below for $n = 9, 19$ and 39.

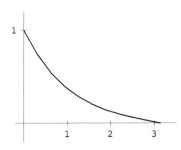

11 Consider the function $G(c) = w_c(1/2) - 1/4$, that returns the value of the boundary value problem

$$\begin{cases} y'' = cy(1 - y) \\ y(0) = 0 \\ y(1) = 1 \end{cases}$$

at $t = 1/2$, minus $1/4$. Newton's Method can be used to approximate the solution w of the nonlinear BVP. Check that $G(10)G(15) < 0$, implying a root between $c = 10$ and $c = 15$.

Using the Bisection Method, for example, the root can be refined to approximately 11.7856. The number n used in the BVP approximation needs to be fairly large to get this accuracy, although applying extrapolation as in Computer Problems 7 and 8 can reduce the computation needed.

COMPUTER PROBLEMS 7.3   Collocation and the Finite Element Method

1 (a)   Collocation is applied to $y'' = y + \frac{2}{3}e^t$ by expanding the solution into monomial basis functions

$$y(t) = \sum_{j=1}^{n} c_j t^{j-1}.$$

Substituting the boundary conditions gives $c_1 = 0$ and $c_1 + \ldots + c_n = e/3$. The remaining $n - 2$ equations use the differential equation:

$$\sum_{j=1}^{n} c_j \left[(j-1)(j-2)t_i^{j-3} - t_i^{j-1} \right] = \frac{2}{3}e^{t_i}$$

for $i = 2, \ldots, n - 2$. Using evenly-spaced base points $t_i = (i-1)/(n-1)$ results in n equations in the n unknowns c_j. After solving for c_j by Gaussian elimination, the solution $y(t) = \sum c_j t^{j-1}$ is plotted on $[0, 1]$ for $n = 8$ and 16, shown below. In addition, the differences between the approximate and exact solution are plotted for $n = 8$. The differences for $n = 16$ are near machine epsilon (not shown).

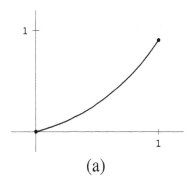

(a)

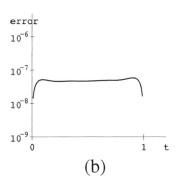

(b)

1 (b)   Similar to (a). The first and last equations are $c_1 = 1$ and $c_1 + \ldots + c_n = e$. The remaining $n - 2$ equations are

$$\sum_{j=1}^{n} c_j \left[(j-1)(j-2)t_i^{j-3} - 2t_i^{j-1} - 4t_i^2 t_i^{j-1} \right] = 0.$$

Substituting $t_i = (i-1)/(n-1)$ for $i = 2, \ldots, n-1$ and solving for c_j gives the approximate solutions shown below.

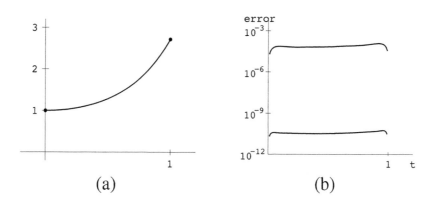

(a)   (b)

3 (a)   For a positive integer n, set the step size $h = 1/(n+1)$, grid points $t_i = ih$, and use the boundary conditions $c_0 = 0, c_{n+1} = e/3$. Consider the Finite Element Method equations (7.22) with linear B-splines:

$$
\begin{aligned}
0 &= \int_0^1 \left[\phi_i(t) \left(\sum_{j=0}^{n+1} c_j \phi_j(t) + \frac{2}{3} e^t \right) + \phi_i'(t) \sum_{j=0}^{n+1} c_j \phi_j'(t) \right] dt \\
&= \frac{2}{3} \int_0^1 \phi_i(t) e^t \, dt + \sum_{j=0}^{n+1} c_j \left[\int_0^1 \phi_i(t) \phi_j(t) \, dt + \int_0^1 \phi_i'(t) \phi_j'(t) \, dt \right].
\end{aligned}
$$

for $i = 1, \ldots, n$. Using the B-spline definition, we calculate $\displaystyle\int_0^1 \phi_i(t) e^t \, dt = e^{t_i} \frac{e^h - 2 + e^{-h}}{h}$ for each i. We must solve the tridiagonal system

$$
\begin{bmatrix}
\alpha & \beta & 0 & \cdots & 0 \\
\beta & \alpha & \ddots & \ddots & \vdots \\
0 & \beta & \ddots & \beta & 0 \\
\vdots & \ddots & \ddots & \alpha & \beta \\
0 & \cdots & 0 & \beta & \alpha
\end{bmatrix}
\begin{bmatrix}
c_1 \\ c_2 \\ \vdots \\ c_{n-1} \\ c_n
\end{bmatrix}
=
\begin{bmatrix}
-y_a \beta \\ 0 \\ \vdots \\ 0 \\ -y_b \beta
\end{bmatrix}
- \frac{2(e^h - 2 + e^{-h})}{3h}
\begin{bmatrix}
e^h \\ e^{2h} \\ \vdots \\ e^{(n-1)h} \\ e^{nh}
\end{bmatrix}
$$

where

$$
\alpha = \frac{2}{3} h + \frac{2}{h} \quad \text{and} \quad \beta = \frac{h}{6} - \frac{1}{h}.
$$

Solving for the values $c_1, \ldots, c_n$ of the approximate solution results in the plots below for $n = 8$ and 16 in (a), and the errors as a function of t in (b).

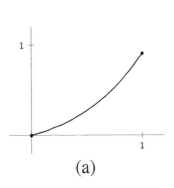

(a)

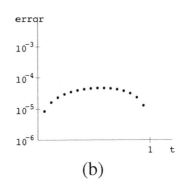

(b)

3 (b)   For a positive integer n, set the step size $h = 1/(n+1)$, grid points $t_i = ih$, and use the boundary conditions $c_0 = 1, c_{n+1} = e$. The FEM equations for $i = 1, \ldots, n$ are:

$$
\begin{aligned}
0 &= \int_0^1 \left[\phi_i(t) \left(2 + 4t^2 \right) \sum_{j=0}^{n+1} c_j \phi_j(t) + \phi_i'(t) \sum_{j=0}^{n+1} c_j \phi_j'(t) \right] \, dt \\
&= \sum_{j=0}^{n+1} c_j \left[\int_0^1 (2 + 4t^2) \phi_i(t) \phi_j(t) \, dt + \int_0^1 \phi_i'(t) \phi_j'(t) \, dt \right].
\end{aligned}
$$

We calculate $\int_0^1 t^2 \phi_i(t) \phi_{i+1}(t) \, dt = \dfrac{h^3}{20} + \dfrac{ht_i^2}{6} + \dfrac{h^2 t_i}{6}$ and $\int_0^1 t^2 \phi_i(t)^2 \, dt = \dfrac{h^3}{15} + \dfrac{2}{3} ht_i^2$ for each i. The c_j satisfy the tridiagonal system

$$
\begin{bmatrix}
\alpha_1 & \beta_1 & 0 & \cdots & 0 \\
\beta_1 & \alpha_2 & \ddots & \ddots & \vdots \\
0 & \beta_2 & \ddots & \ddots & 0 \\
\vdots & \ddots & \ddots & \alpha_{n-1} & \beta_{n-1} \\
0 & \cdots & 0 & \beta_{n-1} & \alpha_n
\end{bmatrix}
\begin{bmatrix}
c_1 \\
c_2 \\
\vdots \\
c_{n-1} \\
c_n
\end{bmatrix}
=
\begin{bmatrix}
-y_a \beta_0 \\
0 \\
\vdots \\
0 \\
-y_b \beta_{n+1}
\end{bmatrix}
$$

where $\alpha_i = \frac{4}{3} h + \frac{4}{15} h^3 + \frac{8}{3} ht_i^2 + \frac{2}{h}$ and $\beta_i = \frac{h}{3} + 4h \left(\frac{h^2}{20} + \frac{t_i^2}{6} + \frac{ht_i}{6} \right) - \frac{1}{h}$. Solutions follow:

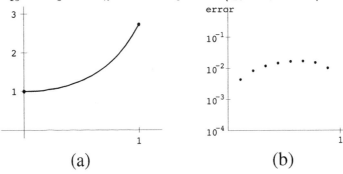

(a)   (b)

CHAPTER 8
Partial Differential Equations

EXERCISES 8.1   Parabolic Equations

1 (a) $u_t = 2e^{2t+x} + 2e^{2t-x}$ and $u_{xx} = e^{2t+x} + e^{2t-x}$, so the heat equation $u_t = 2u_{xx}$ holds. Substitute $t = 0, x = 0$ and $x = 1$, respectively, to check the boundary conditions.

1 (b) $u_t = 2e^{2t+x}$ and $u_{xx} = e^{2t+x}$, so $u_t = 2u_{xx}$ holds. The boundary conditions are easily checked.

3 $u_t = cf''(x)$ and $u_{xx} = f''(x)$, since the fourth derivative of $f(x)$ is zero. Substituting $t = 0$ verifies the initial condition.

5 Set $x = \pi j/(m+1)$. For $i = 1, \ldots, m$, the ith row of Tv_j is the left side of (8.11), by the definitions of T and v_j in (8.10) and (8.12). (Notice that when $i = 1$, $\sin(i-1)x = 0$, and when $i = m$, $\sin(i+1)x = \sin(m+1)\pi j/(m+1) = \sin \pi j = 0$.) Thus (8.13) holds because its right-hand side matches the right-hand side of (8.11).

COMPUTER PROBLEMS 8.1

1 Program 8.1 can be used after adjusting $c = 2$ and the initial/boundary conditions $f(x), l(t)$ and $r(t)$. Setting the `axis` command to expand in the z direction allows more of the solutions to be seen. Theorem 8.2 requires $k < (0.1)^2/4 = 0.0025$ for stability; if $k > 0.003$ is used, the solution becomes noticeably unstable.

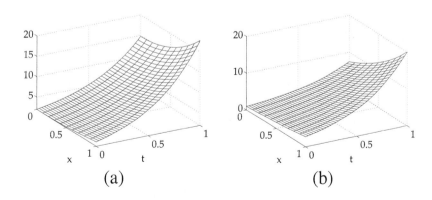

(a)   (b)

3 Program 8.2 implements the Backward Difference Method. The exact solution u and the computed solutions w are:

(a)

h	k	$u(0.5, 1)$	$w(0.5, 1)$	error
0.02	0.02	16.6642	16.7023	0.0381
0.02	0.01	16.6642	16.6834	0.0192
0.02	0.005	16.6642	16.6642	0.0097

(b)

h	k	$u(0.5, 1)$	$w(0.5, 1)$	error
0.02	0.02	12.1825	12.2104	0.0279
0.02	0.01	12.1825	12.1965	0.0140
0.02	0.005	12.1825	12.1896	0.0071

5   Program 8.4 adjusted for the correct initial and boundary conditions can be used. The exact solution u and the computed solutions w are:

(a)

h	k	$u(0.5, 1)$	$w(0.5, 1)$	error
0.02	0.02	16.664183	16.664504	0.000321
0.01	0.01	16.664183	16.664263	0.000080
0.005	0.005	16.664183	16.664203	0.000020

(b)

h	k	$u(0.5, 1)$	$w(0.5, 1)$	error
0.02	0.02	12.182494	12.182728	0.000235
0.01	0.01	12.182494	12.182553	0.000059
0.005	0.005	12.182494	12.182509	0.000015

7   Program 8.4 can be used to generate solutions with $D = 1$ and the domain $[0, 10]$. For $C > \pi^2/100$, the population survives.

EXERCISES 8.2   Hyperbolic Equations

1 (a)   The partial derivatives are $u_{tt} = -16\pi^2 \sin \pi x \cos 4\pi t$ and $u_{xx} = -\pi^2 \sin \pi x \cos 4\pi t$, so u satisfies the wave equation. The initial and boundary conditions are easily checked.

1 (b)   The partial derivatives are $u_{tt} = 4e^{-x-2t}$ and $u_{xx} = e^{-x-2t}$, so u satisfies the wave equation. The initial and boundary conditions also check.

1 (c)   The partial derivatives are $u_{tt} = u_{xx} = -(1 + x + t)^{-2}$. The initial and boundary conditions also check.

3   We check the equation by finding the partial derivatives of $u_1(x,t)$, which are $(u_1)_{tt} = -c^2\alpha^2 \sin \alpha x \cos c\alpha t$ and $(u_1)_{xx} = -\alpha^2 \sin \alpha x \cos c\alpha t$. Therefore u_1 satisfies the wave equation with wave velocity c. The partial derivatives of $u_2(x,t)$ are $(u_2)_{tt} = c^2 e^{x+ct}$ and $(u_2)_{xx} = e^{x+ct}$, so u_2 also satisfies the wave equation.

5 Note that $A = (2 - \sigma^2)I - \sigma^2 T$, where the matrix T in (8.10) has eigenvalues between -1 and 3. The eigenvectors x of A are the same as those of T, since $Ax = (2 - \sigma^2)x - \sigma^2 Tx = (2 - \sigma^2 - \sigma^2\lambda)x$, where λ is the corresponding eigenvalue of T. Therefore the eigenvalues of A lie between $2 - \sigma^2 - \sigma^2(-1) = 2$ and $(2 - \sigma^2) - \sigma^2(3) = 2 - 4\sigma^2$.

COMPUTER PROBLEMS 8.2

1 Set $\sigma = ck/h$, where $h = 0.05$ and $k = h/c$ to satisfy the CFL condition. Iterating the step (8.31) and plotting the solution with the `mesh` command of MATLAB gives the following.

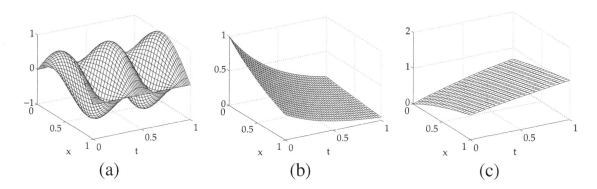

(a) (b) (c)

3 Using the iteration (8.34), the value of the wave equation solution at $(1/4, 3/4)$ at the given step sizes are as follows.

(a)

h	k	$w(1/4, 3/4)$	error
2^{-4}	2^{-6}	-0.70710678	0.0
2^{-5}	2^{-7}	-0.70710678	0.0
2^{-6}	2^{-8}	-0.70710678	0.0
2^{-7}	2^{-9}	-0.70710678	0.0
2^{-8}	2^{-10}	-0.70710678	0.0

(b)

h	k	$w(1/4, 3/4)$	error
2^{-4}	2^{-5}	0.17367424	0.00009971
2^{-5}	2^{-6}	0.17374901	0.00002493
2^{-6}	2^{-7}	0.17376771	0.00000623
2^{-7}	2^{-8}	0.17377238	0.00000156
2^{-8}	2^{-9}	0.17377355	0.00000039

(c)

h	k	$w(1/4, 3/4)$	error
2^{-4}	2^{-4}	0.69308400	0.00006318
2^{-5}	2^{-5}	0.69313136	0.00001582
2^{-6}	2^{-6}	0.69314323	0.00000396
2^{-7}	2^{-7}	0.69314619	0.00000099
2^{-8}	2^{-8}	0.69314693	0.00000025

EXERCISES 8.3 Elliptic Equations

1 The x-partial derivatives are $u_x = \dfrac{2x}{x^2 + y^2}$ and $u_{xx} = \dfrac{2(y^2 - x^2)}{(x^2 + y^2)^2}$. Similarly, $u_{yy} = $

$\frac{2(x^2-y^2)}{(x^2+y^2)^2}$. Therefore $u(x,y)$ satisfies the Laplace equation $\Delta u = 0$. Checking the conditions on the boundary of the square $[0,1] \times [1,2]$ is achieved by substitution into $\ln(x^2+y^2)$.

3 (a) The partial derivatives are $u_{xx} = -\pi^2 e^{-\pi y} \sin \pi x$ and $u_{yy} = \pi^2 e^{-\pi y} \sin \pi x$, so u satisfies the Laplace equation. The boundaries' conditions are easily checked.

3 (b) The partial derivatives are $u_{xx} = \pi^2 \sinh \pi x \sin \pi y$ and $u_{yy} = -\pi^2 \sinh \pi x \sin \pi y$, so u satisfies the Laplace equation. The boundary conditions are easily checked.

5 (a) The partial derivatives are $u_{xx} = -\frac{x^2 y^2}{4} \sin \frac{\pi}{2} xy$ and $u_{yy} = -\frac{\pi^2 x^2}{4} \sin \frac{\pi}{2} xy$, so that $\Delta u = -\frac{\pi^2}{4}(x^2+y^2)u$. The boundary conditions are easily checked.

5 (b) The partial derivatives are $u_{xx} = y^2 e^{xy}$ and $u_{yy} = x^2 e^{xy}$, and $\Delta u = (x^2+y^2)e^{xy}$. The boundary conditions are checked by substitution.

7 Since $\bar{x} = (x_1+x_2+x_3)/3, \bar{y} = (y_1+y_2+y_3)/3$ and $\phi(x,y) = ax+by+c$ is linear,

$$\begin{aligned} \phi(\bar{x},\bar{y}) &= \phi(\frac{x_1+x_2+x_3}{3}, \frac{y_1+y_2+y_3}{3}) \\ &= a\frac{x_1+x_2+x_3}{3} + b\frac{y_1+y_2+y_3}{3} + c \\ &= \frac{1}{3}(ax_1+by_1+c) + \frac{1}{3}(ax_2+by_2+c) + \frac{1}{3}(ax_3+by_3+c) \\ &= \frac{1}{3}(\phi(x_1,y_1)+\phi(x_2,y_2)+\phi(x_3,y_3)) = \frac{1}{3}. \end{aligned}$$

COMPUTER PROBLEMS 8.3

1 Program 8.5 can be used on the square $0 \le x,y \le 1$. For the Laplace equation, the right-hand side is $f(x,y) = 0$. The boundary conditions g1, g2, g3 and g4 in Program 8.5 are set to the given functions. The three-dimensional plots from the mesh command follow.

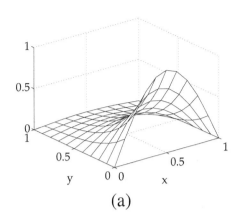
(a)

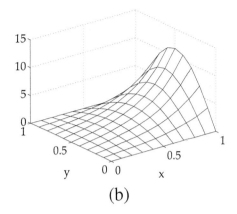
(b)

3 Program 8.5 can be used on the square $0 \le x, y \le 1$ with $f(x,y) = 0$, setting the boundary conditions g1, g2, g3 and g4. The three-dimensional plots from the mesh command follow.

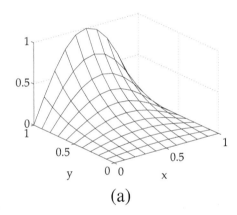
(a)

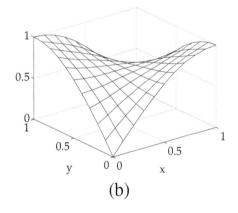
(b)

5 Program 8.5 can be used on the square $0 \le x \le 2, 0 \le y \le 1$ with $f(x,y) = 0$. Setting $h = k = 0.1$ returns the hydraulic head as 0.0114, or 11.4 meters, at $(x,y) = (1, 1/2)$.

7 Using Program 8.5 to generate the solution and evaluating at $(x,y) = (1/4, 3/4)$, yields

(a)

h	k	$w(1/4, 3/4)$	error
2^{-2}	2^{-2}	0.072692	0.005672
2^{-3}	2^{-3}	0.068477	0.001457
2^{-4}	2^{-4}	0.067387	0.000367
2^{-5}	2^{-5}	0.067112	0.000092

(b)

h	k	$w(1/4, 3/4)$	error
2^{-2}	2^{-2}	0.673903	0.059660
2^{-3}	2^{-3}	0.629543	0.015300
2^{-4}	2^{-4}	0.618094	0.003851
2^{-5}	2^{-5}	0.615207	0.000964

9 The Finite Element Method Program 8.6 can be applied on the square $0 \le x, y \le 1$ with $f(x,y) = 0$. Plotting with the MATLAB mesh command gives the following graphs.

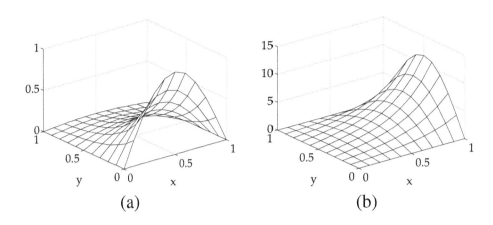

(a)   (b)

11 The Finite Element Method Program 8.6 can be applied on the square $0 \le x, y \le 1$ with $f(x, y) = 0$. Plotting with the MATLAB mesh command gives the following graphs.

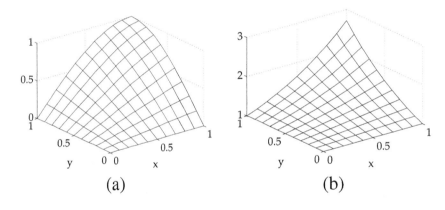

(a)   (b)

13 The Finite Element Method Program 8.6 can be applied. Plotting with the MATLAB mesh command gives the following graphs.

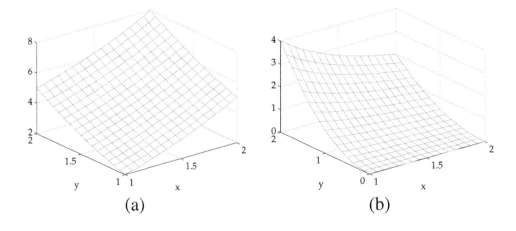

(a)   (b)

15 Using Program 8.6 to generate the solution and evaluating at $(x, y) = (1/4, 3/4)$ yields the tables

(a)

h	k	$w(1/4, 3/4)$	error
2^{-2}	2^{-2}	0.306708	0.016423
2^{-3}	2^{-3}	0.295080	0.004795
2^{-4}	2^{-4}	0.291580	0.001295
2^{-5}	2^{-5}	0.290621	0.000336

(b)

h	k	$w(1/4, 3/4)$	error
2^{-2}	2^{-2}	1.207223	0.000993
2^{-3}	2^{-3}	1.206438	0.000208
2^{-4}	2^{-4}	1.206273	0.000043
2^{-5}	2^{-5}	1.206240	0.000009

17   Use Program 8.6 to generate the approximate solution for $h = 2^{-p}$ for $p = 2, \ldots, 6$, and calculate the error at each point. The maximum error is plotted below.

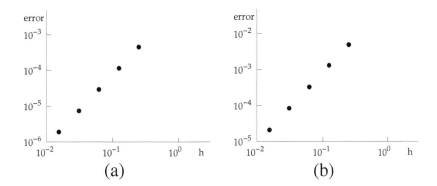

(a)   (b)

EXERCISES 8.4   Nonlinear Partial Differential Equations

1   Since all partial derivatives are zero, Burgers' equation $u_t + uu_x - Du_{xx} = 0$ is automatically satisfied.

3   Direct substitution of the partial derivatives of (8.68) satisfies the Burgers' equation (8.66).

5   Direct substitution of the equilibrium $p = C, q = K/C$ shows that it satisfies the Brusselator equations for any C, K.

COMPUTER PROBLEMS 8.4

1   The Burgers' equation can be solved with Program 8.7. The approximate solutions for $D = 1$ are shown in (a) $h = k = 0.1$ and (b) $h = k = 0.02$. The solution approaches the zero equilibrium as time increases.

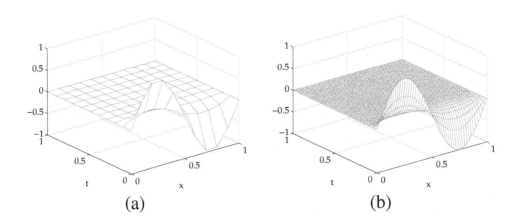

(a)   (b)

3 Fisher's one-dimensional equation can be solved by Program 8.7, replacing the inner loop commands by the code fragment on page 422. The approximate solutions approach the (a) zero equilibrium $u = 0$ and (b) $u = 2$ as time increases.

CHAPTER 9
Random Numbers and Applications

EXERCISES 9.1   Random Numbers

1 (a) The linear congruential generator has the form $x_i = 2x_{i-1} \mod 5, u_i = x_i/5$. Starting with $x_0 = 1$, the LCG cycles through all possible values of $u_1 = \frac{1}{5}$, $u_2 = \frac{2}{5}$, $u_3 = \frac{4}{5}$, $u_4 = \frac{3}{5}$, $u_5 = \frac{1}{5}$. Since $u_1 = u_5$, the period of repetition is 4.

1 (b) The LCG is $x_i = 4x_{i-1} + 1 \mod 9, u_1 = x_i/9$. Starting with $x_0 = 1$, the LCG cycles through $\frac{1}{9}, \frac{5}{9}, \frac{3}{9}, \frac{4}{9}, \frac{8}{9}, \frac{6}{9}, \frac{7}{9}, \frac{2}{9}, 0$, and then repeats with $\frac{1}{9}$. The period is 9.

3 (a) The LCG $x_i = 2x_{i-1} \mod 5$, $u_1 = x_i/5$ provides the x-coordinates $\frac{1}{5}, \frac{2}{5}, \frac{4}{5}, \frac{3}{5}$ before repeating. The area approximation is

$$(1-0)\frac{\left(\frac{1}{5}\right)^2 + \left(\frac{2}{5}\right)^2 + \left(\frac{4}{5}\right)^2 + \left(\frac{3}{5}\right)^2}{4} = \frac{30}{100} = 0.3$$

3 (b) The LCG provides the x-coordinates $\frac{1}{9}, \frac{5}{9}, \frac{3}{9}, \frac{4}{9}, \frac{8}{9}, \frac{6}{9}, \frac{7}{9}, \frac{2}{9}, 0$. The area approximation is

$$(1-0)\frac{(0)^2 + \left(\frac{1}{9}\right)^2 + \left(\frac{2}{9}\right)^2 + \cdots + \left(\frac{8}{9}\right)^2}{8} = 0.28.$$

5 The LCG is $x_i = (2^{24} + 3)x_{i-1} \mod 2^{48}$. We calculate

$$\begin{aligned}
x_{i+2} &= (2^{24} + 3)x_{i+1} \mod 2^{48} \\
&= (2^{24} + 3)(2^{24} + 3)x_i \mod 2^{48} \\
&= (2^{48} + 6 \times 2^{24} + 9)x_i \mod 2^{48} \\
&= (6 \times 2^{24} + 9)x_i \mod 2^{48} \\
x_{i+1} &= (2^{24} + 3)x_i \mod 2^{48}
\end{aligned}$$

Thus

$$\begin{aligned}
x_{i+2} - 6x_{i+1} &= (6 \times 2^{24} + 9 - 6 \times 2^{24} - 18)x_i \mod 2^{48} \\
&= -9x_i \mod 2^{48}.
\end{aligned}$$

COMPUTER PROBLEMS 9.1

1   Implement the Minimal Standard Generator with seed $x_0 = 1$. After generating each three numbers x, y, z, check whether $(x - 1/3)^2 + (y - 1/3)^2 + (z - 1/2)^2 < 0.04$. Of 10^6 triples, 273 satisfy the inequality. The area estimate is therefore 0.000273. The correct volume of a sphere of radius 0.04 is $\frac{4}{3}\pi(0.04)^3 \approx 0.000268$. The error is $\approx 5 \times 10^{-6}$. Of course, different seeds will produce different estimates.

3 (a)   The area between the curves is

$$\int_0^1 -s^2 + x + \frac{1}{2} - (x^2 - x + \frac{1}{2}) \, dx = \int_0^1 (-2x^2 + 2x) \, dx = \frac{1}{3}.$$

3 (b)   Estimates will depend on the random number generator and seed used. As an example, we apply the Minimal Standard Generator with seed $x_0 = 1$. For each uniform random number x in $[0, 1]$, evaluate $P_2(x) - P_1(x)$ and average the results to approximate the area. The results are given below.

3 (c)   As a Type 2 Monte-Carlo problem, generate two uniform random numbers (x, y) and decide whether the two-dimensional point lies in the region by checking $P_1(x) < y < P_2(x)$. The proportion of points that satisfy the inequality is the approximate area.

<table>
<tr><td></td><td>n</td><td>Type 1 estimate</td><td>error</td><td></td><td>n</td><td>Type 2 estimate</td><td>error</td></tr>
<tr><td rowspan="5">(b)</td><td>10^2</td><td>0.327290</td><td>0.006043</td><td rowspan="5">(c)</td><td>10^2</td><td>0.28</td><td>0.053333</td></tr>
<tr><td>10^3</td><td>0.342494</td><td>0.009161</td><td>10^3</td><td>0.354</td><td>0.020667</td></tr>
<tr><td>10^4</td><td>0.332705</td><td>0.000628</td><td>10^4</td><td>0.3406</td><td>0.007267</td></tr>
<tr><td>10^5</td><td>0.333610</td><td>0.000277</td><td>10^5</td><td>0.33382</td><td>0.000487</td></tr>
<tr><td>10^6</td><td>0.333505</td><td>0.000172</td><td>10^6</td><td>0.333989</td><td>0.000656</td></tr>
</table>

5 (a)   As a Type 2 Monte-Carlo estimate, generate pairs of points (x, y) in $[-1, 1] \times [-1, 1]$ and test the inequality. Since the box has area 4, the desired area is the proportion of points that satisfy the inequality divided by 4. The results using the Minimal Standard Generator are given below.

5(b)   Similar to (a). The area is the proportion of random pairs in $[0, 1] \times [0, 1]$ that satisfy the inequality.

<table>
<tr><td></td><td>n</td><td>Type 2 estimate</td><td>error</td><td></td><td>n</td><td>Type 2 estimate</td><td>error</td></tr>
<tr><td rowspan="2">(a)</td><td>10^4</td><td>0.512800</td><td>0.010799</td><td rowspan="2">(b)</td><td>10^4</td><td>0.174400</td><td>0.000133</td></tr>
<tr><td>10^6</td><td>0.524980</td><td>0.001381</td><td>10^6</td><td>0.174851</td><td>0.000318</td></tr>
</table>

7 (a)   The double integral is

$$\int_0^1 \left(\int_{x^2}^{\sqrt{x}} xy \, dy \right) dx = \frac{1}{2} \int_0^1 (x^2 - x^5) \, dx = \frac{1}{2} \left(\frac{13}{3} - \frac{16}{6} \right) = \frac{1}{12} \approx 0.083333.$$

7 (b)   This is a combination of Type 1 and Type 2 Monte-Carlo problems. For each random pair of numbers in the square $[0, 1] \times [0, 1]$, keep a running sum of the quantity xy if (x, y) is in the integration region, and 0 if not. In essence, the average of the function that is xy in the region of integration and 0 outside is being approximated. Using the Minimal Standard Generator gives the result 0.083566, an error of 0.000232.

9   Program the LCG with $m = 2^{48}, a = 2^{24} + 3$, and $b = 0$. A three-dimensional plot of 10000 points (x_i, x_{i+1}, x_{i+2}) is shown below.

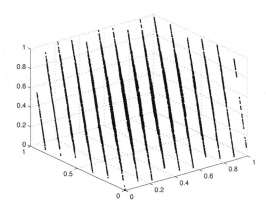

COMPUTER PROBLEMS 9.2   Monte Carlo Simulation

1 (a) $1/3$

1 (b)   Similar to Computer Problem 9.1.3(b), but using the Halton sequence of quasi-random numbers to do the Type 1 Monte-Carlo approximation. Results are shown below.

1 (c)   Similar to Computer Problem 9.1.3(c), but using `halton(2,n)` and `halton(3,n)` for the x and y coordinates.

(b)

n	Type 1 estimate	error
10^2	0.335414	0.002080
10^3	0.333514	0.000181
10^4	0.333339	0.000006
10^5	0.333334	0.000001

(c)

n	Type 1 estimate	error
10^2	0.35	0.016667
10^3	0.333	0.000333
10^4	0.3339	0.000567
10^5	0.33338	0.000047

3   Similar to Computer Problem 9.1.5, but with quasi-random numbers from a Halton sequence. Results are:

(a)

n	Type 2 estimate	error
10^4	0.5232	0.000399
10^5	0.52396	0.000361

(b)

n	Type 2 estimate	error
10^4	0.1743	0.000233
10^5	0.17455	0.000017

5 Generate 4-tuples (x, y, z, w) of uniform random numbers in the four-dimensional cube $[0, 1]^4$. Since the cube has volume 2^4, the volume of the four-dimensional ball can be approximated by multiplying the proportion of 4-tuples that satisfy $x^2+y^2+z^2+w^2 < 1$ by 16. Comparing with the correct volume $\pi^2/2$, typical results are: Monte-Carlo estimate 4.9656, error $= 0.030798$; quasi-Monte-Carlo estimate 4.92928, error $= 0.005522$.

7 (a)   For every matrix $\begin{bmatrix} a & b \\ c & d \end{bmatrix}$ there is a matrix $\begin{bmatrix} b & a \\ d & c \end{bmatrix}$ whose determinant has opposite sign. The probability is 0.5 that the determinant is positive. An example pseudo-Monte-Carlo estimate with $n = 10^6$ matrices gives 0.500313.

7 (b)   The determinant of the symmetric matrix with non-negative entries $\begin{bmatrix} x & z \\ z & y \end{bmatrix}$ is $xy - z^2$, which is positive if $z < \sqrt{xy}$. If x, y, z are uniform in $[0, 1]$, this corresponds to the volume in the cube $[0, 1]^3$ lying under the surface $z = \sqrt{xy}$, or

$$\int_0^1 \int_0^1 \sqrt{x}\sqrt{y}\, dy\, dx = \int_0^1 \frac{2}{3}\sqrt{x}\, dx = \frac{4}{9}.$$

An example Monte-Carlo estimate with $n = 10^6$ matrices gives 0.444486.

9   The exact answer is $\dfrac{1}{4}\dfrac{1}{3}\dfrac{1}{2} = \dfrac{1}{24} \approx 4.167$ percent. A Monte-Carlo simulation can be done by loading matrices with uniform random numbers from $[0, 1]$ and applying the MATLAB lu command to calculate the PA=LU factorization. The proportion of times that P is the identity matrix is the desired quantity.

COMPUTER PROBLEMS 9.3   Discrete and Continuous Brownian Motion

1 (a)   Each random walk starts at zero and increases or decreases by one at each step. For example, one can generate a uniform random number x in $[0, 1]$, increasing the random walk if $x < 0.5$ and decreasing otherwise. After each step, test to see if the random walk has reached either boundary of the interval $[-b, a]$, in which case the walk is terminated. Example results after repeating 10^4 times using the minimal standard LCG with seed $x_0 = 1$ are that the top 5 was reached before the bottom -2 a total of 2907 times. We calculate the probability as 0.2907, which compares with the theoretical answer of $2/7 \approx 0.2857$. The error is $= 0.0050$.

1 (b)   Similar to (a), for interval $[-5, 3]$. Monte-Carlo approximation of probability of reaching the top is 0.6323 with error 0.0073.

1 (c)   Similar to (a), for interval $[-8, 3]$. Monte-Carlo approximation of probability of reaching the top is 0.7322 with error 0.0049.

3 (a)   The same program can be used as in Computer Problem 1, but the random walk should increase if the uniform random number x in $[0, 1]$ satisfies $x < p$, and decrease otherwise. Using the Minimal Standard Generator, the probability of reaching 5 before -2 using bias $p = 0.7$ is estimated to be 0.8199, with error $= 0.0014$ when compared with the theoretical value $[((1 - p)/p)^b - 1]/[((1 - p)/p)^{a+b} - 1]$.

3 (b)   Similar to (a), on the interval $[-5, 3]$. Monte-Carlo estimate of probability of reaching 3 is 0.9871 with error $= 0.0004$.

3 (c)   Similar to (a), on the interval $[-8, 3]$. Monte-Carlo estimate of probability of reaching 3 is 0.9984 with error $= 0.0006$.

5 (a)   The code on page 455 can be used to generate Brownian motion. Starting at zero, using step size $\Delta t = 0.01$, the probability of reaching 5 before -2 is 0.2969, with error $= 0.0112$ when compared with the theoretical value $b/(a + b) = 2/7$.

5 (b)   Similar to (a). Estimated probability of reaching π before -2 is 0.3939, with error $= 0.0049$ when compared with the theoretical value $2/(2 + \pi)$.

5 (c)   Similar to (a). Estimated probability of reaching 3 before $-8/3$ is 0.4600, with error $= 0.0106$ when compared with the theoretical value $8/17$.

7 (a)   Create Brownian motion simulations B_t with step size $\Delta t = 0.01$. Beginning with time t_1, after each time step, calculate the product of the two previous steps B_t and B_{t-1}. If negative, the path has crossed zero. Estimate the probability that at least one crossing occurs between t_1 and t_2 as a Type 2 Monte Carlo simulation with 10^4 realizations. For $t_1 = 3, t_2 = 5$, an example simulation yielded the estimated probability as 0.5848, with error $= 0.0207$ when compared with the theoretical value $(2/\pi) \arcsin \sqrt{3/5}$.

7 (b)   Similar to (a). Estimated probability is 0.3106, error $= 0.0154$.

7 (c)   Similar to (a). Estimated probability is 0.7155, error $= 0.0107$.

EXERCISES 9.4   Stochastic Differential Equations

1 (a)   We apply Ito's Formula (9.17) to $y(t) = f(t, B_t) = tB_t + c$. Note that $f(t, x) = tx + c$. The partial derivatives are

$$\frac{\partial f}{\partial t} = x, \frac{\partial f}{\partial x} = t, \text{ and } \frac{\partial^2 f}{\partial x^2} = 0.$$

Ito's Formula gives $dy = \frac{\partial f}{\partial t}(t, B_t)dt + \frac{\partial f}{\partial x}(t, B_t)dB_t + \frac{1}{2}\frac{\partial^2 f}{\partial x^2}(t, B_t)\, dB_t\, dB_t = B_t\, dt + t\, dB_t$ as required. The initial condition is $y(0) = 0B_t + c = c$.

1 (b)   The partial derivatives of $f(t, x) = x^2 - t + c$ are $\frac{\partial f}{\partial t} = -1, \frac{\partial f}{\partial x} = 2x$, and $\frac{\partial^2 f}{\partial x^2} = 2$. Ito's Formula gives $dy = -1dt + 2B_t\, dB_t + \frac{1}{2}2\, dB_t\, dB_t = -dt + 2B_t\, dB_t + dt = 2B_t\, dB_t$ as required. The initial condition is $y(0) = 0^2 - 0 + c = c$.

3 (a)   The partial derivatives of $f(t,x) = (1+x)e^{\frac{t^2}{2}}$ are $\dfrac{\partial f}{\partial t} = (1+x)te^{\frac{t^2}{2}}, \dfrac{\partial f}{\partial x} = e^{\frac{t^2}{2}}, \dfrac{\partial^2 f}{\partial x^2} = 0.$

Ito's Formula gives $dy = (1+B_t)te^{\frac{t^2}{2}}\, dt + e^{\frac{t^2}{2}}\, dB_t = ty\, dt + e^{\frac{t^2}{2}}\, dB_t$ as required. Moreover, the initial condition is $y(0) = (1+B_0)e^{\frac{0^2}{2}} = 1.$

3 (b)   The partial derivatives of $f(t,x) = x^3 - 3tx$ are $\dfrac{\partial f}{\partial t} = -3x, \dfrac{\partial f}{\partial x} = 3x^2 - 3t,$ and $\dfrac{\partial^2 f}{\partial x^2} = 6x.$

Ito's Formula gives $dy = -3B_t\, dt + (3B_t^2 - 3t)\, dB_t + 3B_t\, dB_t\, dB_t$
$= (-3B_t + 3B_t)\, dt + (3B_t^2 - 3t)\, dB_t = (3B_t^2 - 3t)\, dB_t$ as required. The initial condition is
$y(0) = B_0^3 - 3(0)B_0 = 0.$

5   The partial derivatives of $f(t,x) = \ln(2x + e^{y_0})$ are

$$\frac{\partial f}{\partial t} = 0, \frac{\partial f}{\partial x} = \frac{2}{2x + e^{y_0}}, \text{ and } \frac{\partial^2 f}{\partial x^2} = \frac{-4}{(2x + e^{y_0})^2}.$$

Noting that $e^y = 2x + e^{y_0}$, Ito's Formula gives

$$\begin{aligned}
dy &= \frac{2}{e^y}\, dB_t + \frac{1}{2}\frac{-4}{e^{2y}}\, dB_t\, dB_t \\
&= 2e^{-y}\, dB_t - 2e^{-2y}\, dt
\end{aligned}$$

as required.

COMPUTER PROBLEMS 9.4

1 (a)   We apply the Euler-Maruyama Method to the initial value problem in Exercise 1(a). At time t_{i+1}, we use a Brownian motion realization to generate the new approximation w_{i+1} along with the correct solution $u_{i+1} = t_{i+1}B_{t_{i+1}}$ for that Brownian motion realization. Both are plotted below - they are too close to be distinguished at this resolution. The other graph shows the difference $|u - w|$, plotted on a semilog scale.

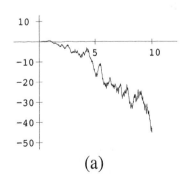

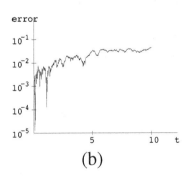

(a)   (b)

1 (b)   Similar to (a). The Euler-Maruyama Method is applied to the initial value problem in Exercise 1(b). At time t_{i+1}, the new approximation w_{i+1} is plotted along with the correct solution $u_{i+1} = B_{t_{i+1}}^2 - t_{i+1}$ for the same Brownian motion realization.

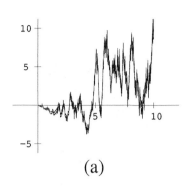
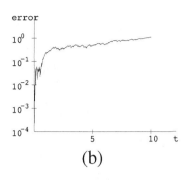

(a)   (b)

3 (a)   Applying the Euler-Maruyama Method to the stochastic differential equation in Exercise 3(a), with initial condition $y(0) = 1$, results in the two realizations in plot (a).

3 (b)   Similar to (a), Euler-Maruyama applied to Exercise 3(b). Two realizations are shown in plot (b).

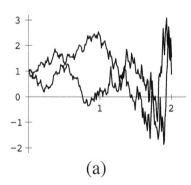
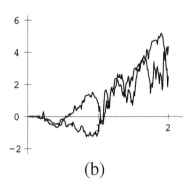

(a)   (b)

5   The Euler-Maruyama Method is applied to the stochastic differential equation. The error at $t = 1$ is averaged over 5000 realizations $h = 10^{-1}, 10^{-2}$ and 10^{-3}. Typical results are shown in the table:

n	avg. error
10^{-1}	0.2657
10^{-2}	0.0925
10^{-3}	0.0256

The results show approximate order $1/2$.

7   The Milstein Method applied to the SDE $dy = B_t \, dt + 9^{1/3} y^{2/3} \, dB_t$ is

$$
\begin{aligned}
w_{i+1} &= w_i + B_i(\Delta t_i) + 9^{1/3} w_i^{2/3} (\Delta B_i) + \frac{1}{2} 9^{1/3} w_i^{2/3} 9^{1/3} \frac{2}{3} w_i^{-1/3} ((\Delta B_i)^2 - \Delta t_i) \\
&= w_i + B_i(\Delta t_i) + 9^{1/3} w_i^{2/3} (\Delta B_i) + 3^{1/3} w_i^{1/3} ((\Delta B_i)^2 - \Delta t_i).
\end{aligned}
$$

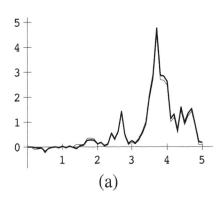
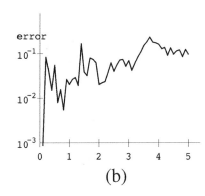

(a)   (b)

An approximate realization with step size $h = 0.1$ is shown above (thick curve) along with the exact realization using the same Brownian motion path. Also, the difference between the approximate and exact solutions is plotted.

9 The Runge-Kutta Method applied to the SDE $dy = B_t\, dt + 9^{1/3}y^{2/3}\, dB_t$ is

$$
w_{i+1} = w_i + B_i(\Delta t_i) + 9^{1/3}w_i^{2/3}(\Delta B_i)
$$
$$
+ \; \frac{1}{2\sqrt{\Delta t_i}}\left[9^{1/3}((w_i + 9^{1/3}w_i^{2/3})\sqrt{\Delta t_i})^{2/3} - 9^{1/3}w_i^{2/3}\right]\left[(\Delta B_i)^2 - \Delta t_i\right].
$$

In (a), an approximate realization with step size $h = 0.1$ is shown (thick curve) along with the exact realization using the same Brownian motion path. The difference between the approximate and exact solutions is plotted in (b).

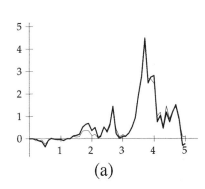
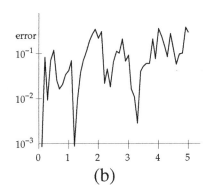

(a)   (b)

11 Similar to Computer Problem 5, but using the Milstein Method. Typical results are shown in the table:

h	avg. error
10^{-1}	0.1394
10^{-2}	0.0202
10^{-3}	0.0026

The results show approximate order 1.

CHAPTER 10
Trigonometric Interpolation and the FFT

EXERCISES 10.1   The Fourier Transform

1 (a)   The 4×4 Fourier matrix is

$$F_4 = \frac{1}{\sqrt{4}} \begin{bmatrix} \omega^0 & \omega^0 & \omega^0 & \omega^0 \\ \omega^0 & \omega^1 & \omega^2 & \omega^3 \\ \omega^0 & \omega^2 & \omega^4 & \omega^6 \\ \omega^0 & \omega^3 & \omega^6 & \omega^9 \end{bmatrix} = \frac{1}{2} \begin{bmatrix} 1 & 1 & 1 & 1 \\ 1 & -i & -1 & i \\ 1 & -1 & 1 & -1 \\ 1 & i & -1 & -i \end{bmatrix}$$

where $\omega = e^{-i2\pi/4} = -i$. The DFT of $[0, 1, 0, -1]$ is

$$F_4 \begin{bmatrix} 0 \\ 1 \\ 0 \\ -1 \end{bmatrix} = \frac{1}{2} \begin{bmatrix} 1 & 1 & 1 & 1 \\ 1 & -i & -1 & i \\ 1 & -1 & 1 & -1 \\ 1 & i & -1 & -i \end{bmatrix} \begin{bmatrix} 0 \\ 1 \\ 0 \\ -1 \end{bmatrix} = i \begin{bmatrix} 0 \\ -1 \\ 0 \\ 1 \end{bmatrix}.$$

1 (b)   The DFT of $[1, 1, 1, 1]$ is

$$F_4 \begin{bmatrix} 1 \\ 1 \\ 1 \\ 1 \end{bmatrix} = \frac{1}{2} \begin{bmatrix} 1 & 1 & 1 & 1 \\ 1 & -i & -1 & i \\ 1 & -1 & 1 & -1 \\ 1 & i & -1 & -i \end{bmatrix} \begin{bmatrix} 1 \\ 1 \\ 1 \\ 1 \end{bmatrix} = \begin{bmatrix} 2 \\ 0 \\ 0 \\ 0 \end{bmatrix}.$$

1 (c)   The DFT of $[0, -1, 0, 1]$ is

$$F_4 \begin{bmatrix} 0 \\ -1 \\ 0 \\ 1 \end{bmatrix} = \frac{1}{2} \begin{bmatrix} 1 & 1 & 1 & 1 \\ 1 & -i & -1 & i \\ 1 & -1 & 1 & -1 \\ 1 & i & -1 & -i \end{bmatrix} \begin{bmatrix} 0 \\ -1 \\ 0 \\ 1 \end{bmatrix} = i \begin{bmatrix} 0 \\ 1 \\ 0 \\ -1 \end{bmatrix}.$$

1 (d)   The 8×8 Fourier matrix is

$$F_8 = \frac{1}{\sqrt{8}} \begin{bmatrix} \omega^0 & \omega^0 & \omega^0 & \omega^0 & \omega^0 & \omega^0 & \omega^0 & \omega^0 \\ \omega^0 & \omega^1 & \omega^2 & \omega^3 & \omega^4 & \omega^5 & \omega^6 & \omega^7 \\ \omega^0 & \omega^2 & \omega^4 & \omega^6 & \omega^8 & \omega^{10} & \omega^{12} & \omega^{14} \\ \omega^0 & \omega^3 & \omega^6 & \omega^9 & \omega^{12} & \omega^{15} & \omega^{18} & \omega^{21} \\ \omega^0 & \omega^4 & \omega^8 & \omega^{12} & \omega^{16} & \omega^{20} & \omega^{24} & \omega^{28} \\ \omega^0 & \omega^5 & \omega^{10} & \omega^{15} & \omega^{20} & \omega^{25} & \omega^{30} & \omega^{35} \\ \omega^0 & \omega^6 & \omega^{12} & \omega^{18} & \omega^{24} & \omega^{30} & \omega^{36} & \omega^{42} \\ \omega^0 & \omega^7 & \omega^{14} & \omega^{21} & \omega^{28} & \omega^{35} & \omega^{42} & \omega^{49} \end{bmatrix}$$

where $\omega = e^{-i2\pi/8} = \sqrt{2}/2 - i\sqrt{2}/2$. Note $w^2 = -i$. The DFT of $[0, 1, 0, -1, 0, 1, 0, -1]$ is

$$F_8 \begin{bmatrix} 0 \\ 1 \\ 0 \\ -1 \\ 0 \\ 1 \\ 0 \\ -1 \end{bmatrix} = \frac{1}{\sqrt{8}} \begin{bmatrix} 0 \\ \omega^1 - \omega^3 + \omega^5 - \omega^7 \\ \omega^2 - \omega^6 + \omega^{10} - \omega^{14} \\ \omega^3 - \omega^9 + \omega^{15} - \omega^{21} \\ \omega^4 - \omega^{12} + \omega^{20} - \omega^{28} \\ \omega^5 - \omega^{15} + \omega^{25} - \omega^{35} \\ \omega^6 - \omega^{18} + \omega^{30} - \omega^{42} \\ \omega^7 - \omega^{21} + \omega^{35} - \omega^{49} \end{bmatrix} = i \begin{bmatrix} 0 \\ 0 \\ -\sqrt{2} \\ 0 \\ 0 \\ 0 \\ \sqrt{2} \\ 0 \end{bmatrix}.$$

3 (a)   The inverse of the 4×4 Fourier matrix is

$$F_4^{-1} = \frac{1}{\sqrt{4}} \begin{bmatrix} \omega^0 & \omega^0 & \omega^0 & \omega^0 \\ \omega^0 & \omega^{-1} & \omega^{-2} & \omega^{-3} \\ \omega^0 & \omega^{-2} & \omega^{-4} & \omega^{-6} \\ \omega^0 & \omega^{-3} & \omega^{-6} & \omega^{-9} \end{bmatrix} = \frac{1}{2} \begin{bmatrix} 1 & 1 & 1 & 1 \\ 1 & i & -1 & -i \\ 1 & -1 & 1 & -1 \\ 1 & -i & -1 & i \end{bmatrix}$$

where $\omega = -i$. The inverse DFT of $[1, 0, 0, 0]$ is

$$F_4^{-1} \begin{bmatrix} 1 \\ 0 \\ 0 \\ 0 \end{bmatrix} = \frac{1}{2} \begin{bmatrix} 1 & 1 & 1 & 1 \\ 1 & i & -1 & -i \\ 1 & -1 & 1 & -1 \\ 1 & -i & -1 & i \end{bmatrix} \begin{bmatrix} 1 \\ 0 \\ 0 \\ 0 \end{bmatrix} = \begin{bmatrix} 1/2 \\ 1/2 \\ 1/2 \\ 1/2 \end{bmatrix}.$$

3 (b)   The inverse DFT of $[1, 1, -1, 1]$ is

$$F_4^{-1} \begin{bmatrix} 1 \\ 1 \\ -1 \\ 1 \end{bmatrix} = \frac{1}{2} \begin{bmatrix} 1 & 1 & 1 & 1 \\ 1 & i & -1 & -i \\ 1 & -1 & 1 & -1 \\ 1 & -i & -1 & i \end{bmatrix} \begin{bmatrix} 1 \\ 1 \\ -1 \\ 1 \end{bmatrix} = \begin{bmatrix} 1 \\ 1 \\ -1 \\ 1 \end{bmatrix}.$$

3 (c)   The inverse DFT of $[1, -i, 1, i]$ is

$$F_4^{-1} \begin{bmatrix} 1 \\ -i \\ 1 \\ i \end{bmatrix} = \frac{1}{2} \begin{bmatrix} 1 & 1 & 1 & 1 \\ 1 & i & -1 & -i \\ 1 & -1 & 1 & -1 \\ 1 & -i & -1 & i \end{bmatrix} \begin{bmatrix} 1 \\ -i \\ 1 \\ i \end{bmatrix} = \begin{bmatrix} 1 \\ 1 \\ 1 \\ -1 \end{bmatrix}.$$

3 (d) The 8×8 inverse Fourier matrix is

$$F_8^{-1} = \frac{1}{\sqrt{8}} \begin{bmatrix} \omega^0 & \omega^0 & \omega^0 & \omega^0 & \omega^0 & \omega^0 & \omega^0 & \omega^0 \\ \omega^0 & \omega^{-1} & \omega^{-2} & \omega^{-3} & \omega^{-4} & \omega^{-5} & \omega^{-6} & \omega^{-7} \\ \omega^0 & \omega^{-2} & \omega^{-4} & \omega^{-6} & \omega^{-8} & \omega^{-10} & \omega^{-12} & \omega^{-14} \\ \omega^0 & \omega^{-3} & \omega^{-6} & \omega^{-9} & \omega^{-12} & \omega^{-15} & \omega^{-18} & \omega^{-21} \\ \omega^0 & \omega^{-4} & \omega^{-8} & \omega^{-12} & \omega^{-16} & \omega^{-20} & \omega^{-24} & \omega^{-28} \\ \omega^0 & \omega^{-5} & \omega^{-10} & \omega^{-15} & \omega^{-20} & \omega^{-25} & \omega^{-30} & \omega^{-35} \\ \omega^0 & \omega^{-6} & \omega^{-12} & \omega^{-18} & \omega^{-24} & \omega^{-30} & \omega^{-36} & \omega^{-42} \\ \omega^0 & \omega^{-7} & \omega^{-14} & \omega^{-21} & \omega^{-28} & \omega^{-35} & \omega^{-42} & \omega^{-49} \end{bmatrix}$$

where $\omega = e^{-i2\pi/8} = \sqrt{2}/2 - i\sqrt{2}/2$. Note that $\omega^2 = -i$. The inverse DFT of the vector $[1, 0, 0, 0, 3, 0, 0, 0]$ is

$$F_8 \begin{bmatrix} 1 \\ 0 \\ 0 \\ 0 \\ 3 \\ 0 \\ 0 \\ 0 \end{bmatrix} = \frac{1}{\sqrt{8}} \begin{bmatrix} 4 \\ 1 + 3\omega^4 \\ 1 + 3\omega^8 \\ 1 + 3\omega^{12} \\ 1 + 3\omega^{16} \\ 1 + 3\omega^{20} \\ 1 + 3\omega^{24} \\ 1 + 3\omega^{28} \end{bmatrix} = \frac{1}{\sqrt{8}} \begin{bmatrix} 4 \\ -2 \\ 4 \\ -2 \\ 4 \\ -2 \\ 4 \\ -2 \end{bmatrix} = \frac{1}{\sqrt{2}} \begin{bmatrix} 2 \\ -1 \\ 2 \\ -1 \\ 2 \\ -1 \\ 2 \\ -1 \end{bmatrix}$$

5 (a) The fourth roots of unity are $1, -i, -1, i$. Since $1^1 = 1$ and $(-1)^2 = 1$, 1 and -1 are not primitive. But $i^4 = 1$ and 4 is the lowest such power, so i is a primitive fourth root. The same is true for $-i$.

5 (b) The 7th roots of unity are $r_k = \omega^k$ where $\omega = e^{-i2\pi/7}$ and $0 \le k \le 6$. The root $r_0 = 1$ is a first root of unity and is not primitive. For r_k to fail to be primitive for $k > 0$, there must be an integer $j < 7$ such that $1 = r_k^j = e^{-i2\pi jk/7}$, which implies $jk/7$ is an integer. If a prime number like 7 divides evenly into jk, it must divide either j or k. Neither is possible since both j and k are less than 7, so r_k is primitive for all $k > 0$. The primitive 7th roots of unity are $\omega, \omega^2, \ldots, \omega^6$, where $\omega = e^{-i2\pi/7}$.

5 (c) Use the argument in part (b) applied to the prime number p instead of 7. If a prime number divides evenly into the product of integers jk, then it must divide either j or k. It follows that the $p - 1$ primitive pth roots of unity are $\omega, \omega^2, \ldots, \omega^{p-1}$. There are $p - 1$ in total.

7 (a) The DFT of a real four-dimensional vector has form

$$F_4 x = \begin{bmatrix} a_0 \\ a_1 + ib_1 \\ a_2 \\ a_1 - ib_1 \end{bmatrix} = \begin{bmatrix} 0 \\ -i \\ 0 \\ i \end{bmatrix}.$$

Matching coefficients gives $a_0 = a_1 = a_2 = 0$ and $b_1 = -1$.

7 (b) Similar to (a). Matching coefficients with the DFT $[2, 0, 0, 0]^T$ results in $a_0 = 2, a_1 = a_2 = b_1 = 0$.

7 (c) Similar to (a). Matching coefficients with the DFT $[0, i, 0, -i]^T$ results in $a_0 = a_1 = a_2 = 0, b_1 = 1$.

7 (d) The DFT of a real eight-dimensional vector has form

$$
F_4 x = \begin{bmatrix} a_0 \\ a_1 + ib_1 \\ a_2 + ib_2 \\ a_3 + ib_3 \\ a_4 \\ a_3 - ib_3 \\ a_2 - ib_2 \\ a_1 - ib_1 \end{bmatrix} = \begin{bmatrix} 0 \\ 0 \\ -i\sqrt{2} \\ 0 \\ 0 \\ 0 \\ i\sqrt{2} \\ 0 \end{bmatrix}.
$$

Matching coefficients gives $a_0 = a_1 = a_2 = a_3 = a_4 = 0$ and $b_1 = 0, b_2 = -\sqrt{2}, b_3 = 0$.

EXERCISES 10.2   Trigonometric Interpolation

1 (a) The data given lies in the interval $[c, d] = [0, 1]$. Applying the DFT to $[0, 1, 0, -1]^T$ gives

$$
F_4 \begin{bmatrix} 0 \\ 1 \\ 0 \\ -1 \end{bmatrix} = \frac{1}{2} \begin{bmatrix} 1 & 1 & 1 & 1 \\ 1 & -i & -1 & i \\ 1 & -1 & 1 & -1 \\ 1 & i & -1 & -i \end{bmatrix} \begin{bmatrix} 0 \\ -1 \\ 0 \\ -1 \end{bmatrix} = i \begin{bmatrix} 0 \\ -1 \\ 0 \\ 1 \end{bmatrix},
$$

so $a_0 = a_1 = a_2 = 0$ and $b_1 = -1$. Corollary 10.8 says that

$$
\begin{aligned}
P_4(t) &= \frac{a_0}{2} + a_1 \cos 2\pi t - b_1 \sin 2\pi t + \frac{a_2}{2} \cos 4\pi t \\
&= \sin 2\pi t.
\end{aligned}
$$

1 (b) Similar to (a). The DFT of $[1, 1, -1, -1]^T$ is $[0, 1 - i, 0, 1 + i]^T$, and the coefficients are $a_0 = 0, a_1 = 1, a_2 = 0, b_1 = -1$. Therefore the trigonometric interpolating polynomial is

$$
\begin{aligned}
P_4(t) &= \frac{a_0}{2} + a_1 \cos 2\pi t - b_1 \sin 2\pi t + \frac{a_2}{2} \cos 4\pi t \\
&= \cos 2\pi t + \sin 2\pi t.
\end{aligned}
$$

1 (c) Similar to (a). The DFT of the vector $[-1, 1, -1, 1]^T$ is $[0, 0, -2, 0]^T$, and the coefficients are $a_0 = 0, a_1 = 0, a_2 = -2, b_1 = 0$. Therefore the trigonometric interpolating polynomial is $P_4(t) = -\cos 4\pi t$.

1 (d)   Similar to (a). The DFT of the vector $[1, 1, 1, 1]^T$ is $[2, 0, 0, 0]^T$, and the coefficients are $a_0 = 2, a_1 = 0, a_2 = 0, b_1 = 0$. Therefore the trigonometric interpolating polynomial is $P_4(t) = 1$.

3 (a)   The data given lies in the interval $[c, d] = [0, 1]$. Applying the DFT to $[0, 1, 0, -1, 0, 1, 0, -1]^T$ gives

$$
F_8 \begin{bmatrix} 0 \\ 1 \\ 0 \\ -1 \\ 0 \\ 1 \\ 0 \\ -1 \end{bmatrix} = \frac{1}{\sqrt{8}} \begin{bmatrix} 0 \\ \omega^1 - \omega^3 + \omega^5 - \omega^7 \\ \omega^2 - \omega^6 + \omega^{10} - \omega^{14} \\ \omega^3 - \omega^9 + \omega^{15} - \omega^{21} \\ \omega^4 - \omega^{12} + \omega^{20} - \omega^{28} \\ \omega^5 - \omega^{15} + \omega^{25} - \omega^{35} \\ \omega^6 - \omega^{18} + \omega^{30} - \omega^{42} \\ \omega^7 - \omega^{21} + \omega^{35} - \omega^{49} \end{bmatrix} = i \begin{bmatrix} 0 \\ 0 \\ -\sqrt{2} \\ 0 \\ 0 \\ 0 \\ \sqrt{2} \\ 0 \end{bmatrix},
$$

so $a_0 = a_1 = a_2 = a_3 = a_4 = b_1 = 0, b_2 = -\sqrt{2}, b_3 = 0$. Corollary 10.8 says that

$$
\begin{aligned}
P_8(t) &= \frac{a_0}{\sqrt{8}} + \frac{1}{\sqrt{2}} \left(a_1 \cos 2\pi t - b_1 \sin 2\pi t \right) + \frac{1}{\sqrt{2}} \left(a_2 \cos 4\pi t - b_2 \sin 4\pi t \right) \\
&\quad + \frac{1}{\sqrt{2}} \left(a_3 \cos 6\pi t - b_3 \sin 6\pi t \right) + \frac{a_4}{2} \cos 8\pi t \\
&= \sin 4\pi t.
\end{aligned}
$$

3 (b)   Similar to part (a). Applying the DFT to $[1, 2, 1, 0, 1, 2, 1, 0]^T$ gives

$$
F_8 \begin{bmatrix} 1 \\ 2 \\ 1 \\ 0 \\ 1 \\ 2 \\ 1 \\ 0 \end{bmatrix} = \frac{1}{\sqrt{8}} \begin{bmatrix} 8 \\ \omega^0 + 2\omega^1 + \omega^2 + \omega^4 + 2\omega^5 + \omega^6 \\ \omega^0 + 2\omega^2 + \omega^4 + \omega^8 + 2\omega^{10} + \omega^{12} \\ \omega^0 + 2\omega^3 + \omega^6 + \omega^{12} + 2\omega^{15} + \omega^{18} \\ \omega^0 + 2\omega^4 + \omega^8 + \omega^{16} + 2\omega^{20} + \omega^{24} \\ \omega^0 + 2\omega^5 + \omega^{10} + \omega^{20} + 2\omega^{25} + \omega^{30} \\ \omega^0 + 2\omega^6 + \omega^{12} + \omega^{24} + 2\omega^{30} + \omega^{36} \\ \omega^0 + 2\omega^7 + \omega^{14} + \omega^{28} + 2\omega^{35} + \omega^{42} \end{bmatrix} = \begin{bmatrix} \sqrt{8} \\ 0 \\ -\sqrt{2}i \\ 0 \\ 0 \\ 0 \\ \sqrt{2}i \\ 0 \end{bmatrix},
$$

so $a_0 = \sqrt{8}, a_1 = a_2 = a_3 = a_4 = b_1 = 0, b_2 = -\sqrt{2}, b_3 = 0$. Corollary 10.8 says that

$$
\begin{aligned}
P_8(t) &= \frac{a_0}{\sqrt{8}} + \frac{1}{\sqrt{2}} \left(a_1 \cos 2\pi t - b_1 \sin 2\pi t \right) + \frac{1}{\sqrt{2}} \left(a_2 \cos 4\pi t - b_2 \sin 4\pi t \right) \\
&\quad + \frac{1}{\sqrt{2}} \left(a_3 \cos 6\pi t - b_3 \sin 6\pi t \right) + \frac{a_4}{2} \cos 8\pi t \\
&= 1 + \sin 4\pi t.
\end{aligned}
$$

3 (c) Similar to part (a). Applying the DFT to $[1, 1, 1, 1, 0, 0, 0, 0]^T$ gives

$$F_8 \begin{bmatrix} 1 \\ 1 \\ 1 \\ 1 \\ 0 \\ 0 \\ 0 \\ 0 \end{bmatrix} = \frac{1}{\sqrt{8}} \begin{bmatrix} 4 \\ 1 - (\sqrt{2}+1)i \\ 0 \\ 1 + (\sqrt{2}-1)i \\ 0 \\ 1 - (\sqrt{2}-1)i \\ 0 \\ 1 + (\sqrt{2}+1)i \end{bmatrix},$$

so $a_0 = \sqrt{2}, a_1 = a_3 = 1/\sqrt{8}, a_2 = a_4 = 0, b_1 = -(1+\sqrt{2})/\sqrt{8}, b_2 = 0, b_3 = (\sqrt{2}-1)/\sqrt{8}$. Corollary 10.8 says that

$$
\begin{aligned}
P_8(t) &= \frac{a_0}{\sqrt{8}} + \frac{1}{\sqrt{2}}\left(a_1 \cos 2\pi t - b_1 \sin 2\pi t\right) + \frac{1}{\sqrt{2}}\left(a_2 \cos 4\pi t - b_2 \sin 4\pi t\right) \\
&\quad + \frac{1}{\sqrt{2}}\left(a_3 \cos 6\pi t - b_3 \sin 6\pi t\right) + \frac{a_4}{2} \cos 8\pi t \\
&= \frac{1}{2} + \frac{1}{4}\cos 2\pi t + \frac{\sqrt{2}+1}{4}\sin 2\pi t + \frac{1}{4}\cos 6\pi t + \frac{\sqrt{2}-1}{4}\sin 6\pi t.
\end{aligned}
$$

3 (d) Similar to part (a). Applying the DFT to $[1, -1, 1, -1, 1, -1, 1, -1]^T$ gives

$$F_8 \begin{bmatrix} 1 \\ -1 \\ 1 \\ -1 \\ 1 \\ -1 \\ 1 \\ -1 \end{bmatrix} = \frac{1}{\sqrt{8}} \begin{bmatrix} 0 \\ 0 \\ 0 \\ 0 \\ 8 \\ 0 \\ 0 \\ 0 \end{bmatrix},$$

so $a_0 = a_1 = a_2 = a_3 = 0, a_4 = \sqrt{8}, b_1 = b_2 = b_3 = 0$. Corollary 10.8 says that $P_8(t) = \cos 8\pi t$.

5 Start with the DFT Interpolation Theorem 10.6. If $x = [x_0, \ldots, x_{n-1}]$ is real, then the function

$$P(t) = \frac{1}{\sqrt{n}} \sum_{k=0}^{n-1} \left(a_k \cos \frac{2k\pi(t-c)}{d-c} - b_k \sin \frac{2k\pi(t-c)}{d-c} \right)$$

satisfies $P(t_j) = x_j$ for $j = 0, \ldots, n-1$, where $(t_j - c)/(d-c) = j/n$. Then for each integer j, k,

$$a_k \cos \frac{2k\pi(t_j - c)}{d-c} = a_k \cos \frac{2\pi k j}{n} = a_k \cos \frac{2\pi(n-k)j}{n} = a_k \cos \frac{2\pi(n-k)(t_j - c)}{d-c}$$

by Lemma 10.7, and $a_k = a_{n-k}$ due to Lemma 10.4. This shows that at $t = t_j$, the cosine terms in $P(t)$ for $k = \frac{n+1}{2}, \ldots, n-1$ are duplicates of the terms for $k = 1, \ldots, \frac{n-1}{2}$, in reverse order, and so we may discard the former, multiply the latter by 2, and still interpolate the data at the t_j. A similar argument can be made for the sine terms. For each integer j, k,

$$b_k \sin \frac{2k\pi(t_j - c)}{d - c} = b_k \sin \frac{2\pi k j}{n} = -b_k \sin \frac{2\pi(n-k)j}{n} = -b_k \sin \frac{2\pi(n-k)(t_j - c)}{d - c}$$

by Lemma 10.7, and $b_k = -b_{n-k}$ due to Lemma 10.4. This verifies that at $t = t_j$, the sine terms in $P(t)$ for $k = \frac{n+1}{2}, \ldots, n-1$ are also exact duplicates of the terms for $k = 1, \ldots, \frac{n-1}{2}$ in reverse order, and so again we may throw away the former and multiply the latter by 2. Therefore the version of (10.19) for an odd integer n is that

$$P_n(t) = \frac{a_0}{\sqrt{n}} + \frac{2}{\sqrt{n}} \sum_{k=1}^{(n-1)/2} \left(a_k \cos \frac{2k\pi(t - c)}{d - c} - b_k \sin \frac{2k\pi(t - c)}{d - c} \right),$$

satisfies $P(t_j) = x_j$ for $j = 0, \ldots, n-1$.

COMPUTER PROBLEMS 10.2

1 (a) Applying the DFT to $[0, 1, 2, 3, 4, 5, 6, 7]^T$ gives

$$F_8 \begin{bmatrix} 0 \\ 1 \\ 2 \\ 3 \\ 4 \\ 5 \\ 6 \\ 7 \end{bmatrix} = \frac{1}{\sqrt{8}} \begin{bmatrix} 28 \\ -4 + 4(1 + \sqrt{2})i \\ -4 + 4i \\ -4 + 4(\sqrt{2} - 1)i \\ -4 \\ -4 - 4(\sqrt{2} - 1)i \\ -4 - 4i \\ -4 - 4(1 + \sqrt{2})i \end{bmatrix},$$

so $a_0 = 7\sqrt{2}, a_1 = a_2 = a_3 = a_4 = -\sqrt{2}, b_1 = \sqrt{2} + 2, b_2 = \sqrt{2}, b_3 = 2 - \sqrt{2}$. Corollary 10.8 implies that

$$P_8(t) = \tfrac{7}{2} - \cos 2\pi t - (1 + \sqrt{2}) \sin 2\pi t - \cos 4\pi t - \sin 4\pi t - \cos 6\pi t + (1 - \sqrt{2}) \sin 6\pi t - \tfrac{1}{2} \cos 8\pi t.$$

The interpolating function can be plotted using the MATLAB program `dftinterp`. The interpolant and the data points are plotted in panel (a) below.

1 (b) Applying the DFT to $[2, -1, 0, 1, 1, 3, -1, -1]^T$ gives

$$F_8 \begin{bmatrix} 2 \\ -1 \\ 0 \\ 1 \\ 1 \\ 3 \\ -1 \\ -1 \end{bmatrix} = \frac{1}{\sqrt{8}} \begin{bmatrix} 4 \\ 1 - 3\sqrt{2} + (\sqrt{2} - 1)i \\ 4 - 2i \\ 1 + 3\sqrt{2} + (\sqrt{2} + 1)i \\ 0 \\ 1 + 3\sqrt{2} - (\sqrt{2} + 1)i \\ 4 + 2i \\ 1 - 3\sqrt{2} - (\sqrt{2} - 1)i \end{bmatrix},$$

so $a_0 = \sqrt{2}, a_1 = (-6 + \sqrt{2})/4, a_2 = \sqrt{2}, a_3 = (6 + \sqrt{2})/4, a_4 = 0, b_1 = (2 - \sqrt{2})/4, b_2 = -\sqrt{2}/2, b_3 = (2 + \sqrt{2})/4$. Corollary 10.8 implies that
$P_8(t) = \frac{1}{2} + \frac{1-3\sqrt{2}}{4} \cos 2\pi t + \frac{1-\sqrt{2}}{4} \sin 2\pi t + \cos 4\pi t + \frac{1}{2} \sin 4\pi t + \frac{1+3\sqrt{2}}{4} \cos 6\pi t - \frac{1+\sqrt{2}}{4} \sin 6\pi t$.
See panel (b) for the plot from `dftinterp`.

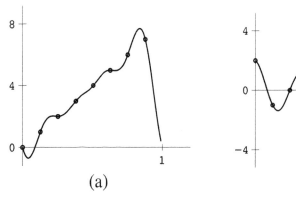
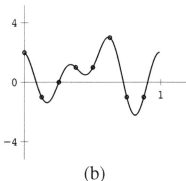

(a)   (b)

1 (c) Applying the DFT to $[3, 1, 4, 2, 3, 1, 4, 2]^T$ gives

$$F_8 \begin{bmatrix} 3 \\ 1 \\ 4 \\ 2 \\ 3 \\ 1 \\ 4 \\ 2 \end{bmatrix} = \frac{1}{\sqrt{8}} \begin{bmatrix} 20 \\ 0 \\ -2 + 2i \\ 0 \\ 8 \\ 0 \\ -2 - 2i \\ 0 \end{bmatrix},$$

so $a_0 = 5\sqrt{2}, a_1 = a_3 = 0, a_2 = -\sqrt{2}/2, a_4 = 2\sqrt{2}, b_1 = b_3 = 0, b_2 = \sqrt{2}/2$. In Corollary 10.8, $c = 0$ and $d = 8$. Equation (10.19) becomes

$$P_8(t) = \frac{5}{2} - \frac{1}{2} \cos \frac{\pi}{2} t - \frac{1}{2} \sin \frac{\pi}{2} t + \cos \pi t.$$

The interpolant is plotted in panel (c) below.

1 (d) Applying the DFT to $[1, -2, 5, 3, -2, -3, 1, 2]^T$ gives

$$F_8 \begin{bmatrix} 1 \\ -2 \\ 5 \\ 3 \\ -2 \\ -3 \\ 1 \\ 2 \end{bmatrix} = \frac{1}{\sqrt{8}} \begin{bmatrix} 5 \\ 3 - (4 + \sqrt{2})i \\ -7 + 10i \\ 3 + (4 - \sqrt{2})i \\ 5 \\ 3 - (4 - \sqrt{2})i \\ -7 - 10i \\ 3 + (4 + \sqrt{2})i \end{bmatrix}.$$

In Corollary 10.8, $c = 1$ and $d = 9$. Equation (10.19) becomes

$$\begin{aligned} P_8(t) &= \frac{5}{8} - \frac{3}{4}\cos\frac{\pi}{4}(t-1) + (1 + \frac{\sqrt{2}}{4})\sin\frac{\pi}{4}(t-1) - \frac{7}{4}\cos\frac{\pi}{2}(t-1) - \frac{5}{2}\sin\frac{\pi}{2}(t-1) \\ &+ \frac{3}{4}\cos\frac{3\pi}{4}(t-1) - (1 - \frac{\sqrt{2}}{4})\sin\frac{3\pi}{4}(t-1) + \frac{5}{8}\cos\pi(t-1). \end{aligned}$$

The trigonometric interpolant is plotted in panel (d).

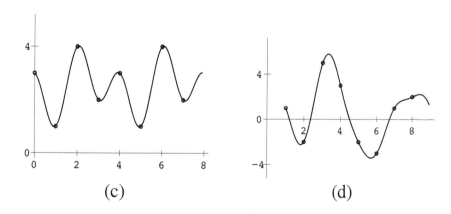

(c) (d)

3 Apply the 8×8 DFT to the data $(0, e^0), (\frac{1}{8}, e^{1/8}), \dots, (\frac{7}{8}, e^{7/8})$ and use Corollary 10.8 with $[c, d] = [0, 1]$. The trigonometric interpolant is

$$\begin{aligned} P_8(t) &= 1.6131 - 0.1253\cos 2\pi t - 0.5050\sin 2\pi t - 0.1881\cos 4\pi t - 0.2131\sin 4\pi t \\ &\quad -0.1991\cos 6\pi t - 0.0886\sin 6\pi t - 0.1007\cos 8\pi t. \end{aligned}$$

A plot of $P_8(t)$ follows.

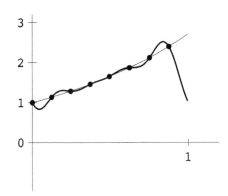

5 Similar to Computer Problem 3, but interpolating the function $f(t) = \ln t$ at the evenly-spaced points $1, 9/8, 10/8, \ldots, 15/8$. The trigonometric interpolating function is

$$
\begin{aligned}
P_8(t) \;=\; & 0.3423 - 0.1115\cos 2\pi(t-1) - 0.2040\sin 2\pi(t-1) \\
& -0.0943\cos 4\pi(t-1) - 0.0859\sin 4\pi(t-1) \\
& -0.0912\cos 6\pi(t-1) - 0.0357\sin 6\pi(t-1) \\
& -0.0453\cos 8\pi(t-1).
\end{aligned}
$$

A plot of $P_8(t)$ follows.

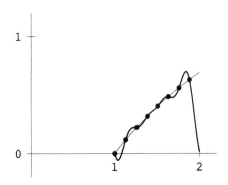

EXERCISES 10.3   The FFT and Signal Processing

1 (a) According to Theorem 10.11, the order 2 least square approximation results from dropping all but the first two terms in the trigonometric interpolating function $P_4(t) = 0 + 0\cos 2\pi t + \sin 2\pi t + 0\cos 2\pi t$. Therefore the approximating function is $P_2(t) = 0$.

1 (b) Similar to (a). Dropping all but the first two terms from the trigonometric interpolating function $P_4(t) = \cos 2\pi t + \sin 2\pi t$ yields $P_2(t) = \cos 2\pi t$.

1 (c) Similar to (a). Dropping all but the first two terms from the trigonometric interpolating function $P_4(t) = -\cos 4\pi t$ yields $P_2(t) = 0$.

1 (d)   Similar to (a). Dropping all but the first two terms from the trigonometric interpolating function $P_4(t) = 1$ yields $P_2(t) = 1$.

3 (a)   The trigonometric interpolating function is

$$
\begin{aligned}
P_8(t) &= \frac{a_0}{\sqrt{8}} + \frac{1}{\sqrt{2}}\left(a_1 \cos 2\pi t - b_1 \sin 2\pi t\right) + \frac{1}{\sqrt{2}}\left(a_2 \cos 4\pi t - b_2 \sin 4\pi t\right) \\
&\quad + \frac{1}{\sqrt{2}}\left(a_3 \cos 6\pi t - b_3 \sin 6\pi t\right) + \frac{a_4}{2}\cos 8\pi t \\
&= \sin 4\pi t.
\end{aligned}
$$

According to Theorem 10.11, the least squares approximating function is obtained by dropping all but the first four terms. Therefore $P_4(t) = 0$.

3 (b)   Similar to part (a). The trigonometric interpolation function is $P_8(t) = 1 + \sin 4\pi t$, so $P_4(t) = 1$.

3 (c)   Similar to part (a). The trigonometric interpolation function is

$$
P_8(t) = \frac{1}{2} + \frac{1}{4}\cos 2\pi t + \frac{\sqrt{2}+1}{4}\sin 2\pi t + \frac{1}{4}\cos 6\pi t + \frac{\sqrt{2}-1}{4}\sin 6\pi t,
$$

and the least squares approximation is $P_4(t) = \frac{1}{2} + \frac{1}{4}\cos 2\pi t + \frac{\sqrt{2}+1}{4}\sin 2\pi t$.

3 (d)   The trigonometric interpolation function is $P_8(t) = \cos 8\pi t$, so $P_4(t) = 0$.

5   Assume that k, l, and $n \geq 1$ are integers. Set $\omega = e^{-i2\pi/n}$, a primitive nth root of unity. Then

$$
\begin{aligned}
\cos\frac{2\pi jk}{n}\cos\frac{2\pi jl}{n} &= \frac{1}{2}\left[e^{i\frac{2\pi jk}{n}} + e^{-i\frac{2\pi jk}{n}}\right]\frac{1}{2}\left[e^{i\frac{2\pi jl}{n}} + e^{-i\frac{2\pi jl}{n}}\right] \\
&= \frac{1}{4}[\omega^{jk} + \omega^{-jk}][\omega^{jl} + \omega^{-jl}] \\
&= \frac{1}{4}[\omega^{j(k+l)} + \omega^{-j(k+l)} + \omega^{j(k-l)} + \omega^{j(l-k)}].
\end{aligned}
$$

Now Lemma 10.1 applies. If both $(k - l)/n$ and $(k + l)/n$ are integers, then so are $(l - k)/n$ and $-(k + l)/n$, so

$$
\begin{aligned}
\sum_{j=0}^{n-1}\cos\frac{2\pi jk}{n}\cos\frac{2\pi jl}{n} &= \frac{1}{4}\sum_{j=0}^{n-1}[\omega^{j(k+l)} + \omega^{-j(k+l)} + \omega^{j(k-l)} + \omega^{j(l-k)}] \\
&= \frac{1}{4}[n + n + n + n] = n.
\end{aligned}
$$

If one or the other of $(k - l)/n$ and $(k + l)/n$ is an integer, then two of the four terms sum to n and the other two sum to zero, leaving $[n + n + 0 + 0]/4 = n/2$. If neither is an integer, then

Lemma 10.1 implies the sum is zero. The same strategy can be applied to the second equality. Note that

$$
\begin{aligned}
\cos \frac{2\pi jk}{n} \sin \frac{2\pi jl}{n} &= \frac{1}{2}\left[e^{i\frac{2\pi jk}{n}} + e^{-i\frac{2\pi jk}{n}}\right]\frac{1}{2i}\left[e^{i\frac{2\pi jl}{n}} - e^{-i\frac{2\pi jl}{n}}\right] \\
&= \frac{1}{4i}[\omega^{jk} + \omega^{-jk}][\omega^{jl} - \omega^{-jl}] \\
&= \frac{1}{4i}[\omega^{j(k+l)} - \omega^{-j(k+l)} - \omega^{j(k-l)} + \omega^{j(l-k)}].
\end{aligned}
$$

Whether $(k + l)/n$ is an integer or not,

$$
\sum_{j=0}^{n-1}(\omega^{j(k+l)} - \omega^{-j(k+l)}) = 0,
$$

by Lemma 10.1. Likewise, whether $(k - l)/n$ is an integer or not,

$$
\sum_{j=0}^{n-1}(\omega^{j(k-l)} - \omega^{j(l-k)}) = 0.
$$

Therefore

$$
\sum_{j=0}^{n-1}\cos \frac{2\pi jk}{n} \sin \frac{2\pi jl}{n} = 0
$$

for all integers $k, l, n \geq 1$. Finally, we can express

$$
\begin{aligned}
\sin \frac{2\pi jk}{n} \sin \frac{2\pi jl}{n} &= \frac{1}{2i}\left[e^{i\frac{2\pi jk}{n}} - e^{-i\frac{2\pi jk}{n}}\right]\frac{1}{2i}\left[e^{i\frac{2\pi jl}{n}} - e^{-i\frac{2\pi jl}{n}}\right] \\
&= -\frac{1}{4}[\omega^{jk} - \omega^{-jk}][\omega^{jl} - \omega^{-jl}] \\
&= -\frac{1}{4}[\omega^{j(k+l)} + \omega^{-j(k+l)} - \omega^{j(k-l)} - \omega^{j(l-k)}].
\end{aligned}
$$

If both $(k - l)/n$ and $(k + l)/n$ are integers, all four contributions sum to n, and the total is $-[n + n - n - n]/4 = 0$. If $(k - l)/n$ is an integer and $(k + l)/n$ is not, then by Lemma 10.1, the sum is $-[0 + 0 - n - n]/4 = n/2$. If $(k + l)/n$ is an integer and $(k - l)/n$ is not, the sum is $-[n + n - 0 - 0]/4 = -n/2$. If neither is an integer, the sum is zero.

COMPUTER PROBLEMS 10.3

1 (a)   The DFT of $[3, 0, -3, 0]^T$ is $[0, 3, 0, 3]^T$. Therefore $a_0 = a_2 = b_1 = 0$ and $a_1 = 3$. The trigonometric interpolating function is $F_4(t) = 3\cos 2\pi t$, and the least squares function of order 2 is $F_2(t) = 3\cos 2\pi t$ by Corollary 10.12. The plot is shown in panel (a) below.

1 (b)   The DFT of $[2, 0, 5, 1]$ is $[4, -3/2 + i/2, 3, -3/2 - i/2]$, so $a_0 = 4, a_1 = 3/2, a_2 = 3, b_1 = 1/2$. Therefore the trigonometric interpolating function is $F_4(t) = 2 - \frac{3}{2}\cos 2\pi t - \frac{1}{2}\sin 2\pi t + \frac{3}{2}\cos 4\pi t$, and the least squares approximating function of order 2 takes the first two terms: $F_2(t) = 2 - \frac{3}{2}\cos 2\pi t$. Plot (b) below shows $F_4(t)$ as the dashed curve and $F_2(t)$ as the solid curve.

1 (c)   The DFT of $[5, 2, 6, 1]$ is $[7, -\frac{1}{2} - \frac{1}{2}i, 4, -\frac{1}{2} + \frac{1}{2}i]$, and $a_0 = 7, a_1 = -1/2, a_2 = 4, b_1 = -1/2$. Therefore $F_4(t) = \frac{7}{2} - \frac{1}{2}\cos \frac{\pi}{2}t + \frac{1}{2}\sin \frac{\pi}{2}t + 2\cos \pi t$, and $F_2(t) = \frac{7}{2} - \frac{1}{2}\cos \frac{\pi}{2}t$. The plot in panel (c) below shows $F_4(t)$ as the dashed curve and $F_2(t)$ as the solid curve.

1 (d)   The least squares functions are $F_4(t) = 2 - 2\cos \frac{\pi}{3}(t - 1) - \cos \frac{2\pi}{3}(t - 1)$, and $F_2(t) = 2 - 2\cos \frac{\pi}{3}(t - 1)$. The plot is in panel (d).

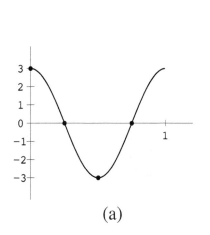

(a)

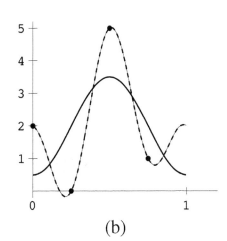

(b)

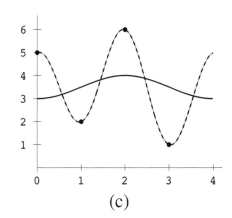

(c)

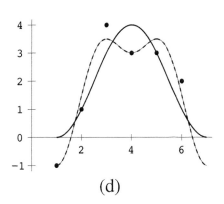

(d)

3 Set $n = 2^{14}$. The order m least squares approximations are shown below for (a) $m = n/2$ (b) $m = n/4$ (c) $m = n/8$ (d) original signal.

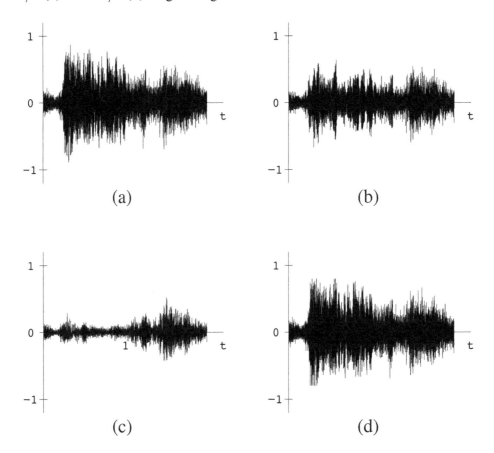

CHAPTER 11
Compression

EXERCISES 11.1   The Discrete Cosine Transform

1 (a)   Begin by applying the DCT to $[3, 3]^T$:

$$y = Cx = \begin{bmatrix} \frac{1}{\sqrt{2}} & \frac{1}{\sqrt{2}} \\ \cos\frac{\pi}{4} & \cos\frac{3\pi}{4} \end{bmatrix} \begin{bmatrix} 3 \\ 3 \end{bmatrix} = \begin{bmatrix} \frac{1}{\sqrt{2}} & \frac{1}{\sqrt{2}} \\ \frac{1}{\sqrt{2}} & -\frac{1}{\sqrt{2}} \end{bmatrix} \begin{bmatrix} 3 \\ 3 \end{bmatrix} = \begin{bmatrix} 3\sqrt{2} \\ 0 \end{bmatrix}$$

Theorem 11.2 provides the interpolating function

$$P_2(t) = \frac{1}{\sqrt{2}}y_0 + y_1 \cos\frac{(2t+1)\pi}{4}$$

for the data $(0, 3), (1, 3)$. Since $y_0 = 3\sqrt{2}$ and $y_1 = 0$, this reduces to $P_2(t) = 3$.

1 (b)   The DCT is

$$y = \begin{bmatrix} \frac{1}{\sqrt{2}} & \frac{1}{\sqrt{2}} \\ \frac{1}{\sqrt{2}} & -\frac{1}{\sqrt{2}} \end{bmatrix} \begin{bmatrix} 2 \\ -2 \end{bmatrix} = \begin{bmatrix} 0 \\ 2\sqrt{2} \end{bmatrix}$$

The interpolating function is

$$\begin{aligned} P_2(t) &= \frac{1}{\sqrt{2}}y_0 + y_1 \cos\frac{(2t+1)\pi}{4} \\ &= 2\sqrt{2}\cos\frac{(2t+1)\pi}{4} \end{aligned}$$

1 (c)   The DCT is

$$y = \begin{bmatrix} \frac{1}{\sqrt{2}} & \frac{1}{\sqrt{2}} \\ \frac{1}{\sqrt{2}} & -\frac{1}{\sqrt{2}} \end{bmatrix} \begin{bmatrix} 3 \\ 1 \end{bmatrix} = \begin{bmatrix} 2\sqrt{2} \\ \sqrt{2} \end{bmatrix}$$

The interpolating function is

$$\begin{aligned} P_2(t) &= \frac{1}{\sqrt{2}}y_0 + y_1 \cos\frac{(2t+1)\pi}{4} \\ &= 2 + \sqrt{2}\cos\frac{(2t+1)\pi}{4}. \end{aligned}$$

1 (d)   The DCT is

$$y = \begin{bmatrix} \frac{1}{\sqrt{2}} & \frac{1}{\sqrt{2}} \\ \frac{1}{\sqrt{2}} & -\frac{1}{\sqrt{2}} \end{bmatrix} \begin{bmatrix} 4 \\ -1 \end{bmatrix} = \begin{bmatrix} \frac{3}{2}\sqrt{2} \\ \frac{5}{2}\sqrt{2} \end{bmatrix}$$

The interpolating function is

$$
\begin{aligned}
P_2(t) &= \frac{1}{\sqrt{2}} y_0 + y_1 \cos \frac{(2t+1)\pi}{4} \\
&= \frac{3}{2} + \frac{5\sqrt{2}}{2} \cos \frac{(2t+1)\pi}{4}
\end{aligned}
$$

3 (a)   Begin by applying the DCT to $[1, 0, 1, 0]^T$:

$$
y = Cx = \begin{bmatrix} a & a & a & a \\ b & c & -c & -b \\ a & -a & -a & a \\ c & -b & b & -c \end{bmatrix} \begin{bmatrix} 1 \\ 0 \\ 1 \\ 0 \end{bmatrix} = \begin{bmatrix} 1 \\ b-c \\ 0 \\ b+c \end{bmatrix}
$$

where

$$
a = \frac{1}{2}, \quad b = \frac{1}{\sqrt{2}} \cos \frac{\pi}{8} = \frac{\sqrt{2+\sqrt{2}}}{2\sqrt{2}}, \quad c = \frac{1}{\sqrt{2}} \cos \frac{3\pi}{8} = \frac{\sqrt{2-\sqrt{2}}}{2\sqrt{2}}.
$$

According to Theorem 11.2, the interpolating function is

$$
\begin{aligned}
P_4(t) &= \frac{1}{2} y_0 + \frac{1}{\sqrt{2}} \left[y_1 \cos \frac{(2t+1)\pi}{8} + y_2 \cos \frac{2(2t+1)\pi}{8} + y_3 \cos \frac{3(2t+1)\pi}{8} \right] \\
&= \frac{1}{2} + \frac{b-c}{\sqrt{2}} \cos \frac{(2t+1)\pi}{8} + \frac{b+c}{\sqrt{2}} \cos \frac{3(2t+1)\pi}{8}.
\end{aligned}
$$

3 (b)   The DCT of $[1, 1, 1, 1]^T$ is

$$
y = Cx = \begin{bmatrix} a & a & a & a \\ b & c & -c & -b \\ a & -a & -a & a \\ c & -b & b & -c \end{bmatrix} \begin{bmatrix} 1 \\ 1 \\ 1 \\ 1 \end{bmatrix} = \begin{bmatrix} 4a \\ 0 \\ 0 \\ 0 \end{bmatrix} = \begin{bmatrix} 2 \\ 0 \\ 0 \\ 0 \end{bmatrix}
$$

The interpolating function is

$$
P_4(t) = \frac{1}{2} y_0 + \frac{1}{\sqrt{2}} \left[y_1 \cos \frac{(2t+1)\pi}{8} + y_2 \cos \frac{2(2t+1)\pi}{8} + y_3 \cos \frac{3(2t+1)\pi}{8} \right] = 1.
$$

3 (c)   The DCT of $[1, 0, 0, 0]^T$ is

$$
y = Cx = \begin{bmatrix} a & a & a & a \\ b & c & -c & -b \\ a & -a & -a & a \\ c & -b & b & -c \end{bmatrix} \begin{bmatrix} 1 \\ 0 \\ 0 \\ 0 \end{bmatrix} = \begin{bmatrix} 1/2 \\ b \\ 1/2 \\ c \end{bmatrix}
$$

The interpolating function is

$$P_4(t) = \frac{1}{2}y_0 + \frac{1}{\sqrt{2}}\left[y_1 \cos\frac{(2t+1)\pi}{8} + y_2 \cos\frac{2(2t+1)\pi}{8} + y_3 \cos\frac{3(2t+1)\pi}{8}\right]$$
$$= \frac{1}{4} + \frac{b}{\sqrt{2}}\cos\frac{(2t+1)\pi}{8} + \frac{1}{2\sqrt{2}}\cos\frac{2(2t+1)\pi}{8} + \frac{c}{\sqrt{2}}\cos\frac{3(2t+1)\pi}{8}.$$

3 (d) The DCT of $[1, 2, 3, 4]^T$ is

$$y = Cx = \begin{bmatrix} a & a & a & a \\ b & c & -c & -b \\ a & -a & -a & a \\ c & -b & b & -c \end{bmatrix}\begin{bmatrix} 1 \\ 2 \\ 3 \\ 4 \end{bmatrix} = \begin{bmatrix} 5 \\ -c - 3b \\ 0 \\ b - 3c \end{bmatrix}.$$

The interpolating function is

$$P_4(t) = \frac{1}{2}y_0 + \frac{1}{\sqrt{2}}\left[y_1 \cos\frac{(2t+1)\pi}{8} + y_2 \cos\frac{2(2t+1)\pi}{8} + y_3 \cos\frac{3(2t+1)\pi}{8}\right]$$
$$= \frac{5}{2} - \frac{c + 3b}{\sqrt{2}}\cos\frac{(2t+1)\pi}{8} + \frac{b - 3c}{\sqrt{2}}\cos\frac{3(2t+1)\pi}{8}.$$

5 The half-angle formula for cosine is

$$\cos\frac{\theta}{2} = \sqrt{\frac{1 + \cos\theta}{2}}.$$

Therefore

$$b = \cos\frac{\pi}{8} = \sqrt{\frac{1 + \cos\frac{\pi}{4}}{2}} = \frac{\sqrt{2 + \sqrt{2}}}{2}$$
$$c = \cos\frac{3\pi}{8} = \sqrt{\frac{1 + \cos\frac{3\pi}{4}}{2}} = \frac{\sqrt{2 - \sqrt{2}}}{2}$$

Using the identities $\cos(2\pi - \theta) = \cos\theta$ and $\cos(\pi - \theta) = -\cos\theta$, the rest of the matrix entries can be identified with $\pm a, b$ or c.

COMPUTER PROBLEMS 11.1

1 Compute $y = Cx$, where C is the 4×4 DCT matrix. Then plot the interpolating function from Theorem 11.2. The results are shown below.

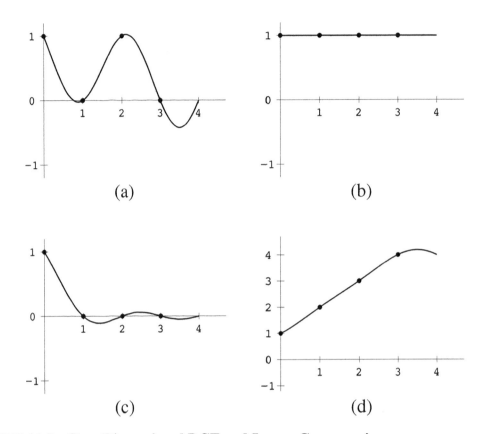

$$\text{(a)} \qquad\qquad\qquad\qquad \text{(b)}$$

$$\text{(c)} \qquad\qquad\qquad\qquad \text{(d)}$$

EXERCISES 11.2   Two-Dimensional DCT and Image Compressions

1 (a)   The 2D-DCT is obtained by $Y = CXC^T$, where C is the 2×2 DCT matrix.

$$Y = \begin{bmatrix} \frac{1}{\sqrt{2}} & \frac{1}{\sqrt{2}} \\ \frac{1}{\sqrt{2}} & -\frac{1}{\sqrt{2}} \end{bmatrix} \begin{bmatrix} 1 & 0 \\ 0 & 0 \end{bmatrix} \begin{bmatrix} \frac{1}{\sqrt{2}} & \frac{1}{\sqrt{2}} \\ \frac{1}{\sqrt{2}} & -\frac{1}{\sqrt{2}} \end{bmatrix} = \begin{bmatrix} \frac{1}{2} & \frac{1}{2} \\ \frac{1}{2} & \frac{1}{2} \end{bmatrix}.$$

The interpolating function is given by Theorem 11.6:

$$\begin{aligned}
P_2(s,t) &= \sum_{k=0}^{1}\sum_{l=0}^{1} y_{kl} a_k a_l \cos \frac{k(2s+1)\pi}{4} \cos \frac{l(2t+1)\pi}{4} \\
&= \frac{1}{4} + \frac{1}{2}\frac{1}{\sqrt{2}} \cos \frac{(2t+1)\pi}{4} + \frac{1}{2}\frac{1}{\sqrt{2}} \cos \frac{(2s+1)\pi}{4} \\
&\quad + \frac{1}{2} \cos \frac{(2s+1)\pi}{4} \cos \frac{(2t+1)\pi}{4}
\end{aligned}$$

1 (b)

$$Y = \begin{bmatrix} \frac{1}{\sqrt{2}} & \frac{1}{\sqrt{2}} \\ \frac{1}{\sqrt{2}} & -\frac{1}{\sqrt{2}} \end{bmatrix} \begin{bmatrix} 1 & 0 \\ 1 & 0 \end{bmatrix} \begin{bmatrix} \frac{1}{\sqrt{2}} & \frac{1}{\sqrt{2}} \\ \frac{1}{\sqrt{2}} & -\frac{1}{\sqrt{2}} \end{bmatrix} = \begin{bmatrix} 1 & 1 \\ 0 & 0 \end{bmatrix}.$$

The interpolating function is given by Theorem 11.6:

$$P_2(s,t) = \frac{1}{2} + \frac{1}{\sqrt{2}} \cos \frac{(2t+1)\pi}{4}$$

1 (c)

$$Y = \begin{bmatrix} \frac{1}{\sqrt{2}} & \frac{1}{\sqrt{2}} \\ \frac{1}{\sqrt{2}} & -\frac{1}{\sqrt{2}} \end{bmatrix} \begin{bmatrix} 1 & 1 \\ 1 & 1 \end{bmatrix} \begin{bmatrix} \frac{1}{\sqrt{2}} & \frac{1}{\sqrt{2}} \\ \frac{1}{\sqrt{2}} & -\frac{1}{\sqrt{2}} \end{bmatrix} = \begin{bmatrix} 2 & 0 \\ 0 & 0 \end{bmatrix}.$$

The interpolating function is $P_2(s,t) = 1$

1 (d)

$$Y = \begin{bmatrix} \frac{1}{\sqrt{2}} & \frac{1}{\sqrt{2}} \\ \frac{1}{\sqrt{2}} & -\frac{1}{\sqrt{2}} \end{bmatrix} \begin{bmatrix} 1 & 0 \\ 0 & 1 \end{bmatrix} \begin{bmatrix} \frac{1}{\sqrt{2}} & \frac{1}{\sqrt{2}} \\ \frac{1}{\sqrt{2}} & -\frac{1}{\sqrt{2}} \end{bmatrix} = \begin{bmatrix} 1 & 0 \\ 0 & 1 \end{bmatrix}.$$

The interpolating function is

$$P_2(s,t) = \frac{1}{2} + \cos \frac{(2s+1)\pi}{4} \cos \frac{(2t+1)\pi}{4}$$

3 (a)   The 2D-DCT is

$$Y = CXC^T \begin{bmatrix} 0 & 2(c+b) & 2 & 2(c-b) \\ 0 & 0 & 0 & 0 \\ 0 & 0 & 0 & 0 \\ 0 & 0 & 0 & 0 \end{bmatrix},$$

where

$$b = \frac{1}{\sqrt{2}} \cos \frac{\pi}{8} = \frac{\sqrt{2+\sqrt{2}}}{2\sqrt{2}}, \quad c = \frac{1}{\sqrt{2}} \cos \frac{3\pi}{8} = \frac{\sqrt{2-\sqrt{2}}}{2\sqrt{2}}.$$

The least squares approximation is composed of the first three terms of the interpolating function given by Theorem 11.6, corresponding to the three upper-left-most entries in the transform Y. Substituting the values from Y, we find

$$P(t) = \frac{b+c}{\sqrt{2}} \cos \frac{(2t+1)\pi}{8}.$$

3 (b)   Similar to part (a). The 2D-DCT is

$$\begin{bmatrix} 1 & 0 & 0 & 0 \\ 0 & 1 & 0 & 0 \\ 0 & 0 & 1 & 0 \\ 0 & 0 & 0 & 1 \end{bmatrix},$$

and the least squares approximating function is $P(t) = 1/4$.

3 (c) The 2D-DCT is

$$\begin{bmatrix} 1 & 0 & -1 & 0 \\ 0 & 0 & 0 & 0 \\ -1 & 0 & 1 & 0 \\ 0 & 0 & 0 & 0 \end{bmatrix},$$

and the least squares approximating function is $P(t) = 1/4$.

3 (d) The 2D-DCT is

$$\begin{bmatrix} 8 & 0 & 4 & 0 \\ 4(b-c) & 0 & -4(b-c) & 0 \\ 0 & 0 & 0 & 0 \\ 4(b+c) & 0 & -4(b+c) & 0 \end{bmatrix}.$$

The interpolating function is

$$P_4(s, t) = 2 + \sqrt{2}(b - c) \cos \frac{(2s + 1)\pi}{8}.$$

COMPUTER PROBLEMS 11.2

1 (a) The 2D-DCT is computed as

$$Y = CXC^T = \begin{bmatrix} 0 & -3.8268 & 0 & -9.2388 \\ 0 & 1.7071 & 0 & 4.1213 \\ 0 & 0.0000 & 0 & 0.0000 \\ 0 & 0.1213 & 0 & 0.2929 \end{bmatrix}.$$

1 (b)

$$Y = CXC^T = \begin{bmatrix} 0.0000 & 0.0000 & 0.0000 & 0.0000 \\ 0.0000 & 2.1213 & -0.7654 & -0.8787 \\ 0.0000 & 0.0000 & 0.0000 & 0.0000 \\ 0.0000 & 5.1213 & -1.8478 & -2.1213 \end{bmatrix}$$

1 (c)

$$Y = CXC^T = \begin{bmatrix} 4.7500 & 1.4419 & 0.2500 & 0.2146 \\ -0.7886 & 0.5732 & -1.4419 & -1.0910 \\ 0.2500 & 2.6363 & -2.2500 & -0.8214 \\ 0.0560 & -2.0910 & -0.2146 & 0.9268 \end{bmatrix}$$

1 (d)

$$Y = CXC^T = \begin{bmatrix} 0 & -4.4609 & 0 & -0.3170 \\ -4.4609 & 0 & 0 & 0 \\ 0 & 0 & 0 & 0 \\ -0.3170 & 0 & 0 & 0 \end{bmatrix}$$

EXERCISES 11.3   Huffman Coding

1 (a)   Of the eight symbols, A appears 2 times, B appears 5 times, and C one time. The empirical probabilities are $P(A) = 2/8 = 1/4, P(B) = 5/8$, and $P(C) = 1/8$. The Shannon information is

$$I = -\sum_{i=1}^{3} p_i \log_2 p_i = -\frac{1}{4}\log_2\frac{1}{4} - \frac{5}{8}\log_2\frac{5}{8} - \frac{1}{8}\log_2\frac{1}{8} \approx 1.30.$$

1 (b)   The empirical probabilities are $P(A) = 3/8, P(B) = 1/4$, and $P(C) = 3/8$. The Shannon information is

$$I = -\sum_{i=1}^{3} p_i \log_2 p_i = -\frac{3}{8}\log_2\frac{3}{8} - \frac{1}{4}\log_2\frac{1}{4} - \frac{3}{8}\log_2\frac{3}{8} \approx 1.56.$$

1 (c)   The empirical probabilities are $P(A) = 1/2, P(B) = 3/8$, and $P(C) = 1/8$. The Shannon information is

$$I = -\sum_{i=1}^{3} p_i \log_2 p_i = -\frac{1}{2}\log_2\frac{1}{2} - \frac{3}{8}\log_2\frac{3}{8} - \frac{1}{8}\log_2\frac{1}{8} \approx 1.41.$$

3 (a)   The empirical probabilities of the symbols are

A	B	C	R	M	U	Y	!	–
$\frac{3}{11}$	$\frac{1}{11}$	$\frac{1}{11}$	$\frac{1}{11}$	$\frac{1}{11}$	$\frac{1}{11}$	$\frac{1}{11}$	$\frac{1}{11}$	$\frac{1}{11}$

The Shannon information is

$$I = -\sum_{i=1}^{2} p_i \log_2 p_i = -\left(\frac{3}{11}\log_2\frac{3}{11} + \frac{8}{11}\log_2\frac{1}{11}\right) \approx 3.03.$$

The Huffman tree is

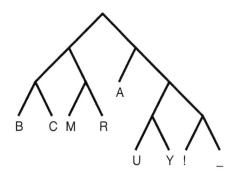

The bit stream representing the message AY CARUMBA! is

$$10\ 1101\ 1111\ 001\ 10\ 011\ 1100\ 010\ 000\ 10\ 1110$$

The stream contains 34 bits, or $34/11 \approx 3.09$ bits/symbol.

3 (b) The empirical probabilities of the symbols are

A	C	E	G	H	I	M	O	P	R	S	T	−
$\frac{1}{19}$	$\frac{1}{19}$	$\frac{3}{19}$	$\frac{1}{19}$	$\frac{1}{19}$	$\frac{1}{19}$	$\frac{2}{19}$	$\frac{1}{19}$	$\frac{1}{19}$	$\frac{1}{19}$	$\frac{5}{19}$	$\frac{1}{19}$	$\frac{2}{19}$

The Shannon information is

$$I = -\sum_{i=1}^{3} p_i \log_2 p_i \approx 3.42.$$

A Huffman tree is

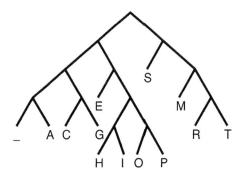

The bit stream representing COMPRESS THIS MESSAGE is

0010 01110 110 01111 1110 010 10 10 0000
1111 01100 01101 10 0000
110 010 10 10 0001 0011 010

The stream contains 73 bits, or $73/21 \approx 3.48$ bits/symbol.

3 (c) The empirical probabilities of the symbols are

A	B	E	H	L	O	R	S	T	Y	−
$\frac{2}{35}$	$\frac{1}{35}$	$\frac{1}{5}$	$\frac{4}{35}$	$\frac{4}{35}$	$\frac{1}{35}$	$\frac{1}{35}$	$\frac{8}{35}$	$\frac{1}{35}$	$\frac{1}{35}$	$\frac{1}{7}$

The Shannon information is

$$I = -\sum_{i=1}^{3} p_i \log_2 p_i \approx 3.04.$$

A Huffman tree is

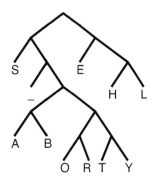

The bit stream representing SHE SELLS SEASHELLS BY THE SEASHORE is

00 110 10 010 00 10 111 111 00 010 00 10 01100 00 110 10 111 111 00 010

01101 011111 010 011110 110 10 010 00 10 01100 00 110 011100 011101 10

The stream contains 108 bits, or $108/35 \approx 3.09$ bits/symbol.

EXERCISES 11.4   Modified DCT and Audio Compression

1 (a) If x is a four-dimensional vector, the MDCT is

$$Mx = E \begin{bmatrix} -Rx_3 - x_4 \\ x_1 - Rx_2 \end{bmatrix} = E \begin{bmatrix} -x_3 - x_4 \\ x_1 - x_2 \end{bmatrix}$$

where E is the 2×2 DCT4 matrix

$$E = \begin{bmatrix} b & c \\ c & -b \end{bmatrix}$$

with entries $b = \cos \pi/8, c = \cos 3\pi/8$. Therefore

$$M \begin{bmatrix} 1 \\ 3 \\ 5 \\ 7 \end{bmatrix} = E \begin{bmatrix} -x_3 - x_4 \\ x_1 - x_2 \end{bmatrix} = \begin{bmatrix} b & c \\ c & -b \end{bmatrix} \begin{bmatrix} -12 \\ -2 \end{bmatrix} = \begin{bmatrix} -12b - 2c \\ -12c + 2b \end{bmatrix}.$$

1 (b) Similar to (a). The MDCT is

$$M \begin{bmatrix} -2 \\ -1 \\ 1 \\ 2 \end{bmatrix} = \begin{bmatrix} b & c \\ c & -b \end{bmatrix} \begin{bmatrix} -3 \\ -1 \end{bmatrix} = \begin{bmatrix} -3b - c \\ -3c + b \end{bmatrix}.$$

1 (c)   Similar to (a). The MDCT is

$$M \begin{bmatrix} 4 \\ -1 \\ 3 \\ 5 \end{bmatrix} = \begin{bmatrix} b & c \\ c & -b \end{bmatrix} \begin{bmatrix} -8 \\ 5 \end{bmatrix} = \begin{bmatrix} -8b + 5c \\ -5b - 8c \end{bmatrix}.$$

3 (a)   To quantize to 4 bits on $(-1, 1)$, we divide by $q = 2M/(2^b - 1) = 2/15$ and round. Given $y = 2/3$,

$$z = \text{round} \left(\frac{2/3}{2/15} \right) = 5 = +101.$$

Dequantizing is multiplication by q:

$$\overline{y} = qz = \frac{2}{15}5 = \frac{2}{3},$$

and the quantization error is 0.

3 (b)   Divide by $2/15$ and round.

$$z = \text{round} \left(\frac{0.6}{2/15} \right) = 5 = +101.$$

Dequantizing is multiplication by q:

$$\overline{y} = qz = \frac{2}{15}5 = \frac{2}{3},$$

and the quantization error is $|2/3 - 3/5| = 1/15$.

3 (c)   Divide by $2/15$ and round.

$$z = \text{round} \left(\frac{3/7}{2/15} \right) = 3 = +011.$$

Dequantizing is multiplication by q:

$$\overline{y} = qz = \frac{2}{15}3 = \frac{2}{5},$$

and the quantization error is $|2/5 - 3/7| = 1/35$.

5 (a)   To quantize to 8 bits on $(-4, 4)$, we divide by $q = 2(4)/(2^8 - 1) = 8/255$ and round. Given $y = 3/2$,

$$z = \text{round} \left(\frac{3/2}{8/255} \right) = 48 = +0110000.$$

Dequantization:

$$\overline{y} = qz = \frac{8}{255}48 = \frac{384}{255},$$

quantization error $= 384/255 - 3/2 = 1/170$.

5 (b) Divide by $8/255$ and round.

$$z = \text{round}\left(\frac{-7/5}{8/255}\right) = -45 = -0101101.$$

Dequantization:

$$\overline{y} = qz = \frac{8}{255}(-45) = -\frac{72}{51},$$

and the quantization error is $|72/51 + 7/5| = 1/85$.

5 (c) Divide by $8/255$ and round.

$$z = \text{round}\left(\frac{2.9}{8/255}\right) = 92 = +1011100.$$

Dequantization:

$$\overline{y} = qz = \frac{8}{255}92 = \frac{736}{255},$$

and the quantization error is $|736/255 - 2.9| = 7/510$.

5 (d) Divide by $8/255$ and round.

$$z = \text{round}\left(\frac{\pi}{8/255}\right) = 100 = +1100100.$$

Dequantization:

$$\overline{y} = qz = \frac{8}{255}100 = \frac{160}{51},$$

and the quantization error is $|160/51 - \pi| \approx 0.0043$.

7 (a) To quantize to 4 bits on $(-6, 6)$, we divide by $q = 2(6)/(2^4 - 1) = 4/5$ and round.

$$v_1 = M \begin{bmatrix} -3 \\ -2 \\ -1 \\ 1 \end{bmatrix} = \begin{bmatrix} -c \\ b \end{bmatrix} \approx \begin{bmatrix} -0.3827 \\ 0.9239 \end{bmatrix} \longrightarrow \begin{bmatrix} 0 \\ 1 \end{bmatrix},$$

$$v_2 = M \begin{bmatrix} -1 \\ 1 \\ 2 \\ 3 \end{bmatrix} = \begin{bmatrix} -5b - 2c \\ 2b - 5c \end{bmatrix} \approx \begin{bmatrix} -5.3848 \\ -0.0657 \end{bmatrix} \longrightarrow \begin{bmatrix} -7 \\ 0 \end{bmatrix}$$

Dequantization:

$$\bar{v}_1 = \frac{4}{5}\begin{bmatrix} 0 \\ 1 \end{bmatrix} = \begin{bmatrix} 0.0 \\ 0.8 \end{bmatrix}, \quad \bar{v}_2 = \frac{4}{5}\begin{bmatrix} -7 \\ 0 \end{bmatrix} = \begin{bmatrix} -5.6 \\ 0.0 \end{bmatrix}$$

$$\begin{bmatrix} w_1 \\ w_2 \end{bmatrix} = N\bar{v}_1 = \begin{bmatrix} -0.7391 \\ 0.7391 \\ -0.3061 \\ -0.3061 \end{bmatrix}$$

$$\begin{bmatrix} w_3 \\ w_4 \end{bmatrix} = N\bar{v}_2 = \begin{bmatrix} -2.1430 \\ 2.1430 \\ 5.1737 \\ 5.1737 \end{bmatrix}$$

The reconstruction is

$$u_2 = \frac{1}{2}(w_2 + w_3) = \frac{1}{2}\left(\begin{bmatrix} -0.3061 \\ -0.3061 \end{bmatrix} + \begin{bmatrix} -2.1430 \\ 2.1430 \end{bmatrix} \right) = \begin{bmatrix} -1.2246 \\ 0.9184 \end{bmatrix},$$

compared to the original overlapped data $[-1, 1]$.

7 (b) Similar to part (a).

$$v_1 = M\begin{bmatrix} 1 \\ -2 \\ 2 \\ -1 \end{bmatrix} = \begin{bmatrix} -b + 3c \\ -3b - c \end{bmatrix} \approx \begin{bmatrix} 0.2242 \\ -3.1543 \end{bmatrix} \longrightarrow \begin{bmatrix} 0 \\ -4 \end{bmatrix},$$

$$v_2 = M\begin{bmatrix} 2 \\ -1 \\ 3 \\ 0 \end{bmatrix} = \begin{bmatrix} -3b + 3c \\ -3b - 3c \end{bmatrix} \approx \begin{bmatrix} -1.6236 \\ -3.9197 \end{bmatrix} \longrightarrow \begin{bmatrix} -2 \\ -5 \end{bmatrix}$$

Dequantization:

$$\bar{v}_1 = \frac{4}{5}\begin{bmatrix} 0 \\ -4 \end{bmatrix} = \begin{bmatrix} 0.0 \\ -3.2 \end{bmatrix}, \quad \bar{v}_2 = \frac{4}{5}\begin{bmatrix} -2 \\ -5 \end{bmatrix} = \begin{bmatrix} -1.6 \\ -4.0 \end{bmatrix}$$

$$\begin{bmatrix} w_1 \\ w_2 \end{bmatrix} = N\bar{v}_1 = \begin{bmatrix} 2.9564 \\ -2.9564 \\ 1.2246 \\ 1.2246 \end{bmatrix}$$

$$\begin{bmatrix} w_3 \\ w_4 \end{bmatrix} = N\bar{v}_1 = \begin{bmatrix} 3.0832 \\ -3.0832 \\ 3.0089 \\ 3.0089 \end{bmatrix}$$

The reconstruction is

$$u_2 = \frac{1}{2}(w_2 + w_3) = \frac{1}{2}\left(\begin{bmatrix} 1.2246 \\ 1.2246 \end{bmatrix} + \begin{bmatrix} 3.0832 \\ -3.0832 \end{bmatrix}\right) = \begin{bmatrix} 2.1539 \\ -0.9293 \end{bmatrix},$$

compared to the original overlapped data $[2, -1]$.

7 (c) Similar to part (a).

$$v_1 = M \begin{bmatrix} 4 \\ 1 \\ -2 \\ -3 \end{bmatrix} = \begin{bmatrix} 5b + 3c \\ -3b + 5c \end{bmatrix} \approx \begin{bmatrix} 5.7674 \\ -0.8582 \end{bmatrix} \longrightarrow \begin{bmatrix} 7 \\ -1 \end{bmatrix},$$

$$v_2 = M \begin{bmatrix} -2 \\ -3 \\ 0 \\ 3 \end{bmatrix} = \begin{bmatrix} -3b + c \\ -b - 3c \end{bmatrix} \approx \begin{bmatrix} -2.3890 \\ -2.0719 \end{bmatrix} \longrightarrow \begin{bmatrix} -3 \\ -3 \end{bmatrix}$$

Dequantization:

$$\bar{v}_1 = \frac{4}{5}\begin{bmatrix} 7 \\ -1 \end{bmatrix} = \begin{bmatrix} 5.6 \\ -0.8 \end{bmatrix}, \quad \bar{v}_2 = \frac{4}{5}\begin{bmatrix} -3 \\ -3 \end{bmatrix} = \begin{bmatrix} -2.4 \\ -2.4 \end{bmatrix}$$

$$\begin{bmatrix} w_1 \\ w_2 \end{bmatrix} = N\bar{v}_1 = \begin{bmatrix} 2.8821 \\ -2.8821 \\ -4.8676 \\ -4.8676 \end{bmatrix}$$

$$\begin{bmatrix} w_3 \\ w_4 \end{bmatrix} = N\bar{v}_1 = \begin{bmatrix} 1.2989 \\ -1.2989 \\ 3.1358 \\ 3.1358 \end{bmatrix}$$

The reconstruction is

$$u_2 = \frac{1}{2}(w_2 + w_3) = \frac{1}{2}\left(\begin{bmatrix} -4.8676 \\ -4.8676 \end{bmatrix} + \begin{bmatrix} 1.2989 \\ -1.2989 \end{bmatrix}\right) = \begin{bmatrix} -1.7844 \\ -3.0832 \end{bmatrix}.$$

9 It is clear from the definition (11.27) that $c_{j+4n} = c_j$ for each integer j. By Lemma 11.10, the c_j for $-n \le j \le 3n - 1$ are equal to $\pm c_{k'}$ for some $0 \le k' \le n - 1$, and so it holds for all j. In particular, $c_{5n} = c_n = -c_{2n-1-n} = -c_{n-1}$ by Lemma 11.10(b), and $c_{6n} = c_{2n} = -c_{2n-1-2n} = -c_{-1} = -c_{-1-(-1)} = -c_0$ by Lemma 11.10 (b) and (a).

COMPUTER PROBLEMS 11.4

1   A MATLAB program that carries out the computations of Example 11.9 is the following:

```
function xout=mdctexample(x,n)
len=length(x);    % input column vector x
for i=1:n
  for j=1:2*n
    M(i,j)=sqrt(2/n)*cos((i-0.5)*(j-0.5+n/2)*pi/n);
  end
end
N=M';
xout=[];
for k= 1:len/n-2
  v1=M*x((k-1)*n+1:(k+1)*n);
  v2=M*x(k*n+1:(k+2)*n);
  wa=N*v1;
  wb=N*v2;
  w2=wa(n+1:2*n);
  w3=wb(1:n);
  u2=(w2+w3)/2;
  xout=[xout;u2];
end
```

Applying the code to part (a), for example, would use the MATLAB command

```
>> x=(1:12)';xout=mdctexample(x,4)

xout =

    5.0000
    6.0000
    7.0000
    8.0000
```

CHAPTER 12
Eigenvalues and Singular Values

EXERCISES 12.1   Power Iteration Methods

1 (a) The characteristic polynomial is

$$P(\lambda) = \det(A - \lambda I) = \det \begin{bmatrix} 3.5 - \lambda & -1.5 \\ -1.5 & 3.5 - \lambda \end{bmatrix} = \lambda^2 - 7\lambda + 10 = (\lambda - 2)(\lambda - 5).$$

The eigenvalues are the roots 2 and 5. To find an eigenvector corresponding to $\lambda = 2$, solve

$$0 = (A - 2I)v = \begin{bmatrix} 1.5 & -1.5 \\ -1.5 & 1.5 \end{bmatrix}$$

for $v = [1, 1]^T$. An eigenvector corresponding to $\lambda = 5$ is the solution of

$$0 = (A - 5I)v = \begin{bmatrix} -1.5 & -1.5 \\ -1.5 & -1.5 \end{bmatrix}$$

or $v = [1, -1]^T$.

1 (b) The characteristic polynomial is $P(\lambda) = (-\lambda)(-\lambda) - 4 = (\lambda + 2)(\lambda - 2)$. Solving as in part (a), eigenvalues corresponding to -2 and 2 are $[1, -1]^T$ and $[1, 1]^T$, respectively.

1 (c) The characteristic polynomial is $P(\lambda) = (0.2 - \lambda)(1.2 - \lambda) - 5.76 = (\lambda - 3)(\lambda + 2)$. Eigenvalues corresponding to -2 and 3 are $[4, 3]^T$ and $[-3, 4]^T$, respectively.

1 (d) The characteristic polynomial is $P(\lambda) = (136 - \lambda)(164 - \lambda) - 48^2 = (\lambda - 100)(\lambda - 200)$. Eigenvalues corresponding to 100 and 200 are $[4, 3]^T$ and $[-3, 4]^T$, respectively.

3 (a) The characteristic polynomial is

$$P(\lambda) = \det(A - \lambda I) = \det \begin{bmatrix} 1 - \lambda & 0 & 1 \\ 0 & 3 - \lambda & -2 \\ 0 & 0 & 2 - \lambda \end{bmatrix} = (1 - \lambda)(2 - \lambda)(3 - \lambda).$$

The eigenvalues are the roots $1, 2$ and 3. Corresponding eigenvectors are $[1, 0, 0]^T, [1, 2, 1]^T$ and $[0, 1, 0]^T$.

3 (b) The characteristic polynomial is

$$P(\lambda) = \det(A - \lambda I) = \det \begin{bmatrix} 1 - \lambda & 0 & -\frac{1}{3} \\ 0 & 1 - \lambda & \frac{2}{3} \\ -1 & 1 & 1 - \lambda \end{bmatrix} = (1 - \lambda)(\lambda)(\lambda - 2).$$

The eigenvalues are the roots $0, 1$ and 2. Corresponding eigenvectors are $[1, -2, 3]^T, [1, 1, 0]^T$ and $[-1, 2, 3]^T$.

3 (c) The characteristic polynomial is

$$P(\lambda) = \det(A - \lambda I) = \det \begin{bmatrix} \frac{1}{2} - \lambda & -\frac{1}{2} & -\frac{1}{6} \\ -1 & 0 - \lambda & \frac{1}{3} \\ -\frac{1}{2} & \frac{1}{2} & \frac{1}{2} - \lambda \end{bmatrix} = -(\lambda + 1)(\lambda)(\lambda - 1).$$

The eigenvalues are the roots $-1, 0$ and 1. Corresponding eigenvectors are $[1, 1, 0]^T, [1, -2, 3]^T$ and $[-1, 2, 3]^T$.

5 (a) For almost every initial condition, Power Iteration converges to the eigenvalue of largest magnitude $\lambda_1 = 4$. The convergence rate is the ratio $|\lambda_2/\lambda_1| = 3/4$.

5 (b) For almost every initial condition, Power Iteration converges to $\lambda_1 = -4$, with convergence rate $|\lambda_2/\lambda_1| = 3/4$.

5 (c) Power Iteration generally converges to $\lambda_1 = 4$, with convergence rate $|\lambda_2/\lambda_1| = 2/4$.

5 (d) For almost every initial condition, Power Iteration converges to $\lambda_1 = 10$, with convergence rate $|\lambda_2/\lambda_1| = 9/10$.

7 (a) With shift $s = 0$, the eigenvalues of $(A - sI)^{-1}$ are $1/3, 1, 1/4$. Under almost all initial conditions, Inverse Power Iteration will converge to the dominant eigenvalue 1, corresponding to the smallest eigenvalue 1 of A, with convergence rate constant equal to the ratio of the two largest eigenvalues of $(A - sI)^{-1}$, $S = (1/3)/1 = 1/3$.

7 (b) Similar to part (a). The eigenvalues of $(A - sI)^{-1}$ are $1/3, 1, -1/4$. Under almost all initial conditions, Inverse Power Iteration will converge to the dominant eigenvalue 1, corresponding to the smallest eigenvalue 1 of A, with convergence rate constant equal to the ratio of the two largest eigenvalues of $(A - sI)^{-1}$, $S = (1/3)/1 = 1/3$.

7 (c) The eigenvalues of $(A - sI)^{-1}$ are $-1, 1/2, 1/4$. Under almost all initial conditions, Inverse Power Iteration will converge to the dominant eigenvalue -1, corresponding to the smallest eigenvalue -1 of A, with convergence rate constant equal to the ratio of the two largest eigenvalues of $(A - sI)^{-1}$, $S = (1/2)/1 = 1/2$.

7 (d) With $s = 6$, the eigenvalues of $A - sI$ are $-5, 3, 4$, and the eigenvalues of $(A - sI)^{-1}$ are $-1/5, 1/3, 1/4$. Under almost all initial conditions, Inverse Power Iteration will converge to the dominant eigenvalue $1/3$, corresponding to the eigenvalue of A nearest to the shift $s = 6$, which is $1/(1/3) + 6 = 9$. The convergence rate constant is equal to the ratio of the two largest eigenvalues of $(A - sI)^{-1}$, $S = (1/4)/(1/3) = 3/4$.

9 (a) The characteristic polynomial of A is $\lambda^2 - 4\lambda - 5 = (\lambda - 5)(\lambda + 1)$. The eigenvalues are 5 and -1 with corresponding eigenvectors $[1, 2]^T$ and $[-1, 1]^T$, respectively.

9 (b) Three steps of Power Iteration:

$$x_1 \;=\; Au_0 = \begin{bmatrix} 1 & 2 \\ 4 & 3 \end{bmatrix}\begin{bmatrix} 1 \\ 0 \end{bmatrix} = \begin{bmatrix} 1 \\ 4 \end{bmatrix}$$

$$\lambda_1 \;=\; u_0^T x_1 = \begin{bmatrix} 1 & 0 \end{bmatrix}\begin{bmatrix} 1 \\ 4 \end{bmatrix} = 1, \quad u_1 = \frac{x_1}{\|x_1\|_2} = \begin{bmatrix} 1/\sqrt{17} \\ 4/\sqrt{17} \end{bmatrix}$$

$$x_2 \;=\; Au_1 = \begin{bmatrix} 1 & 2 \\ 4 & 3 \end{bmatrix}\begin{bmatrix} \frac{1}{\sqrt{17}} \\ \frac{4}{\sqrt{17}} \end{bmatrix} = \begin{bmatrix} \frac{9}{\sqrt{17}} \\ \frac{16}{\sqrt{17}} \end{bmatrix},$$

$$\lambda_2 \;=\; u_1^T x_2 = \frac{73}{17} \approx 4.2941, \quad u_2 = \frac{x_2}{\|x_2\|_2} \approx \begin{bmatrix} 0.4903 \\ 0.8716 \end{bmatrix}$$

$$x_3 \;=\; Au_2 = \begin{bmatrix} 1 & 2 \\ 4 & 3 \end{bmatrix}\begin{bmatrix} 0.4903 \\ 0.8716 \end{bmatrix} = \begin{bmatrix} 2.2334 \\ 4.5758 \end{bmatrix}$$

$$\lambda_3 \;=\; u_2^T x_3 = 5.0831$$

9 (c) Convergence to eigenvalue nearest to $s = 0$, which is -1.

9 (d) Convergence to eigenvalue nearest to $s = 3$, which is 5.

11 (a) For almost all initial vectors, Power Iteration will converge to the dominant eigenvalue 7.

11 (b) For almost all initial vectors, Inverse Power Iteration will converge to the eigenvalue closest to the shift $s = 4$, in this case 5.

11 (c) The convergence rate of the iteration in (a) will be $|\lambda_1|/|\lambda_2| = 6/7$. The convergence rate of the iteration in (b) will be the ratio of the two largest eigenvalues of $(A - sI)^{-1}$. The eigenvalues are $-1/10, -1/7, -1/3, -1/2, 1, 1/3$, and the ratio is $1/2$. Therefore the iteration in (b) with shift $s = 4$ converges faster than the iteration in (a).

COMPUTER PROBLEMS 12.1

1 (a) For example, if initial vector $x_0 = [0, 0, 1]^T$ is used in MATLAB Program 12.1 `powerit`, some of the Rayleigh quotients are $\lambda_7 = 4.0911, \lambda_8 = 4.0680, \lambda_9 = 4.0507, \lambda_{10} = 4.0380$. The eigenvector approximations converge to $[1, 1, -1]$ and the Rayleigh quotients converge to 4, in agreement with Exercise 5(a). The ratios of errors at successive steps are approximately $3/4$, in agreement with Theorem 12.2.

1 (b) Similar to part (a). The eigenvector approximations converge to $[1, 1, -1]$ and the Rayleigh quotients converge to -4, in agreement with Exercise 5(b).

1 (c) The eigenvector approximations converge to $[1, 1, -1]$ and the Rayleigh quotients converge to 4, in agreement with Exercise 5(c).

1 (d) The eigenvector approximations converge to $[1, 1, -1]$ and the Rayleigh quotients converge to 10, in agreement with Exercise 5(d).

3 (a)   For example, assume that initial vector $x_0 = [0, 0, 1]^T$ is used in MATLAB Program 12.2 `invpowerit`. After inverting and adding the shift $s = 5$ to the Rayleigh quotients, approximations are $\lambda_5 = 4.0166\lambda_6 = 4.0080\lambda_7 = 4.0040\lambda_8 = 4.0020$ The eigenvector approximations converge to $[1, 1, -1]$ and the eigenvalue approximations converge to 4 with convergence rate constant $S \approx 1/2$, in agreement with Exercise 6(a).

3 (b)   Similar to part (a). The eigenvector approximations converge to $[0, 1, -2]$ and the eigenvalue approximations converge to 3.

3 (c)   The eigenvector approximations converge to $[2, 1, 1]$ and the eigenvalue approximations converge to 2.

3 (d)   The eigenvector approximations converge to $[2, 1, 1]$ and the eigenvalue approximations converge to 9.

EXERCISES 12.2   QR Algorithm

1 (a)   To find a Householder reflector for $[1, 1]^T$, set $v = \begin{bmatrix} 1 \\ 1 \end{bmatrix} + \begin{bmatrix} \sqrt{2} \\ 0 \end{bmatrix}$,

$$\hat{H} = I - \frac{2vv^T}{v^Tv} = \begin{bmatrix} 1 & 0 \\ 0 & 1 \end{bmatrix} - \begin{bmatrix} 1 + \frac{\sqrt{2}}{2} & \frac{\sqrt{2}}{2} \\ \frac{\sqrt{2}}{2} & 1 - \frac{\sqrt{2}}{2} \end{bmatrix}$$
$$= \begin{bmatrix} -\frac{\sqrt{2}}{2} & -\frac{\sqrt{2}}{2} \\ -\frac{\sqrt{2}}{2} & \frac{\sqrt{2}}{2} \end{bmatrix}$$

Then the upper Hessenberg matrix is

$$HAH = \begin{bmatrix} 1 & 0 & 0 \\ 0 & -\frac{\sqrt{2}}{2} & -\frac{\sqrt{2}}{2} \\ 0 & -\frac{\sqrt{2}}{2} & \frac{\sqrt{2}}{2} \end{bmatrix} \begin{bmatrix} 1 & 0 & 1 \\ 1 & 1 & 0 \\ 1 & 0 & 0 \end{bmatrix} \begin{bmatrix} 1 & 0 & 0 \\ 0 & -\frac{\sqrt{2}}{2} & -\frac{\sqrt{2}}{2} \\ 0 & -\frac{\sqrt{2}}{2} & \frac{\sqrt{2}}{2} \end{bmatrix} = \begin{bmatrix} 1 & -\frac{\sqrt{2}}{2} & \frac{\sqrt{2}}{2} \\ -\sqrt{2} & \frac{1}{2} & \frac{1}{2} \\ 0 & \frac{1}{2} & \frac{1}{2} \end{bmatrix}$$

1 (b)   To find a Householder reflector for $[0, 1]^T$, set $v = \begin{bmatrix} 0 \\ 1 \end{bmatrix} - \begin{bmatrix} 1 \\ 0 \end{bmatrix} = \begin{bmatrix} -1 \\ 1 \end{bmatrix}$,

$$\hat{H} = I - \frac{2vv^T}{v^Tv} = \begin{bmatrix} 1 & 0 \\ 0 & 1 \end{bmatrix} - \frac{2}{2} \begin{bmatrix} 1 & -1 \\ -1 & 1 \end{bmatrix} = \begin{bmatrix} 0 & 1 \\ 1 & 0 \end{bmatrix}.$$

Then the upper Hessenberg matrix is

$$HAH = \begin{bmatrix} 1 & 0 & 0 \\ 0 & 0 & 1 \\ 0 & 1 & 0 \end{bmatrix} \begin{bmatrix} 0 & 0 & 1 \\ 0 & 1 & 0 \\ 1 & 0 & 0 \end{bmatrix} \begin{bmatrix} 1 & 0 & 0 \\ 0 & 0 & 1 \\ 0 & 1 & 0 \end{bmatrix} = \begin{bmatrix} 0 & 1 & 0 \\ 1 & 0 & 0 \\ 0 & 0 & 1 \end{bmatrix}$$

1 (c) To find a Householder reflector for $[4, 3]^T$, set $v = \begin{bmatrix} -5 \\ 0 \end{bmatrix} - \begin{bmatrix} 4 \\ 3 \end{bmatrix} = \begin{bmatrix} -9 \\ -3 \end{bmatrix}$,

$$\hat{H} = I - \frac{2vv^T}{v^Tv} = \begin{bmatrix} 1 & 0 \\ 0 & 1 \end{bmatrix} - \frac{2}{90}\begin{bmatrix} 81 & 27 \\ 27 & 9 \end{bmatrix}$$
$$= \begin{bmatrix} -0.8 & -0.6 \\ -0.6 & 0.8 \end{bmatrix}$$

Then the upper Hessenberg matrix is

$$\begin{bmatrix} 1 & 0 & 0 \\ 0 & -0.8 & -0.6 \\ 0 & -0.6 & 0.8 \end{bmatrix} \begin{bmatrix} 2 & 1 & 0 \\ 4 & 1 & 1 \\ 3 & 0 & 1 \end{bmatrix} \begin{bmatrix} 1 & 0 & 0 \\ 0 & -0.8 & -0.6 \\ 0 & -0.6 & 0.8 \end{bmatrix} = \begin{bmatrix} 2.00 & -0.80 & -0.60 \\ -5.00 & 1.48 & -0.64 \\ 0.00 & 0.36 & 0.52 \end{bmatrix}$$

1 (d) To find a Householder reflector for $[2, 2]^T$, set $v = \begin{bmatrix} -\sqrt{8} \\ 0 \end{bmatrix} - \begin{bmatrix} 2 \\ 2 \end{bmatrix} = \begin{bmatrix} -2\sqrt{2} - 2 \\ -2 \end{bmatrix}$,

$$\hat{H} = I - \frac{2vv^T}{v^Tv} = \begin{bmatrix} 1 & 0 \\ 0 & 1 \end{bmatrix} - \frac{2}{16 + 8\sqrt{2}}\begin{bmatrix} 12 + 8\sqrt{2} & 4 + 4\sqrt{2} \\ 4 + 4\sqrt{2} & 4 \end{bmatrix} = \begin{bmatrix} -\frac{\sqrt{2}}{2} & -\frac{\sqrt{2}}{2} \\ -\frac{\sqrt{2}}{2} & \frac{\sqrt{2}}{2} \end{bmatrix}.$$

Then the upper Hessenberg matrix is

$$HAH = \begin{bmatrix} 1 & 0 & 0 \\ 0 & -\frac{\sqrt{2}}{2} & -\frac{\sqrt{2}}{2} \\ 0 & -\frac{\sqrt{2}}{2} & \frac{\sqrt{2}}{2} \end{bmatrix} \begin{bmatrix} 1 & 1 & 0 \\ 2 & 3 & 1 \\ 2 & 1 & 0 \end{bmatrix} \begin{bmatrix} 1 & 0 & 0 \\ 0 & -\frac{\sqrt{2}}{2} & -\frac{\sqrt{2}}{2} \\ 0 & -\frac{\sqrt{2}}{2} & \frac{\sqrt{2}}{2} \end{bmatrix} = \begin{bmatrix} 1 & -\frac{\sqrt{2}}{2} & -\frac{\sqrt{2}}{2} \\ -2\sqrt{2} & \frac{5}{2} & \frac{3}{2} \\ 0 & \frac{3}{2} & \frac{1}{2} \end{bmatrix}$$

3 The matrix A is in upper Hessenberg form if and only if $a_{ij} = 0$ for $i \geq j + 2$. If in addition A is symmetric, then $a_{ij} = a_{ji} = 0$ for $j \geq i + 2$, or $i \leq j - 2$. Since $a_{ij} = 0$ unless $j - 1 \leq i \leq j + 1$, A is tridiagonal.

5 (a) Normalized Simultaneous Iteration gives

$$\overline{Q}_0 = I$$
$$A\overline{Q}_0 = \begin{bmatrix} 0 & 1 \\ 1 & 0 \end{bmatrix} = \overline{Q}_1R_1 = \begin{bmatrix} 0 & 1 \\ 1 & 0 \end{bmatrix}\begin{bmatrix} 1 & 0 \\ 0 & 1 \end{bmatrix}$$
$$A\overline{Q}_1 = \begin{bmatrix} 1 & 0 \\ 0 & 1 \end{bmatrix} = \overline{Q}_2R_2 = \begin{bmatrix} 1 & 0 \\ 0 & 1 \end{bmatrix}\begin{bmatrix} 1 & 0 \\ 0 & 1 \end{bmatrix}$$
$$A\overline{Q}_2 = \begin{bmatrix} 0 & 1 \\ 1 & 0 \end{bmatrix} = \overline{Q}_3R_3 = \begin{bmatrix} 0 & 1 \\ 1 & 0 \end{bmatrix}\begin{bmatrix} 1 & 0 \\ 0 & 1 \end{bmatrix}$$

and so forth, showing failure of convergence of the columns of $\overline{Q}_j$.

5 (b)   Normalized Simultaneous Iteration gives

$$
\begin{aligned}
\overline{Q}_0 &= I \\
A\overline{Q}_0 &= \begin{bmatrix} 0 & 1 \\ -1 & 0 \end{bmatrix} = \overline{Q}_1 R_1 = \begin{bmatrix} 0 & -1 \\ 1 & 0 \end{bmatrix}\begin{bmatrix} 1 & 0 \\ 0 & 1 \end{bmatrix} \\
A\overline{Q}_1 &= \begin{bmatrix} -1 & 0 \\ 0 & -1 \end{bmatrix} = \overline{Q}_2 R_2 = \begin{bmatrix} 1 & 0 \\ 0 & 1 \end{bmatrix}\begin{bmatrix} -1 & 0 \\ 0 & -1 \end{bmatrix} \\
A\overline{Q}_2 &= \begin{bmatrix} 0 & 1 \\ -1 & 0 \end{bmatrix} = \overline{Q}_3 R_3 = \begin{bmatrix} 0 & 1 \\ -1 & 0 \end{bmatrix}\begin{bmatrix} 1 & 0 \\ 0 & 1 \end{bmatrix}
\end{aligned}
$$

and so forth, showing failure of convergence of the columns of $\overline{Q}_j$.

7 (a)   The matrix is already in upper Hessenberg form. The preliminary version of the shifted QR Algorithm gives:

$$
\begin{aligned}
A_0 &= \begin{bmatrix} 1 & 0 & 0 \\ 0 & 0 & 1 \\ 0 & 1 & 0 \end{bmatrix} = Q_1 R_1 = \begin{bmatrix} 1 & 0 & 0 \\ 0 & 0 & 1 \\ 0 & 1 & 0 \end{bmatrix}\begin{bmatrix} 1 & 0 & 0 \\ 0 & 1 & 0 \\ 0 & 0 & 1 \end{bmatrix} \\
A_1 &= R_1 Q_1 = \begin{bmatrix} 1 & 0 & 0 \\ 0 & 0 & 1 \\ 0 & 1 & 0 \end{bmatrix}
\end{aligned}
$$

showing that $A_0 = A_1 = \ldots$. The method does not converge to Schur form for this matrix.

7 (b)   Before changing to upper Hessenberg form, the shifted QR Algorithm gives:

$$
\begin{aligned}
A_0 &= \begin{bmatrix} 0 & 0 & 1 \\ 0 & 1 & 0 \\ 1 & 0 & 0 \end{bmatrix} = Q_1 R_1 = \begin{bmatrix} 0 & 0 & 1 \\ 0 & 1 & 0 \\ 1 & 0 & 0 \end{bmatrix}\begin{bmatrix} 1 & 0 & 0 \\ 0 & 1 & 0 \\ 0 & 0 & 1 \end{bmatrix} \\
A_1 &= R_1 Q_1 = \begin{bmatrix} 0 & 0 & 1 \\ 0 & 1 & 0 \\ 1 & 0 & 0 \end{bmatrix}
\end{aligned}
$$

showing that $A_0 = A_1 = \ldots$. The method does not converge to Schur form. To convert A to upper Hessenberg form, we use a Householder reflector

$$
A' = HAH = \begin{bmatrix} 1 & 0 & 0 \\ 0 & 0 & 1 \\ 0 & 1 & 0 \end{bmatrix}\begin{bmatrix} 0 & 0 & 1 \\ 0 & 1 & 0 \\ 1 & 0 & 0 \end{bmatrix}\begin{bmatrix} 1 & 0 & 0 \\ 0 & 0 & 1 \\ 0 & 1 & 0 \end{bmatrix} = \begin{bmatrix} 0 & 1 & 0 \\ 1 & 0 & 0 \\ 0 & 0 & 1 \end{bmatrix}
$$

Applying the preliminary shifted QR Algorithm to A' yields

$$A'_0 = Q_1 R_1 = \begin{bmatrix} 0 & 1 & 0 \\ 1 & 0 & 0 \\ 0 & 0 & 1 \end{bmatrix} \begin{bmatrix} 1 & 0 & 0 \\ 0 & 1 & 0 \\ 0 & 0 & 1 \end{bmatrix}$$

$$A'_1 = R_1 Q_1 = \begin{bmatrix} 0 & 1 & 0 \\ 1 & 0 & 0 \\ 0 & 0 & 1 \end{bmatrix}$$

showing that $A'_0 = A'_1 = \ldots$, so the preliminary version of the QR algorithm does not isolate the eigenvalues. (However, note that the matrix A' is already in Schur form, and the eigenvalues can be easily read, as in the general QR algorithm.)

COMPUTER PROBLEMS 12.2

1 (a) The MATLAB Program 12.6 `shiftedqr0` may be used to converge to the eigenvalues $-6, 4, -2$ of the matrix. The tolerance `tol=1e-14` suffices.
1 (b) Similar to part (a). The eigenvalues are $6, 4, 2$.
1 (c) Similar to part (a). The eigenvalues are $20, 18, 16$.
1 (d) Similar to part (a). The eigenvalues are $10, 2, 1$.

2 (a) $5.7742, 2.1794, -0.9536$
2 (b) $-6.1962, 4.1962, 3$
2 (c) $5.5545, -0.2773 \pm 1.0017i$
2 (d) $6.2915, 6, -4.2915$

3 (a) The MATLAB Program 12.7 `shiftedqr` may be used to converge to the repeated eigenvalues $3, 3, 3$ of the matrix.
3 (b) Similar to part (a). The program `shiftedqr` returns the eigenvalues $\{1, 9, 10\}$.
3 (c) Similar to part (a). The eigenvalues are $\{3, 3, 18\}$.
3 (d) Similar to part (a). The eigenvalues are $\{-2, 2, 0\}$.

5 (a) The MATLAB program Program 12.7 `shiftedqr` converges to the eigenvalues $\{2, i, -i\}$
5 (b) Similar to part (a). The eigenvalues are $\{1, i, -i\}$
5 (c) Similar to part (a). The eigenvalues are $\{2 + 3i, 2 - 3i, 1\}$
5 (d) Similar to part (a). The eigenvalues are $\{5, 4 + 3i, 4 - 3i\}$

EXERCISES 12.3   Singular Value Decomposition

1 (a) The eigenvalues are $-3, 2$; the singular values are the absolute values $s_1 = 3, s_2 = 2$. The eigenvectors $v_1 = [1, 0]^T$ and $v_2 = [0, 1]^T$ are the right singular vectors, and the left singular vectors are $u_1 = [-1, 0]^T$ and $u_2 = [0, 1]^T$. Putting the information together, the SVD is

$$\begin{bmatrix} -3 & 0 \\ 0 & 2 \end{bmatrix} = A = USV^T = \begin{bmatrix} -1 & 0 \\ 0 & 1 \end{bmatrix} \begin{bmatrix} 3 & 0 \\ 0 & 2 \end{bmatrix} \begin{bmatrix} 1 & 0 \\ 0 & 1 \end{bmatrix}.$$

The SVD is not quite unique; another correct factorization is

$$\begin{bmatrix} -3 & 0 \\ 0 & 2 \end{bmatrix} = A = USV^T = \begin{bmatrix} 1 & 0 \\ 0 & 1 \end{bmatrix} \begin{bmatrix} 3 & 0 \\ 0 & 2 \end{bmatrix} \begin{bmatrix} -1 & 0 \\ 0 & 1 \end{bmatrix}.$$

Multiplication by the matrix expands vectors by factor of 3 and flips along x-axis, expands by factor of 2 along y-axis.

1 (b)   The singular values are the eigenvalues $s_1 = 3, s_2 = 0$. The eigenvectors are $u_1 = v_1 = [0, 1]^T$ and $u_2 = v_2 = [1, 0]^T$. The SVD is

$$\begin{bmatrix} 0 & 0 \\ 0 & 3 \end{bmatrix} = A = USV^T = \begin{bmatrix} 0 & 1 \\ 1 & 0 \end{bmatrix} \begin{bmatrix} 3 & 0 \\ 0 & 0 \end{bmatrix} \begin{bmatrix} 0 & 1 \\ 1 & 0 \end{bmatrix}.$$

Projects onto y axis and expands by 3 in y-direction.

1 (c)   The eigenvalues are $s_1 = 2, s_2 = 1$, with corresponding unit eigenvectors $u_1 = v_1 = [1/\sqrt{2}, -1/\sqrt{2}]^T$ and $u_2 = v_2 = [1/\sqrt{2}, 1/\sqrt{2}]^T$. The SVD is

$$\begin{bmatrix} \frac{3}{2} & -\frac{1}{2} \\ -\frac{1}{2} & \frac{3}{2} \end{bmatrix} = A = USV^T = \begin{bmatrix} \frac{1}{\sqrt{2}} & \frac{1}{\sqrt{2}} \\ -\frac{1}{\sqrt{2}} & \frac{1}{\sqrt{2}} \end{bmatrix} \begin{bmatrix} 2 & 0 \\ 0 & 1 \end{bmatrix} \begin{bmatrix} \frac{1}{\sqrt{2}} & -\frac{1}{\sqrt{2}} \\ \frac{1}{\sqrt{2}} & \frac{1}{\sqrt{2}} \end{bmatrix}.$$

Another correct factorization is

$$\begin{bmatrix} \frac{3}{2} & -\frac{1}{2} \\ -\frac{1}{2} & \frac{3}{2} \end{bmatrix} = A = USV^T = \begin{bmatrix} -\frac{1}{\sqrt{2}} & \frac{1}{\sqrt{2}} \\ \frac{1}{\sqrt{2}} & \frac{1}{\sqrt{2}} \end{bmatrix} \begin{bmatrix} 2 & 0 \\ 0 & 1 \end{bmatrix} \begin{bmatrix} -\frac{1}{\sqrt{2}} & \frac{1}{\sqrt{2}} \\ \frac{1}{\sqrt{2}} & \frac{1}{\sqrt{2}} \end{bmatrix}.$$

Expands into ellipse with major axis of length 4 along the line $y = -x$.

1 (d)   The eigenvalues are $-2, -1$; the singular values are the absolute values $s_1 = 2, s_2 = 1$. The eigenvectors are $v_1 = [1/\sqrt{2}, -1/\sqrt{2}]^T$ and $v_2 = [1/\sqrt{2}, 1/\sqrt{2}]^T$. According to (13.26), the left singular vectors are $u_1 = [-1/\sqrt{2}, 1/\sqrt{2}]^T$ and $u_2 = [-1/\sqrt{2}, -1/\sqrt{2}]^T$. The SVD is

$$\begin{bmatrix} -\frac{3}{2} & \frac{1}{2} \\ \frac{1}{2} & -\frac{3}{2} \end{bmatrix} = A = USV^T = \begin{bmatrix} -\frac{1}{\sqrt{2}} & -\frac{1}{\sqrt{2}} \\ \frac{1}{\sqrt{2}} & -\frac{1}{\sqrt{2}} \end{bmatrix} \begin{bmatrix} 2 & 0 \\ 0 & 1 \end{bmatrix} \begin{bmatrix} \frac{1}{\sqrt{2}} & -\frac{1}{\sqrt{2}} \\ \frac{1}{\sqrt{2}} & \frac{1}{\sqrt{2}} \end{bmatrix}.$$

Same as (c), but with a 180 degree rotation.

1 (e)   The eigenvalues are $2, -1/2$; the singular values are the absolute values $s_1 = 2, s_2 = 1/2$. The eigenvectors are $v_1 = [1/\sqrt{2}, 1/\sqrt{2}]^T$ and $v_2 = [1/\sqrt{2}, -1/\sqrt{2}]^T$. According to (13.26), the left singular vectors are $u_1 = [1/\sqrt{2}, 1/\sqrt{2}]^T$ and $u_2 = [-1/\sqrt{2}, 1/\sqrt{2}]^T$. The SVD is

$$\begin{bmatrix} \frac{3}{4} & \frac{5}{4} \\ \frac{5}{4} & \frac{3}{4} \end{bmatrix} = A = USV^T = \begin{bmatrix} \frac{1}{\sqrt{2}} & -\frac{1}{\sqrt{2}} \\ \frac{1}{\sqrt{2}} & \frac{1}{\sqrt{2}} \end{bmatrix} \begin{bmatrix} 2 & 0 \\ 0 & \frac{1}{2} \end{bmatrix} \begin{bmatrix} \frac{1}{\sqrt{2}} & \frac{1}{\sqrt{2}} \\ \frac{1}{\sqrt{2}} & -\frac{1}{\sqrt{2}} \end{bmatrix}.$$

As usual, a different choice on the signs of the eigenvectors would lead to a different factorization, for example

$$\begin{bmatrix} \frac{3}{4} & \frac{5}{4} \\ \frac{5}{4} & \frac{3}{4} \end{bmatrix} = \begin{bmatrix} -\frac{1}{\sqrt{2}} & \frac{1}{\sqrt{2}} \\ -\frac{1}{\sqrt{2}} & -\frac{1}{\sqrt{2}} \end{bmatrix} \begin{bmatrix} 2 & 0 \\ 0 & \frac{1}{2} \end{bmatrix} \begin{bmatrix} \frac{1}{\sqrt{2}} & -\frac{1}{\sqrt{2}} \\ -\frac{1}{\sqrt{2}} & -\frac{1}{\sqrt{2}} \end{bmatrix}.$$

Expands by factor of 2 along line $y = x$ and contracts by factor of 2 along line $y = -x$.

3 Four:

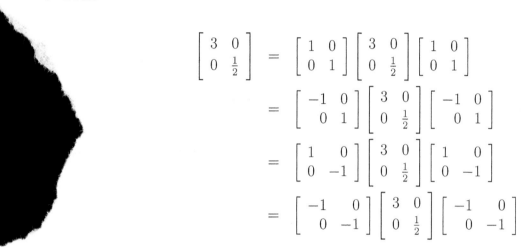

$$\begin{bmatrix} 3 & 0 \\ 0 & \frac{1}{2} \end{bmatrix} = \begin{bmatrix} 1 & 0 \\ 0 & 1 \end{bmatrix} \begin{bmatrix} 3 & 0 \\ 0 & \frac{1}{2} \end{bmatrix} \begin{bmatrix} 1 & 0 \\ 0 & 1 \end{bmatrix}$$

$$= \begin{bmatrix} -1 & 0 \\ 0 & 1 \end{bmatrix} \begin{bmatrix} 3 & 0 \\ 0 & \frac{1}{2} \end{bmatrix} \begin{bmatrix} -1 & 0 \\ 0 & 1 \end{bmatrix}$$

$$= \begin{bmatrix} 1 & 0 \\ 0 & -1 \end{bmatrix} \begin{bmatrix} 3 & 0 \\ 0 & \frac{1}{2} \end{bmatrix} \begin{bmatrix} 1 & 0 \\ 0 & -1 \end{bmatrix}$$

$$= \begin{bmatrix} -1 & 0 \\ 0 & -1 \end{bmatrix} \begin{bmatrix} 3 & 0 \\ 0 & \frac{1}{2} \end{bmatrix} \begin{bmatrix} -1 & 0 \\ 0 & -1 \end{bmatrix}$$

COMPUTER PROBLEMS 12.4   Applications of the SVD

1 (a)   The MATLAB command `svd` calculates the singular value decomposition. To find the best rank-one approximation of the matrix A, replace s_i with 0 for $i > 1$ and recalculate the product:

```
>> A = [1 2;2 3];
>> [U,S,V] = svd(A);
>> S(2:end,2:end)=0;
>> A1 = U*S*V';
```

The result is $\begin{bmatrix} 1.1708 & 1.8944 \\ 1.8944 & 3.0652 \end{bmatrix}$.

1 (b)   Similar to part (a). The rank-one approximation is $\begin{bmatrix} 1.5607 & 3.7678 \\ 1.3536 & 3.2678 \end{bmatrix}$.

1 (c)   Similar to part (a). The rank-one approximation is $\begin{bmatrix} 1.0107 & 2.5125 & 3.6436 \\ 0.9552 & 2.3746 & 3.4436 \\ 0.1787 & 0.4442 & 0.6441 \end{bmatrix}$.

1 (d)   Similar to part (a). The rank-one approximation is $\begin{bmatrix} -0.5141 & 5.2343 & 1.9952 \\ 0.2070 & -2.1076 & -0.8033 \\ -0.1425 & 1.4510 & 0.5531 \end{bmatrix}$.

3 (a)   According to section 12.4.2, the best least squares one-dimensional subspace is found by finding the SVD of the data matrix

$$A = \begin{bmatrix} 1 & 1 & 2 \\ 4 & 5 & 4 \end{bmatrix} = USV^T.$$

Set the entry $S_{22} = 0$ to form S_1 and recalculate to find the best line:

$$A_1 = US_1V^T = \begin{bmatrix} 1.1934 & 1.4707 & 1.2774 \\ 3.9415 & 4.8575 & 4.2188 \end{bmatrix}.$$

The best line is $y = 3.3028x$, projections are $\begin{bmatrix} 1.1934 \\ 3.9415 \end{bmatrix}, \begin{bmatrix} 1.4707 \\ 4.8575 \end{bmatrix}, \begin{bmatrix} 1.2774 \\ 4.2188 \end{bmatrix}$

3 (b)   Best line $y = 0.3620x$, projections are $\begin{bmatrix} 1.7682 \\ 0.6402 \end{bmatrix}, \begin{bmatrix} 3.8565 \\ 1.3963 \end{bmatrix}, \begin{bmatrix} 3.2925 \\ 1.1921 \end{bmatrix}.$

3 (c)   Similar to part (a). Best line $[x(t), y(t), z(t)] = [0.3015, 0.3416, 0.8902]t$, projections

$$\begin{bmatrix} 1.3702 \\ 1.5527 \\ 4.0463 \end{bmatrix}, \begin{bmatrix} 1.8325 \\ 2.0764 \\ 5.4111 \end{bmatrix}, \begin{bmatrix} 1.8949 \\ 2.1471 \\ 5.5954 \end{bmatrix}, \begin{bmatrix} 0.9989 \\ 1.1319 \\ 2.9498 \end{bmatrix}.$$

5 Exact factorizations given in solutions to Exercise 12.3.2.

CHAPTER 13
Optimization

EXERCISES 13.1   Unconstrained Optimization without Derivatives

1 (a)   The derivative is $f'(x) = e^x - e^{-x}$, which is zero if and only if $x = 0$. Furthermore, $f'(x) < 0$ for $x < 0$ and $f'(x) > 0$ for $x > 0$. Therefore f is unimodal on $(-\infty, \infty)$ and has an absolute minimum at $(x, y) = (0, 2)$.

(b)   The expression x^6 is positive if and only if $x \neq 0$, and equals zero at $x = 0$. Therefore $(0, 0)$ is the absolute minimum. The derivative is $f'(x) = 6x^5$, which is negative for $x < 0$ and positive for $x > 0$, so f is unimodal on $(-\infty, \infty)$.

The derivative $f'(x) = 8x^3 + 1$ is equal to zero if and only if $x = -1/2$, is negative for $x < -1/2$, and is positive for $x > -1/2$. Therefore $(-1/2, -3/8)$ is the absolute minimum of the unimodal function.

(d)   The derivative is $f'(x) = 1 - 1/x$, which equals zero if and only if $x = 1$, is negative for $0 < x < 1$, and positive for $x > 1$. Thus f is unimodal on $(0, \infty)$ and the absolute minimum occurs at $(1, 1)$.

COMPUTER PROBLEMS 13.1

1 (a)   The plot shows that the interval $[0, 1]$ contains a relative minimum. According to Theorem 13.2, the number k of Golden Section Search steps needed satisfies

$$\frac{g^k(1 - 0)}{2} < 0.5 \times 10^{-5},$$

where $g = (\sqrt{5} - 1)/2$. The inequality holds for $k \geq 24$. Program 13.1 is an implementation of Golden Section Search that can be used to find the minimum. The command

```
>> x=gss(@(x) 2*x^4+3*x^2-4*x+5,0,1,24)
```

results in convergence to the minimum $x = 1/2$.

1 (b)   From the plot below, there are two relative minima. The intervals $[-2.5, -1.5]$ and $[0.5, 1.5]$ each contain a minimum. The number of steps needed for each interval is 24, as in (a). The minima $x = -2$ and $x = 1$ are found by **gss**.

1 (c)   Similar to (a). The interval $[0, 1]$ contains a relative minimum. Applying 24 steps of **gss** gives the approximation $x = 0.47033$.

1 (d)   Similar to (a). The interval $[1, 2]$ contains a relative minimum. Applying 24 steps of **gss** provides the approximation $x = 1.43791$.

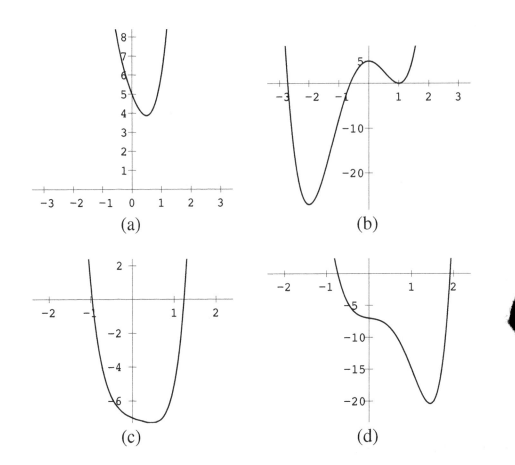

3 (a) The squared distance from the point $(x, 1/x)$ to $(2, 3)$ is $D(x) = (x - 2)^2 + (1/x - 3)^2$. The derivative is

$$D'(x) = 2x - 4 - \frac{2}{x^3} + \frac{6}{x^2}.$$

Newton's Method applied to find a root of $D'(x)$ converges to $r = 0.358555$, corresponding to a distance of 2.788973.

3 (b) Applying Golden Section Search on the interval $[0, 1]$

```
>> x=gss(@(x) (x-2)^2+(1/x-3)^2,0,1,30)
```

produces $x = 0.358555$ as in part (a).

5 Program 13.3 can be applied as

```
x=neldermead(@(x) exp(-x(1)^2*x(2)^2)+(x(1)-1)^2+(x(2)-1)^2,[1;1],1,60)
```

to converge to $(1.20881759, 1.20881759)$ within 8 decimal places.

7 Program 13.3 can be applied as

```
x=neldermead(@(x) 100*(x(2)-x(1)^2)^2+(x(1)-1)^2,[0;0],1,100)
```

to converge to $(1,1)$.

COMPUTER PROBLEMS 13.2   Unconstrained Optimization with Derivatives

1 Minimum is $(1.2088176, 1.2088176)$. Different initial conditions will yield answers that differ by about $\epsilon^{1/2}$.

(a) Newton's Method when applied to the gradient of the Rosenbrock function $F(x_1, x_2) = 100(x_2 - x_1^2)^2 + (x_1 - 1)^2$ converges to the minimum $(x_1, x_2) = (1, 1)$. Newton's method will be accurate to machine precision since it is finding a simple root.

Steepest Descent also converges to $(1, 1)$, but about 8 digits of accuracy in double precision, ce error is of size $\approx \epsilon^{1/2}$.

) Implement Conjugate Gradient Search as on page 596, using Successive Parabolic Interpolation as the one-dimensional minimizer. Using initial guess $(1, -1)$, the method converges to the minimum $(1.132638, -0.465972)$. Using initial guess $(-1, 1)$, the method converges to the minimum $(-0.465972, 1.132638)$.

5 (b) Similar to (a). Conjugate Gradient Search with SPI converges, depending on initial guess, to the two minima $(0.6763, 0.6763)$ and $(-0.6763, -0.6763)$.